PHILIP'S

KT-371-690

STREET ATLAS

Aberdeenshire

First published 2004 by

Philip's, a division of
Octopus Publishing Group Ltd
2-4 Heron Quays, London E14 4JP

First edition 2004
First impression 2004

ISBN-10   0-540-08654-1 (pocket)
ISBN-13   978-0-540-08654-2 (pocket)

© Philip's 2004

Ordnance Survey®

This product includes mapping data licensed from
Ordnance Survey® with the permission of the
Controller of Her Majesty's Stationery Office.
© Crown copyright 2004. All rights reserved.
Licence number 100011710.

Printed and bound in Italy by Rotolito

Contents

III **Key to map symbols**

IV **Key to map pages**

VI **Route planning**

X **Administrative and Postcode boundaries**

1 **Street maps** at 1⅓ inches to 1 mile

139 **Street maps** at 2⅔ inches to 1 mile

190 **Street map of Aberdeen city centre**
at 5⅓ inches to 1 mile

191 **Index** of towns and villages

193 **Index** of streets, hospitals, industrial estates, railway
stations, schools, shopping centres, universities
and places of interest

Digital Data

The exceptionally high-quality mapping found in this atlas is available as digital data in TIFF
format, which is easily convertible to other bitmapped (raster) image formats.

The index is also available in digital form as a standard database table. It contains all the details
found in the printed index together with the National Grid reference for the map square in which
each entry is named.

For further information and to discuss your requirements, please contact Philip's on
020 7644 6932 or james.mann@philips-maps.co.uk

Motorway with junction number (22a)	
Primary route – dual/single carriageway	
A road – dual/single carriageway	
B road – dual/single carriageway	
Minor road – dual/single carriageway	
Other minor road – dual/single carriageway	
Road under construction	
Tunnel, covered road	
Rural track, private road or narrow road in urban area	
Gate or obstruction to traffic (restrictions may not apply at all times or to all vehicles)	
Path, bridleway, byway open to all traffic, road used as a public path	
Pedestrianised area	
DY7 Postcode boundaries	
County and unitary authority boundaries	
Railway, tunnel, railway under construction	
Tramway, tramway under construction	
Miniature railway	
Walsall Railway station	
Private railway station	
South Shields Metro station	
Tram stop, tram stop under construction	
Bus, coach station	

Ambulance station	
Coastguard station	
Fire station	
Police station	
Accident and Emergency entrance to hospital	
H Hospital	
+ Place of worship	
i Information Centre (open all year)	
P P&R Parking, Park and Ride	
PO Post Office	
Camping site	
Caravan site	
Golf course	
Picnic site	
Prim Sch Important buildings, schools, colleges, universities and hospitals	
Built up area	
Woods	
River Ouse Tidal water, water name	
Non-tidal water – lake, river, canal or stream	
Lock, weir, tunnel	
Church Non-Roman antiquity	
ROMAN FORT Roman antiquity	

Abbr	Full	Abbr	Full	Abbr	Full
Acad	Academy	Inst	Institute	Recn Gd	Recreation Ground
Allot Gdns	Allotments	Ct	Law Court	Resr	Reservoir
Cemy	Cemetery	L Ctr	Leisure Centre	Ret Pk	Retail Park
C Ctr	Civic Centre	LC	Level Crossing	Sch	School
CH	Club House	Liby	Library	Sh Ctr	Shopping Centre
Coll	College	Mkt	Market	TH	Town Hall/House
Crem	Crematorium	Meml	Memorial	Trad Est	Trading Estate
Ent	Enterprise	Mon	Monument	Univ	University
Ex H	Exhibition Hall	Mus	Museum	W Twr	Water Tower
Ind Est	Industrial Estate	Obsy	Observatory	Wks	Works
IRB Sta	Inshore Rescue Boat Station	Pal	Royal Palace	YH	Youth Hostel
		PH	Public House		

87	Adjoining page indicators and overlap bands The colour of the arrow and the band indicates the scale of the adjoining or overlapping page (see scales below)
228	

Enlarged mapping only

Railway or bus station building	
Place of interest	
Parkland	

■ The small numbers around the edges of the maps identify the 1 kilometre National Grid lines
■ The dark grey border on the inside edge of some pages indicates that the mapping does not continue onto the adjacent page

The scale of the maps on the pages numbered in blue is 4.2 cm to 1 km • 2⅔ inches to 1 mile • 1: 23810

0	¼	½	¾	1 mile
0	250 m	500 m	750 m	1 kilometre

The scale of the maps on pages numbered in green is 1.96 cm to 1 km • 1⅛ inches to 1 mile • 1: 50688

0	¼	½	¾	1 mile
0	250m	500m	750m	1kilometre

The scale of the maps on pages numbered in red is 8.4 cm to 1 km • 5⅓ inches to 1 mile • 1: 11900

0	220 yards	440 yards	660 yards	½ mile
0	125m	250m	375m	½ kilometre

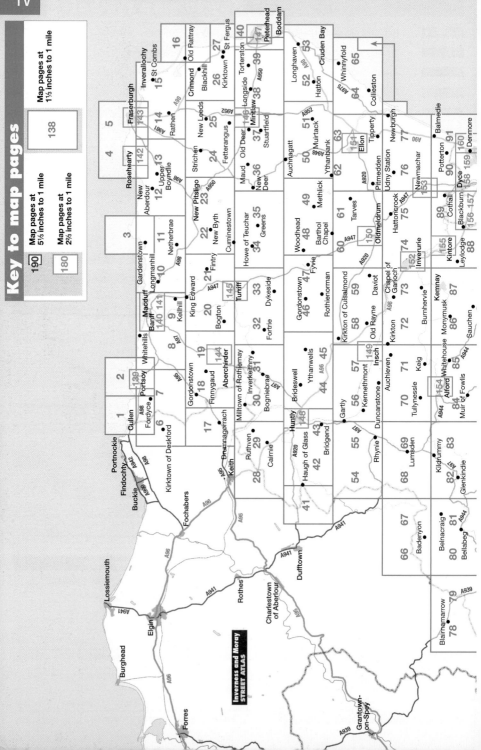

Key to map pages

Map pages at
5⅓ inches to 1 mile

190

Map pages at
2⅔ inches to 1 mile

180

Map pages at
1⅓ inches to 1 mile

138

Inverness and Moray
STREET ATLAS

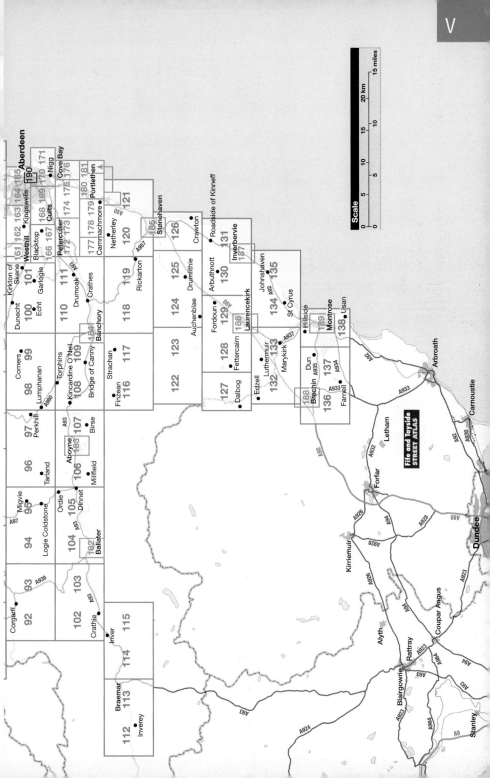

V

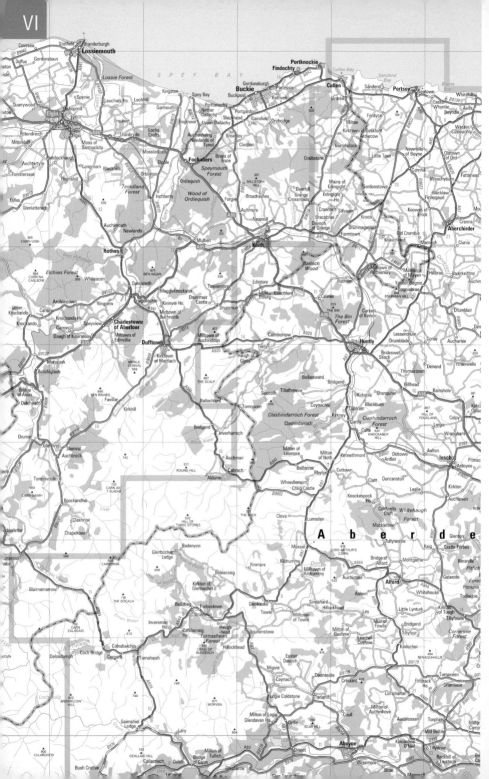

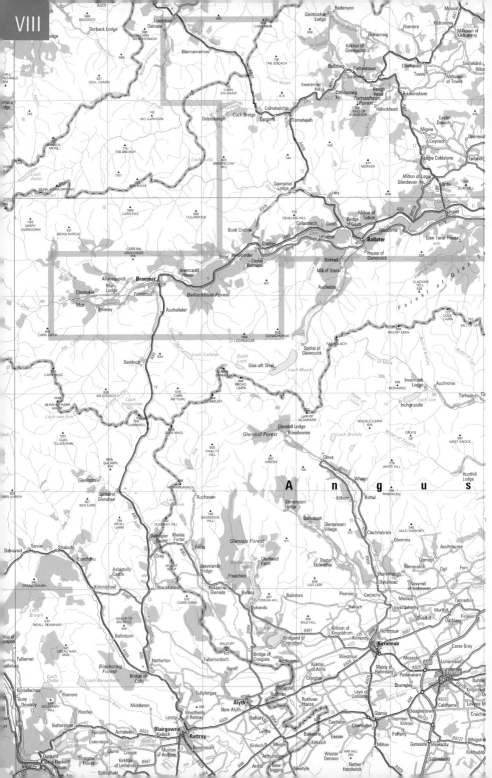

Administrative and Postcode boundaries

County and unitary authority boundaries
Postcode boundaries
Area covered by this atlas

B4
1 SOUTH CASTLE ST
2 YORK PL
3 NORTH DESKFORD ST
4 SOUTH DESKFORD ST
5 QUEEN'S DR
6 BINVIEW RD
7 BINVIEW TER
8 JUDY'S LA
9 GLEBE PARK CR

B5
1 CAMPBELL ST
2 LOWER BLANTYRE ST
3 STATION RD
4 SEAFIELD ST
5 THE SQUARE
6 REIDHAVEN PL
7 REIDHAVEN ST
8 BLANTYRE ST
9 NEW VIEW CT
10 ALBERT TER
11 LOGIE AV
12 BAYVIEW RD
13 NORTH CASTLE ST
14 GRANT ST

Cullen
Golf
Course
CH
Cullen Bay

Lighthouse
Cemy
Harbour
Seatown
Logie Head

A98 Fochabers (196)
A98
CASTLE TER
Cullen Bay
Hotel
Castle Hill
Motte
Chy
Cullen Library
Cullen Prim Sch
SEAFIELD ST
SEAFIELD RD
OLD CHURCH RD

Claypot's
Bridge

Old
Cullen
Cullen
House

Betty's
Well
Weir
GRANT ST

CULLEN
Seafield
Farm
Cemetery

Logie
House

Crannoch
Hill

Sunnyside

Findlater Castle
(rems of)
Viewpoint

Crathie
Point

Fort

Garron
Point

Dovecot

Barnyards of
Findlater

Broom

Harbour

Sandend
Bay

Sandend

Brankanentham

Crannoch-hill
Wood

Hillocks
Plantation

Dytach
Bridge

Sandend
Bridge

THE
BENTS

SLAVERY RD

B9018
TOCHIENEAL CR
SEAFIELD RD
BURNSIDE

Lintmill
Tochieneal
Ford

Kilnhillock

Kilnhillock
Wood

Scattery Burn

Dytach

A98

Weir

Kirstie's
Well
Weir
Shirralds

Low Glen
Plantation

Chy

Mill of
Towle

Birkenbog

Birkenbog
Wood

AB45

Mains of
Glassaugh

Shirralds
Wood

AB56

Clune Hill

Mains of
Birkenbog

Porterstown

Little Dytach

Nicholson
Park

Church
(rems of)

Burnsford

Gallows
Well

Clunehill

Clune
Leitchestown

Ley

Cairnton

Fordyce

PO
Fordyce Joiner's
Workshop and
Visitor Centre

Castle
Fordyce
Prim Sch

THE LOAN
EAST CHURCH ST
WEST CHURCH ST

Fordyce
Cemetery

B9018
Ha'burn

Nether
Blairock

Milton

Castle
(rems of)

Towie
Wood

Ha'burn Bridge

Braxy Burn
Burn of Cullen

Burn of Fordyce

F1
1 PITCHAIDLIE PL
2 BRIDGE ST
3 CHURCH ST
4 CASTLE LA
5 BACK ST
6 ST TARQUINS PL
7 THE SQUARE

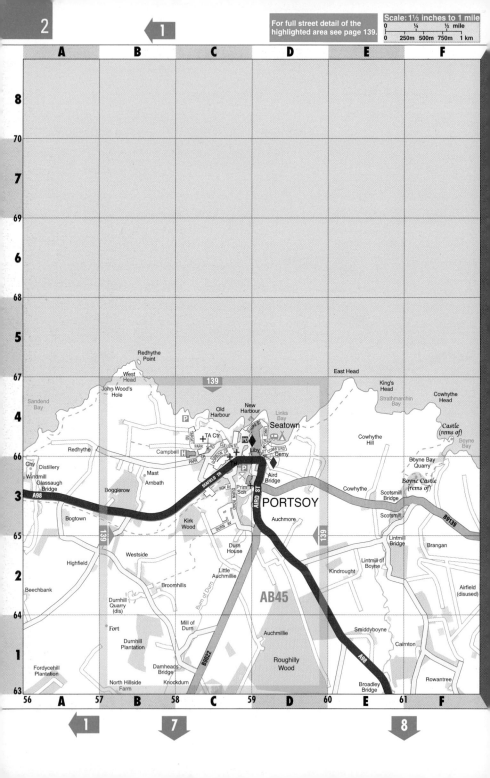

For full street detail of the highlighted area see page 139.

Scale: 1⅓ inches to 1 mile

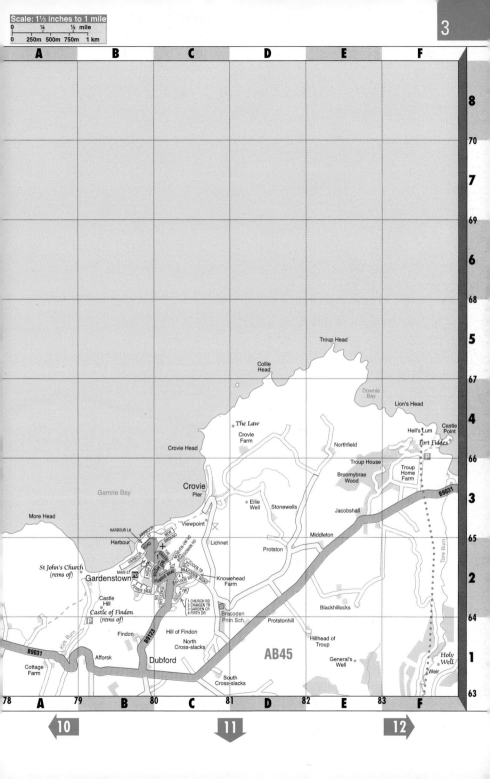

Scale: 1⅓ inches to 1 mile

0   ¼   ½ mile
0 250m 500m 750m 1 km

A   B   C   D   E   F

8

70

7

69

6

68

5

67

4

66

3

65

2

64

1

63

Troup Head

Collie
Head

Downie
Bay

Lion's Head

The Law

Crovie
Farm

Hell's Lum

Castle
Point

Crovie Head

Northfield

Fort Fiddes

Troup House

Troup
Home
Farm

Broombrae
Wood

Crovie

Pier

Gamrie Bay

Ellie
Well

Stonewells

Jacobshall

Viewpoint

Middleton

B9031

More Head

HARBOUR LA

Harbour

Lichnet

Protston

HARBOUR ROAD

NEW GROUND

MID HIGH
RD

FISH ST

SEATOWN
HIGH ST

GAMRIE BRAE

CASTLE TR

MAIN ST

BRACODEN TR

MERVIEW AV
MERVIEW RD

BRACODEN RD

BAYVIEW RD

St John's Church
(rems of)

Gardenstown

BAYVIEW RD

Knowehead
Farm

Tore Burn

Castle
Hill

Castle of Findon
(rems of)

FENNIE BRAE

1 CHURCH RD
2 CRAIGEN TR
3 GARDEN CR
4 FIRTH DR

Bracoden
Prim Sch

Protstonhill

Blackhillocks

B9122

Findon

Hill of Findon

North
Cross-slacks

Protstonhill

Hillhead of
Troup

Hillhead of
Troup

General's
Well

Holy
Well

Kirk Burn

B9031

Afforsk

Dubford

AB45

Weir

Cottage
Farm

South
Cross-slacks

Kirk Burn

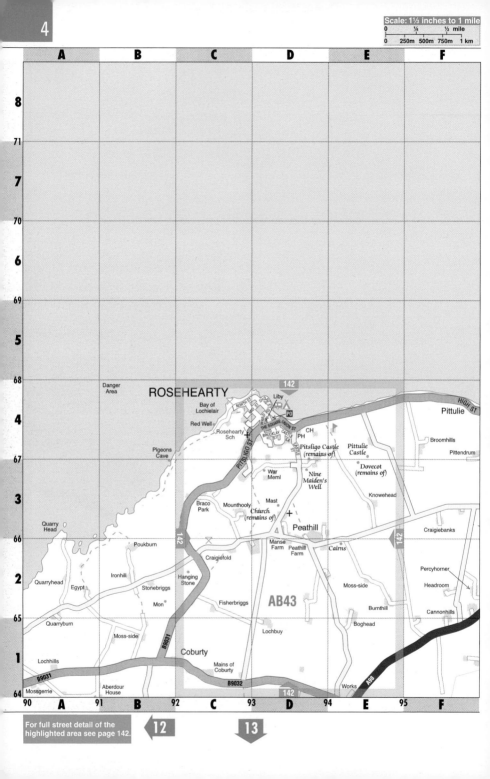

Scale: 1½ inches to 1 mile

0   ¼   ½ mile
0   250m 500m 750m 1 km

ROSEHEARTY

Danger Area

Bay of Lochielair

Red Well

Pigeons Cave

Rosehearty Sch

PITSLIGO ST

NORTH ST
SHORE ST
WHARF ST
THE SQUARE UNION ST
BRUCKLAY CASTLE ST
BRUCKLAY CASTLE ST

Liby

PO

CH
PH

Pitsligo Castle
(remains of)

Pittulie Castle

HIGH ST

Pittulie

Broomhills

Pittendrum

War Meml

Nine Maiden's Well

Dovecot
(remains of)

Braco Park

Mounthooly

Mast

Church
(remains of)

Peathill

Knowehead

Craigiebanks

Quarry Head

Poukburn

142

Craigiefold

Manse Farm

Peathill Farm

Cairns

142

Percyhorner

Ironhill

Hanging Stone

Moss-side

Headroom

Quarryhead

Egypt

Stonebriggs

Mon

Fisherbriggs

AB43

Burnthill

Cannonhills

Quarryburn

Moss-side

Lochbuy

Boghead

Lochhills

Coburty

Mains of Coburty

Works

A98

B9031

Aberdour House

B9032

Mossgerrie

142

90   A   91   B   92   C   93   D   94   E   95   F

For full street detail of the highlighted area see page 142.

12

13

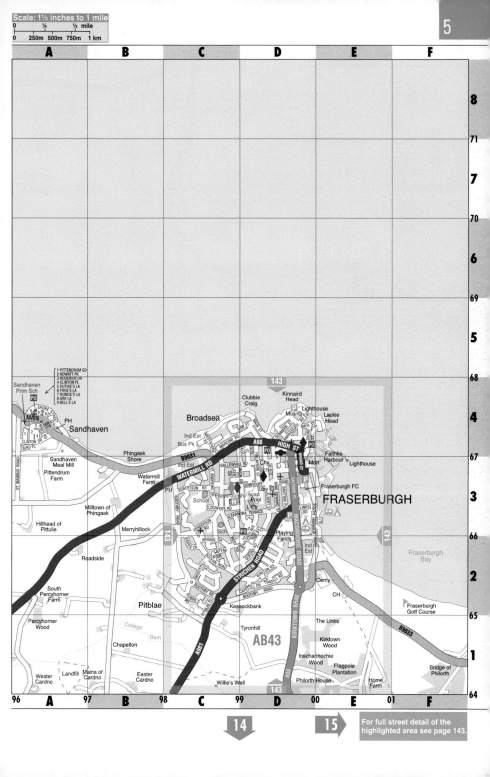

Scale: 1⅓ inches to 1 mile

0 ¼ ½ mile
0 250m 500m 750m 1 km

1 PITTENDRUM GD
2 HOWATT PK
3 RODERICK DR
4 CLINTON PL
5 PIRIE'S LA
6 PIRIE'S LA
7 RUNCIE'S LA
8 ARK LA
9 BELL'S LA

Sandhaven
Prim Sch

Sandhaven

Broadsea

Clubbie
Craig

Kinnaird
Head

Lighthouse
Mus

Lackie
Head

Faithlie
Harbour

Lighthouse

Phingask
Shore

Sandhaven
Meal Mill

Pittendrum
Farm

Ind Est
Bus Pk

Ind Est

A98

HIGH ST

Men

FRASERBURGH

Watermill
Farm

Chy

Gallowhill Rd

Fraserburgh FC

Milltown of
Phingask

School

Fraserburgh
Pool

L Ctr

Hillhead of
Pittulie

Merryhillock

ALEXANDRA TERRACE

Sch

Sch

Playing
Fields

Ind
Est

Roadside

STRICHEN ROAD

Cemy

Fraserburgh
Bay

South
Percyhorner
Farm

Pitblae

CH

Fraserburgh
Golf Course

Kessockbank

Percyhorner
Wood

College
Burn

Tyronhill

AB43

The Links

B9033

Kirktown
Wood

Chapelton

Inschannochie
Wood

Bridge of
Philorth

Wester
Cardno

Landfill

Mains of
Cardno

Easter
Cardno

Willie's Well

Flagpole
Plantation

Philorth House

Home
Farm

For full street detail of the
highlighted area see page 143.

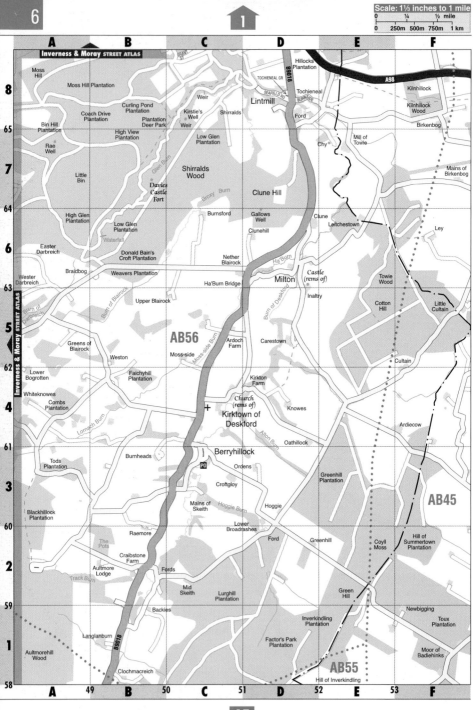

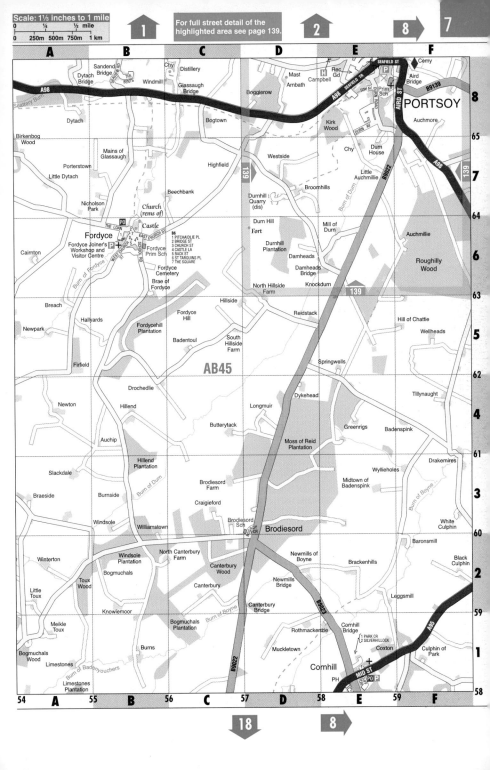

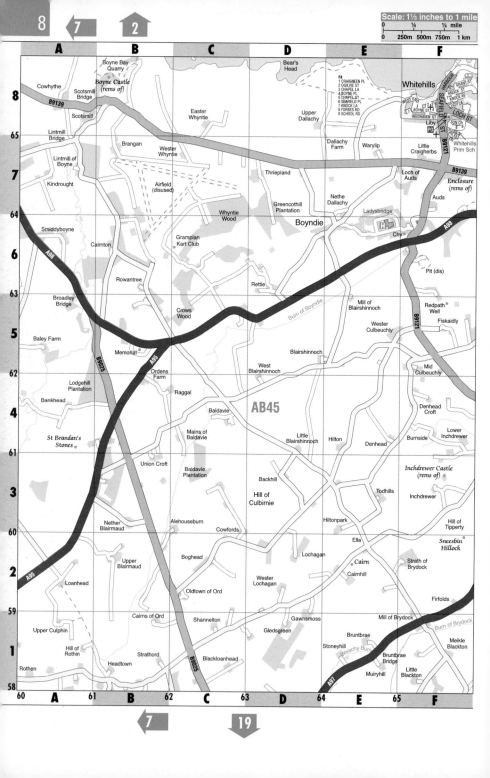

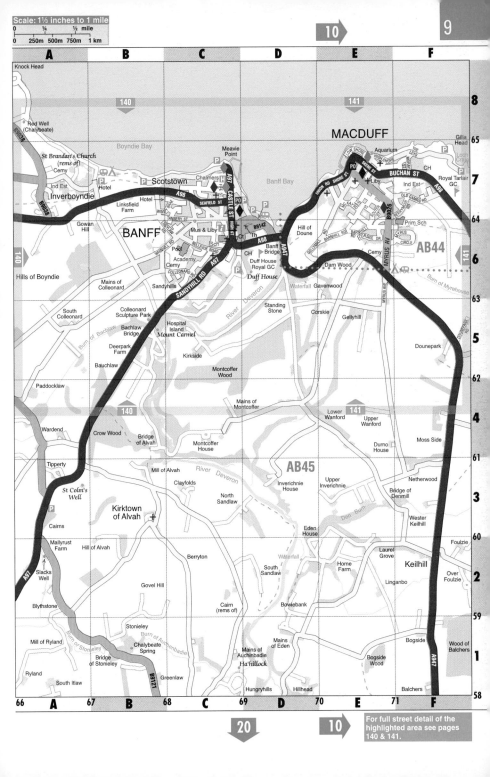

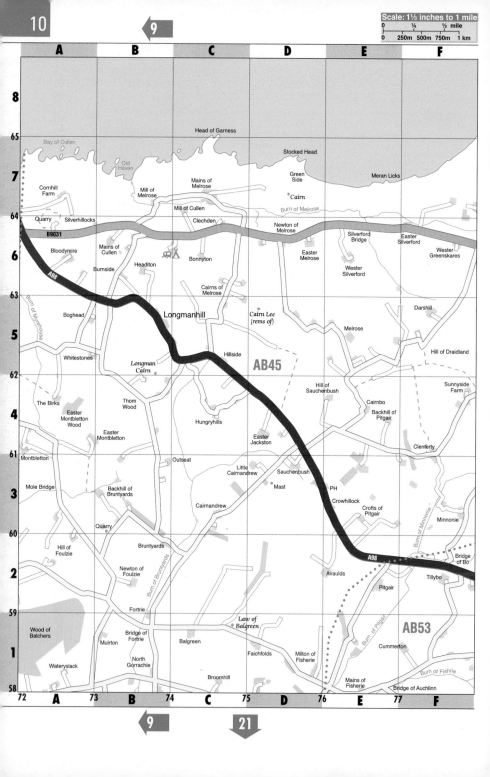

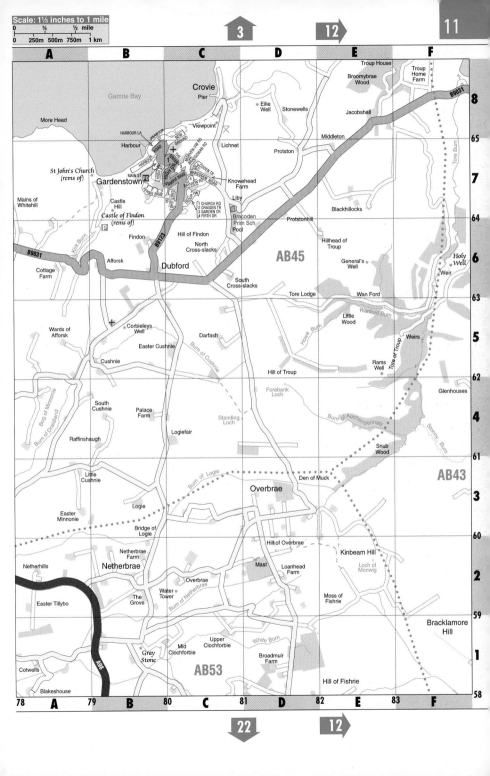

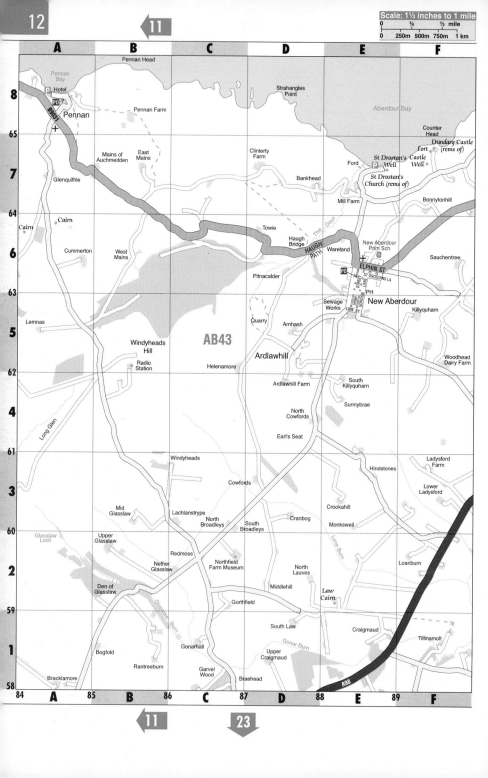

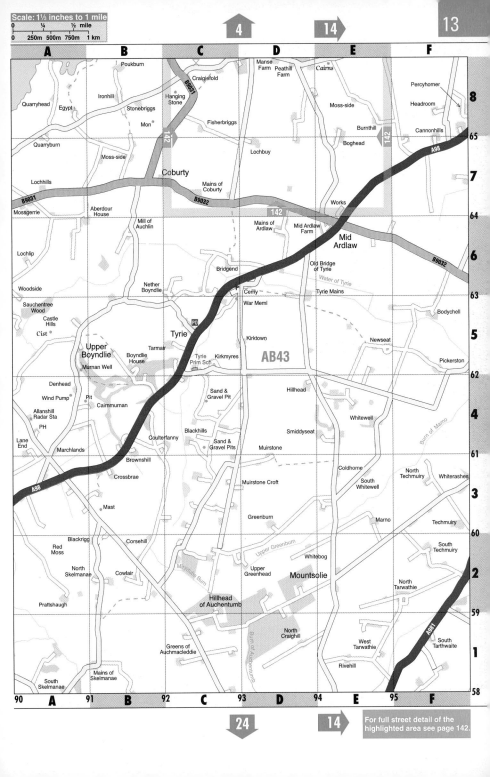

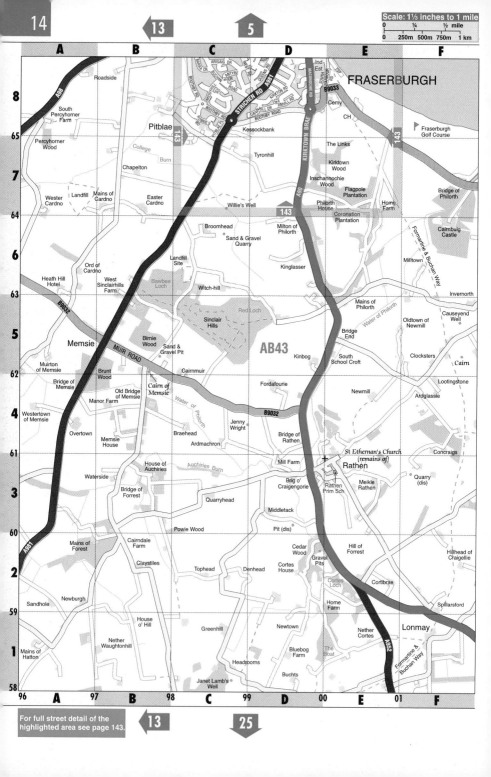

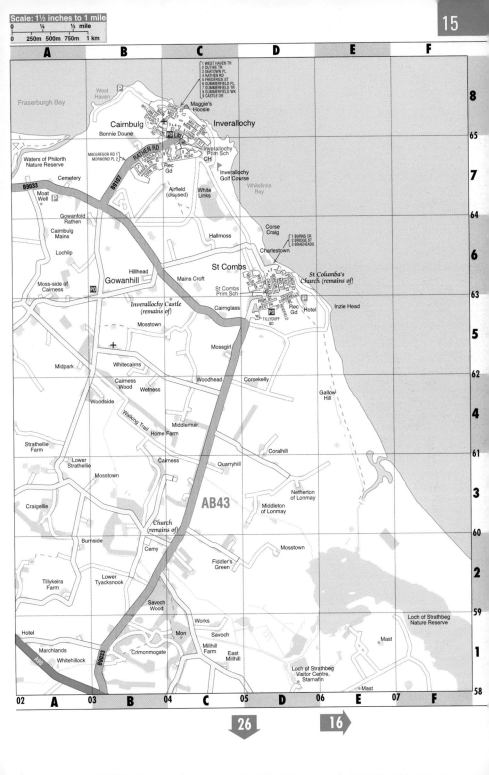

Scale: 1⅓ inches to 1 mile

| 0 | ¼ | ½ mile |
| 0 | 250m | 500m | 750m | 1 km |

A   **B**   **C**   **D**   **E**   **F**

Fraserburgh Bay

West Haven

1 WEST HAVEN TR
2 DUTHIE ST
3 SEATOWN PL
4 RATHEN RD
5 FREDERICK ST
6 SUMMERFIELD PL
7 SUMMERFIELD TR
8 SUMMERFIELD WK
9 CASTLE DR

Maggie's Hoosie

Cairnbulg

Inverallochy

Bonnie Doune

MACGREGOR RD 1
MORMOND PL 2

RATHEN RD

Waters of Philorth Nature Reserve

Cemetery

B9033

Moat Well

B9107

ALLOCHY ROAD

Inverallochy Prim Sch

CH

Rec Gd

Inverallochy Golf Course

Whitelinks Bay

Airfield (disused)

White Links

Gowanfold Rathen

Cairnbulg Mains

Lochlip

Hallmoss

Corse Craig

Charlestown

1 BURNS CR
2 BRIDGE ST
3 BRAEHEADS

St Columba's Church (remains of)

Moss-side of Cairness

Gowanhill

Hillhead

Mains Croft

St Combs

St Combs Prim Sch

Cairnglass

HIGH ST

WEST PK

Rec Gd

Hotel

Inzie Head

TILLYDUFF GD

Inverallochy Castle (remains of)

Mosstown

Mossgirl

Midpark

Whitecairns

Cairness Wood

Wetness

Woodhead

Corsekelly

Gallow Hill

Woodside

Walking Trail

Middlemuir

Home Farm

Strathellie Farm

Lower Strathellie

Mosstown

Cairness

Quarryhill

Coralhill

Netherton of Lonmay

AB43

Middleton of Lonmay

Craigellie

Church (remains of)

Burnside

Cemy

Fiddler's Green

Mosstown

Tillykeira Farm

Lower Tyacksnook

Savoch Wood

Hotel

Marchlands

A90

Whitehillock

B9033

Crimonmogate

Mon

Works

Savoch

Millhill Farm

East Millhill

Loch of Strathbeg Nature Reserve

Mast

Loch of Strathbeg Visitor Centre, Starnafin

Mast

8
65
7
64
6
63
5
62
4
61
3
60
2
59
1
58

02   **A**   03   **B**   04   **C**   05   **D**   06   **E**   07   **F**

26
16

Scale: 1⅓ inches to 1 mile

0   ¼   ½   mile
0 250m 500m 750m 1 km

8

61

7

60

6

59

Black Bar

AB43

Maut Craig

5

The Hassy

Loch of
Strathbeg
Nature
Reserve

Castle
Earthworks

The Skellies

58

Old
Rattray

Seatown

Rattray Head

Jetty

The Ron
Lighthouse

4

St Mary's Chapel
(remains of)

Rattray Head
Lighthouse Shore
Station

57

Ryehill

*Burgh of Rattray
(site of)*

Middleton of
Rattray

3

Greenmyre

AB42

Rattray
House

56

Rattray
Wood

Home Farm

2

55

Mast

1

Gas Terminal

Middle
Essie

54

A   08   09   B   10   C   11   D   12   E   13   F

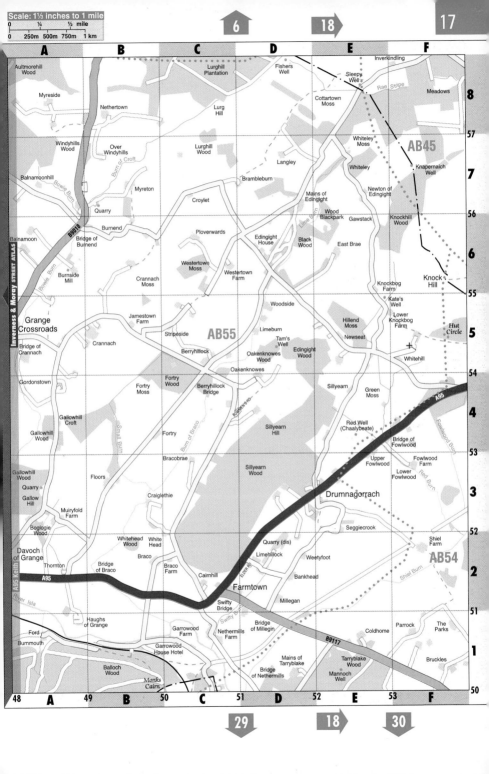

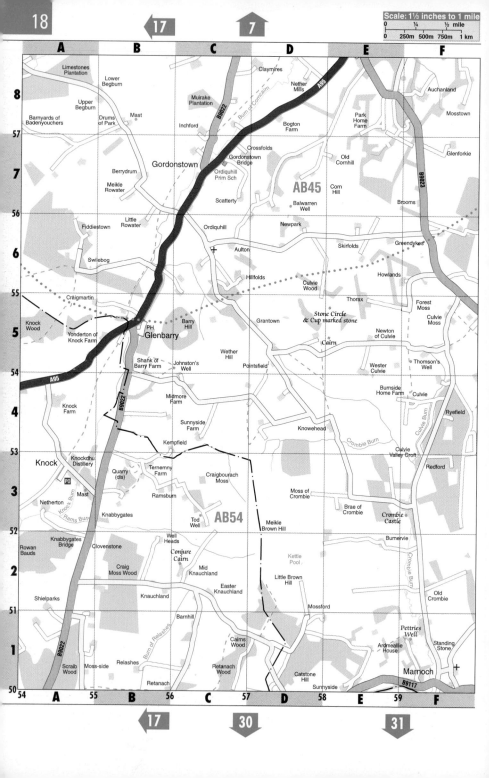

8

20

A   B   C   D   E   F

Blackhills

Gammie's Bridge
Newton of Deershaw
Loanhead

Reidside Farm
Blackhills Moss
Dens of Muiryhill

8

Reidside Moss
Cormickhillock
Ladysheets
Burn of Muiryhill

57

Peterden
Sheriffseat
Middle Weachyburn
Coldhome

Drywells

AB45

7

Fishermen's Moss
Hill of Maunderlea
Herodhill

Torston
Auchinderran Moss
Milbethill
Barbethill

56

Blacklaw
Little Deuchries

Finnygaud Farm
Auchinderran
Gledfield
Dogshillock Farm
Hilltown
Lower Deuchries
Burngrains Farm

6

Burn of Backieley
Kebholes
Craigaithry Wood

55

B9023
Finnygaud
Spring Garden Farm
Littlefield
Dogshillock
Upper Backieley
Castlebrae
Black Law
Craigathray

5

144

Lootcherbrae Bridge
Backieley Croft
Alliehar

Auchintoul Moss
Wester Corskie
Upper Crannabog
Gallow Hill
Sweerburn
Boghead

54

Knowes of Elrick

AB54

North Cranna
Rotten Moss
Rowantree

B9025

4

Craigiebrae Farm
Mains of Corskie
Burn of Alrland

53

Leachkiln Wood
Newton of Auchintoul
Aberchirder Prim Sch
Mains of Cranna

Monedie
CORNHILL RD
B9023
NORTH ST
Liby
ABERCHIRDER
Hillhead

3

Home Farm Auchintoul
PH
MAIN ST
South Cranna
Woodside

144
Bronchall Well
PO
MAIN ST
Skeebhill Bridge
Skeibhill

52

Auchintoul Home Farm
Cleanhill Wood
Little Haven Well
South Brownhill

Westside of Carnousie

2

SOUTH ST
Cleanhill
Quarryhill

Whitemuir
White Stone
Mill of Auchintoul
North Braeside Farm
Muiryfield
Bogharvey
Castlehill
Auldtown Hill

51

Whitemuir Plantation
Janefield
Forgieston
Backhill of Clunie
AB53
Yonderton

Bellman's Wood
Sheep Park
Myreside Stone Circle (rems of)
Craig Well
144
Dubiton
Mains of Knockorth
Clunie Hill
Brokenfolds

1

Clasduff Well
Mosshead
Dundee Farm
Home Farm of Clunie
Crans Wood

50

60   A   61   B   62   C   63   D   64   E   65   F   66

31

32

20

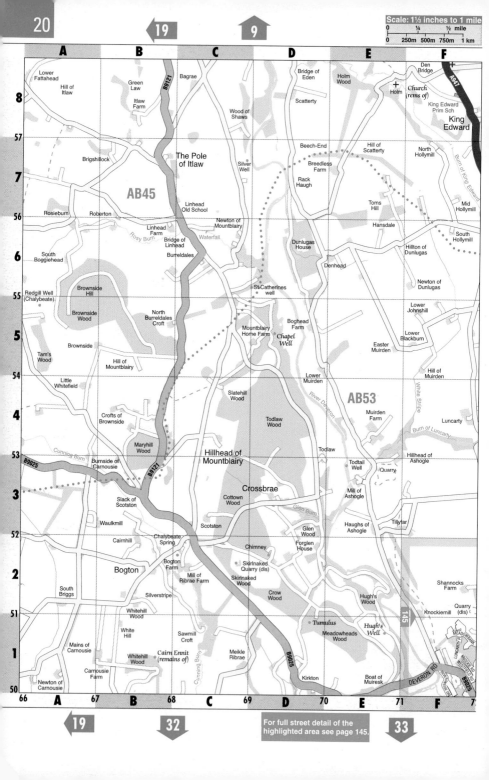

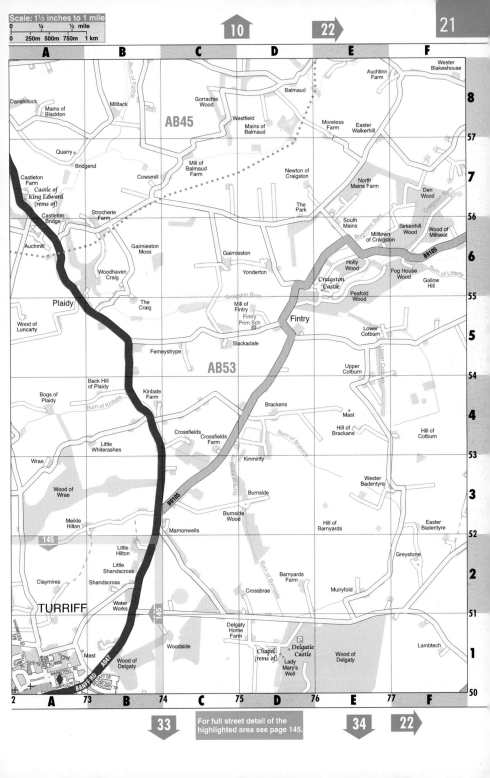

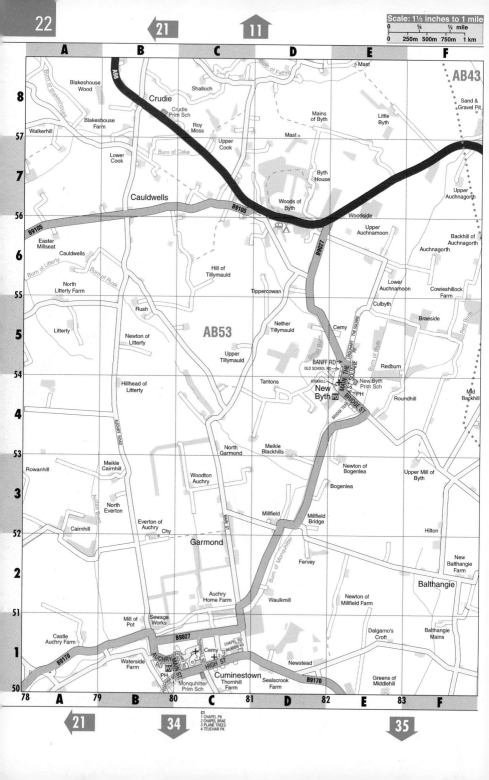

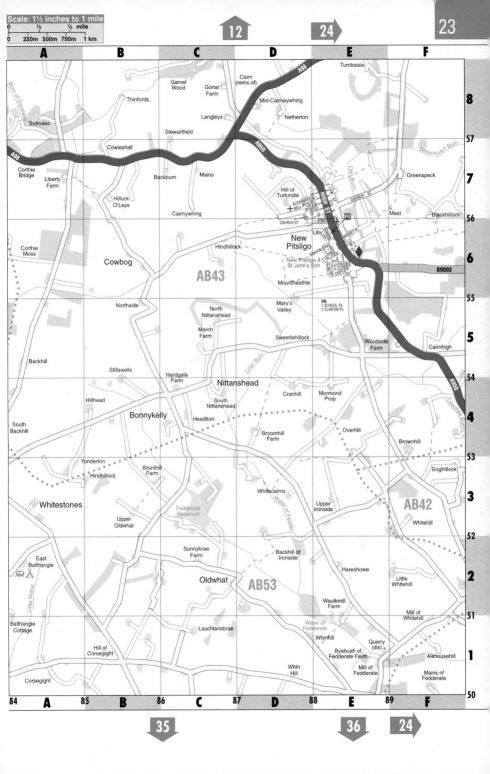

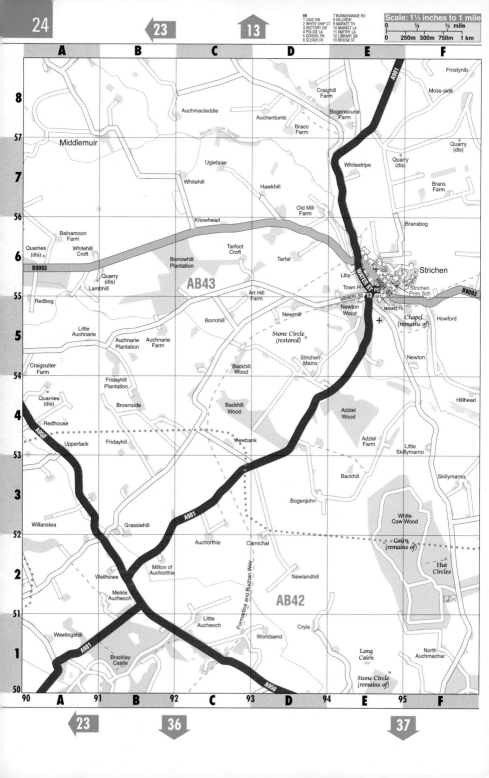

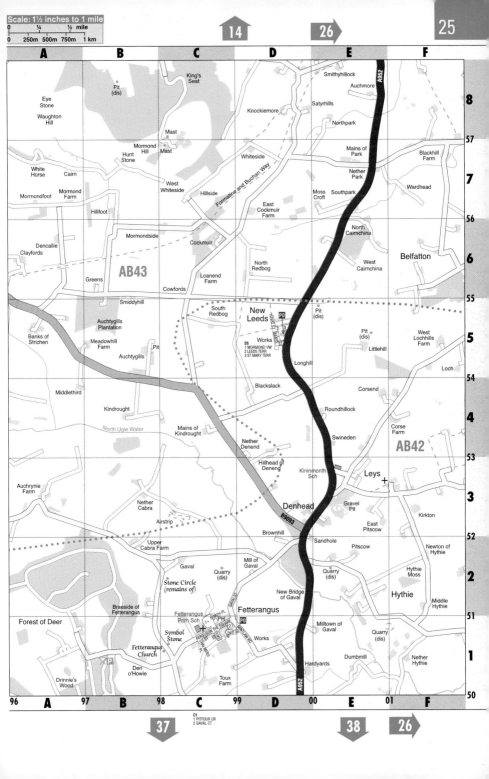

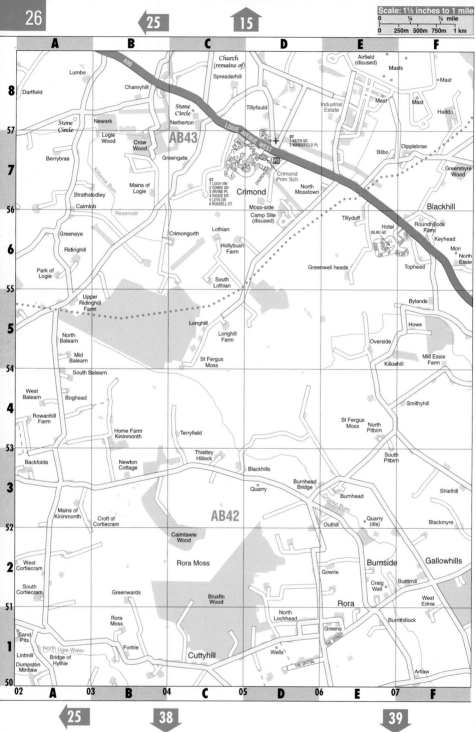

AB43
Old Rattray
Jetty
St Mary's Chapel
(remains of)
Ryehill
Burgh of Rattray
(site of)
Middleton of
Rattray
Greenmyre
Rattray Head
The Ron
Lighthouse
Rattray Head
Lighthouse Shore
Station
Rattray
House
Home Farm
Rattray
Wood
A90
Mast
Middle
Essie
Gas Terminal
Black Water
Newseat
Essie
Mast
AB42
Netherhill
South
Essie
St Fergus
Prim Sch
Kirktown
Corhill
SCHOOL ROAD
LINKS RD
NETHERHILL LA
KINLOCH ROAD
NEWTON RD
Recn
Gd

1 COWIE CR
2 SEAVIEW RD
3 BRAEHEAD RD
4 URQUHART RD
5 URQUHART CR
6 HALL RD
7 LINKS VW
8 ALWYN WIND
9 WISEMAN TR

St Fergus
Scotstown
PH
P0
Mast
P

Mast
Scotstown
Head
St Fergus
Links
Mast
North
Kirkton
Little
Ednie
Kinloch
Inverquinzie
Cotts
Mason
Well
St Fergus's Church
(remains of)
Kirkton
Head
Ednie
A90
South
Kirkton

8
57
7
56
6
55
5
54
4
53
3
52
2
51
1
50

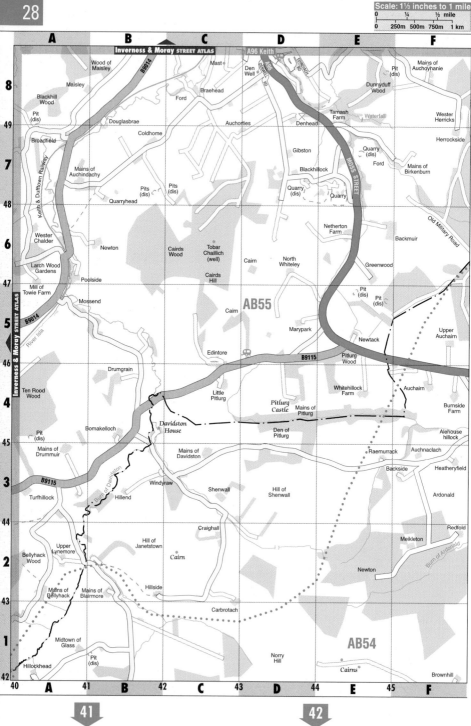

Inverness & Moray STREET ATLAS

A96 Keith

A **B** **C** **D** **E** **F**

8

Wood of Maisley
Maisley
Blackhill Wood
Pit (dis)
Broadfield

Den Well
Mast
Braehead
Ford
Auchorties
Denhead

Pit (dis)
Mains of Auchoyhanie
Dunnyduff Wood
Tarnash Farm
Waterfall
Wester Herricks
Herrockside

49

Douglasbrae
Coldhome
Gibston
Quarry (dis)
Ford
Mains of Birkenburn

7

Keith & Dufftown Railway
Mains of Auchindachy
Pits (dis)
Pits (dis)
Quarryhead
Blackhillock
Quarry (dis)
Quarry
Moss Street

48

6

Wester Chalder
Larch Wood Gardens
Newton
Poolside
Cairds Wood
Tobar Chaillich (well)
Cairds Hill
Cairn
North Whiteley
Netherton Farm
Backmuir
Greenwood
Old Military Road

47

Mill of Towie Farm
Mossend
AB55
Cairn
Pit (dis)
Pit (dis)
Upper Auchairn

5

B9014
River Isla
Maryport
Newtack
Pitlurg Wood
B9115

46

Drumgrain
Edintore
Little Pitlurg
Whitehillock Farm
Auchairn

4

Ten Rood Wood
Pit (dis)
Bomakelloch
Davidston House
Pitlurg Castle
Mains of Pitlurg
Den of Pitlurg
Alehouse hillock
Burnside Farm

45

Mains of Drummuir
Mains of Davidston
Raemurrack
Auchnaclach
Backside
Heatheryfield

3

B9115
Turfhillock
Burn of Davidston
Hillend
Windyraw
Shenwall
Hill of Shenwall
Ardonald

44

Upper Lynemore
Hill of Janetstown
Craighall
Redfold
Meikleton

2

Bellyhack Wood
Cairn
Newton
Burn of Ardonald

Mains of Bellyhack
Mains of Blairmore
Hillside

43

Carbrotach

1

Midtown of Glass
Pit (dis)
AB54
Norry Hill
Cairns
Brownhill

Hillockhead

42

40 **A** **41** **B** **42** **C** **43** **D** **44** **E** **45** **F**

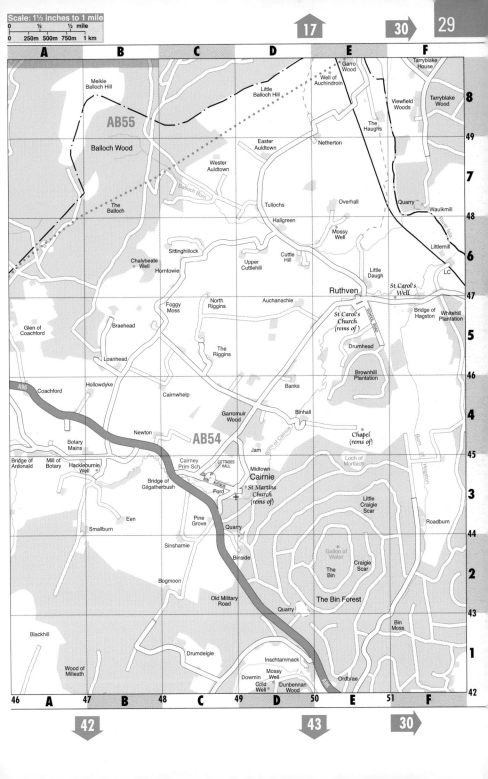

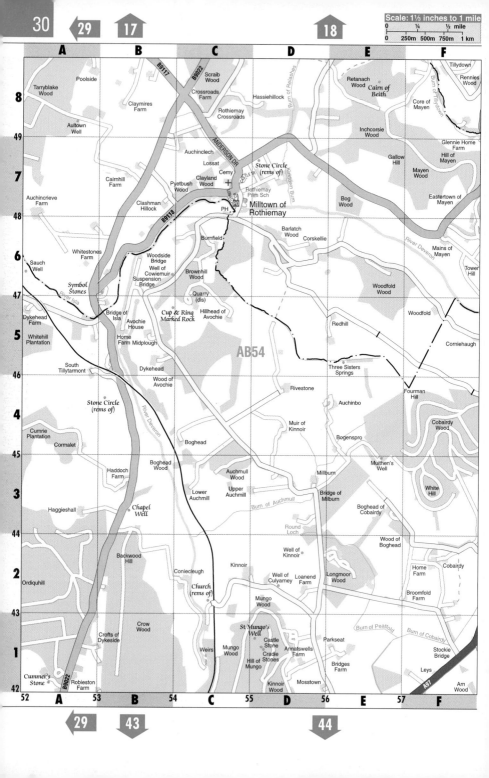

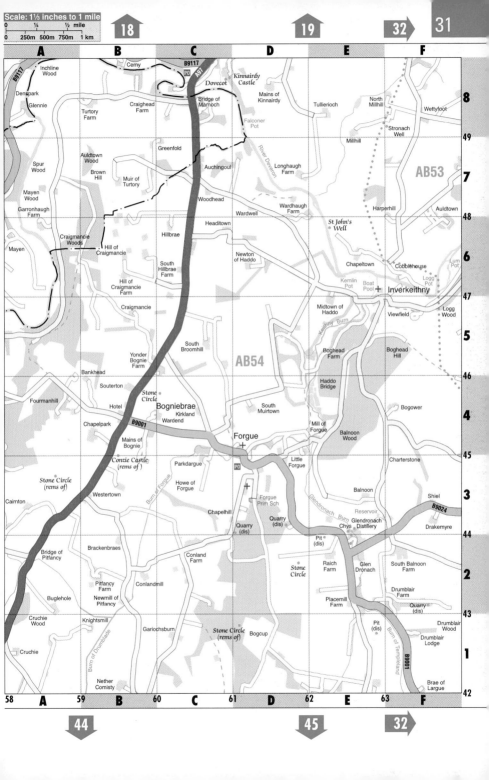

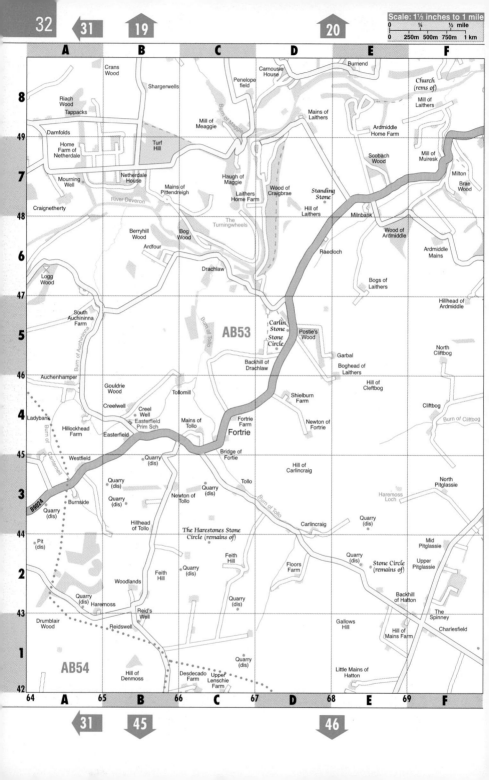

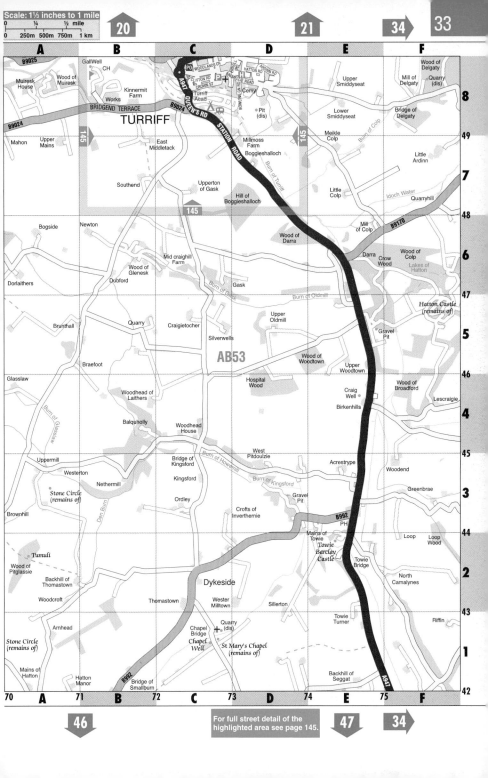

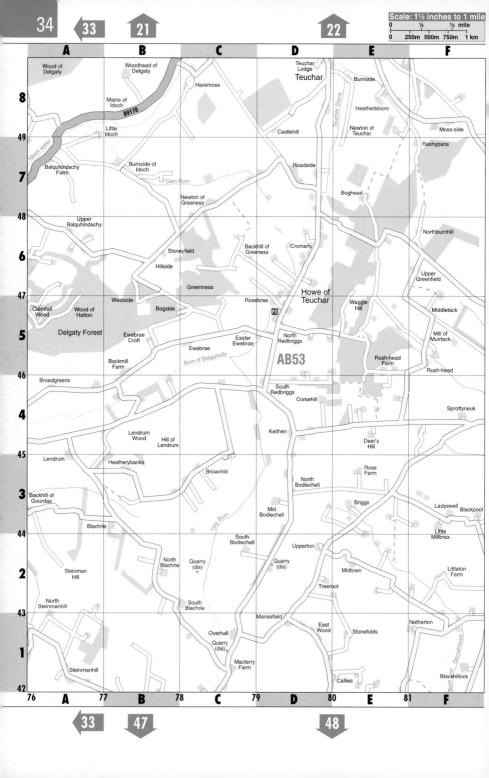

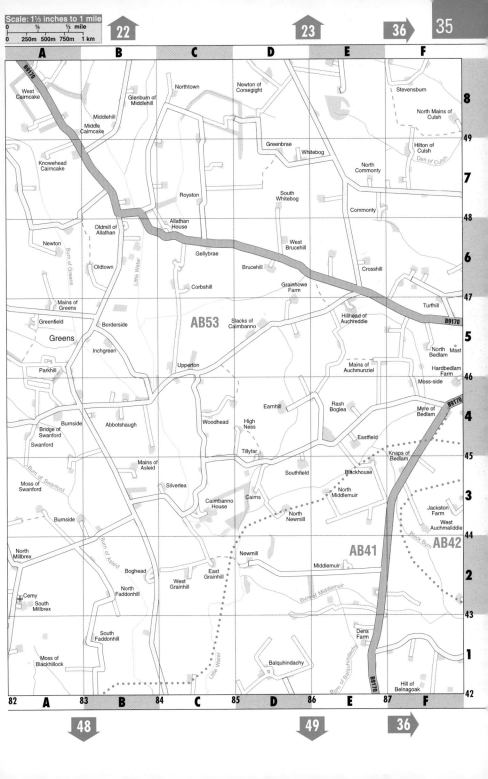

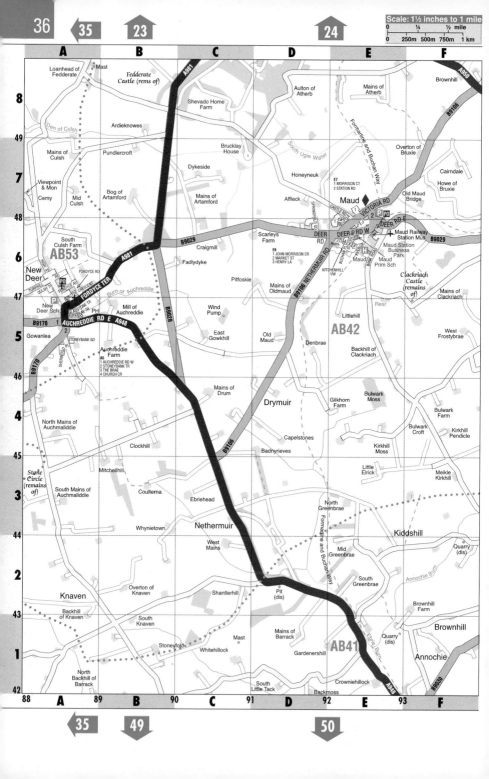

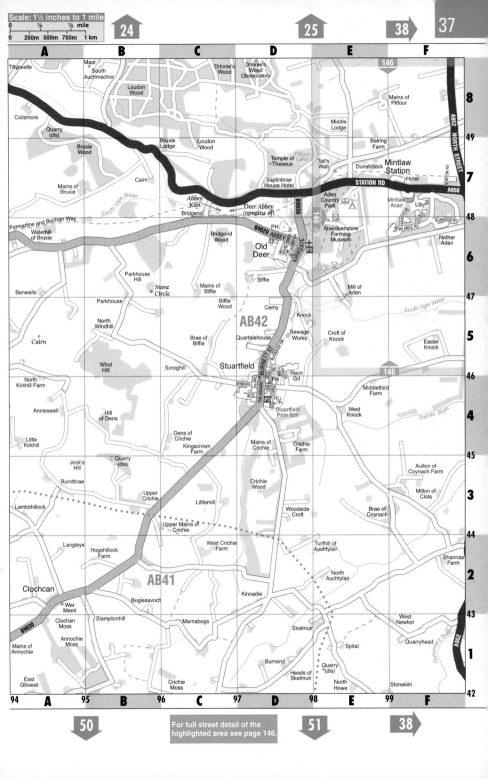

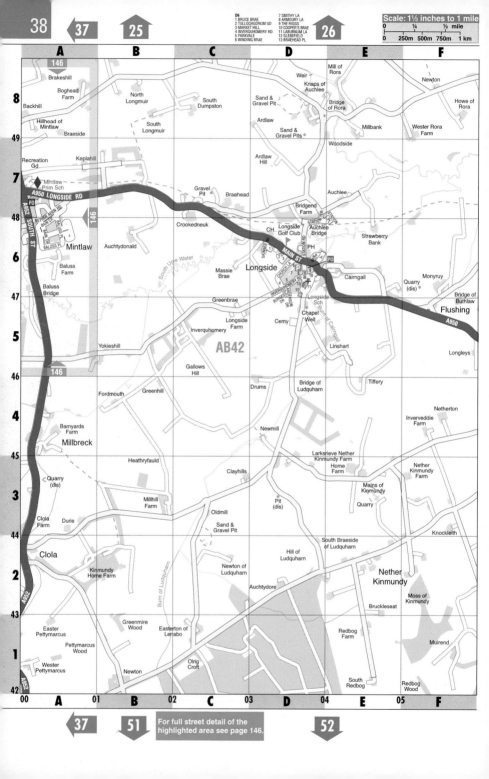

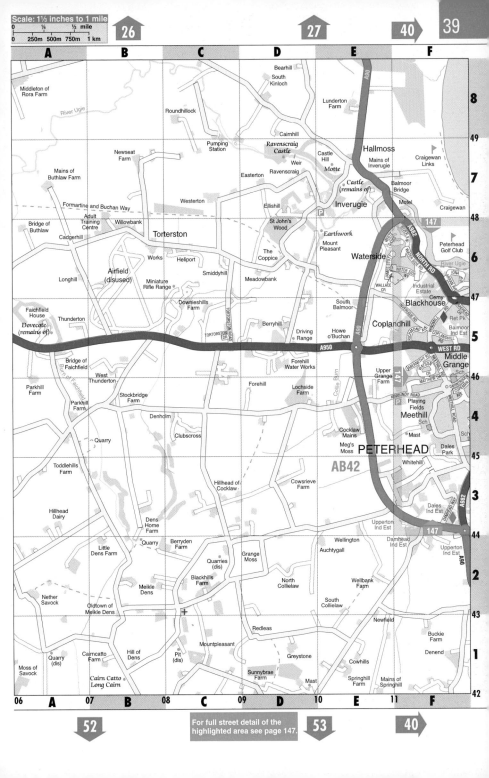

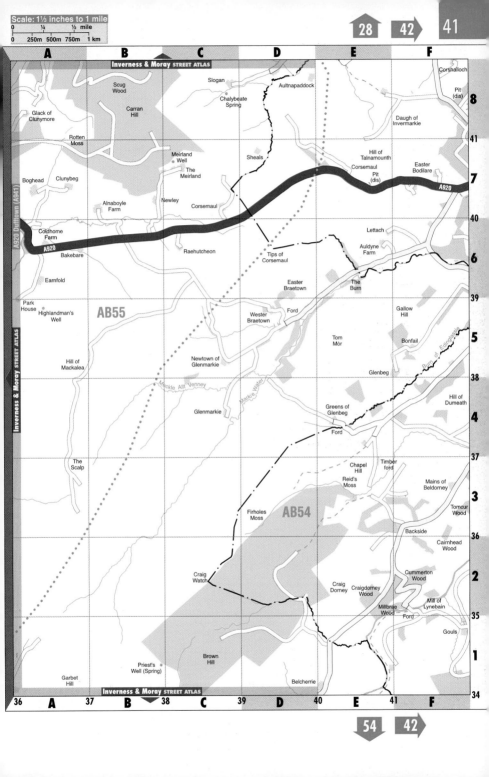

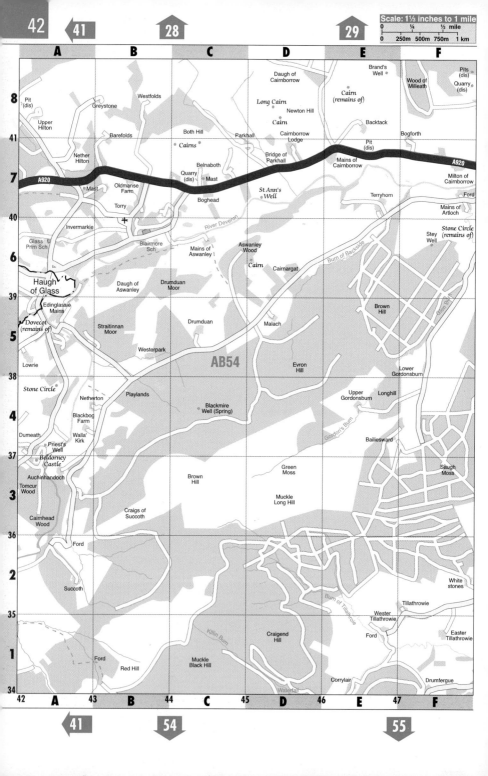

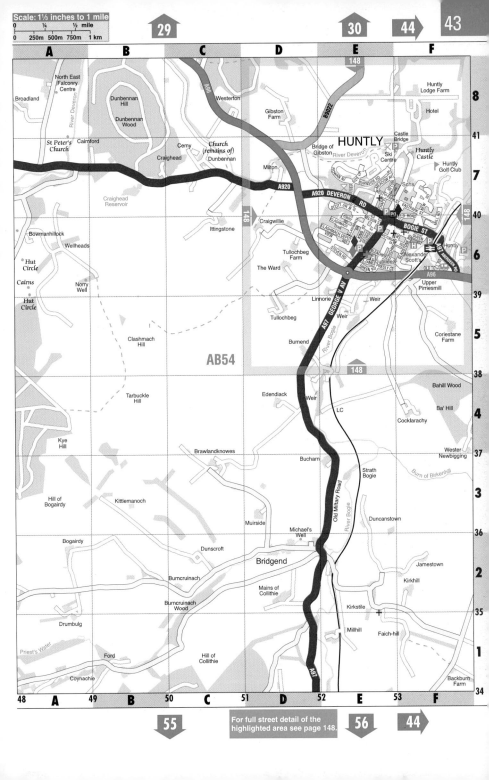

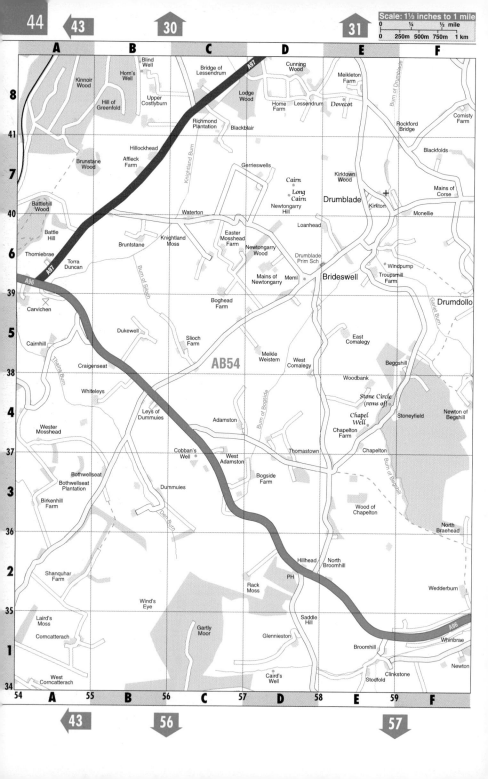

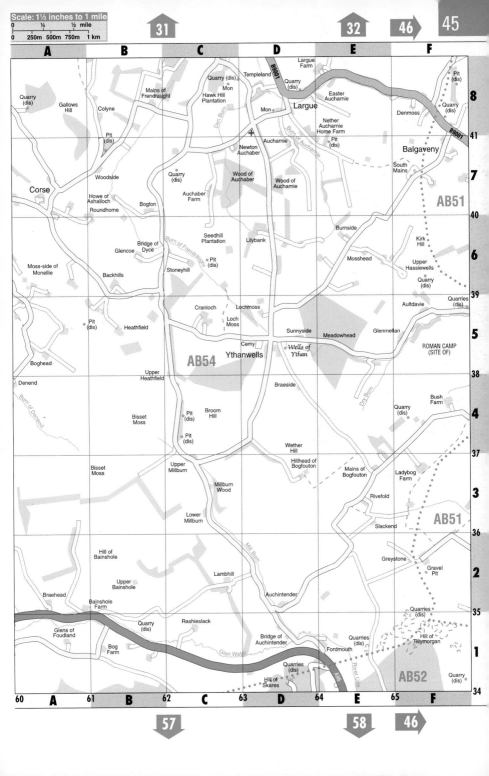

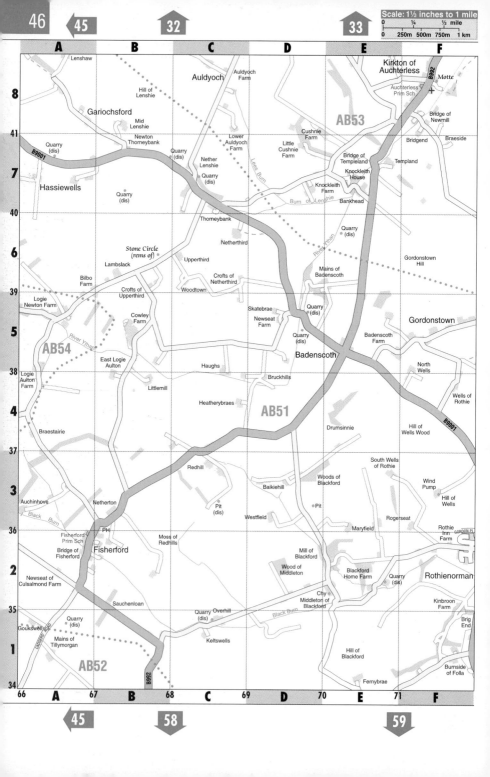

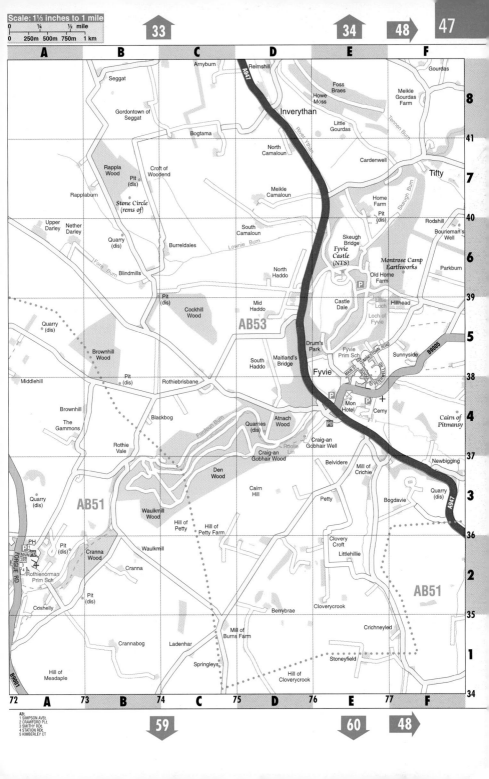

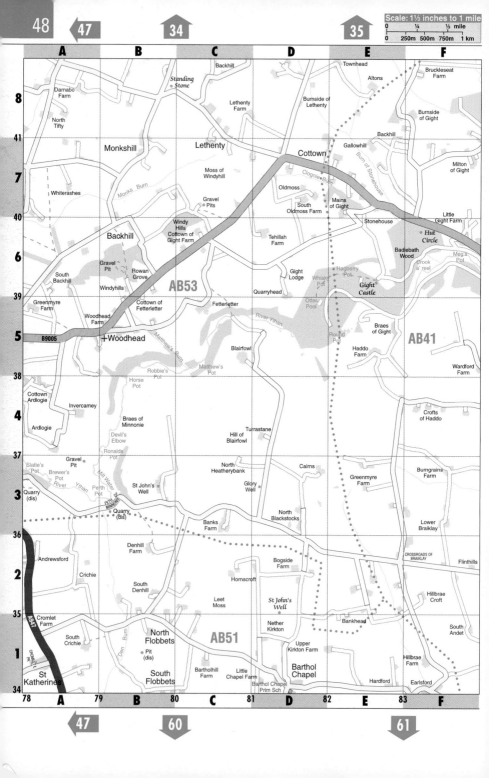

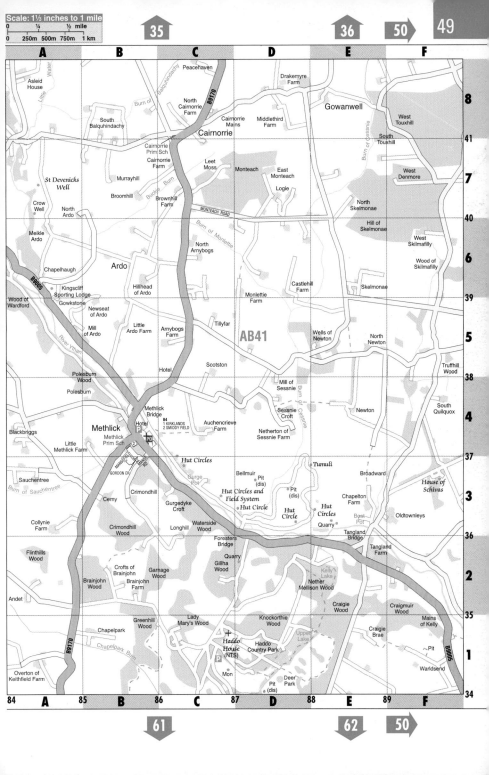

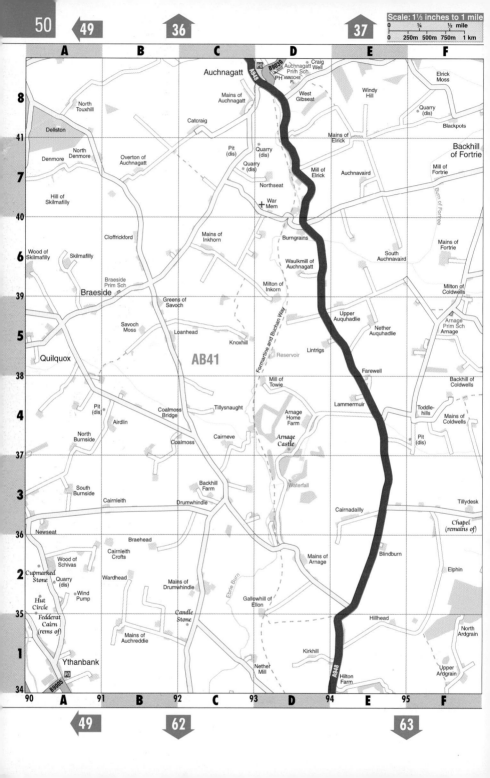

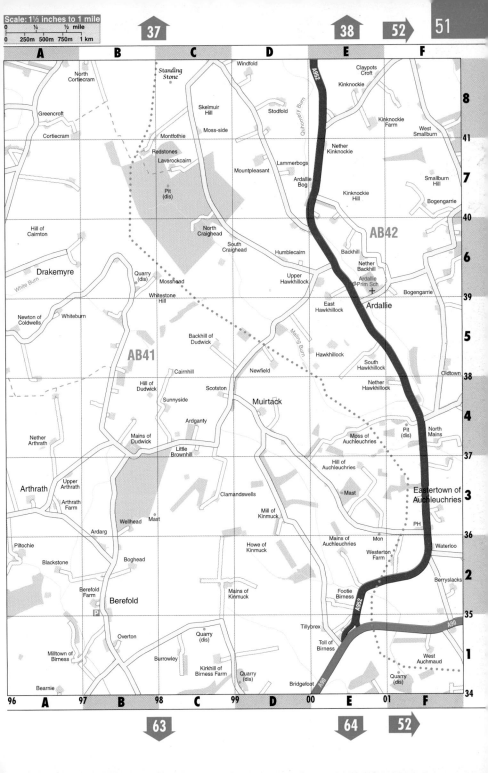

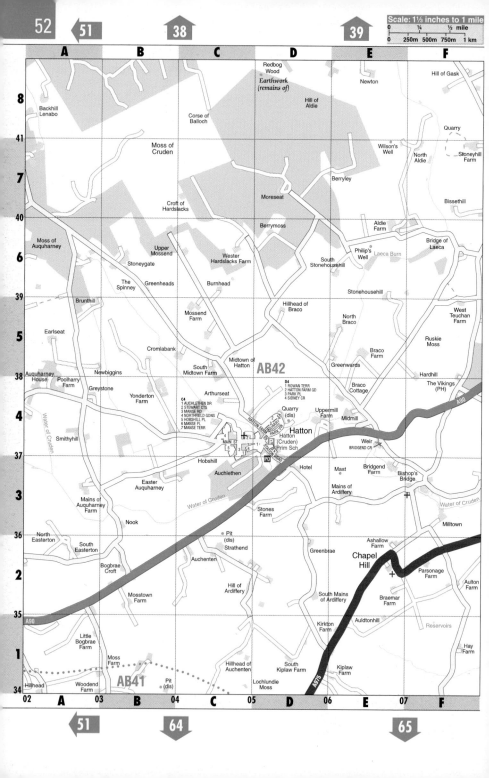

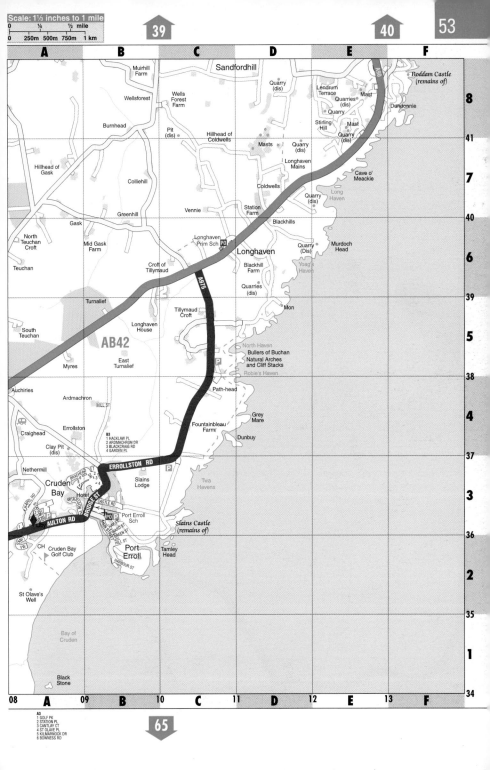

Scale: 1½ inches to 1 mile

0   ¼   ½ mile

0   250m 500m 750m 1 km

A **B** **C** **D** **E** **F**

Muirhill Farm
Sandfordhill
Wellsforest
Wells Forest Farm
Quarry (dis)
Lendrum Terrace
Quarries (dis)
Mast
Boddam Castle (remains of)
Burnhead
Pit (dis)
Hillhead of Coldwells
Quarry (dis)
Quarry
Stirling Hill
Mast
Quarry (dis)
Dundonnie
Hillhead of Gask
Colliehill
Masts
Quarry (dis)
Longhaven Mains
Cave o' Meackie
North Teuchan Croft
Greenhill
Vennie
Coldwells
Quarry (dis)
Long Haven
Gask
Station Farm
Blackhills
Teuchan
Mid Gask Farm
Longhaven Prim Sch
Longhaven
Blackhill Farm
Quarry (Dis)
Murdoch Head
Croft of Tillymaud
Quarries (dis)
Yoag's Haven
Turnalief
Tillymaud Croft
Mon
South Teuchan
Longhaven House
North Haven
Bullers of Buchan Natural Arches and Cliff Stacks
Robie's Haven
Myres
East Turnalief
Auchiries
Path-head
Grey Mare
Ardmachron
HILL ST
Fountainbleau Farm
Dunbuy
Craighead
Errollston
B3
1 HACKLAW PL
2 ARDMACHRON DR
3 BLACKCRAIG RD
4 GARDEN PL
Clay Pit (dis)
ERROLLSTON RD
Nethermill
Slains Lodge
Twa Havens
Cruden Bay
Hotel
CASTLE RD
Port Erroll Sch
AULTON RD
Slains Castle (remains of)
CH
Cruden Bay Golf Club
Port Erroll
Tamley Head
St Olave's Well
HARBOUR ST
Bay of Cruden
Black Stone

AB42

A975

A3
1 GOLF PK
2 STATION PL
3 CANTLAY CT
4 ST OLAVE PL
5 KILMARNOCK DR
6 BOWNESS RD

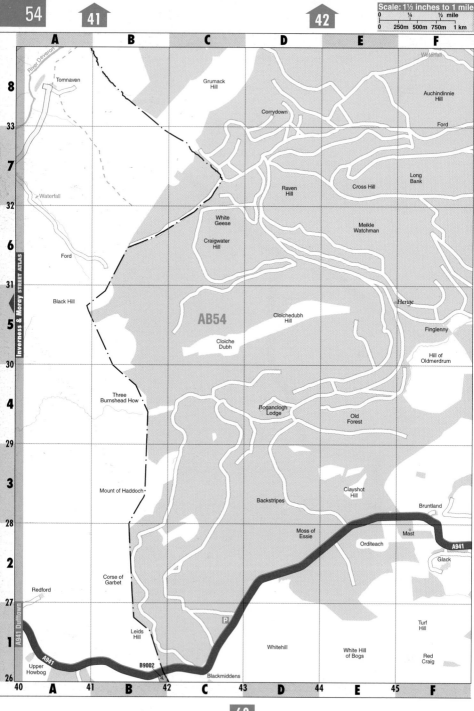

Scale: 1⅓ inches to 1 mile

| 0 | ¼ | ½ mile |
| 0 | 250m | 500m 750m 1 km |

Inverness & Moray STREET ATLAS

A   B   C   D   E   F

River Deveron

Waterfall

Tomnaven

Grumack Hill

Auchindinnie Hill

Corrydown

Ford

8

33

7

Waterfall

Raven Hill

Cross Hill

Long Bank

32

White Geese

Meikle Watchman

6

Ford

Craigwater Hill

31

Black Hill

AB54

Cloichedubh Hill

Henge

Finglenny

5

Cloiche Dubh

Hill of Oldmerdrum

30

Three Burnshead How

Boganclogh Lodge

Old Forest

4

29

Mount of Haddoch

Clayshot Hill

Bruntland

3

Backstripes

Moss of Essie

Mast

28

Corse of Garbet

Orditeach

A941

Glack

2

Redford

A941 Dufftown

Turf Hill

27

Leids Hill

P

1

Whitehill

White Hill of Bogs

Red Craig

Upper Howbog

A941

B9002

Blackmiddens

26

40   A   41   B   42   C   43   D   44   E   45   F

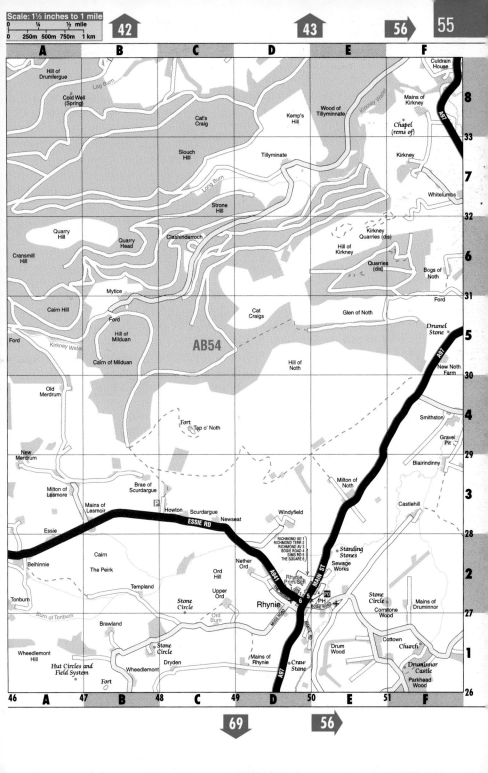

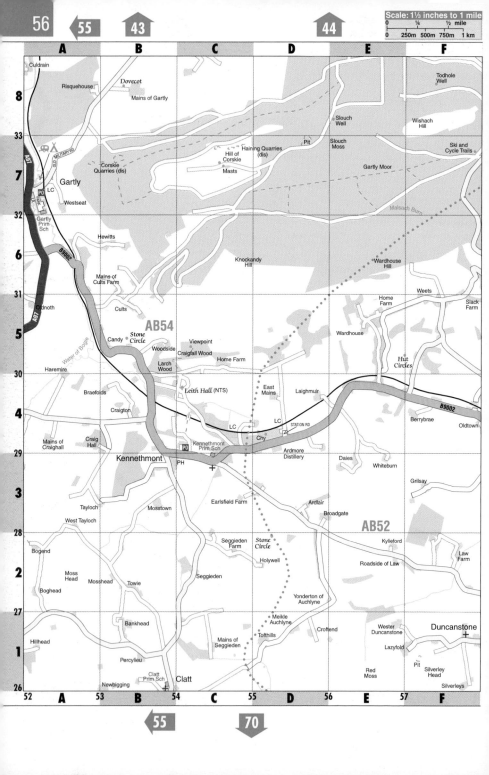

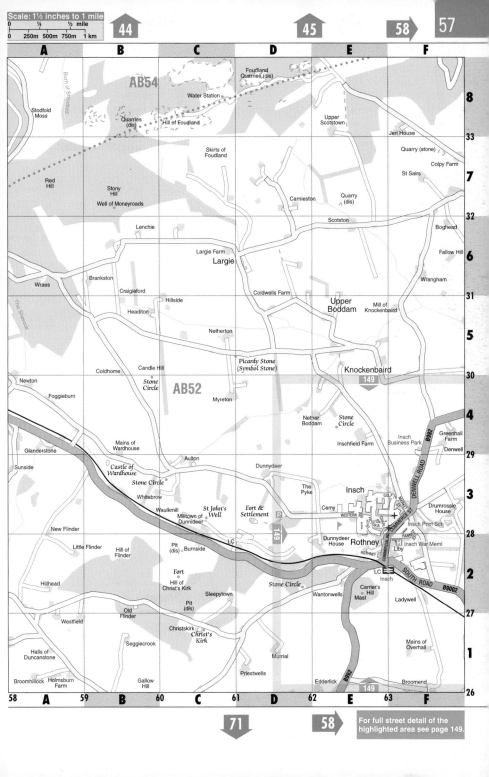

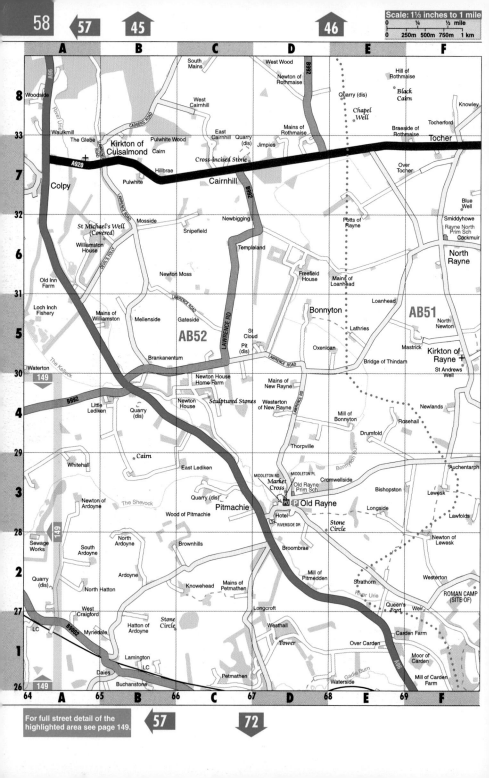

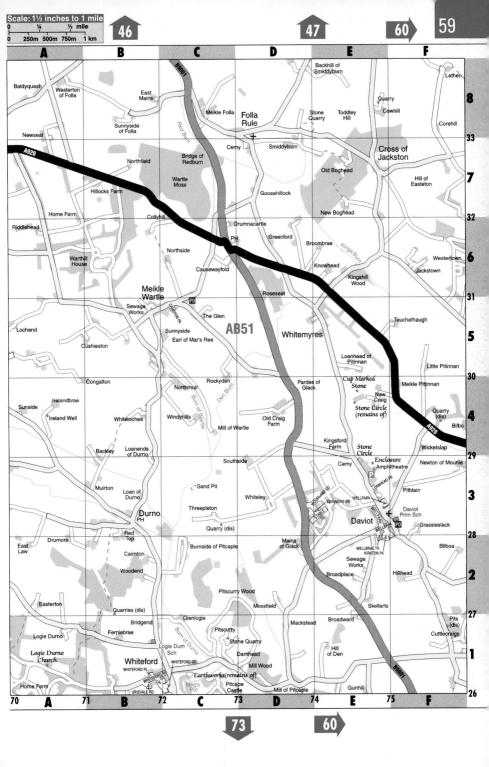

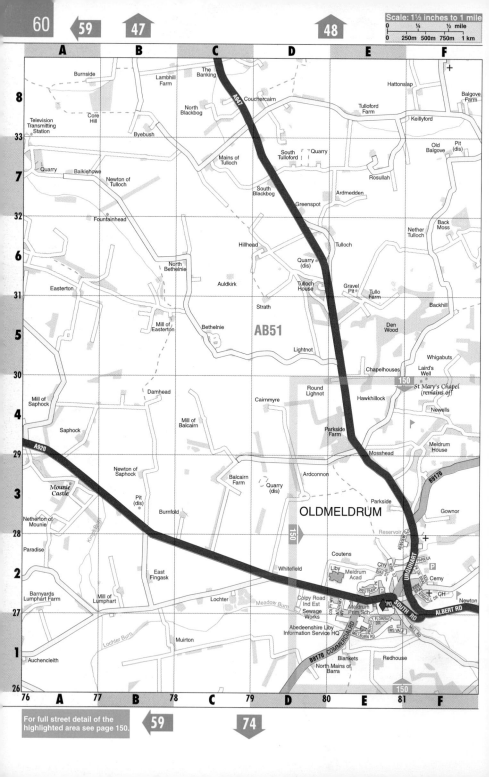

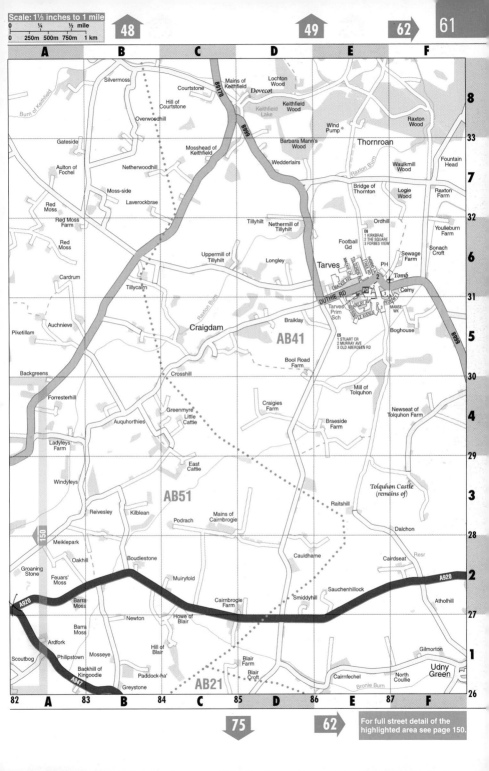

For full street detail of the highlighted area see page 150.

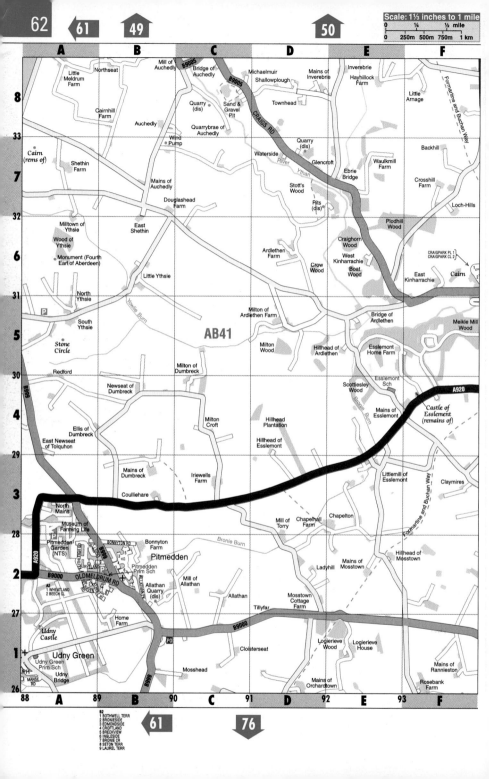

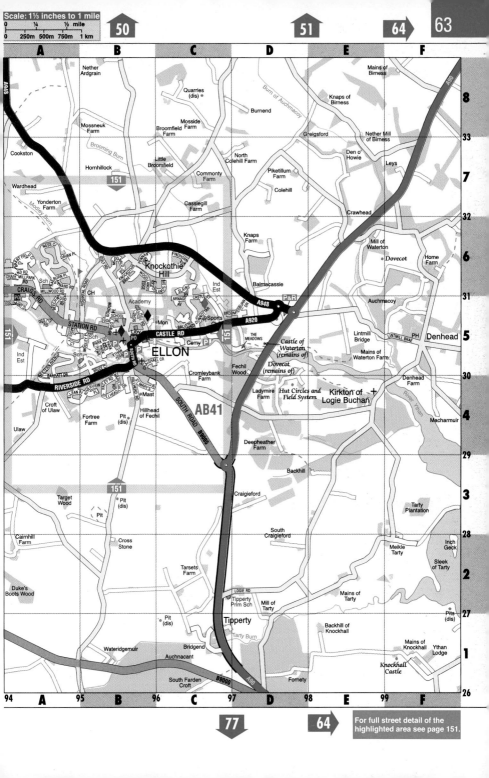

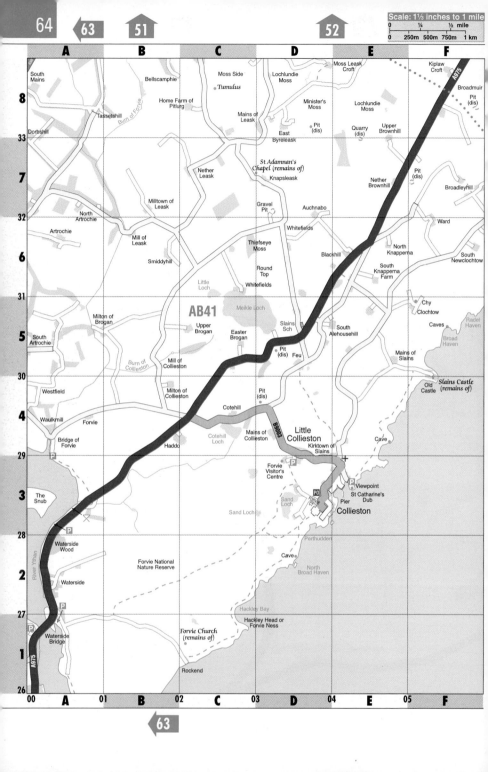

0   ¼   ½ mile
0   250m 500m 750m 1 km

A   B   C   D   E   F

8

South Mains

Bellscamphie

Moss Side

Moss Leask Croft

Kiplaw Croft

Broadmuir

Pit (dis)

A975

Home Farm of Pitlurg

Tassetshill

Tumulus

Lochlundie Moss

Burn of Fogie

Minister's Moss

Lochlundie Moss

33

Dorbshill

Mains of Leask

Pit (dis)

Quarry (dis)

Upper Brownhill

7

Nether Leask

East Byreleask

St Adamnan's Chapel (remains of)

Knapsleask

Nether Brownhill

Pit (dis)

Broadleyhill

32

North Artrochie

Milltown of Leask

Gravel Pit

Auchnabo

Whitefields

Ward

Artrochie

Mill of Leask

Thiefseye Moss

Blackhill

North Knapperna

South Newclochtow

6

Smiddyhill

Round Top

Whitefields

South Knapperna Farm

Chy

Little Loch

Meikle Loch

31

AB41

Clochtow

Caves

Radel Haven

Milton of Brogan

Upper Brogan

Easter Brogan

Slains Sch

South Alehousehill

Mains of Slains

Broad Haven

5

South Artrochie

Mill of Collieston

Pit (dis)

Feu

Slains Castle (remains of)

30

Burn of Collieston

Milton of Collieston

Pit (dis)

Old Castle

Westfield

Cotehill

Little Collieston

4

Waulkmill

Forvie

Cotehill Loch

Mains of Collieston

B9003

Cave

Haddo

Kirktown of Slains

Bridge of Forvie

P

29

Forvie Visitor's Centre

P

Viewpoint

P

St Catharine's Dub

3

The Snub

Sand Loch

PO

Pier

Colliestion

Waterside Wood

P

X

Sand Loch

Perthudden

28

Cave

River Ythan

Forvie National Nature Reserve

North Broad Haven

2

Waterside

Hackley Bay

27

P

Hackley Head or Forvie Ness

Waterside Bridge

P

Forvie Church (remains of)

A975

1

Rockend

26

00   A   01   B   02   C   03   D   04   E   05   F

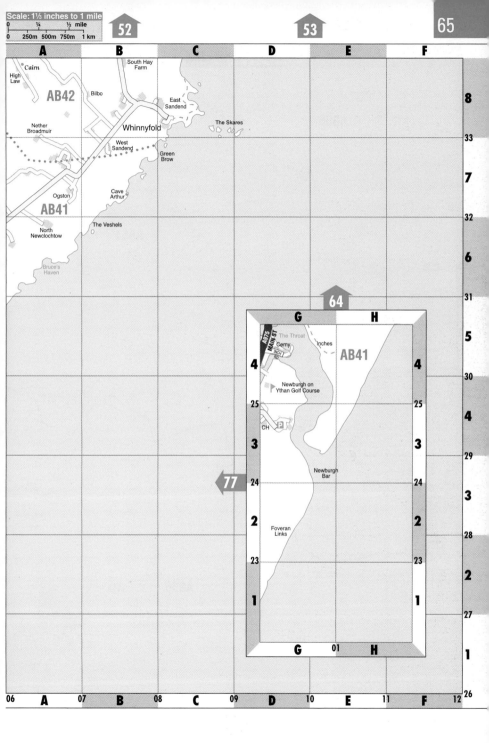

Scale: 1⅓ inches to 1 mile

0   ¼   ½   mile
0 250m 500m 750m 1 km

52   53

A   B   C   D   E   F

High Law
Cairn

AB42

Bilbo

South Hay Farm

East Sandend

The Skares

8

Nether Broadmuir

Whinnyfold

West Sandend

Green Brow

33

7

Ogston

Cave Arthur

AB41

The Veshels

32

North Newclochtow

6

Bruce's Haven

31

64

G   H

The Throat

Cemy

Inches

AB41

5

A975 MAIN ST
INCH RD

4   4

30

Newburgh on Ythan Golf Course

25   25

4

CH   P

3   3

29

Newburgh Bar

77   24   24

3

2   2

28

Foveran Links

23   23

2

1   1

27

G   01   H

1

26

06   A   07   B   08   C   09   D   10   E   11   F   12

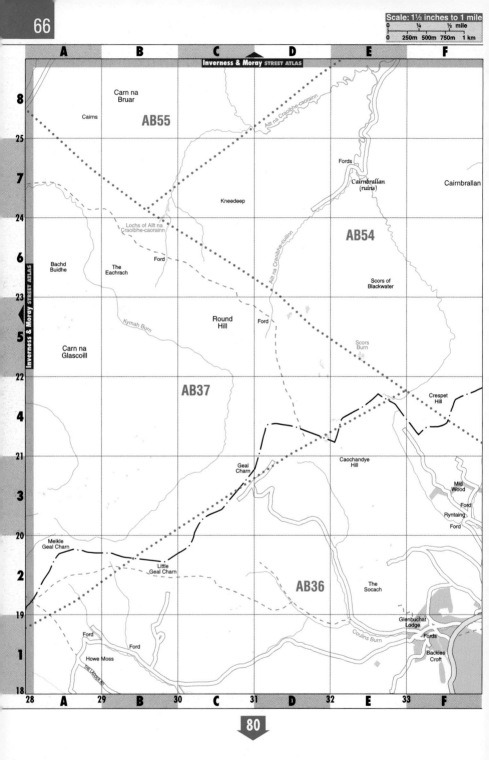

Carn na Bruar

Cairns

AB55

Allt na Craoibhe-caorainn

Fords

Cairnbrallan (ruins)

Cairnbrallan

Kneedeep

Lochs of Allt na Craoibhe-caorainn

Allt na Craoibhe-cuilinn

AB54

Bachd Buidhe

The Eachrach

Ford

Scors of Blackwater

Kymah Burn

Round Hill

Ford

Scors Burn

Carn na Glascoill

AB37

Crespet Hill

Geal Charn

Caochandye Hill

Mid Wood

Ford

Ryntaing

Ford

Meikle Geal Charn

Little Geal Charn

AB36

The Socach

Glenbuchat Lodge

Coulins Burn

Fords

Ford

Ford

Backies Croft

Howe Moss

THE LADDER RD

Inverness & Moray STREET ATLAS

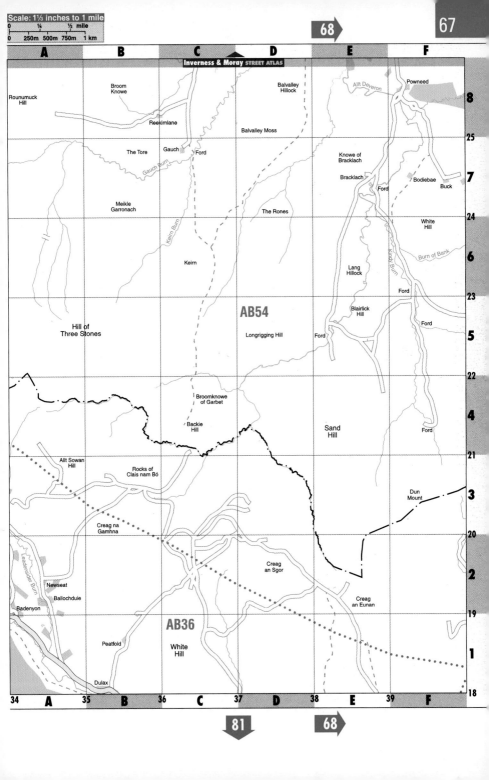

Inverness & Moray STREET ATLAS

Rounumuck Hill

Broom Knowe

Reekimlane

Balvalley Hillock

Powneed

Allt Deveron

8

Balvalley Moss

25

The Tore

Gauch

Ford

Gauch Burn

Knowe of Bracklach

Bracklach

Ford

Bodiebae

Buck

7

Meikle Garronach

Keirn Burn

The Rones

White Hill

24

Keirn

Lang Hillock

Burn of Bank

Kindy Burn

6

Hill of Three Stones

AB54

Longrigging Hill

Blairlick Hill

Ford

Ford

23

Ford

5

22

Broomknowe of Garbet

Backie Hill

Sand Hill

Ford

4

Allt Sowan Hill

Rocks of Clais nam Bó

Dun Mount

21

Creag na Gamhna

3

Newseat

Ballochduie

Creag an Sgor

20

Badenyon

Leadnadec Burn

AB36

White Hill

Creag an Eunan

2

Peatfold

19

Dulax

1

18

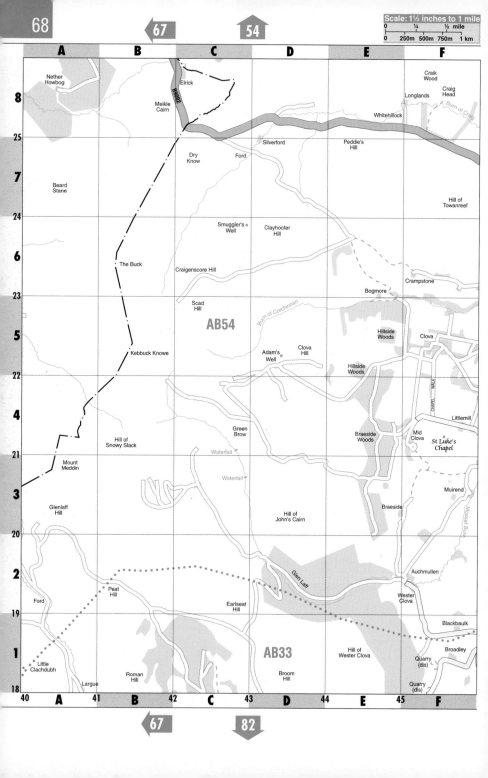

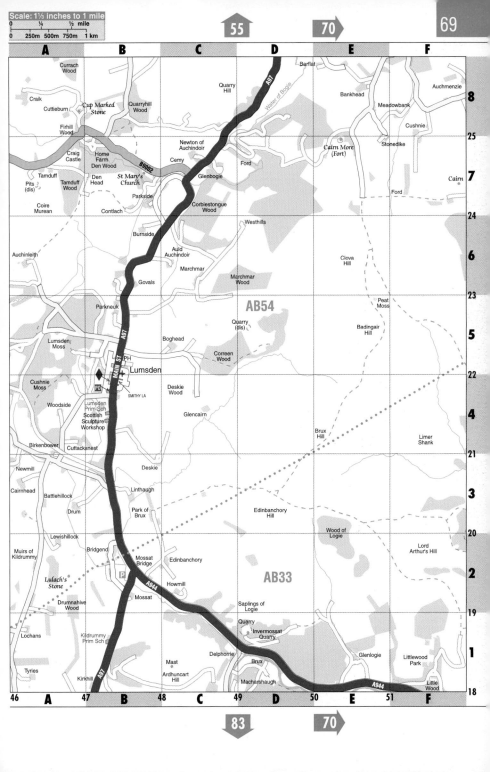

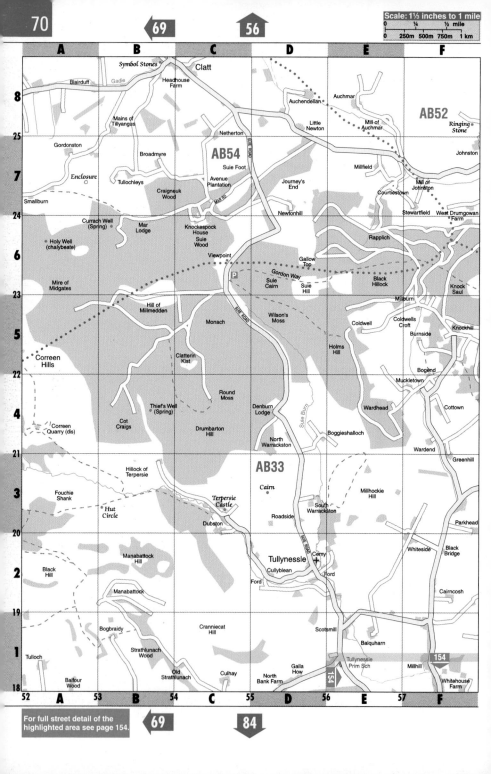

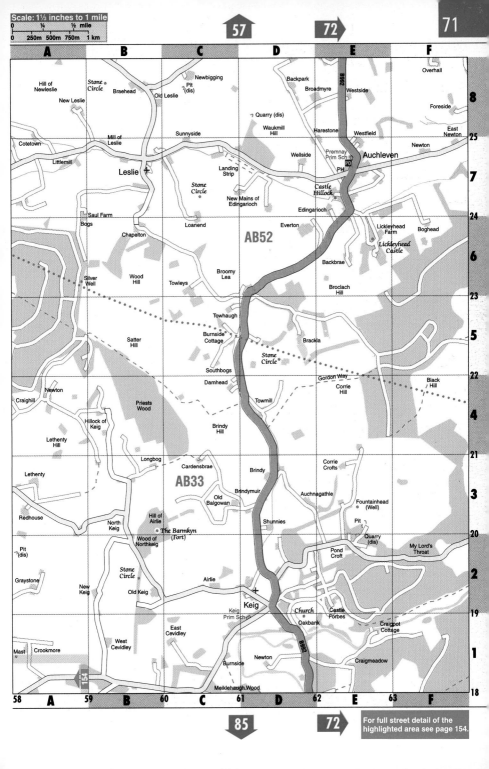

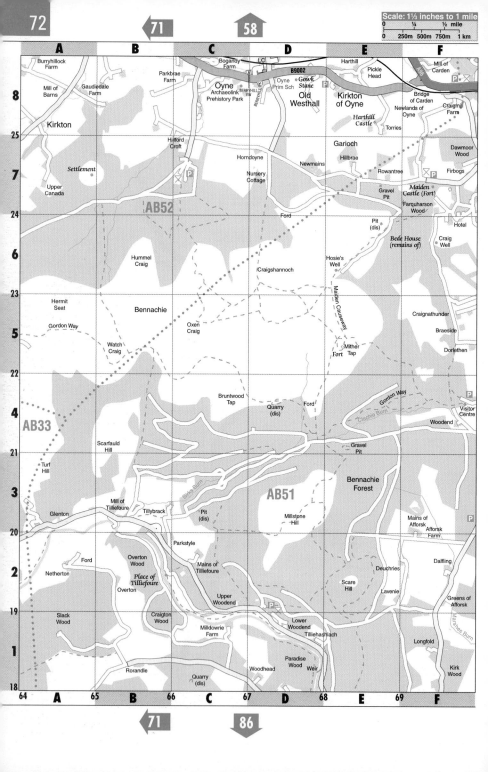

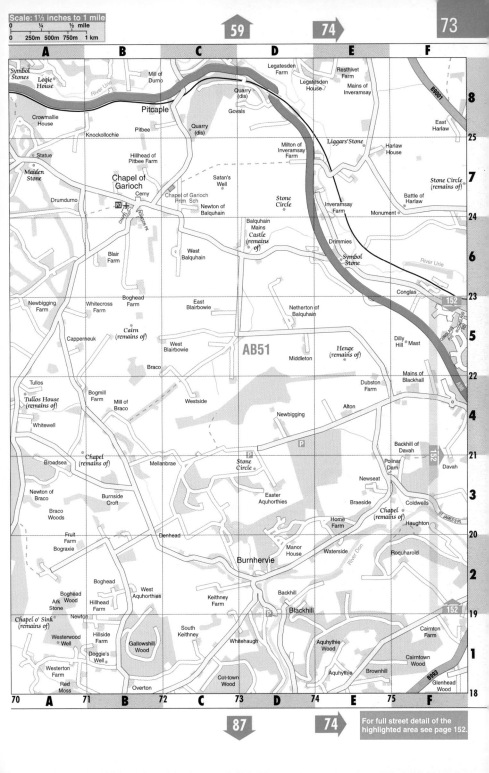

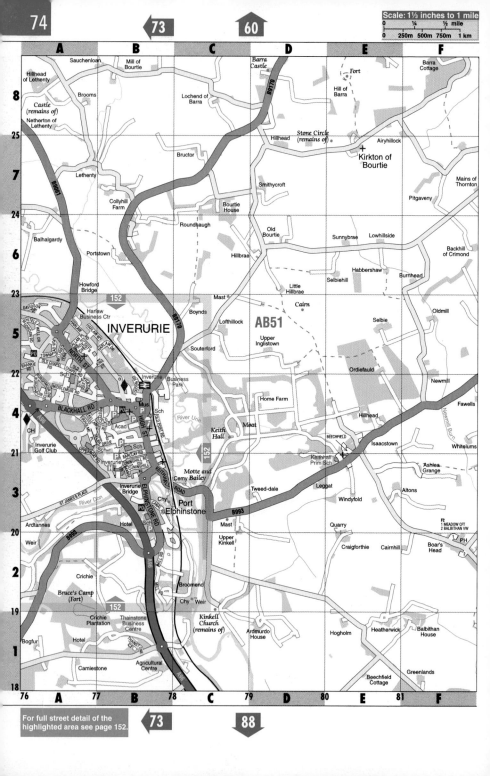

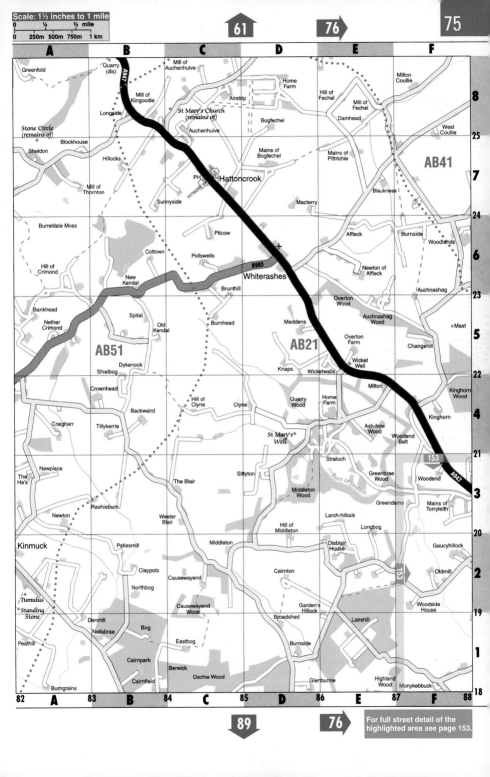

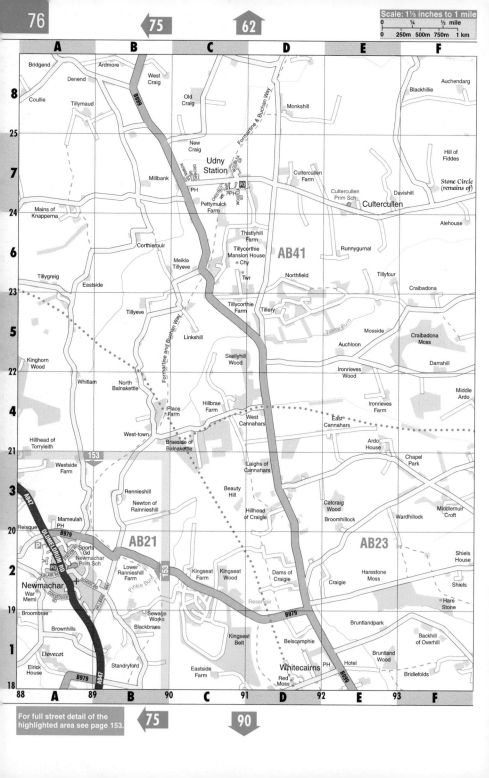

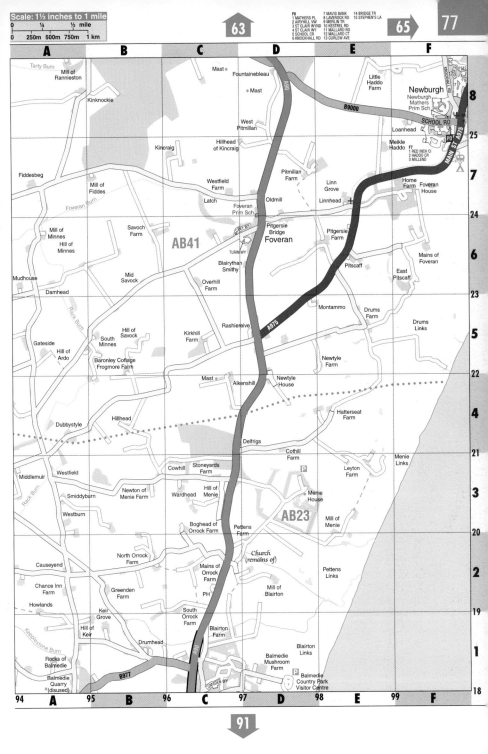

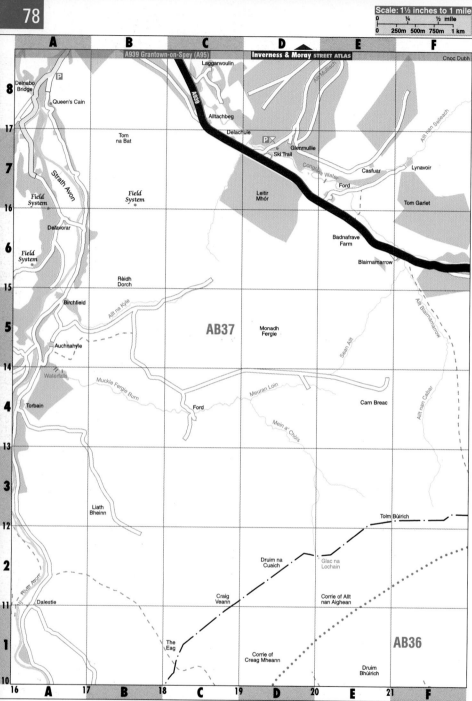

A939 Grantown-on-Spey (A95)

Cnoc Dubh

Lagganvoulin

Delnabo
Bridge

P

Queen's Cain

Alltachbeg

Allt Mulliach

Delachule

P ✗

Glenmullie

Ski Trail

Tom
na Bat

Congiles Water

Casfuar

Lynavoir

Ford

Allt nan Seileach

Strath Avon

Field
System

Field
System

Leitir
Mhór

Tom Garlet

Defavorar

Badnafrave
Farm

Field
System

Blairnamarrow

Rèidh
Dorch

Allt Blairnamarrow

Birchfield

Allt na Kyle

AB37

Monadh
Fergie

Sean Allt

Auchnahyle

Allt nan Cabar

Waterfalls

Muckle Fergie Burn

Meuran Loin

Torbain

Ford

Carn Breac

Mein a' Chòis

Liath
Bheinn

Tolm Bùirich

Druim na
Cuaich

Glac na
Lochain

River Avon

Dalestie

Craig
Veann

Corrie of Allt
nan Aighean

AB36

The
Eag

Corrie of
Creag Mheann

Druim
Bhùirich

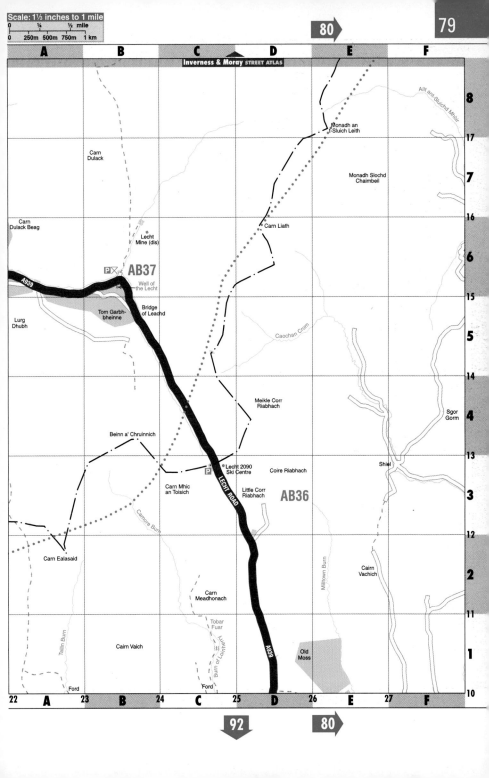

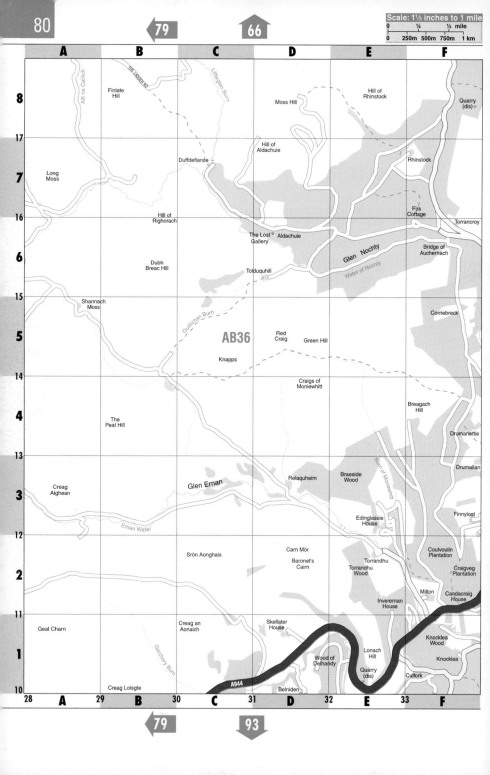

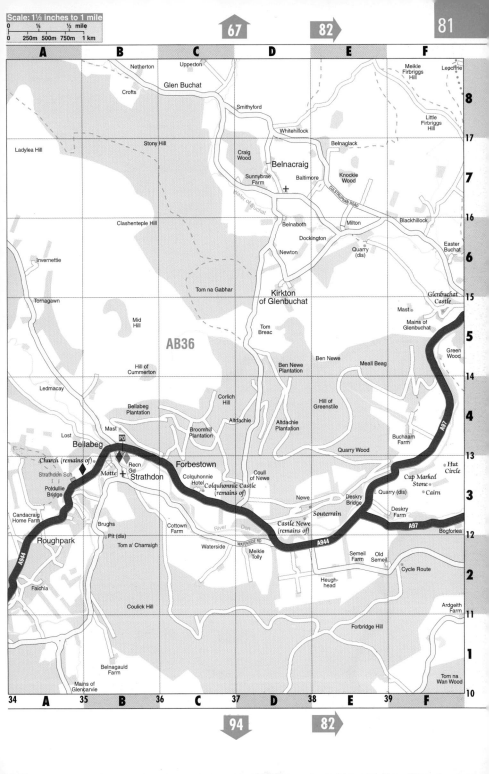

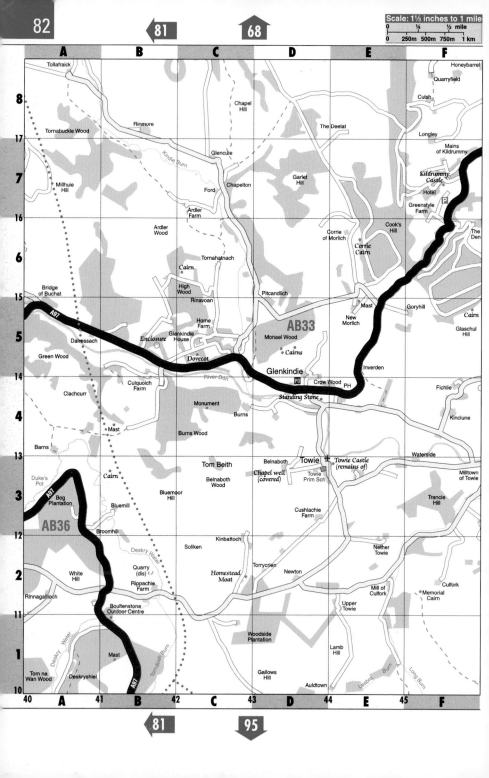

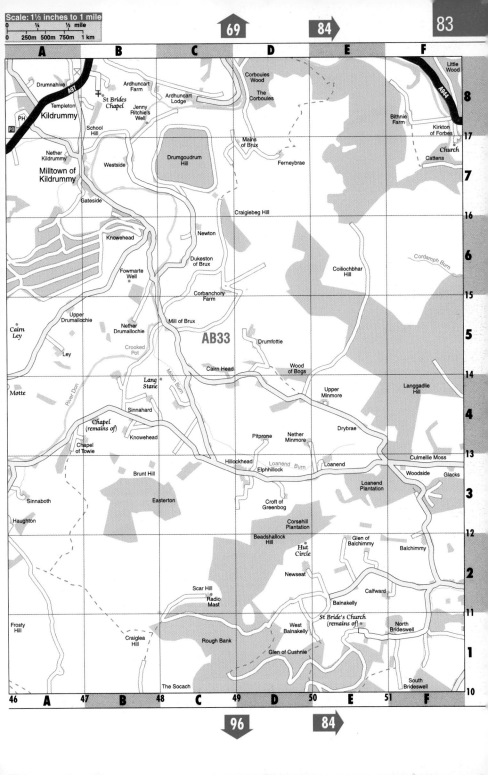

A   B   C   D   E   F

Drumnahive
A97
Templeton
Kildrummy
PH
PO
St Brides Chapel
Ardhuncart Farm
Jenny Ritchie's Well
Ardhuncart Lodge
Corbouies Wood
The Corbouies

8

School Hill
Nether Kildrummy
Milltown of Kildrummy
Westside
Drumgoudrum Hill
Mains of Brux
Ferneybrae
Bithnie Farm
A941
Little Wood
Kirkton of Forbes
Church
Cattens

17

7

Gateside
Craiglebeg Hill

16

Knowehead
Newton
Dukeston of Brux
Coiliochbhar Hill
Cordamph Burn

6

Upper Drumallochie
Fowmarte Well
Corbanchory Farm

15

Cairn Ley
Ley
Nether Drumallochie
Mill of Brux
AB33
Drumfottie
Wood of Bogs

5

Crooked Pot
Cairn Head
Langgadlie Hill

14

Motte
River Don
Lang Stane
Milton Burn
Upper Minmore

4

Chapel (remains of)
Sinnahard
Knowehead
Pitprone
Nether Minmore
Drybrae

Chapel of Towie
Hillockhead
Elphhillock
Loanend Burn
Loanend
Culmellie Moss

13

Brunt Hill
Woodside
Glacks

Sinnaboth
Easterton
Croft of Greenbog
Loanend Plantation

3

Haughton
Corsehill Plantation

Beadshallock Hill
Glen of Balchimmy
Balchimmy

12

Hut Circle
Newseat

2

Scar Hill
Radio Mast
Calfward
Balnakelly

Frosty Hill
Craiglea Hill
Rough Bank
West Balnakelly
St Bride's Church (remains of)
North Brideswell

11

Glen of Cushnie
South Brideswell

1

The Socach

10

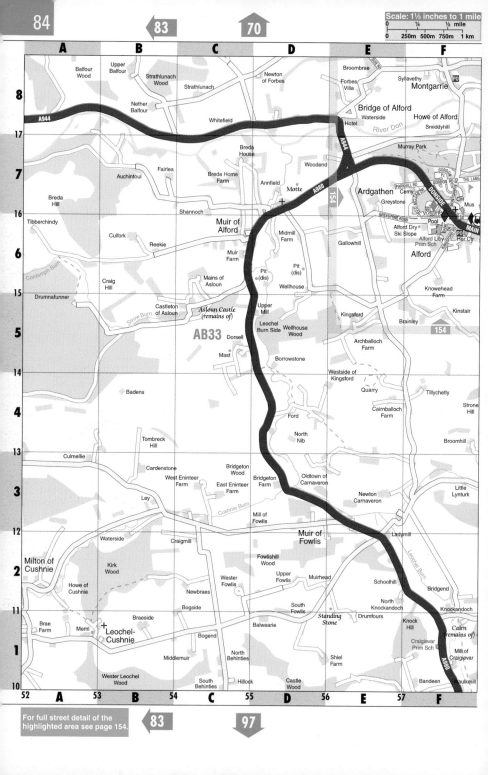

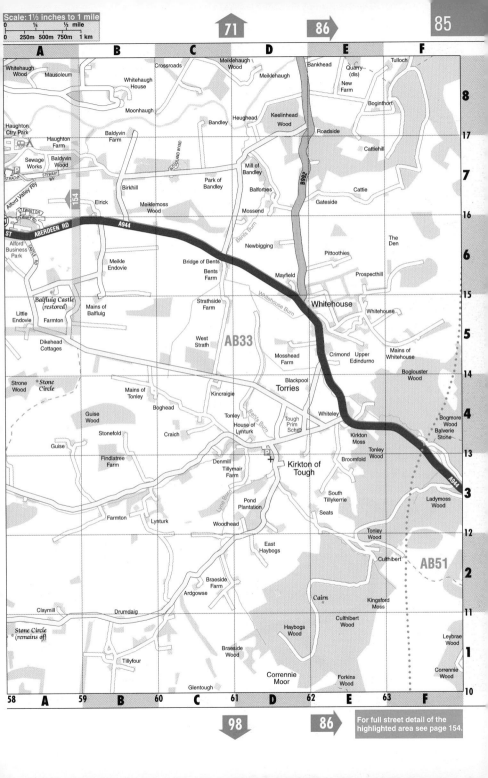

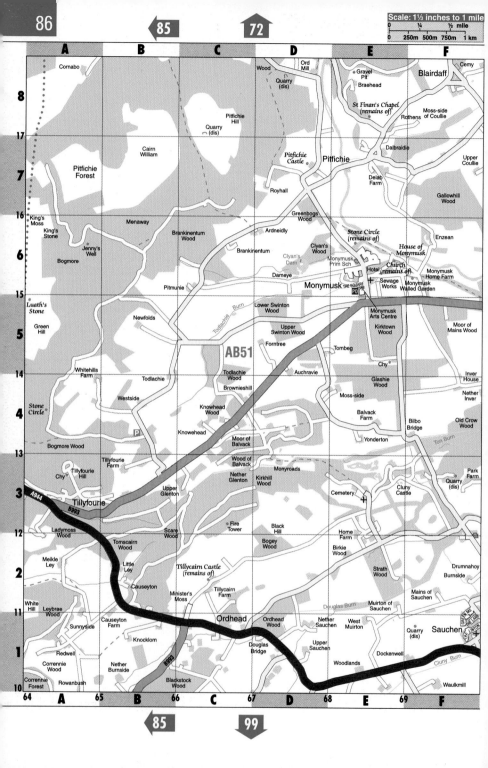

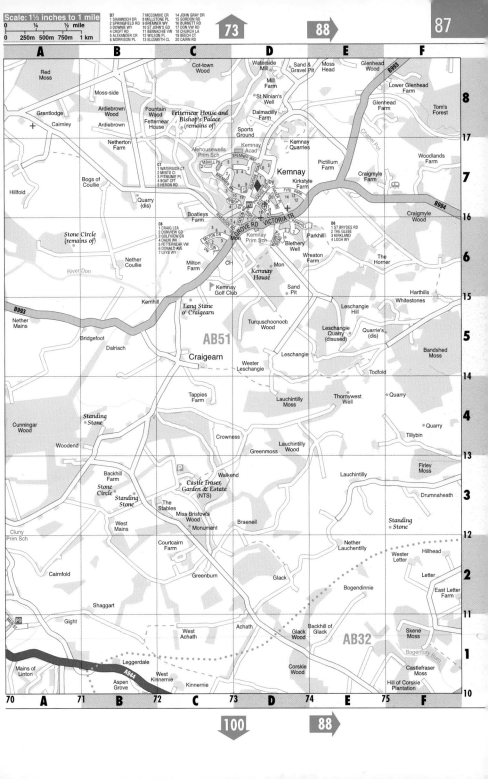

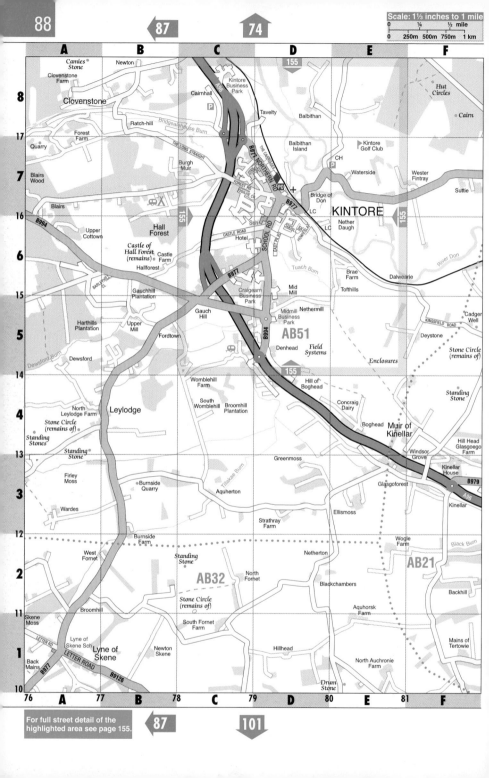

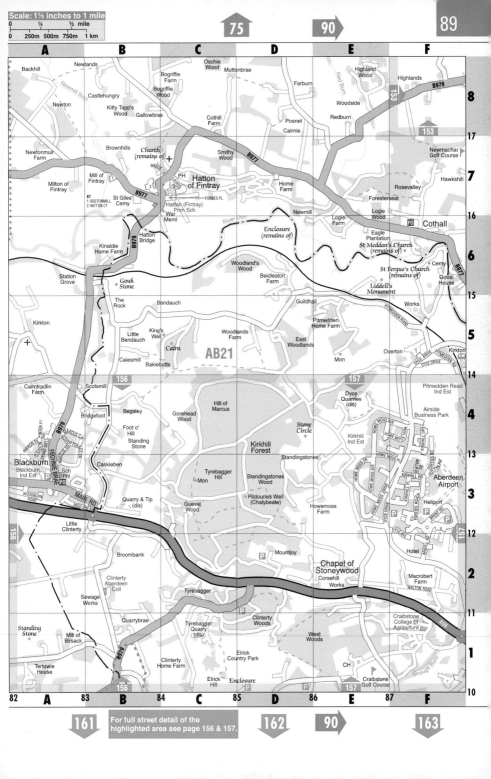

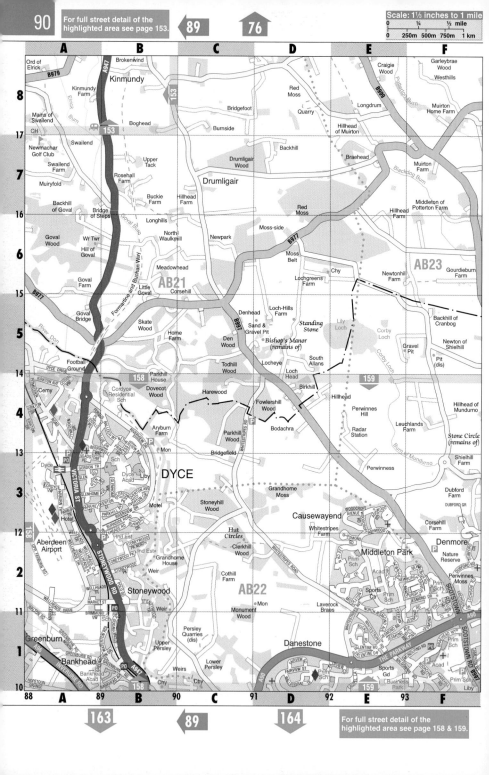

C8
1 WHITEHORSE TR
2 BURNSIDE WY
3 BEACHFIELD WY
4 MENIE CR
5 GEAN CT
6 OAK VW
7 ROWAN DR
8 ASH ROW
9 ELM PL
10 MENIE CL
11 ROBBIE CL
12 KEITH CR

77

Overhill
Balmedie Farm
Belhelvie
Sewage Works
Hare Cairn
Keir Farm
Eigie Burn
Cairntack
Balmedie Prim Sch
Balmedie Country Park
Eigie Links
South Folds Farm
Ctr & Liby
Balmedie
Belhelvie Lodge
CH
East Aberdeenshire Golf Course
Temple Stones
Home Farm
Millden
AB23
Hatton
Milton of Potterton
Potterton House
Millden Burn
Sand Pit
Wester Hatton
Millden Links
Sewage Works
Auld Kirk Art Gall
Sand Pit
Potterton
Blackdog Rifle Range
Laingseat Farm
Sewage Works
Middleton Farm
Middlefield
Blackdog Burn
Blackdog Links
Cranfield Farm
Harehill Farm
Blackdog Ind Ctr
Blackdog
DANGER AREA
North Tarbothill
160
Pit (dis)
Blackdog Rock
Newton of Mundurno
Pit (dis)
Hill of Strabathie
Works
Mundurno Farm
Tarbothill Farm
Motel
Berryhill Farm
Murcar Golf Course
Murcar Ind Est
CH
Cloverhill
Denmore Ind Est
Balgownie Links
Findlay Farm
Technology Park
Prim Sch
THE PARKWAY
ELLON RD
Bridge of Don
Con Ctr
P&R
Royal Aberdeen Golf Club
160

165

160

For full street detail of the highlighted area see page 160.

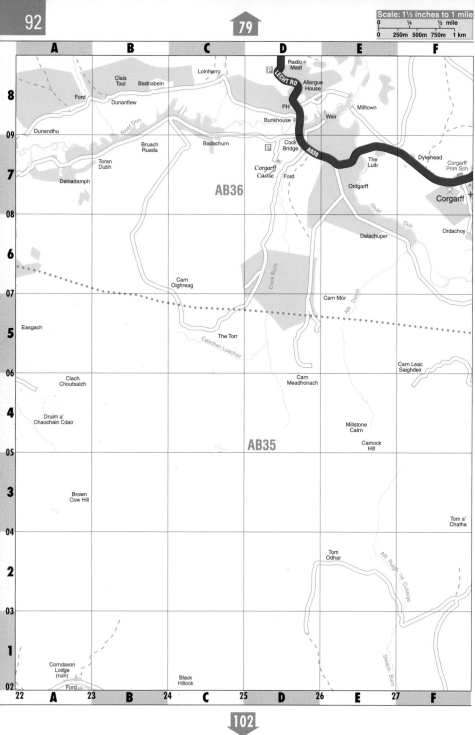

79

Scale: 1⅓ inches to 1 mile

0   ¼   ½ mile
0 250m 500m 750m 1 km

A   B   C   D   E   F

Radio
Mast
P
LECHT RD
Loinherry
Clais
Toul   Badnabein
Allargue
House
8   Milltown
Ford   PH
Dunanflew   Bunkhouse   Weir
Dunandhu   River Don
09   Cock
Bruach   Badochurn Bridge   A939
Ruada   Dykehead
P   Corgarff
Toran   Corgarff   The   Prim Sch
7   Dubh   Castle   Cock   Luib
Delnadamph   Ford   Corgarff
AB36   Ordgarff
08
Delachuper   River
Don   Ordachoy
6
Cock Burn
Carn
07   Carn
Oighreag   Carn Mòr   Allt Deich
Easgach
5   The Torr
Caochan Luachair
Carn Leac
Clach   Saighdeir
06   Choutsaich   Carn
Meadhonach
Druim a'
4   Chaochain Cdair
Millstone
Cairn
AB35   Camock
05   Hill
Brown
3   Cow Hill
Torn a'
04   Chatha

Tom
Odhar   Allt Ruigh na Cuileige
2
Corndavon
Lodge
1   (ruin)   Black
Ford   Hillock   Sleach Burn
02
22   A   23   B   24   C   25   D   26   E   27   F

A   B   C   D   E   F

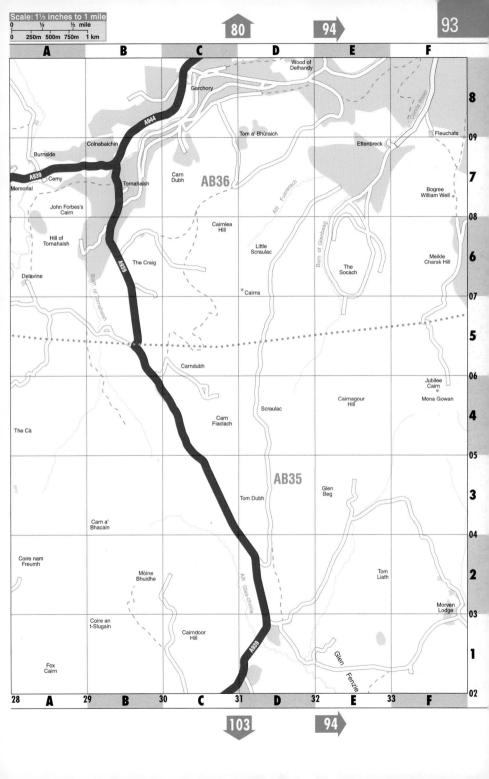

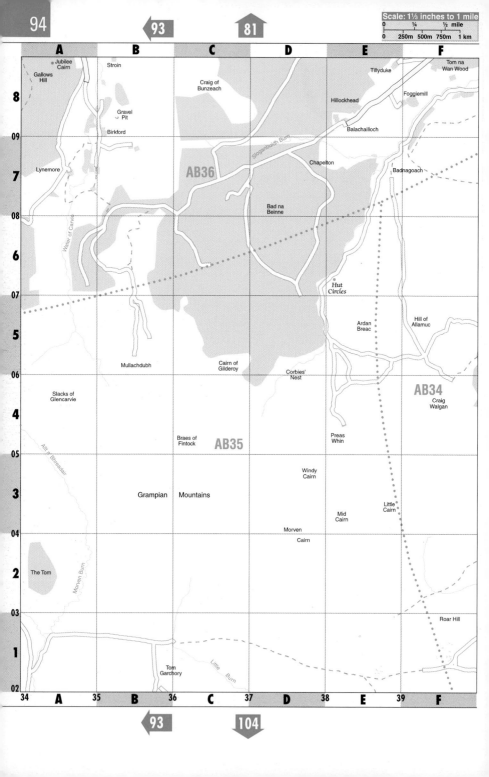

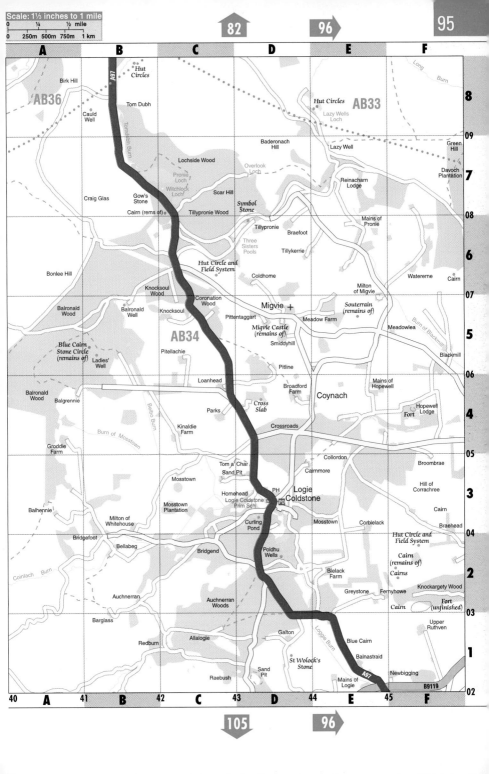

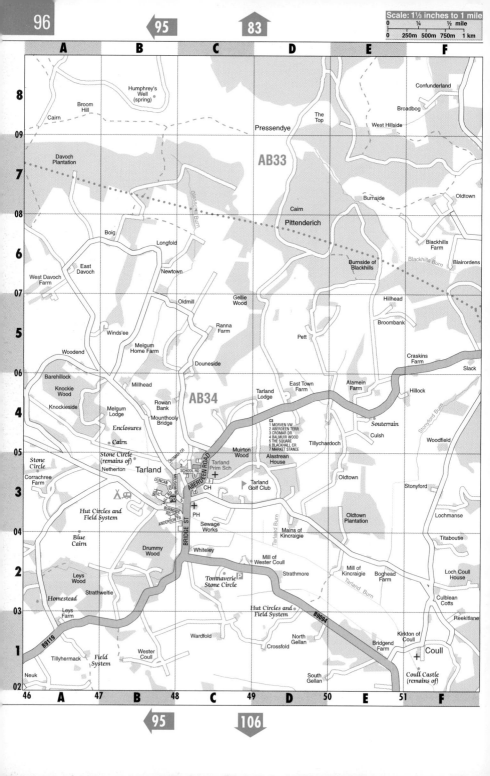

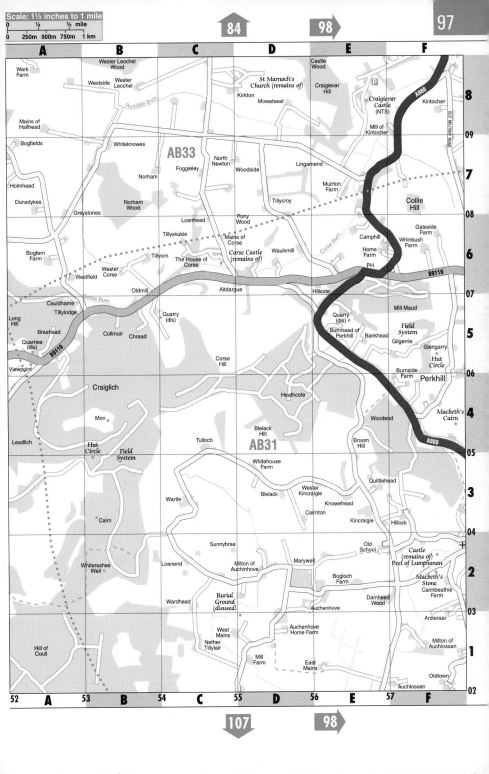

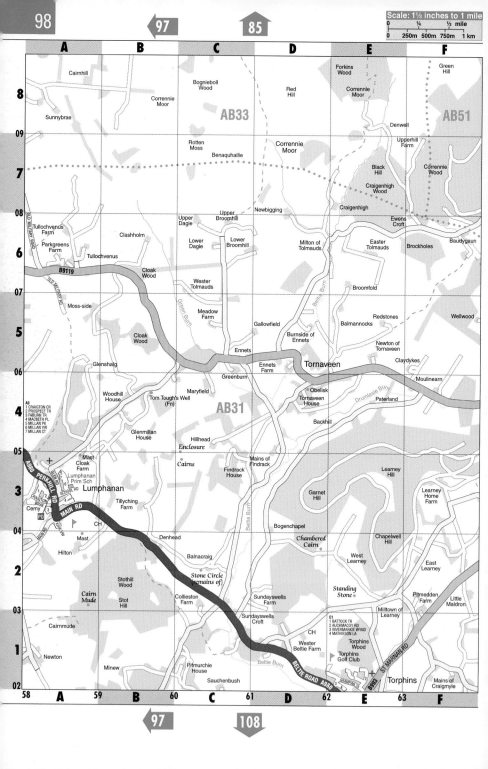

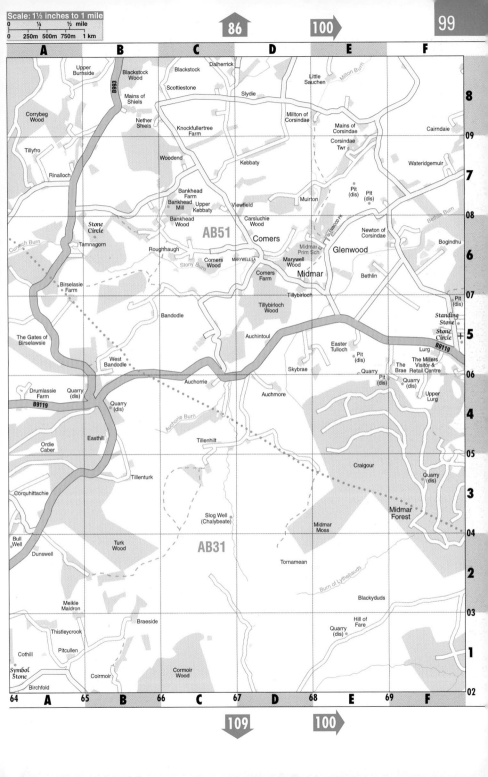

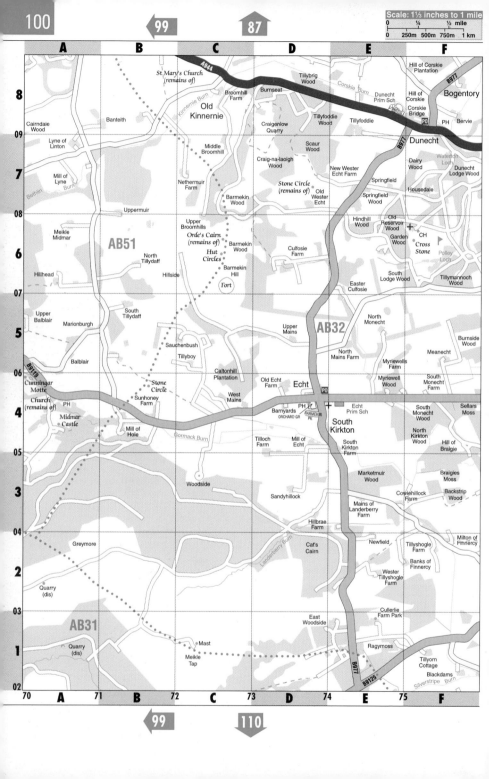

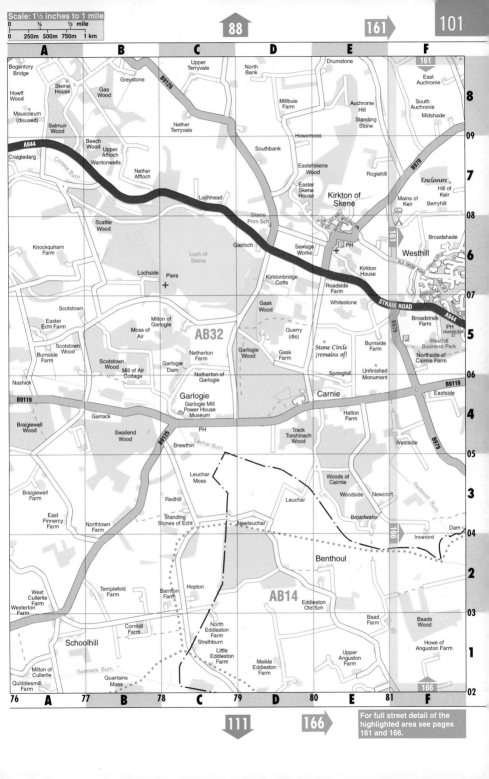

111

166

For full street detail of the
highlighted area see pages
161 and 166.

Column A

Bogentory Bridge
Howff Wood
Skene House
Gas Wood
Greystone
Mausoleum (disused)
Balmuir Wood
A944
Craigiedarg
Corskie Burn
Beech Wood
Upper Affloch
Wantonwells
Nether Affloch
Knockquharn Farm
Scattie Wood
Lochside
Piers
Easter Echt Farm
Scotstown
Scotstown Wood
Burnside Farm
Nashick
Moss of Air
Scotstown Wood
Mill of Air Cottage
B9119
Garrack
Braigiewell Wood
Swailend Wood
Braigiewell Farm
East Finnercy Farm
Northtown Farm
West Cullerlie Farm
Westerton Farm
Templefold Farm
Cornhill Farm
Schoolhill
Milton of Cullerlie
Quiddiesmill Farm
Gormack Burn
Quartains Moss

Column B / C

B9126
Upper Terryvale
Nether Terryvale
Lochhead
North Bank
Millbuie Farm
Southbank
Howemoss
Skene Prim Sch
Gairloch
Loch of Skene
Kirktonbridge Cotts
Milton of Garlogie
Netherton Farm
Garlogie Dam
AB32
Garlogie Wood
Netherton of Garlogie
Garlogie
Garlogie Mill Power House Museum
PH
B9125
Brewthin
Leuchar Burn
Leuchar Moss
Redhill
Standing Stones of Echt
Newleuchar
Barnton Farm
Hopton
AB14
North Eddieston Farm Strathburn
Little Eddieston Farm
Meikle Eddieston Farm

Column D / E / F

Drumstone
East Auchronie
South Auchronie Midshade
Auchronie Hill
Standing Stone
Easterskene Wood
Rogiehill
Enclosure
Hill of Keir
Kirkton of Skene
Mains of Keir
Berryhill
Easter Skene House
Broadshade
Sewage Works
Westhill
Kirkton House
Roadside Farm
Gask Wood
Whitestone
STRAIK ROAD
A944
Quarry (dis)
Stone Circle (remains of)
Broadstraik Farm
PH CRUICKSHANK CT
Burnside Farm
P
Westhill Business Park
Gask Farm
Springhill
Northside of Carnie Farm
Garlogie Wood
Unfinished Monument
B9119
Carnie
Eastside
Hatton Farm
B979
Track Torshinach Wood
Westside
Westdie
Woods of Cairnie
Woodside
Newcroft
Leuchar
Broadwater
Redwell Burn
166
Inverord
Dam
Benthoul
Eddieston Old Sch
Baad Farm
Baads Wood
Howe of Anguston Farm
Upper Anguston Farm
166

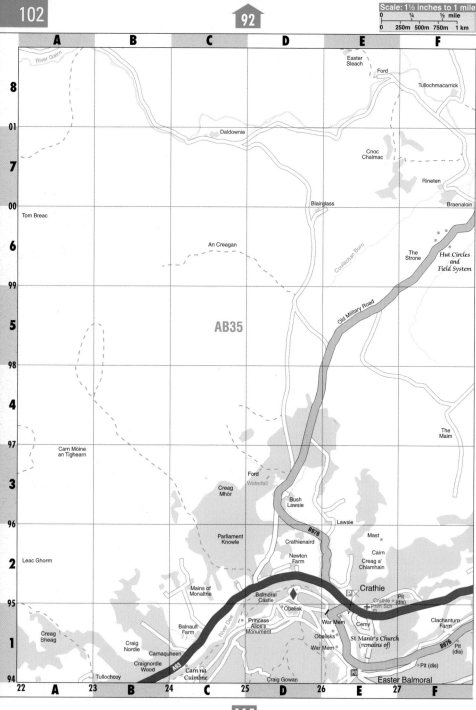

Scale: 1⅓ inches to 1 mile

| 0 | ¼ | ½ mile |
| 0 | 250m 500m 750m | 1 km |

River Gairn

Easter
Sleach

Ford

Tullochmacarrick

Daldownie

Cnoc
Chalmac

Blairglass

Rineten

Braenaloin

Tom Breac

An Creagan

The
Strone

Hut Circles
and
Field System

Coulachan Burn

AB35

Old Military Road

The
Maim

Carn Mòine
an Tighearn

Ford
Waterfall

Creag
Mhòr

Bush
Lawsie

Lawsie

Parliament
Knowle

B976

Mast

Crathienaird

Cairn
Creag a'
Chlamhain

Leac Ghorm

Newton
Farm

Crathie

Mains of
Monaltrie

Balmoral
Castle

P X

Pit
(dis)

Crathie
Prem Scn

Obelisk

Clachanturn
Farm

Creag
Bheag

Balnault
Farm

Princess
Alice's
Monument

Obelisk

War Mem

Cemy

B976

Pit
(dis)

Craig
Nordie

St Manir's Church
(remains of)

River Dee

Carnaqueen

Obelisks

War Mem

Craignordie
Wood

A93

Pit (dis)

Tullochcoy

Carn na
Cuimbric

Craig Gowan

P

Easter Balmoral

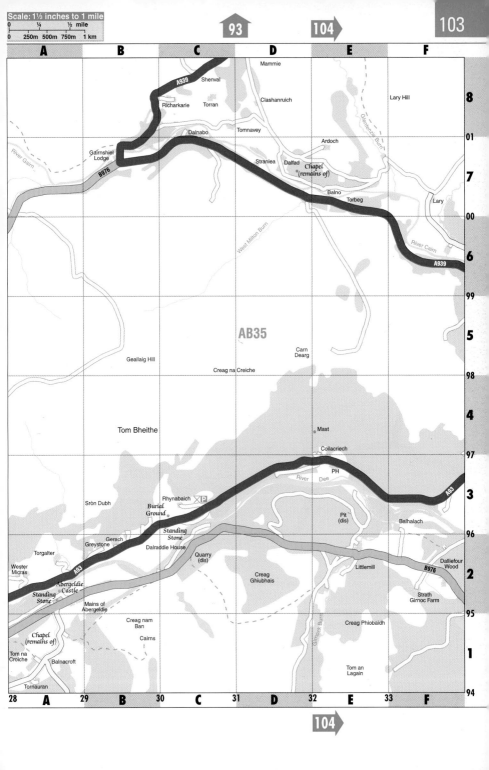

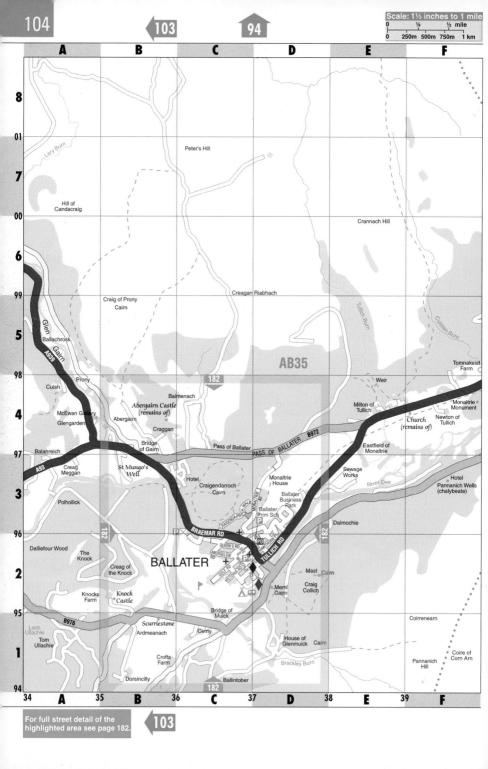

Scale: 1⅓ inches to 1 mile

| 0 | ¼ | ½ mile |
| 0 | 250m | 500m | 750m | 1 km |

A B C D E F

8

01

7

Lary Burn

Peter's Hill

Hill of
Candacraig

00

Crannach Hill

6

Glen Gairn

A939

Ballachrosk

99

Craig of Prony
Cairn

Creagan Riabhach

Tullich Burn

Cuaien Burn

5

AB35

Tomnakeist
Farm

Culsh

Prony

98

182

Balmenach

Weir

Milton of
Tullich

Monaltrie
Monument

McEwan Gallery

Abergairn Castle
(remains of)

Newton of
Tullich

4

Glengarden

Abergairn

Craggan

Church
(remains of)

Balanreich

Bridge
of Gairn

Pass of Ballater

PASS OF BALLATER

B972

Eastfield of
Monaltrie

97

A93

Creag
Meggan

St Mungo's
Well

Hotel

Monaltrie
House

Sewage
Works

River Dee

Hotel
Pannanich Wells
(chalybeate)

3

Polhollick

Craigendarroch
Cairn

Ballater
Business
Park

Dalmochie

96

182

Dalliefour Wood

The
Knock

BRAEMAR RD

P

Ballater
Prim Sch

QUEEN'S RD

PO

TULLICH RD

2

Creag of
the Knock

ABERGELDIE
RD

GOLF RD

BALLATER

Mast

Cairn

Craig
Collich

Knocks
Farm

Knock
Castle

VICTORIA RD

Menu
Cairn

95

B976

Scurriestone

Ardmeanach

Bridge of
Muick

Cemy

House of
Glenmuick

Cairn

Coirrenearn

Loch
Ullachie

Tom
Ullachie

Crofts
Farm

Brackley Burn

Pannanich
Hill

Coire of
Corn Arn

1

Dorsincilly

Ballintober

182

94

34 A 35 B 36 C 37 D 38 E 39 F

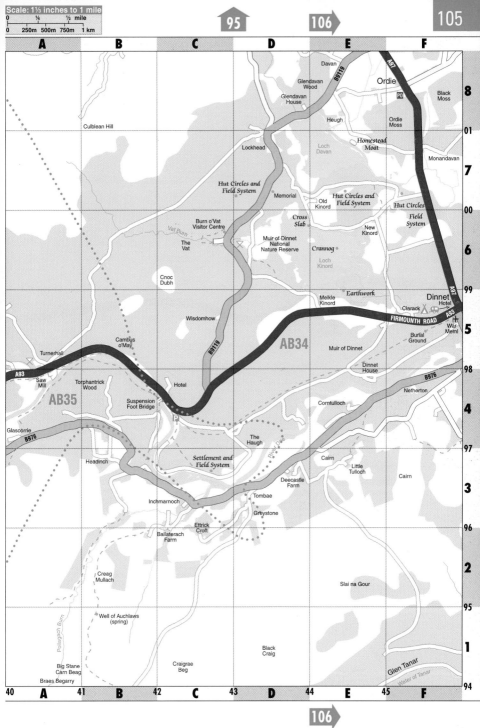

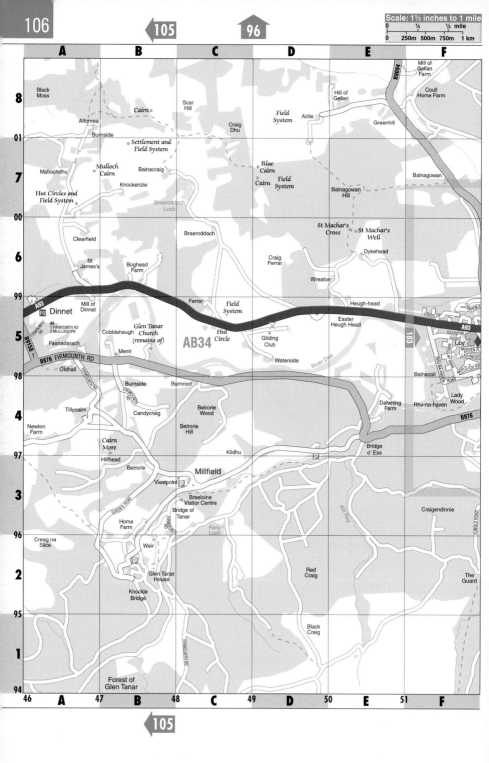

Scale: 1⅓ inches to 1 mile
0 ¼ ½ mile
0 250m 500m 750m 1 km

A **B** **C** **D** **E** **F**

8

Black
Moss

Mill of
Gellan
Farm

B9094

Coull
Home Farm

Hill of
Gellan

Cairn

Scar
Hill

Field
System

Airlie

Greenhill

Altonrea

Craig
Dhu

01

Burnside

Settlement and
Field System

7

Mullochdhu

Mulloch
Cairn

Balnacraig

Blue
Cairn

Balnagowan

Knockenzie

Cairn

Field
System

Balnagowan
Hill

Hut Circles and
Field System

Braeroddach
Loch

00

Clearfield

Braeroddach

St Machar's
Cross

St Machar's
Well

Dykehead

6

St
James's

Craig
Ferrar

Boghead
Farm

Wreaton

99

A93
P0

Dinnet

Mill of
Dinnet

Ferrar

Field
System

Heugh-head

Easter
Heugh Head

ABOYNE DR

A93

B9158

A5
1 FIRMOUNTH RD
2 MULLOCH VW

Aboyne
Acad Lby

MORVEN PL

183

5

Fasnadarach

Glen Tanar
Church
(remains of)

Cobblehaugh

AB34

Hut
Circle

LADYWOOD

MORTLICH GRI

MARR

B976 FIRMOUNTH RD

Meml

Gliding
Club

Balnacoil

Lady
Wood

98

Oldhall

Waterside

River Dee

Rhu-na-haven

4

Tillycairn

Burnside

Burnroot

Belrorie
Wood

Dalwhing
Farm

B976

Candycraig

FIRMOUNTH RD

Newton
Farm

Belrorie
Hill

97

Cairn
More

Kildhu

Bridge
o' Ess

Hillhead

Belrorie

Millfield

3

QUEEN'S ROAD

Viewpoint

Braeloine
Visitor Centre

Craigendinnie

FUNGLE ROAD

Bridge
of Tanar

Fairy
Loch

Allt Roy

96

Creag na
Slice

Home
Farm

Weir

2

Glen Tanar
House

Red
Craig

The
Guard

Knockie
Bridge

95

Black
Craig

1

94

Forest of
Glen Tanar

46 **A** 47 **B** 48 **C** 49 **D** 50 **E** 51 **F**

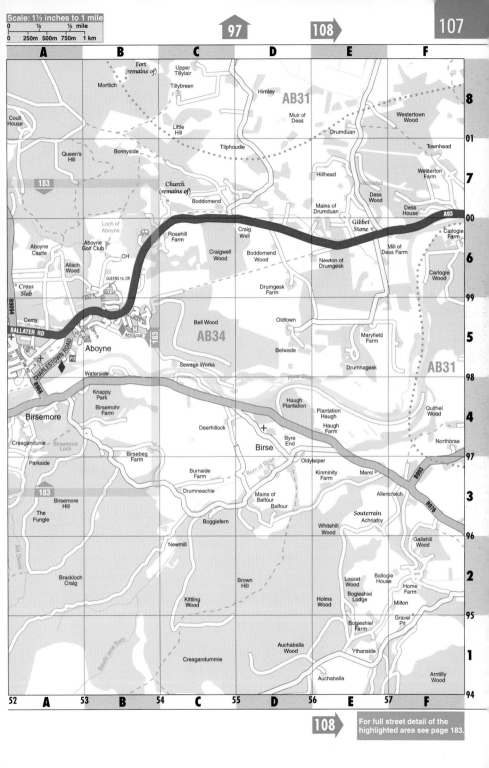

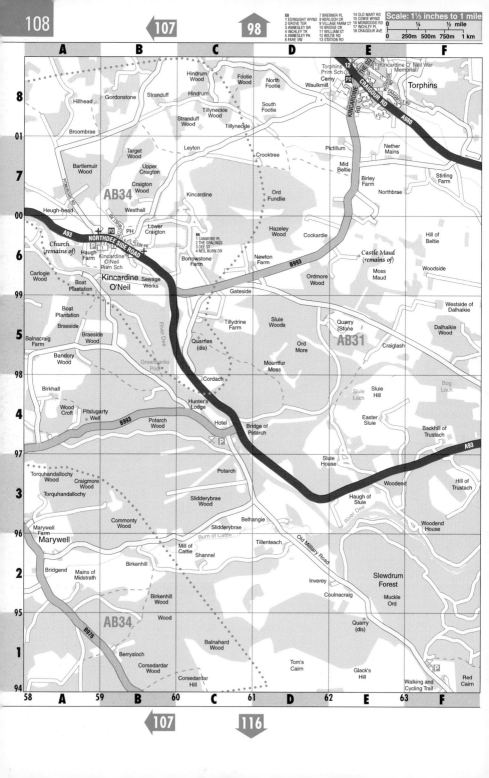

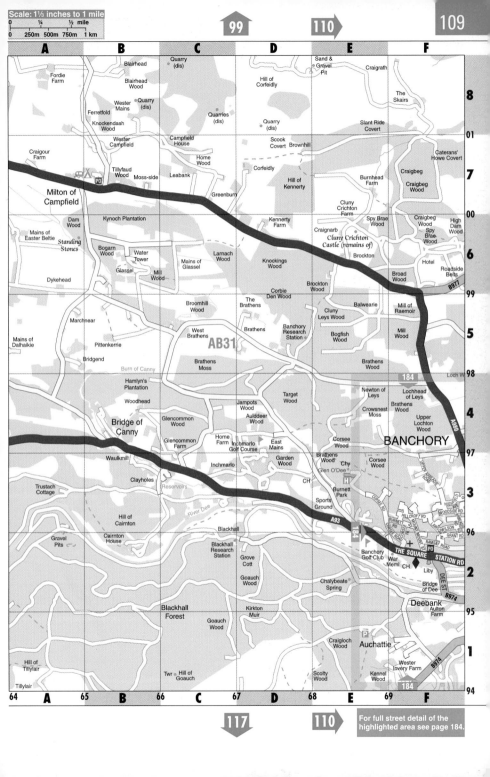

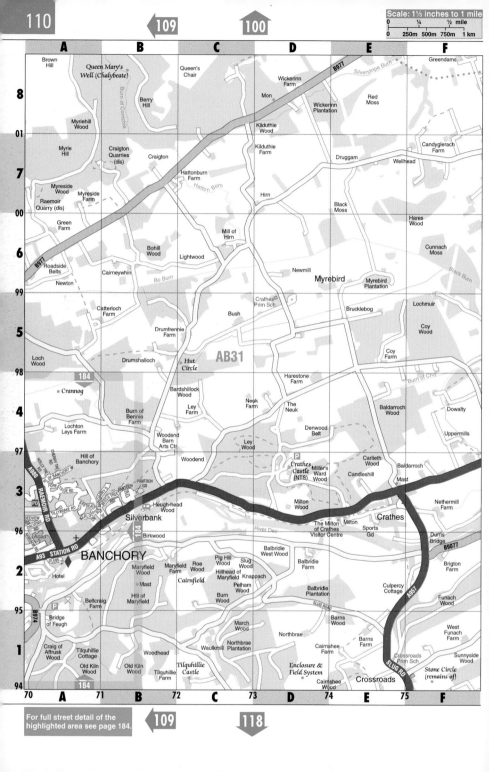

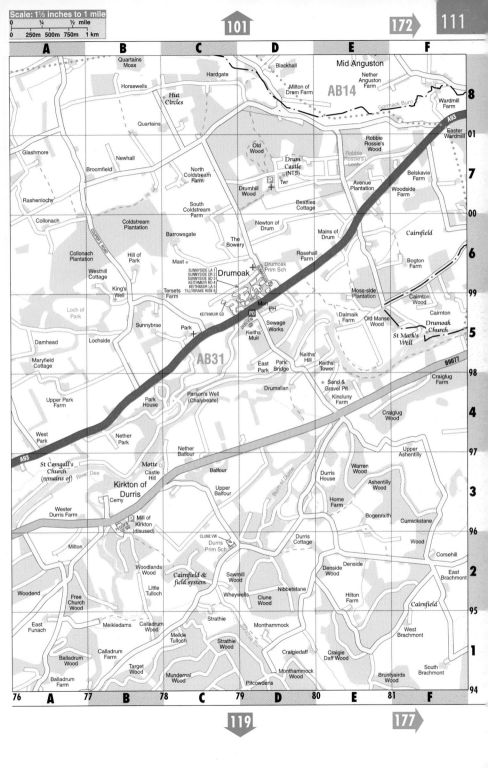

Scale: 1⅓ inches to 1 mile

0   ¼   ½ mile

0   250m 500m 750m 1 km

8

Quartains Moss

Horsewells

Hardgate

Blackhall

Milton of Drum Farm

Mid Anguston

Nether Anguston Farm

AB14

Gormack Burn

Wardmill Farm

Hut Circles

Quartains

A93

Easter Wardmill

01

Glashmore

Newhall

Broomfield

North Coldstream Farm

Old Wood

Drum Castle (NTS)

Twr

Robbie Rossie's Wood

Robbie Rossie's Loch

Avenue Plantation

Belskavie Farm

Woodside Farm

7

Rashenlochy

Drumhill Wood

Collonach

Coldstream Plantation

South Coldstream Farm

Barrowsgate

Newton of Drum

The Bowery

Mains of Drum

Cairnfield

00

Collonach Plantation

Hill of Park

Mast

Drumoak Prim Sch

Rosehall Farm

Bogton Farm

6

Westhill Cottage

SUNNYSIDE LA 1
SUNNYSIDE CR 2
SUNNYSIDE GD 3
KEITHMUIR RD 4
KEITHMUIR LA 5
TILLYBRAKE RISE 6

Drumoak

KEITHMUIR GD

Moss-side Plantation

Cairnton Wood

King's Well

Tersets Farm

Mon

Cairnton

99

Loch of Park

Sunnybrae

Park

KEITHMUIR GD

PO

PH

Dalmaik Farm

Old Manse Wood

St Mark's Well

Drumoak Church

Damhead

Lochside

Keiths' Muir

Sewage Works

Keiths' Hill

5

Maryfield Cottage

AB31

East Park

Park Bridge

Keiths' Tower

B9077

98

Upper Park Farm

Park House

Parson's Well (Chalybeate)

Drumallan

Sand & Gravel Pit

Kincluny Farm

Craiglug Farm

4

West Park

Nether Park

Nether Balfour

Craiglug Wood

Upper Ashentilly

97

A93

St Comgall's Church (remains of)

River Dee

Motte Castle Hill

Balfour

Durris House

Warren Wood

Ashentilly Wood

3

Kirkton of Durris

Cemy

Upper Balfour

Burn o' Durris

Home Farm

Bogenraith

Currackstane

Wester Durris Farm

Milton

Mill of Kirkton (disused)

CLUNE VW

Durris Prim Sch

Durris Cottage

Wood

Corsehill

96

Woodlands Wood

Cairnfield & field system

Sawmill Wood

Denside Wood

Denside

East Brachmont

2

Woodend

Free Church Wood

Little Tulloch

Wheywells

Clune Wood

Nibbetstane

Hilton Farm

Cairnfield

East Funach

Meikledams

Calladrum Wood

Strathie

Monthammock

West Brachmont

95

Balladrum Wood

Calladrum Farm

Meikle Tulloch

Strathie Wood

Strathie Burn

Craigiedaff

Craigie Daff Wood

Bruntyairds Wood

South Brachmont

1

Balladrum Farm

Target Wood

Mundernal Wood

Pitcowdens

Monthammock Wood

94

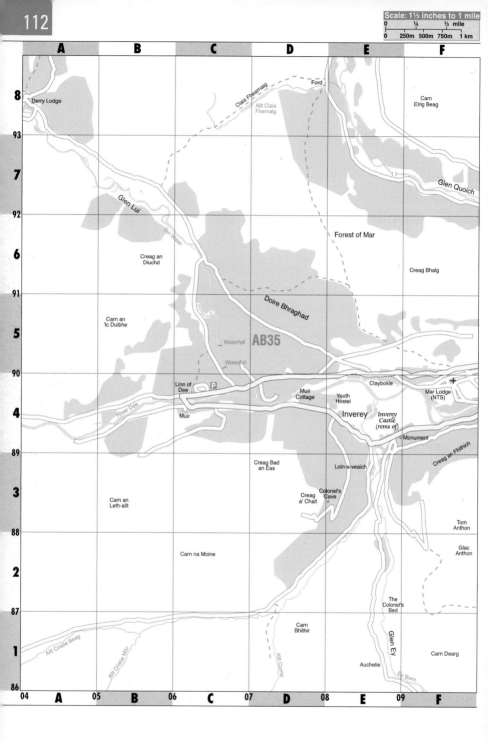

A   B   C   D   E   F

8   Derry Lodge

Clais Fhearnaig
Allt Clais Fhernaig
Ford
Carn Elrig Beag

93

7   Glen Lui
Glen Quoich

92   Lui Water
Forest of Mar

6   Creag an Diuchd
Creag Bhalg

91   Doire Bhraghad

Carn an 'Ic Duibhe

5   Waterfall
AB35

90   Waterfall
Linn of Dee
Claybokie
Mar Lodge (NTS)

P
Muir Cottage
Youth Hostel

4   River Dee
Muir
INVEREY
Inverey Castle (rems of)
Monument

Creag an Fhitich

89   Creag Bad an Eas
Loin-a-veaich

Carn an Leth-allt

3   Creag a' Chait
Colonel's Cave

Tom Anthon

88   Carn na Moine
Glac Anthon

2   The Colonel's Bed

87   Allt Cristie Beag
Carn Bhithir
Glen Ey

1   Allt Cristie Mòr
Allt Corrie
Carn Dearg
Auchelie
Ey Burn

86

04   A   05   B   06   C   07   D   08   E   09   F

A   B   C   D   E   F

8

Carn na
Drochaide

Creag a'
Chleirich

Balnagower
Cottage

93

Carn
Dearg

Monument

F6
1 CAIRNADROCHIT
2 FIFE BRAE
3 INVERCAULD RD
4 BALNELLAN RD
5 BALNELLAN PL
6 CASTLETON TERR
7 CASTLETON PL
8 HILLSIDE DR
9 SCHOOL RD
10 KINDROCHIT DR
11 GLENSHEE RD

Braemar
Castle

7

Quoich Water

West Coultain

East Allt Coltain

Sewage
Works

OLD MILITARY RD

A93

A93

Viewpoint

92

Braemar

Allanmore

E8
1 ST ANDREW'S TERR
2 LINN OF DEE PL

Castleton

Elevenstones
Prim Sch
Braemar
Prim Sch

6

The
Punch Bowl

Allanaquoich

River Dee

Meml
Park

Highland
Her Ctr

Youth
Hostel

Linn of
Quoich

Chapel Brae

Auchendryne

Ski
School

91

An Car

AB35

Tomintoul

Kindrochit
Castle
(rems)

Locham a'
Chreagain

Morrone Birkwood
National Nature Reserve

Viewpoint

CH

Braemar
Golf Club

90

Victoria Bridge

Linn of
Corriemulzie

Coire na
Sqreuchaig

Balintuim

Easter
Auchallater

89

Pit (dis)

A93

Braegarie

Morrone or
Morven

Viewpoint

Coire Allt
a' Chlair

Coldrach Burn

Auchallater

3

Corriemulzie Burn

OLD MILITARY ROAD

Glen Clunie

A93

Sròn Dubh

2

Carn Mòr

Coire na Meanneasg

87

Coire nam
Freumh

Clunie Water

1

Carn na
Drochaide

86

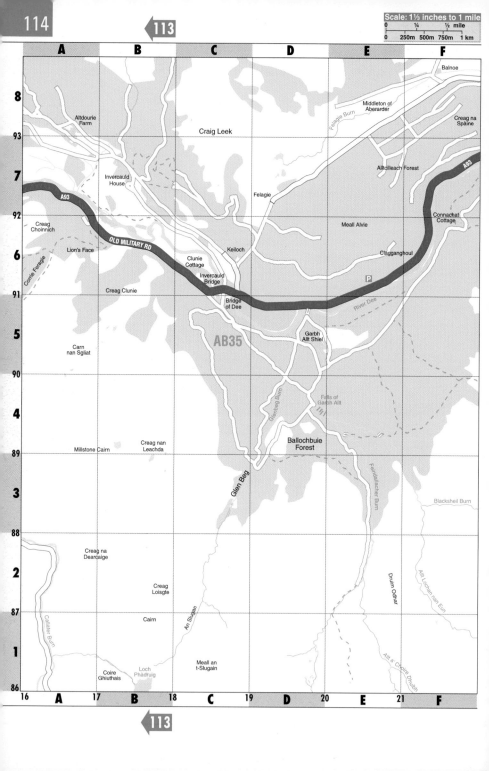

Scale: 1⅓ inches to 1 mile

0   ¼   ½ mile
0   250m 500m 750m 1 km

A **B** **C** **D** **E** **F**

8

93

7

92

6

91

5

90

4

89

3

88

2

87

1

86

Balnoe

Middleton of
Aberarder

Felagie Burn

Creag na
Spàine

Altdourie
Farm

Craig Leek

Alltcilleach Forest

A93

Invercauld
House

Felagie

Meall Alvie

Connachat
Cottage

Creag
Choinnich

A93

OLD MILITARY RD

Lion's Face

Keilloch

Ctagganghoul

Clunie
Cottage

Creag Clunie

Invercauld
Bridge

P

Corrie Feragie

Bridge
of Dee

River Dee

Carn
nan Sgliat

AB35

Garbh
Allt Shiel

Greenbeg Burn

Falls of
Garbh Allt

Ballochbuie
Forest

Millstone Cairn

Creag nan
Leachda

Feindallacher Burn

Blacksheil Burn

Glen Beg

Creag na
Dearcaige

Creag
Loisgte

Druim Odhar

Allt Lochan nan Eun

Cairn

An Slugan

Callater Burn

Coire
Ghiuthais

Loch
Phàdruig

Meall an
t-Slugain

Allt a' Choire Dhuibh

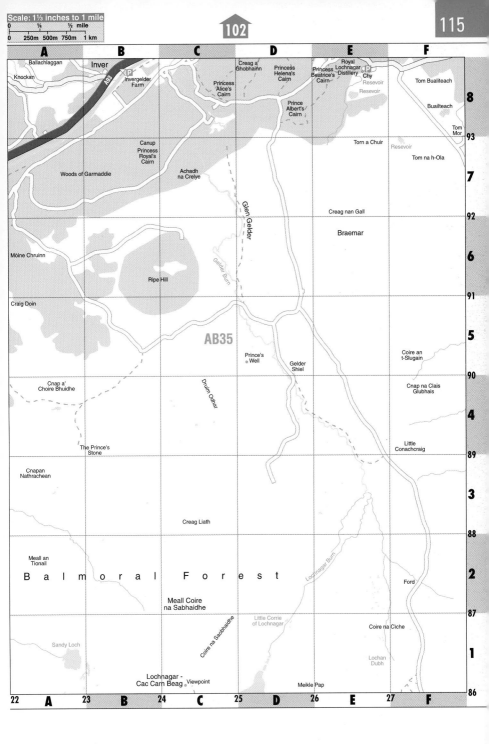

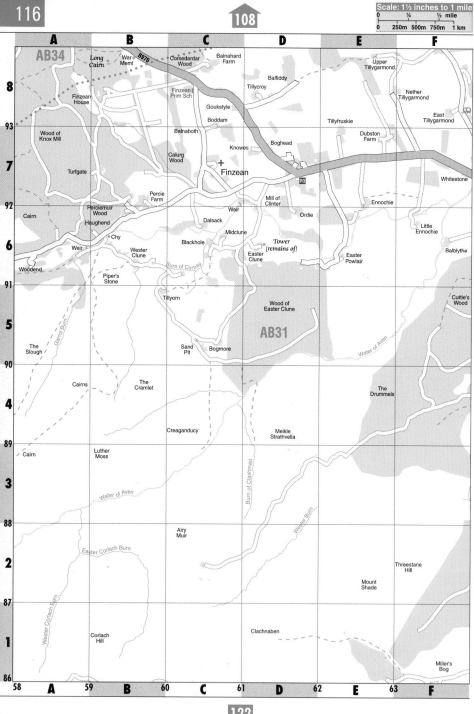

Scale: 1⅓ inches to 1 mile

0   ¼   ½ mile

0   250m   500m   750m   1 km

8

93

7

92

6

91

5

90

4

89

3

88

2

87

1

86

A   B   C   D   E   F

AB34

Long Cairn

War Meml

B976

Corsedardar Wood

Balnahard Farm

Finzean House

Finzean Prim Sch

Tillycroy

Balfiddy

Upper Tillygarmond

Nether Tillygarmond

East Tillygarmond

Goukstyle

Boddam

Tillyfruskie

Wood of Knox Mill

Balnaboth

Knowes

Boghead

Dubston Farm

Calurg Wood

Turfgate

Finzean

PO

Whitestone

Percie Farm

Mill of Clinter

Ennochie

Perciemuir Wood

Weir

Ordie

Little Ennochie

Cairn

Haughend

Dalsack

Easter Powlair

Balblythe

Chy

Midclune

Weir

Blackhole

Tower (remains of)

Woodend

Wester Clune

Burn of Curber

Easter Clune

Piper's Stone

Garrol Burn

Tillyorn

Wood of Easter Clune

Cuttie's Wood

AB31

The Slough

Sand Pit

Bogmore

Water of Aven

Cairns

The Cramlet

The Drummels

Creaganducy

Meikle Strathvella

Burn of Clashmad

Cairn

Luther Moss

Water of Aven

Wester Burn

Airy Muir

Easter Corlach Burn

Threestane Hill

Wester Corlach Burn

Mount Shade

Corlach Hill

Clachnaben

Miller's Bog

A   58   59   B   60   C   61   D   62   E   63   F

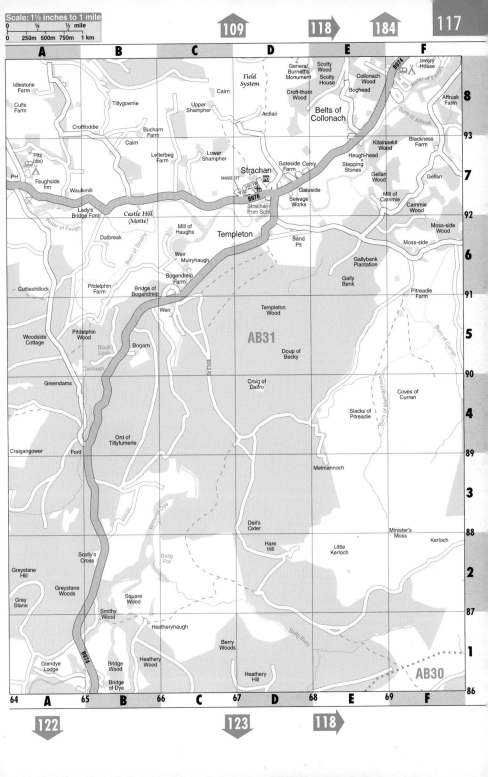

109
118
184

Scale: 1⅓ inches to 1 mile

0   ¼   ½ mile
0   250m 500m 750m 1 km

A   **B**   **C**   **D**   **E**   **F**

Idlestone Farm
Cults Farm
Croftfoddie
Tillygownie
Bucharn Farm
Cairn
Upper Shampher
Cairn
Ardlair

8

Field System

General Burnett's Monument
Scolty Wood
Scolty House
Croft-thorn Wood
Collonach Wood
Boghead
Invery House
B974
Water of Feugh
Affrusk Farm

Belts of Collonach

93

Letterbeg Farm
Cairn
Lower Shampher
Strachan
Gateside Cemy
Gateside Farm
Kitalnaekit Wood
Heugh-head
Stepping Stones
Gellan Wood
Blackness Farm
Gellan

7

PH
Pits (dis)
Feughside Inn
Waulkmill
MANSE CFT
LGH VW
PO
B976
Strachan Prim Sch
Gateside
Sewage Works
Mill of Cammie
Cammie Wood

Water of Feugh
Lady's Bridge Ford
Castle Hill (Motte)
Dalbreak
Mill of Haughs
Templeton
Sand Pit

Moss-side Wood
Moss-side

92

Burn of Sheeoch
Weir
Muiryhaugh
Bogendreip Farm
Bridge of Bogandreip
Weir
Pitdelphin Farm

Gallybank Plantation
Gally Bank
Pitreadie Farm

6

Cuttieshillock

Woodside Cottage
Pitdelphin Wood
Black Loch
Cormech
Bogarn
Templeton Wood

AB31

Doup of Becky

Coves of Curran
Burn of Curran

5

Greendams

Craig of Dalfro

91

Ord of Tillyfumerie
Craigangower
Ford

Melmannoch

Slacks of Pitreadie

4

Water of Dye

Deil's Oxter

Minister's Moss
Kerloch

89

Scolly's Cross

Hare Hill
Little Kerloch

3

Greystane Hill
Greystane Woods
Grey Stane
Square Wood
Smithy Wood
Bullg Pot

Berry Woods
Bullg Burn

88

Heatheryhaugh
Heathery Wood
Glendye Lodge
Bridge Wood
Bridge of Dye
Heathery Hill

AB30

2

87

1

86

A   **B**   **C**   **D**   **E**   **F**
64   65   66   67   68   69

122
123
118

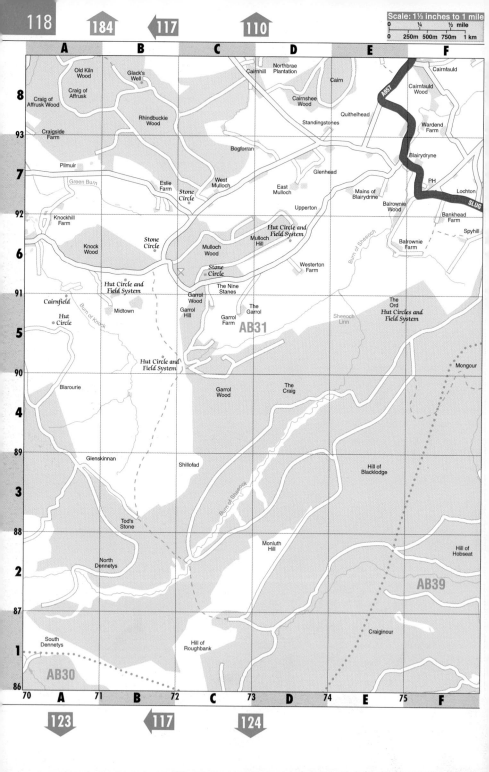

184
117
110

Scale: 1⅓ inches to 1 mile

0   ¼   ½ mile
0   250m 500m 750m 1 km

A   **B**   **C**   **D**   **E**   **F**

8
Old Kiln Wood
Glack's Well
Craig of Affrusk
Craig of Affrusk Wood
Cairnhill
Northbrae Plantation
Cairn
Cairnfauld
Cairnfauld Wood

Rhindbuckie Wood
Cairnshee Wood
Standingstones
Quithelhead
Wardend Farm

93
Craigside Farm
Bogforran
Blairydryne

7
Pilmuir
Green Burn
Eslie Farm
West Mulloch
Glenhead
PH
Lochton

Stone Circle
East Mulloch
Mains of Blairydrine
Balrownie Wood
Bankhead Farm
SLUG

92
Knockhill Farm
Upperton
Spyhill

6
Knock Wood
Stone Circle
Mulloch Wood
Hut Circle and Field System
Mulloch Hill
Balrownie Farm

Stone Circle
Westerton Farm

91
Cairnfield
Hut Circle and Field System
Garrol Wood
The Nine Stanes
The Ord
Hut Circles and Field System

5
Hut Circle
Midtown
Garrol Hill
The Garrol
Garrol Farm
AB31
Sheeoch Linn
Mongour

90
Blarourie
Hut Circle and Field System
Garrol Wood
The Craig

4

89
Glenskinnan
Shillofad
Burn of Sheeoch
Hill of Blacklodge

3

88
Tod's Stone
Monluth Hill
Hill of Hobseat

2
North Dennetys
AB39

87
Craiginour

1
South Dennetys
Hill of Roughbank

86
AB30

70   **A**   **71**   **B**   **72**   **C**   **73**   **D**   **74**   **E**   **75**   **F**

123
117
124

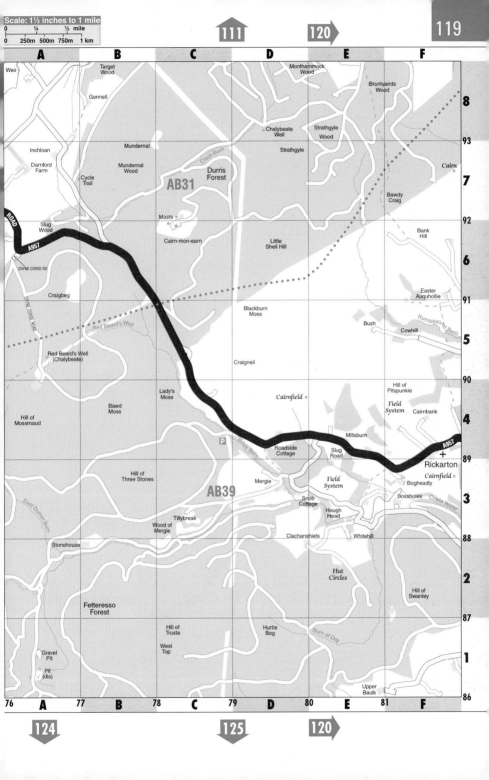

Scale: 1⅓ inches to 1 mile

0   ¼   ½ mile
0 250m 500m 750m 1 km

111

120

119

A   B   C   D   E   F

Weir

Target
Wood

Gennell

Monthammock
Wood

Bruntyairds
Wood

8

Inchloan

Mundernal

Chalybeate
Well

Strathgyle
Wood

93

Darnford
Farm

Mundernal
Wood

Durris
Forest

Strathgyle

Cairn

7

Cycle
Trail

AB31

Bawdy
Craig

ROAD

Masts

Bank
Hill

92

Slug
Wood

Cairn-mon-earn

Little
Sheil Hill

A957

6

CRYNE CORSE RD

Easter
Auquhollie

91

Craigbeg

Blackburn
Moss

Rumbleyo Hill Burn

CRYNE CORSE ROAD

Red Beard's Well

Bush

Cowhill

5

Red Beard's Well
(Chalybeate)

Craigneil

Hill of
Pitspunkie

90

Lady's
Moss

Cairnfield

Field
System

Cairnbank

Bawd
Moss

A957

4

Hill of
Mossmaud

Black Burn

Millsburn

Rickarton

89

P

Roadside
Cottage

Slug
Road

Cairnfield

East Durnar Burn

Hill of
Three Stones

Mergie

Field
System

Bogheadly

Bossholes

Cowie Water

3

AB39

Snob
Cottage

Haugh
Head

Whitehill

Tillybreak

Wood of
Mergie

Clachanshiels

Stonehouse

88

Hut
Circles

2

Fetteresso
Forest

Hill of
Swanley

87

Hill of
Trusta

Hurtie
Bog

Burn of Day

West
Top

1

Gravel
Pit

Pit
(dis)

Upper
Baulk

86

76 A 77 B 78 C 79 D 80 E 81 F

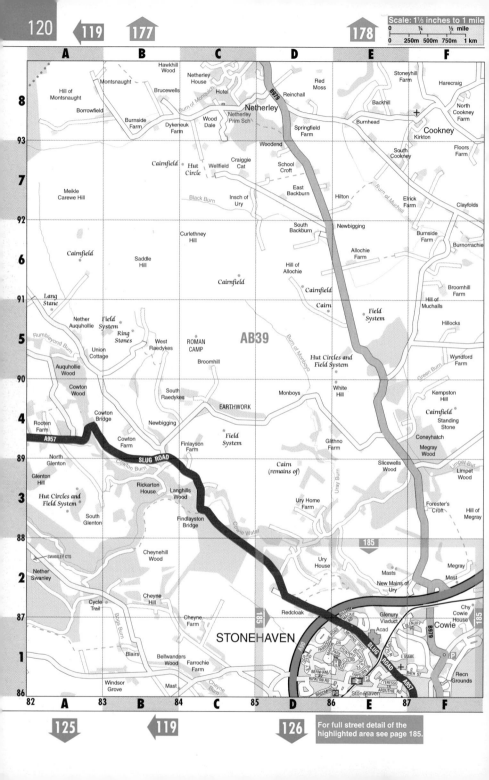

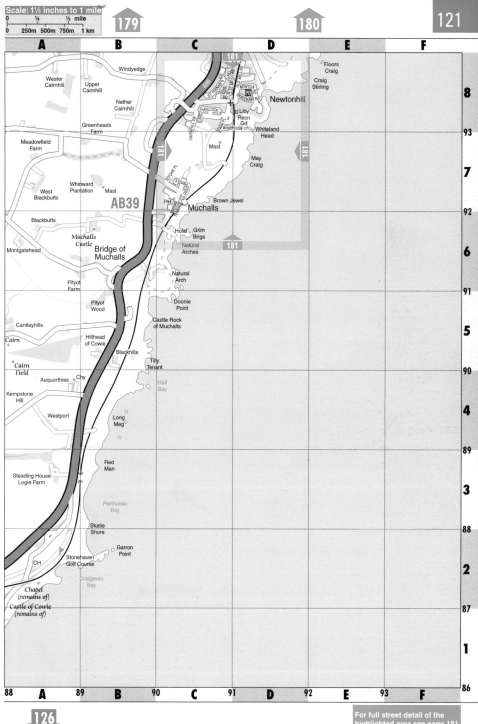

Scale: 1⅓ inches to 1 mile

0   ¼   ½ mile
0   250m 500m 750m 1 km

Wester Cairnhill
Upper Cairnhill
Windyedge
Nether Cairnhill
Floors Craig
Craig Stirling
Newtonhill
Greenheads Farm
Meadowfield Farm
Liby
Recn Gd
Mast
Whiteland Head
West Blackbutts
Whinward Plantation
Mast
May Craig
AB39
Blackbutts
Brown Jewel
PH
Muchalls
Muchalls Castle
Montgatehead
Hotel
Grim Brigs
Bridge of Muchalls
Natural Arches
Pityot Farm
Natural Arch
Pityot Wood
Doonie Point
Cantlayhills
Castle Rock of Muchalls
Cairn
Hillhead of Cowie
Blackhills
Cairn Field
Tilly Tenant
Auquorthies
Chy
Hall Bay
Kempstone Hill
Westport
Long Meg
Red Man
Steading House Logie Farm
Perthumie Bay
Skatie Shore
Garron Point
Stonehaven Golf Course
CH
Craigeven Bay
Chapel (remains of)
Castle of Cowie (remains of)

For full street detail of the highlighted area see page 181.

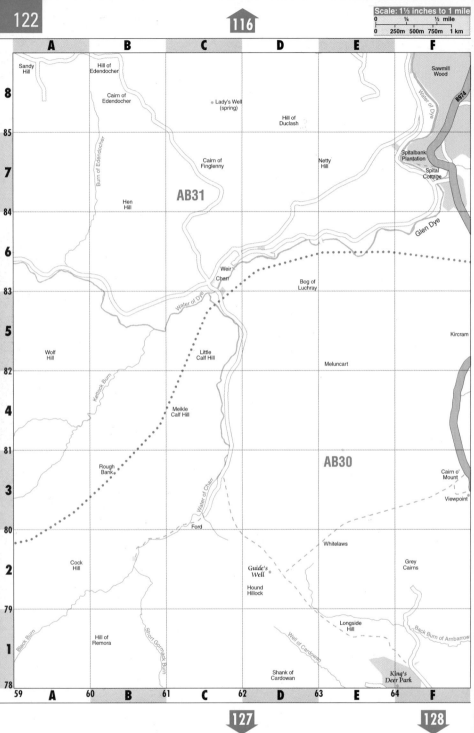

116

Scale: 1⅓ inches to 1 mile

| 0 | ¼ | ½ | mile |

| 0 | 250m | 500m | 750m | 1 km |

A   B   C   D   E   F

8

Sandy
Hill

Hill of
Edendocher

Cairn of
Edendocher

Lady's Well
(spring)

Hill of
Duclash

Sawmill
Wood

B974

85

Burn of Edendocher

Cairn of
Finglenny

Netty
Hill

Spitalbank
Plantation

Spital
Cottage

Water of Dye

7

AB31

Hen
Hill

84

Glen Dye

6

Weir

Charr

Bog of
Luchray

83

Water of Dye

5

Wolf
Hill

Little
Calf Hill

Meluncart

Kircram

Kettock Burn

4

Meikle
Calf Hill

81

Rough
Bank

AB30

Cairn o'
Mount

3

Water of Charr

Viewpoint

80

Ford

Whitelaws

2

Cock
Hill

Guide's
Well

Hound
Hillock

Grey
Cairns

Short Garrock Burn

79

Black Burn

Hill of
Remora

Well of Cardowan

Longside
Hill

Back Burn of Arnbarrow

1

Shank of
Cardowan

King's
Deer Park

78

59   A   60   B   61   C   62   D   63   E   64   F

127

128

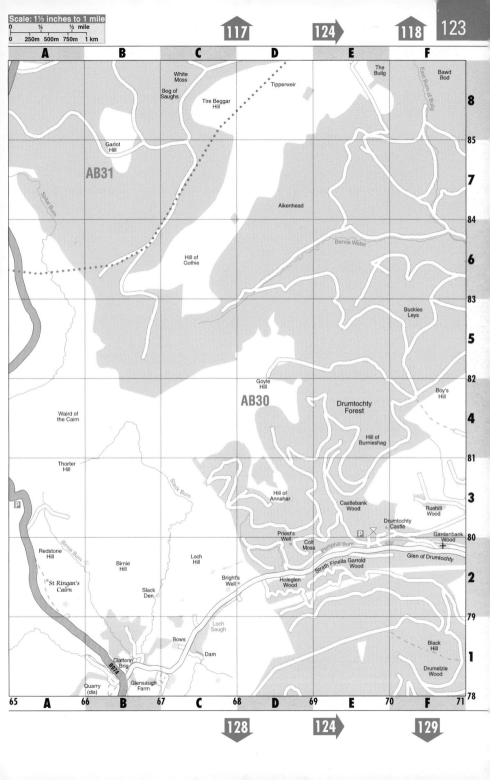

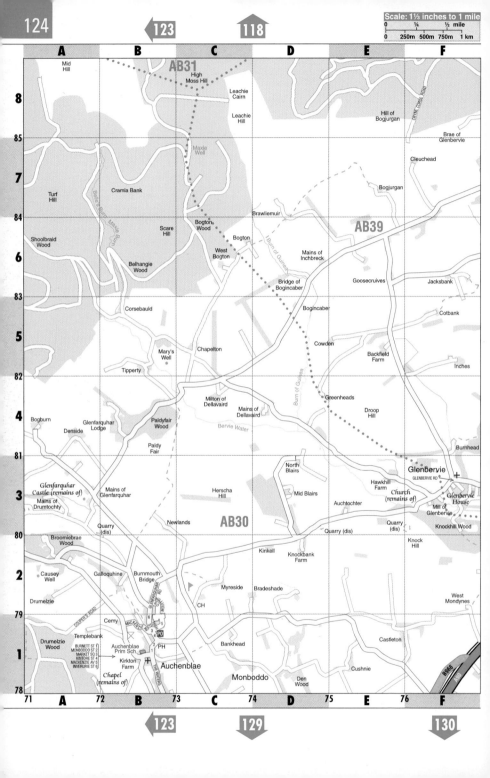

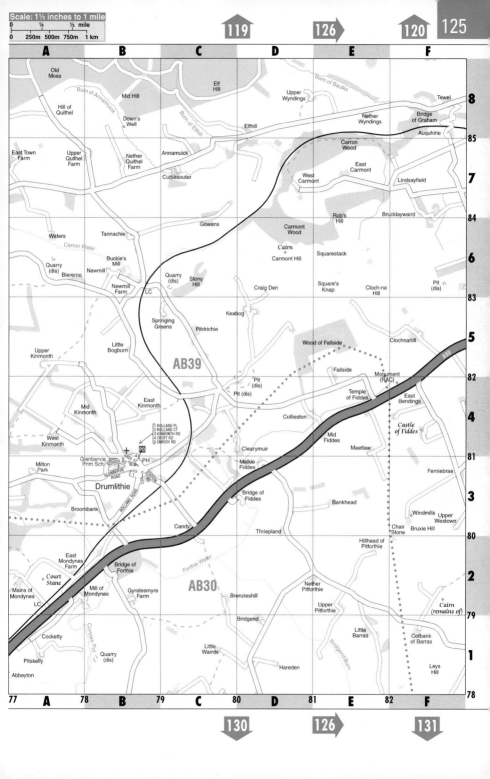

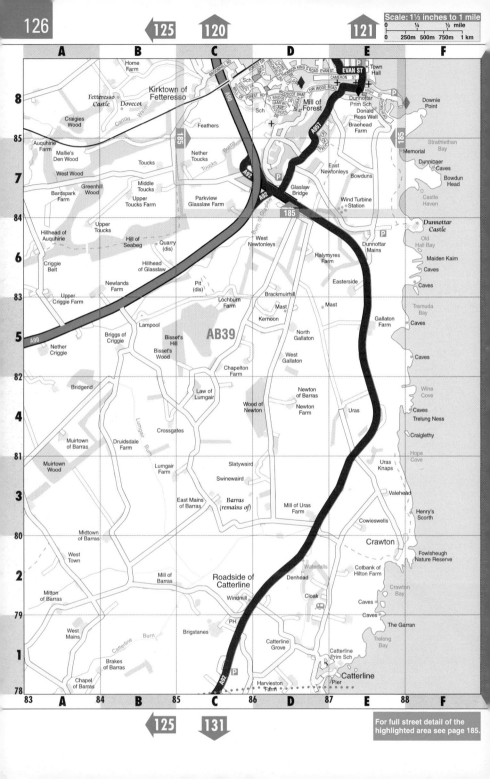

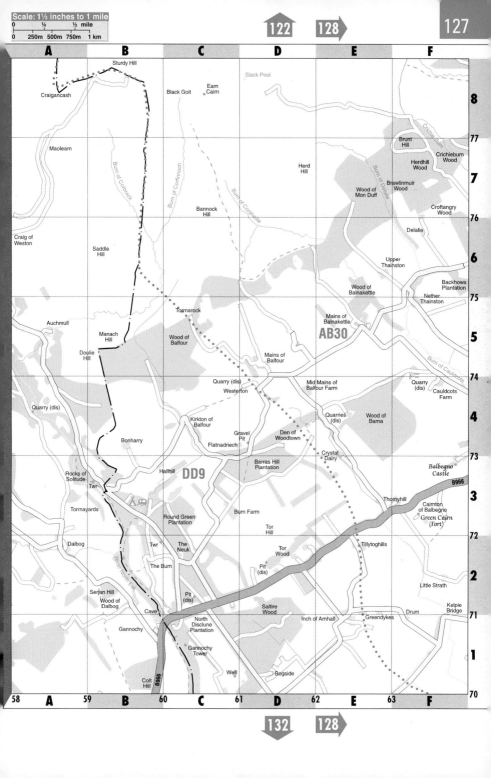

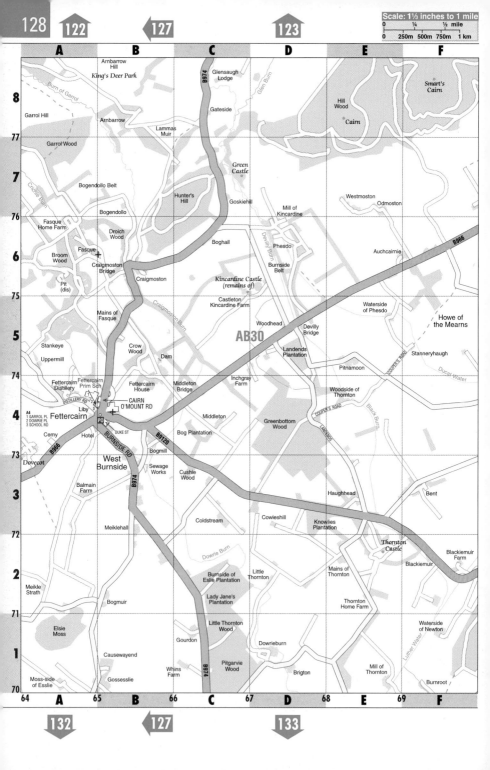

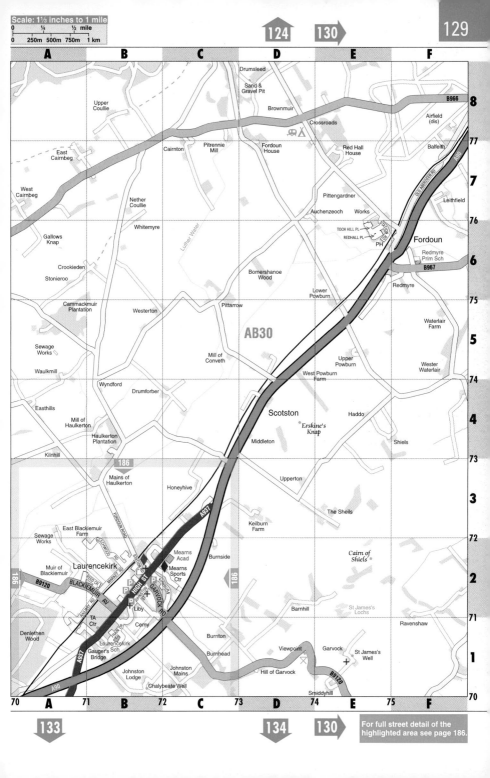

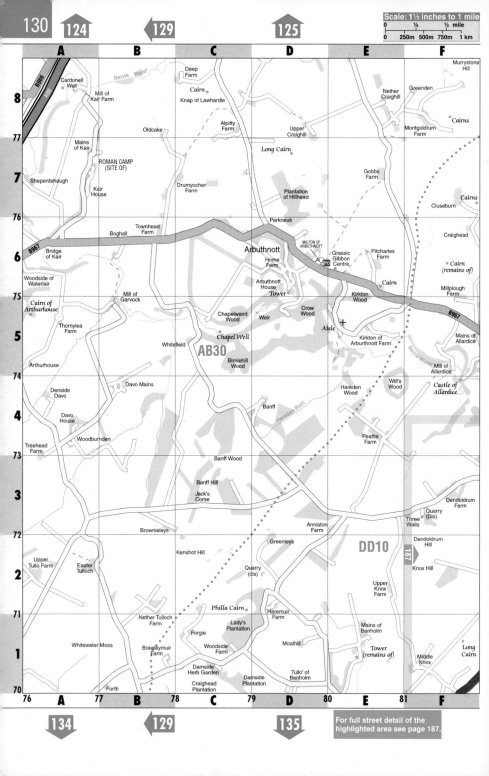

Scale: 1⅓ inches to 1 mile

0 ¼ ½ mile
0 250m 500m 750m 1 km

A **B** **C** **D** **E** **F**

Leys of
Barras

Standing
Stone

AB39

St John's
Knap

Bellfield
Farm

Forley Craig

8

Cairn

St John's
Hill

Fawsyde
Farm

Pit
(dis)

Millhill

Braidon
Bay

Moor of
Auchendreich

Overton

Fernieflatt
Farm

Todhead Point

77

Water Hill

MARTIN TR

PO

Roadside
of Kinneff

Temple

Kinneff
Prim Sch

Hallhill
Farm

Todhead
Lighthouse

7

Auchendreich
Farm

The
Law

SANDY PARK

Powdam Head

The Slunges

76

Largie
Farm

Wardhead

Slains
Park

Rouen Bay

Whistleberry
Castle (remains of)

Scart's
Craig

6

Gallow Hill

Clashendrum

DD10

Whistleberry
Farm

Kinneff

75

Pitcarrie Burn

Harbour
Shields

Crowhillock

Crooked
Haven

5

Pitcarry

Grange
Farm

Castle Hill

Little John's
Haven

74

B967

Seppie
Wood

Cairn

Bervie Brow

Craig David

Darn
Bay

4

Upper Mill

187

Pitcarry
Mill

Big Rob's
Cove

73

The Haughs

Bervie
Prim Sch

Linton
Ind Est

War Meml

King's
Step

3

Townhead

QUEEN'S RD

CHURCH ST

KING ST

WORK BURN

HALLGREEN RD

P

Inverbervie

Bervie Bay

Hallgreen
Castle

72

Hillside of
Dendoldrum

WEST PARK

KING

INCHIBREAK RD

Hallgreen
Mains

Sillyflatt

Linton
Business
Park

187

Horse
Crook Bay

2

BRAE RD

Cemy

Recn Gd

Sch

PO

71

PH

Mus

QUEEN
ST

WILLIAM ST

WEST BAY

SEAFIELD
TERRACE

Gourdon

Doolie Ness

A92

1

Whitehouse

A **B** **C** **D** **E** **F**

82 83 84 85 86 87

70

For full street detail of the
highlighted area see page 187.

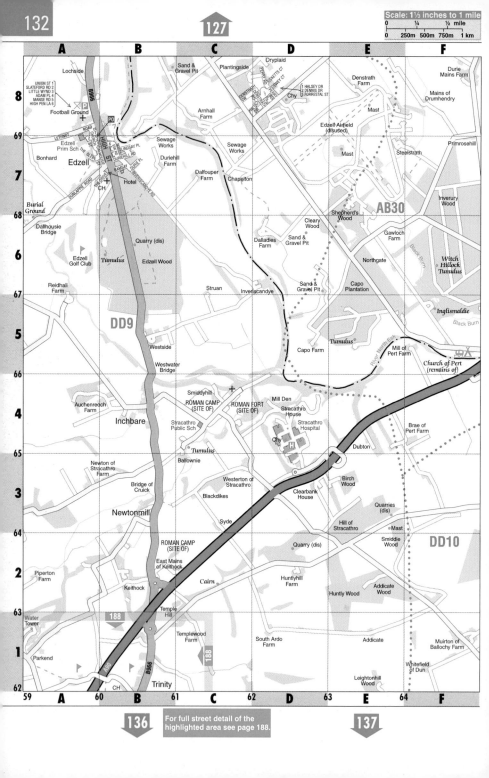

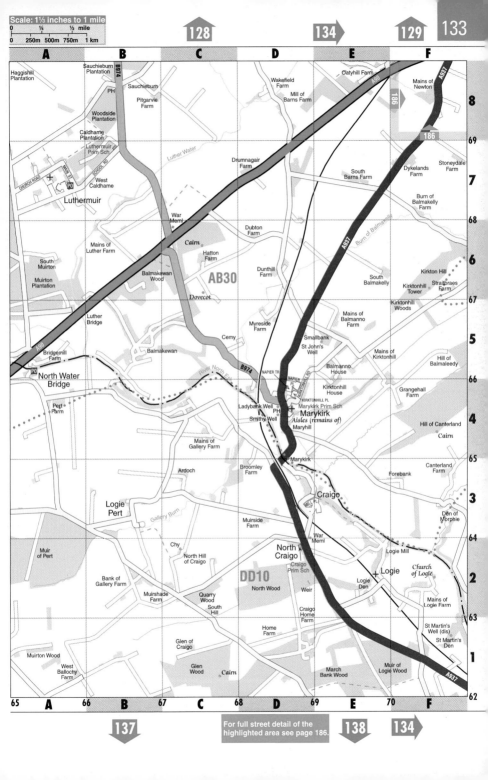

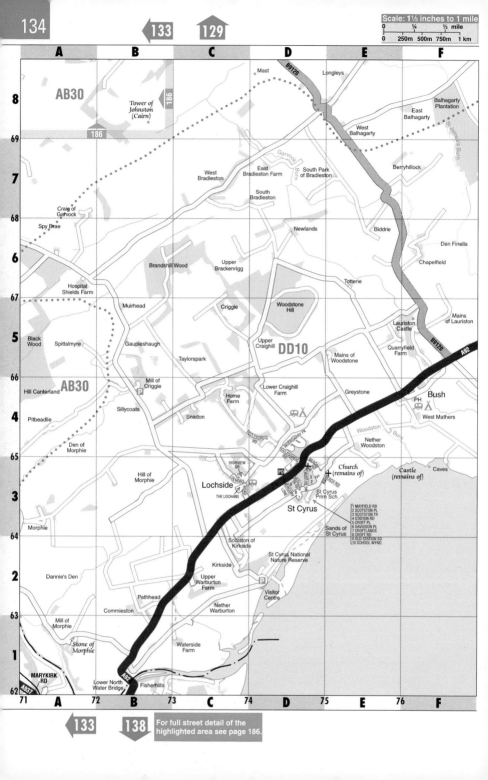

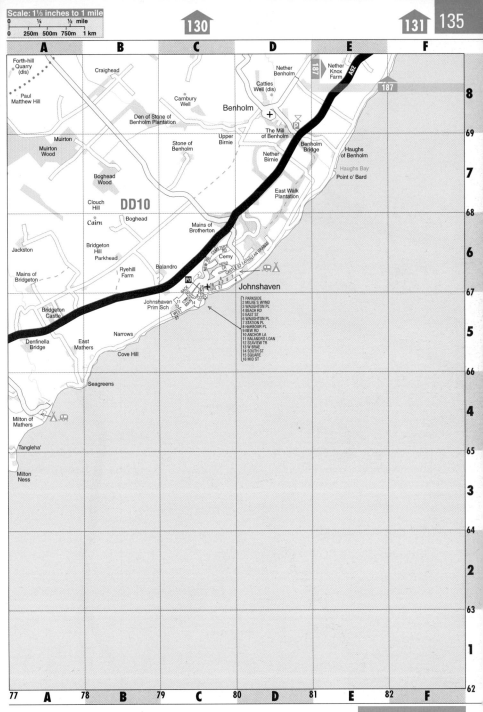

A   B   C   D   E   F

8

Forth-hill Quarry (dis)

Paul Matthew Hill

Craighead

Carnbury Well

Nether Benholm

Catties Well (dis)

Nether Knox Farm

187

A92

187

Benholm

Den of Stone of Benholm Plantation

Stone of Benholm

Upper Birnie

The Mill of Benholm

69

Muirton

Muirton Wood

Benholm Bridge

Nether Birnie

Haughs of Benholm

7

Boghead Wood

Haughs Bay
Point o' Bard

Clouch Hill

DD10

68

Cairn

Boghead

East Walk Plantation

Jackston

Mains of Brotherton

6

Bridgeton Hill
Parkhead

Ryehill Farm

Balandro

NEW RD   CEMETERY RD
Cemy

67

Mains of Bridgeton

PO

CASTLE ST   LATHALLAN GRANGE

HEAD
DYKE

BACK

FORE ST

Johnshaven

Bridgeton Castle

Johnshaven Prim Sch

WEST
ST

MARINE ST

1 PARKSIDE
2 MILNE'S WYND
3 WAUGHTON PL
4 BEACH RD
5 EAST ST
6 WAUGHTON PL
7 STATION PL
8 HARBOUR PL
9 NEW RD
10 ANCHOR LA
11 BALANDRO LOAN
12 SEAVIEW TR
13 W BRAE
14 SOUTH ST
15 SQUARE
16 MID ST

5

Denfinella Bridge

East Mathers

Narrows

Cove Hill

66

Seagreens

4

Milton of Mathers

Tangleha'

65

Milton Ness

3

64

2

63

1

62

77   A   78   B   79   C   80   D   81   E   82   F

For full street detail of the highlighted area see page 187.

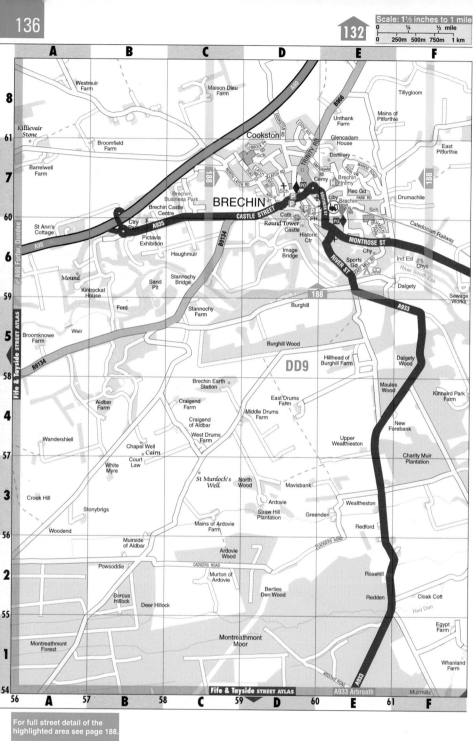

Scale: 1½ inches to 1 mile

0   ¼   ½   mile
0 250m 500m 750m 1 km

BRECHIN

DD9

For full street detail of the highlighted area see page 188.

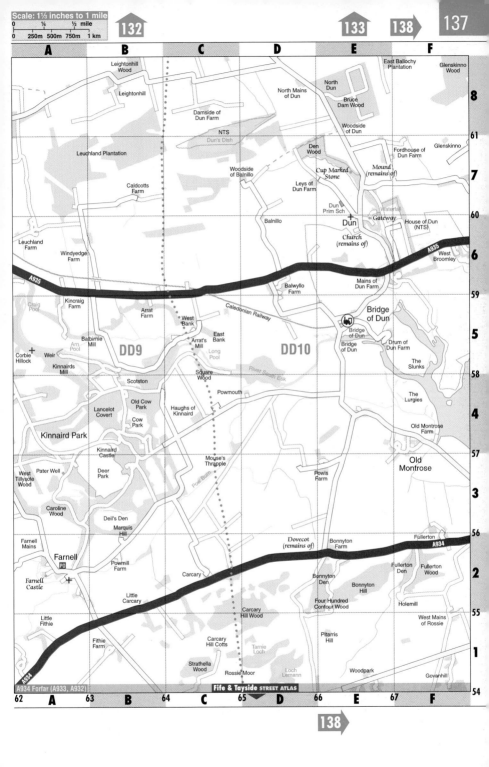

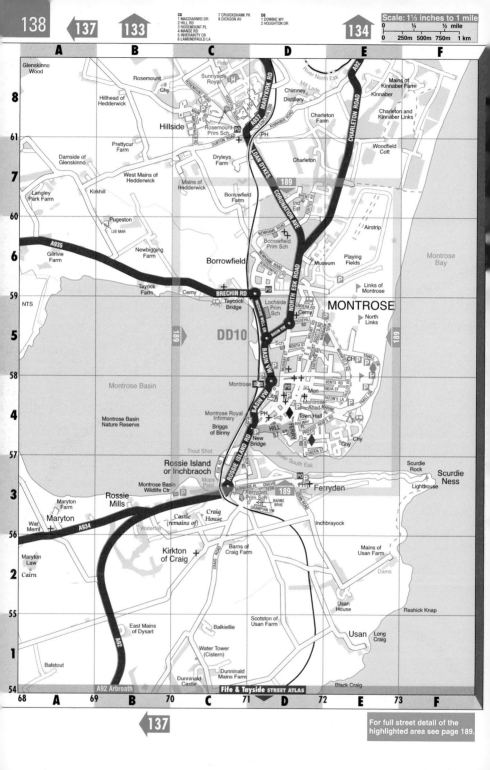

138

137 133 134

C8
1 MACDIARMID DR
2 HILL RD
3 ROSEMOUNT PL
4 MANSE RD
5 INVERARITY CR
6 LAMONDFAULD LA

7 CRUICKSHANK PK
8 DICKSON AV

D8
1 DOWNIE WY
2 HOUGHTON DR

Scale: 1⅓ inches to 1 mile

0   ¼   ½   mile
0 250m 500m 750m 1 km

A   B   C   D   E   F

Glenskinno Wood

8

Rosemount
Chy

Sunnyside Royal

Rest

Hillhead of Hedderwick

Hillside

Rosemount Prim Sch

Chimney
Distillery

Mill Lade

River North Esk

A92

Mains of Kinnaber Farm

Kinnaber

Charleton and Kinnaber Links

61

Prettycur Farm

Dryleys Farm

PH

Charleton Farm

Woodfield Cott

Damside of Glenskinno

West Mains of Hedderwick

Charleton

7

Langley Park Farm

Kirkhill

Mains of Hedderwick

Borrowfield Farm

189

Brent Ind Est

60

Pugeston

LEE MAR

A935

Gilrivie Farm

Newbigging Farm

Borrowfield

Newhame Road

Borrowfield Prim Sch

Museum

Airstrip

Playing Fields

Montrose Bay

6

Tayock Farm

Cemy

BRECHIN RD

Tayock Bridge

Lochside Prim Sch

PO

North Esk Road

Links of Montrose

59

NTS

189

DD10

BASIN VW

Sch

NORTH ST

MONTROSE

North Links

5

Montrose Basin

Montrose

Liby

Montrose Acad

189

58

Montrose Basin Nature Reserve

Montrose Royal Infirmary

Briggs of Binny

PH
Sch

Town Hall
Railway

Mon

Montrose Marine

Chy

4

Trout Shot

New Bridge

HILL ST

FERRY

Chy

57

Rossie Island or Inchbraoch

Montrose Basin Wildlife Ctr

Mops Pool

River South Esk

Ferryden

Scurdie Rock

Scurdie Ness

3

Maryton Farm

Rossie Mills

Burnside Pl

Ferryden Prim Sch

Barns Brae

189

GRAMPIAN VW

Lighthouse

Maryton

War Meml

A934

Castle (remains of)

Craig House

Inchbrayock

56

Maryton Law

Cairn

Waterfall

Kirkton of Craig

Barns of Craig Farm

Mains of Usan Farm

2

East Mains of Dysart

Balkiellie

Scotston of Usan Farm

Dams

55

A92

Water Tower (Cistern)

Usan House

Usan

Long Craig

Rashick Knap

1

Balstout

Dunninald Castle

Dunninald Mains Farm

Black Craig

54

A92 Arbroath

Fife & Tayside STREET ATLAS

68   A   69   B   70   C   71   D   72   E   73   F

137

For full street detail of the highlighted area see page 189.

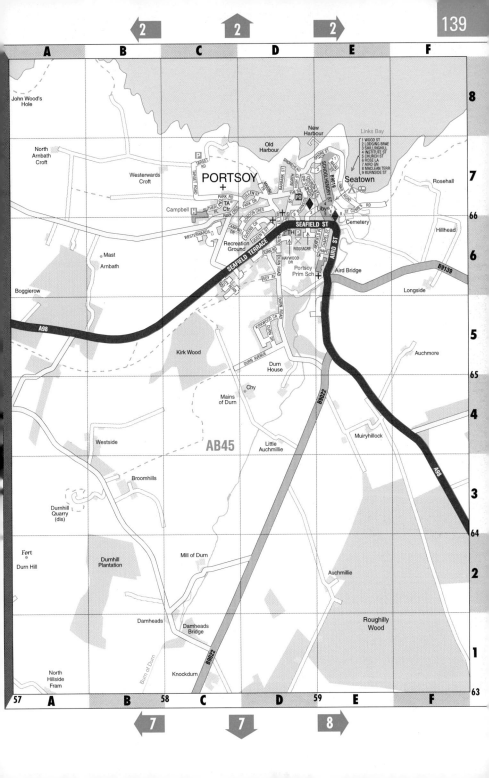

PORTSOY

Seatown

1 WOOD ST
2 LODGING BRAE
3 SHILLINGHILL
4 INSTITUTE ST
5 CHURCH ST
6 ROSE LA
7 AIRD GN
8 MACLEAN TERR
9 BURNSIDE ST

John Wood's Hole

North Arnbath Croft

Westerwards Croft

Campbell

Mast
Arnbath

Boggierow

New Harbour

Old Harbour

Links Bay

Rosehall

Hillhead

SEAFIELD ST

SEAFIELD TERRACE

AIRD ST

Recreation Ground

Roseacre

Haywood Dr

Portsoy Prim Sch

Aird Bridge

Longside

A98

Kirk Wood

Durn House

Chy

Mains of Durn

Little Auchmillie

AB45

Auchmore

Muiryhillock

Westside

Broomhills

Durnhill Quarry (dis)

Fort
Durn Hill

Durnhill Plantation

Mill of Durn

Auchmillie

Roughilly Wood

Damheads

Damheads Bridge

Knockdurn

Burn of Durn

North Hillside Fram

B9139

B9022

B9022

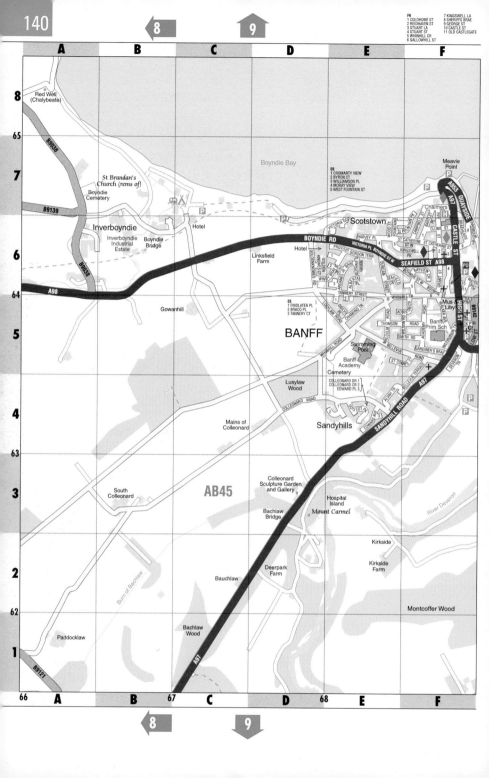

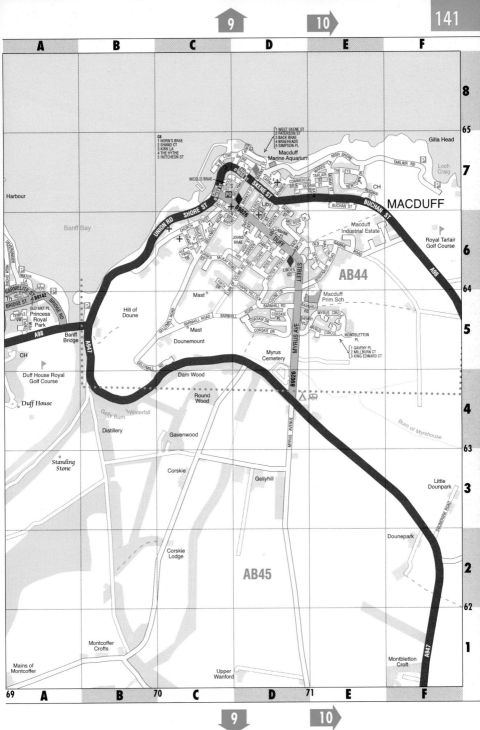

MACDUFF

AB44

AB45

C6
1 HORN'S BRAE
2 SHAND CT
3 KIRK LA
4 THE HYTHE
5 HUTCHEON ST

1 WEST SKENE ST
2 PATERSON ST
3 BACK BRAE
4 BRAEHEADS
5 SIMPSON PL

Macduff
Marine Aquarium

Gilla Head

Loch
Craig

Tarlair Rd

Royal Tarlair
Golf Course

Macduff
Industrial Estate

Macduff
Prim Sch

Myrus Circle

Montbletton
Pl

1 GAVENY PL
2 MILLBURN CT
3 KING EDWARD CT

Myrus
Cemetery

Harbour

Banff Bay

Hill of
Doune

Mast

Mast

Dounemount

Barnhill

Corskie Dr

Corskie Dr

Dam Wood

Round
Wood

Waterfall

Distillery

Gavenwood

Standing
Stone

Corskie

Gellyhill

Little
Dounpark

Dounepark

Corskie
Lodge

Montbletton
Croft

Montcoffer
Crofts

Mains of
Montcoffer

Upper
Wanford

Duff House Royal
Golf Course

Duff House

Banff
Bridge

Princess
Royal Park

Burn of Myrehouse

Gelly Burn

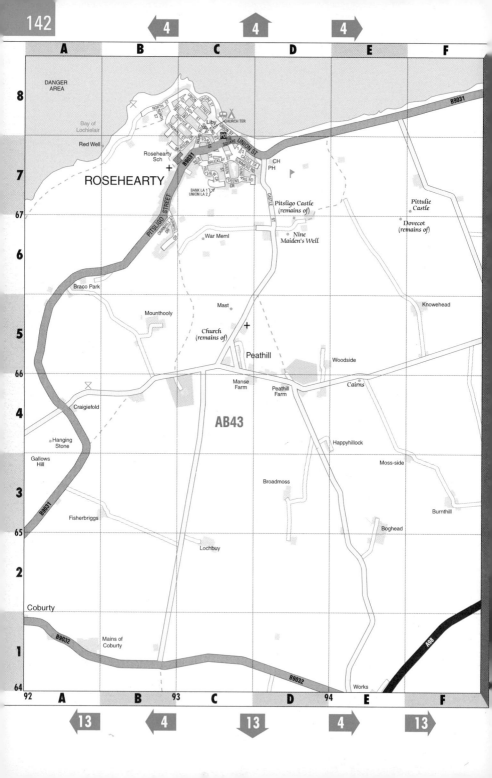

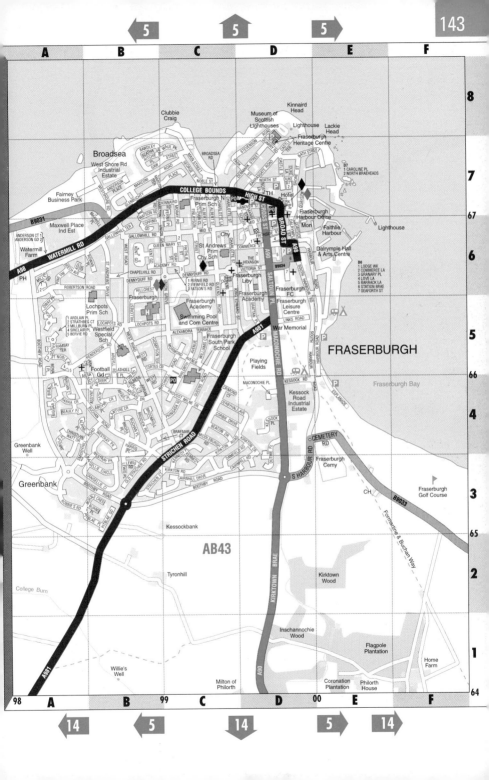

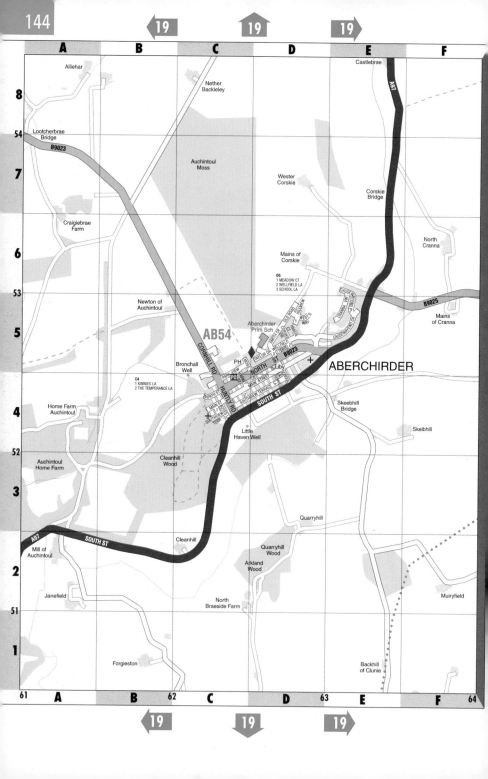

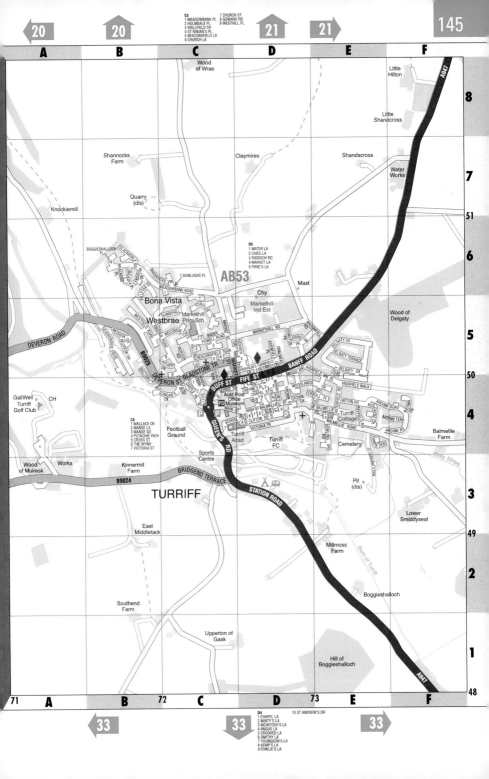

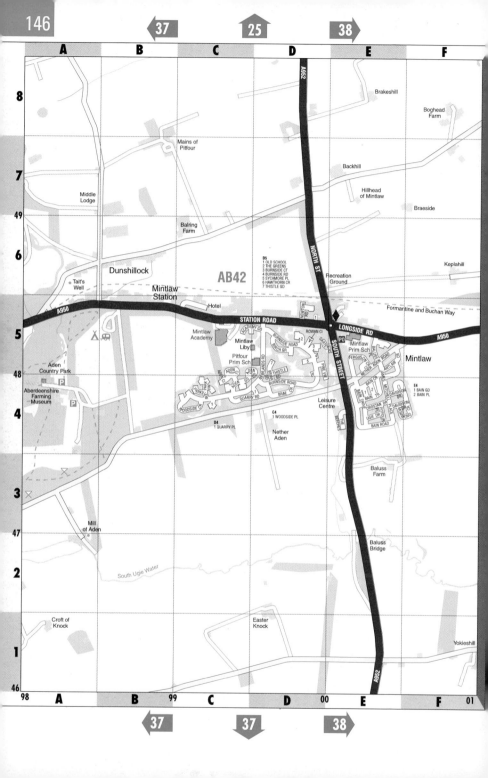

A8
1 BROOKSIDE
2 WHITE GATES

B5
1 GADWALL PL
2 EIDER CT
3 MALLARD DR
4 ST MAGNUS PL
5 HAWTHORN RD

E5
1 CARTERS CL
2 TOLBOOTHWYND
3 THREADNEEDLE ST
4 NARROW LA

Craigewan Links

Waterside

Peterhead
Golf Club

CH

River Ugie

George Birnee
Memorial Footbridge

Peterhead
Ugie

Buchanhaven

Blackhouse
Industrial
Estate

Blackhouse

Balmoor
Cemetery

A6
1 CAPTAIN GRAY PL
2 HAYFIELD PL

Coplandhill

Radio
Mast

Balmoor
Ret Pk
Balmoor
Ind Est

Balmoor Stadium
(Peterhead FC)

BALMOOR TERRACE

Buchanhaven
Prim Sch

E6
1 NORTH STREET
2 ALMANYTHIE RD
3 PORT HENRY RD
4 CORDINER CT
5 SUTHERLAND AVE

Roanheads

F6
1 BATTERY PK
2 GT STUART ST
3 SEAGATE

F5
1 CROOKED LA
2 ROSE ST
3 PARK LA
4 BROAD ST

Swimming
Pool

Peterhead
Acad

TA
Centre

Upper
Grange

Middle
Grange

Farm

A5
1 COPLANDHILL PL
2 ACACIA GR
3 PENNY PL

The Anna
Ritchie Sch

Grange
Gardens

Clerkhill
Prim Sch

Cemetery

Liby
Arbuthnot
Mus

Sheriff
Ct House
Drummers'
Corner

Hotel

Model
Jetty

Works

Willie Wood's
Hole Rock

AB42

Kirktown

Chimney

Keith
Inch

C4
1 SANDFORD CT
2 CLERKHILL PL
3 LINKSFIELD RD
4 FORREST RD

E4
1 UPHILL LA
2 WALLACE ST
3 MERCHANTS QUAY

PLEASURE WK

Clerkhill

Peterhead
Com

PETERHEAD

A4
1 LINGBANK TERR
2 BOSIES BANK WY
3 SILVER PITT GD
4 LOCHSIDE PL

Playing
Fields

Meethill

Peterhead
Bay

North
Breakwater

Clerkhill
Mast

Dales Park
Farm

Meethill
Prim
Sch

B4
1 GRANGE PK PL
2 ROWANBANK
3 GREENBRAE PL

Dales
Park

Peterhead
Maritime Heritage
Centre

Jetty

B3
1 LILAC GR
2 ASHGROVE PL
3 ORCHARD GR

C2
1 AALESUND PL
2 DALES RD

Watersport
Centre

Jetty

South
Breakwater

South Bay
Harbour

Whitehill

Works

Dales Industrial
Estate

Industrial
Estate

Reform
Tower

HM
Prison

Salthouse
Head

Invernettie

Burnhaven
Prim Sch

Upperton
Ind Est

Dales
Ind Est

Damhead
Ind Est

Dales Industrial
Estate

Burnside
Business
Park

Works

The
Skellyis

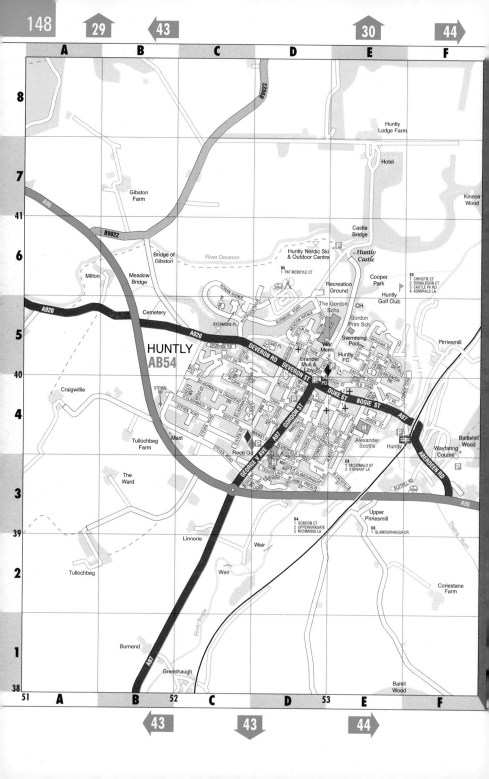

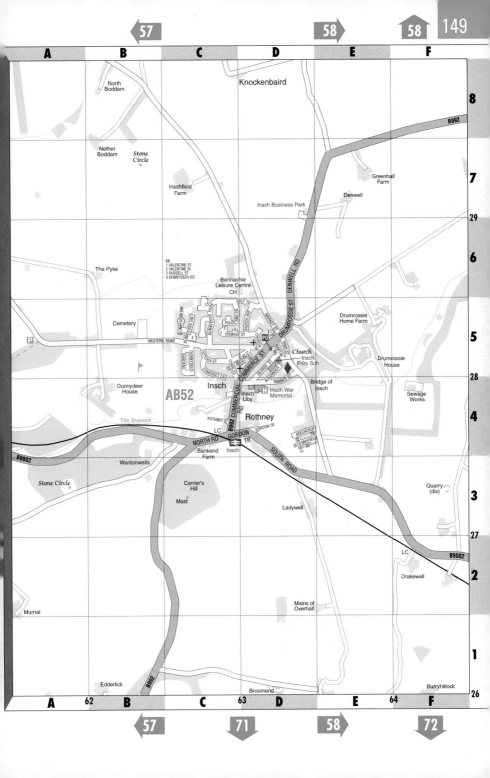

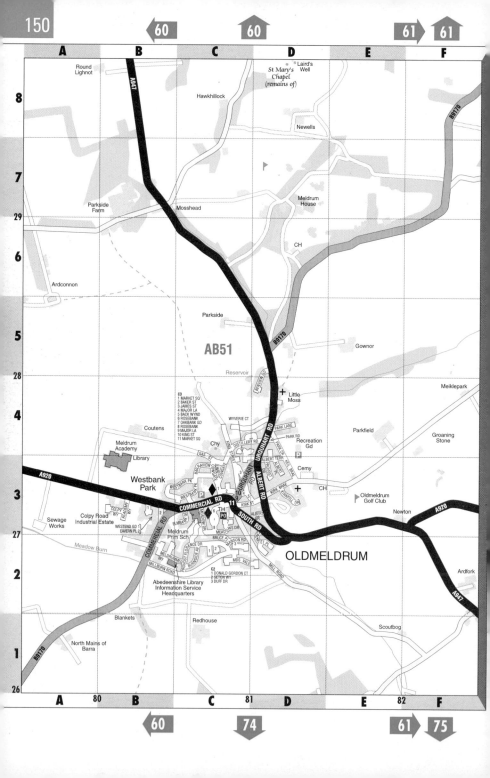

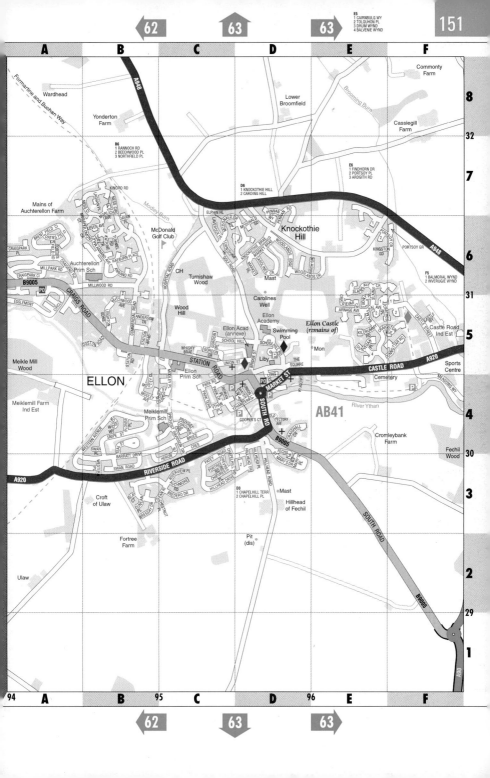

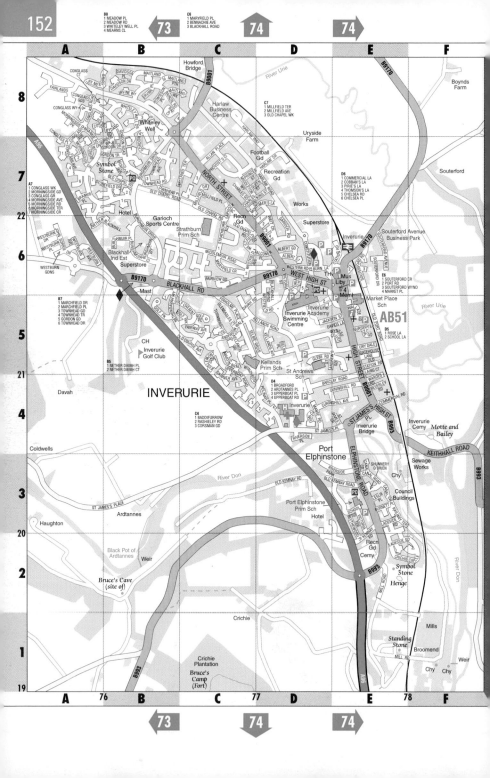

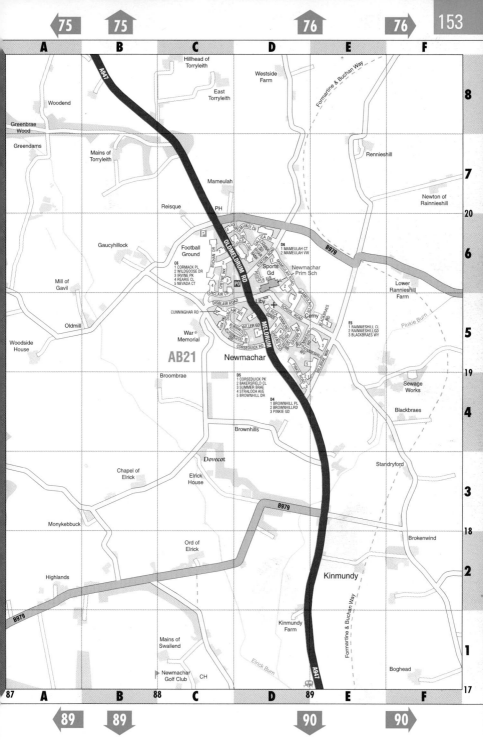

Hillhead of
Torryleith

Westside
Farm

Woodend

Greenbrae
Wood

Greendams

Mains of
Torryleith

East
Torryleith

Rennieshill

Newton of
Rainnieshill

Mameulah

PH

Reisque

Gaucyhillock

Football
Ground

Mill of
Gavil

Oldmill

Woodside
House

War
Memorial

AB21

Newmachar

OLDMELDRUM RD

BUCHAN DR

SINCLAIR DR

DISBLAIR ROAD

CUNNINGHAR RD

MELDRUM RD

CORSEDUICK RD

C6
1 CORMACK PL
2 WILDGOOSE DR
3 IRVINE PK
4 REARIE CL
5 NEVADA CT

D6
1 MAMEULAH CT
2 MAMEULAH VW

Newmachar
Prim Sch

Sports
Gd

Liby

Cemy

E5
1 RAINNIESHILL CL
2 RAINNIESHILLGD
3 BLACKBRAES WY

Lower
Rannieshill
Farm

Pinkie Burn

Sewage
Works

Blackbraes

Broombrae

D5
1 CORSEDUICK PK
2 BAKERSFIELD CL
3 SUMMER BRAE
4 STRALOCH AVE
5 BROWNHILL DR

D4
1 BROWNHILL PL
2 BROWNHILL RD
3 PINKIE GD

Brownhills

Dovecot

Chapel of
Elrick

Elrick
House

Standryford

Monykebbuck

Ord of
Elrick

B979

Brokenwind

Highlands

Kinmundy

Mains of
Swailend

Kinmundy
Farm

Formartine & Buchan Way

Elrick Burn

Newmachar
Golf Club

CH

Boghead

A947

B979

B979

Formartine & Buchan Way

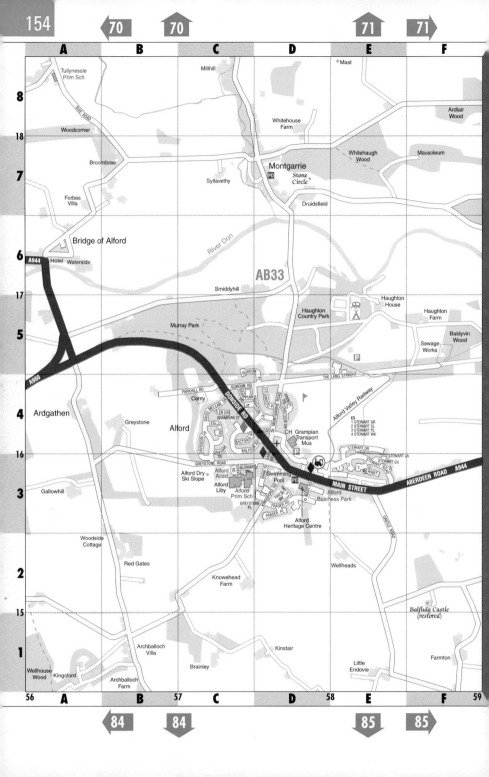

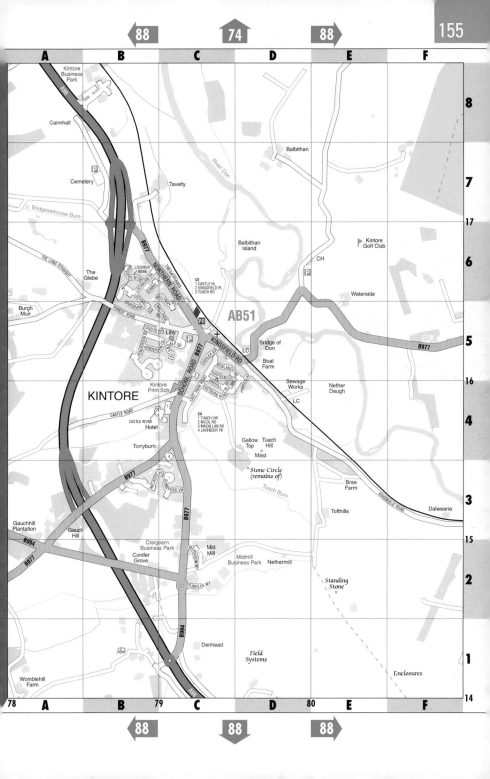

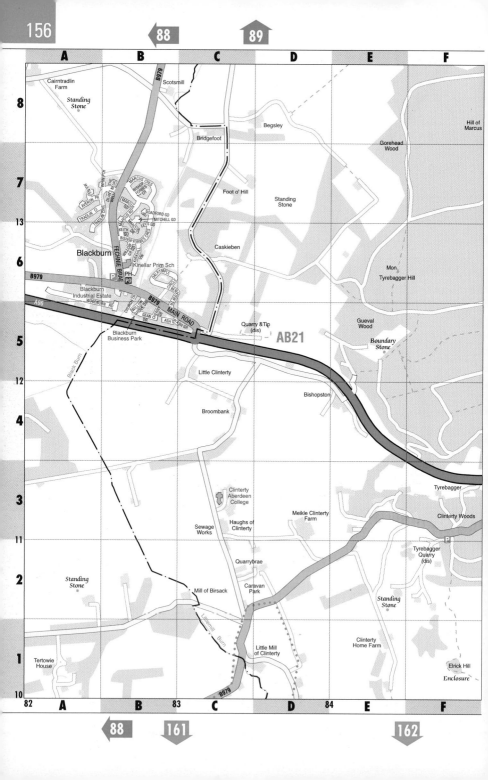

88
89

A B C D E F

8

Cairntradlin Farm

Standing Stone

Scotsmill

Hill of Marcus

Begsley

Bridgefoot

Gorehead Wood

7

MARCUS CRES
BISHOP FORBES CRES

Foot o' Hill

Standing Stone

13

ROADFORD GD
MITCHELL GD

Mon Tyrebagger Hill

Caskieben

6

Blackburn

Kinellar Prim Sch

PH
PO

B979

B979

A96

Blackburn Industrial Estate

WOODBURN RD

MAIN ROAD

GEAN CS
ASH CS ASH GR

Gueval Wood

5

Quarry &Tip (dis)

AB21

Boundary Stone

Blackburn Business Park

Black Burn

12

Little Clinterty

Bishopston

4

Broombank

Tyrebagger

3

Clinterty Aberdeen College

Meikle Clinterty Farm

Clinterty Woods

11

Sewage Works

Haughs of Clinterty

Tyrebagger Quarry (dis)

P

2

Standing Stone

Quarrybrae

Caravan Park

Standing Stone

Mill of Birsack

Unkmill Burn

Little Mill of Clinterty

Clinterty Home Farm

1

Tertowie House

Elrick Hill
Enclosure

10

82 A B 83 C D 84 E F

B979

88
161
162

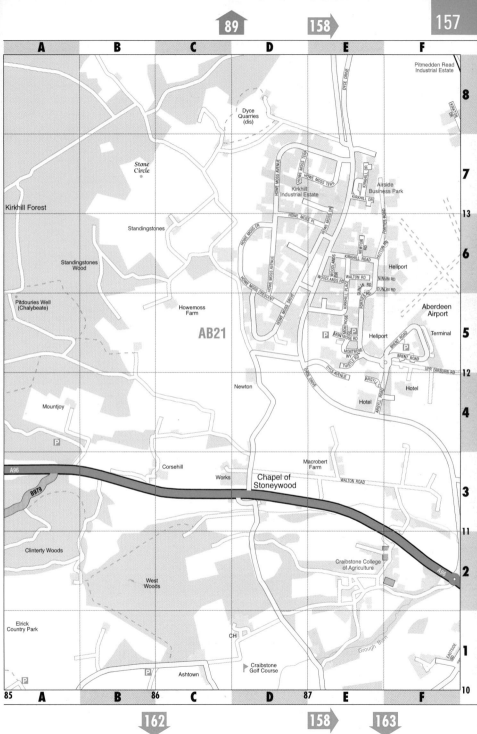

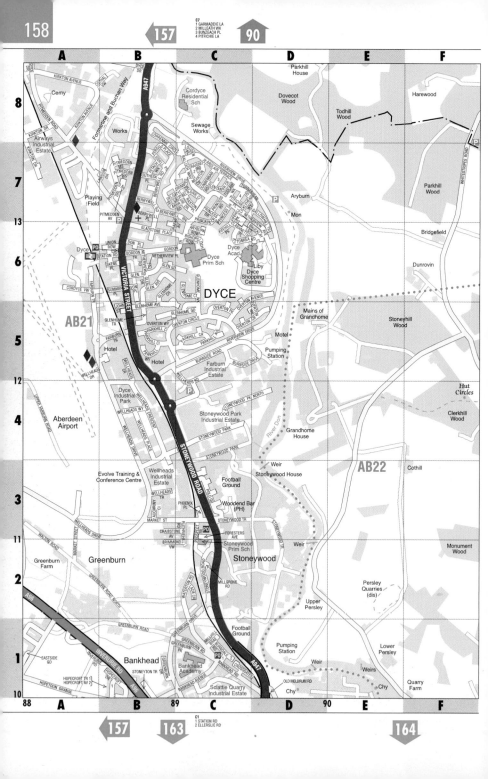

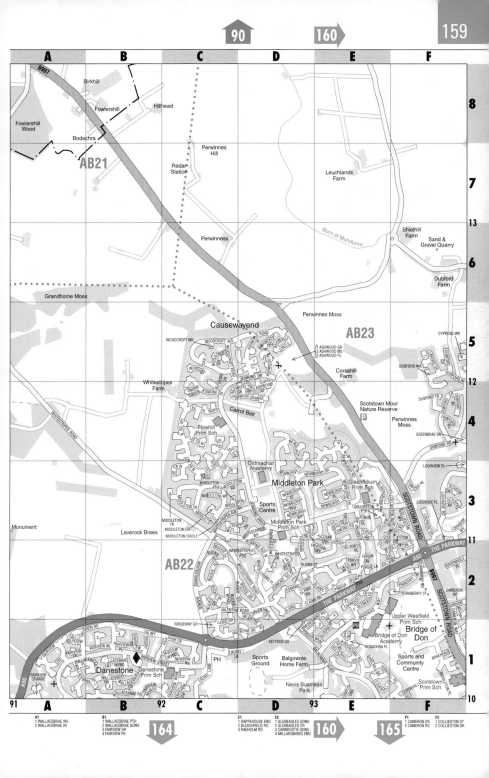

A B C D E F

8 Newton of Mundurno

Hillhead of Mundurno

North Tarbothill

Pit (dis)

Hill of Strabathie

Blackdog Rock

7 Stone Circle (remains of)

Pit (dis)

Works

Munderno

13 Mundurno

Tarbothill Farm

6 Motel

Berryhill

Murcar Golf Course

5 Cypress Wk Cypress Gr

Seaview Av

Seaview Cl

Murcar Industrial Estate

AB23

CH

Cloverhill

12 Denmore

Cres

Balgownie Links

4 Greenbrae Cl

Tern Place

Denmore Place

Greenbrae Gdn N

Denmore Ind Est

Findlay Farm

3 Greenbrae Prim Sch

Lochside Dr

Lochside Rd

Gordon Lennox Cr

Passiefern Av

Rydaid

Playing Field

ELLON ROAD

Claymore Avenue

Technology Park

Claymore Drive

11 THE PARKWAY

Greenhole Pl

Industrial Estate

A90

Woodcroft Road

Exploration Drive

Claymore Drive

2 Silverburn Place

Broadfold Road

Cameron Av

Intown Rd

A956

Parkway E

Exploration Dr

Aberdeen Exhibition & Conference Centre

1 Cameron Place

Broadfold Rd

Aberdeen Coll Balgownie Ctr

Crookfold Gd

ELLON RD

A956

P&R

Bridge of Don

Minden Cl

Alma Rd

Royal Aberdeen Golf Club

10 Fraserfield Gd

North Donside Rd

Corunna Pl

B999

94 A B 95 C D 96 E F

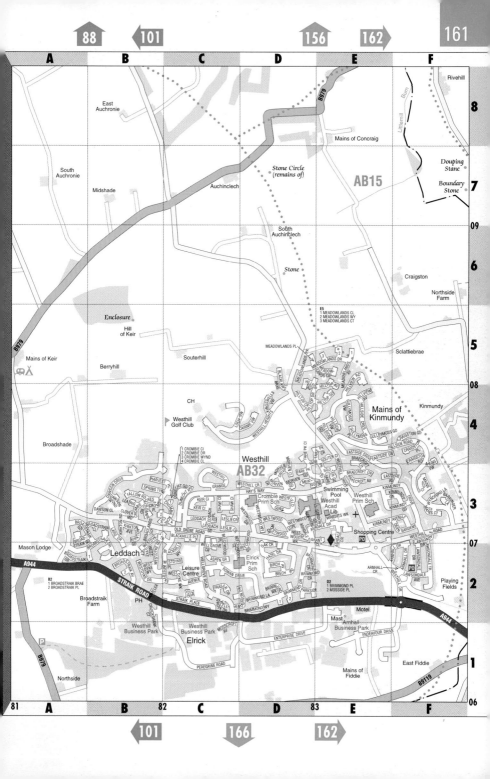

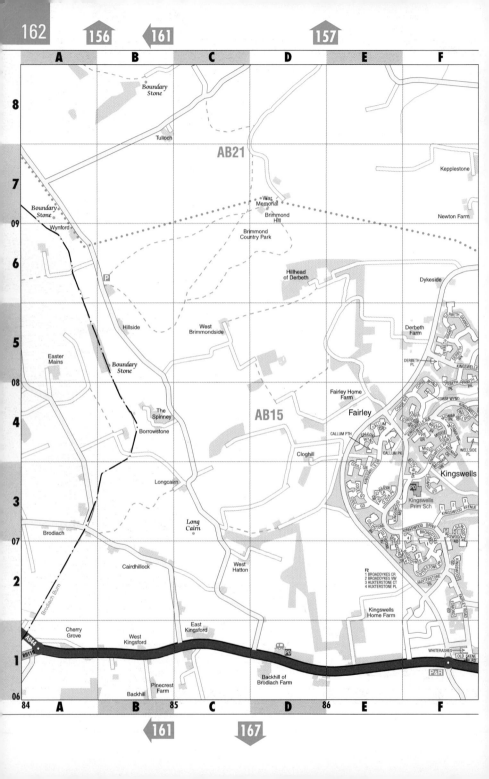

Boundary
Stone

Tulloch

AB21

Kepplestone

War
Memorial

Brimmond
Hill

Boundary
Stone

Wynford

Newton Farm

Brimmond
Country Park

09

Hillhead
of Derbeth

Dykeside

6

Derbeth
Farm

Hillside

West
Brimmondside

Easter
Mains

DERBETH
PL

KINGSWELLS

5

08

Boundary
Stone

Fairley Home
Farm

CORSE WYND

The
Spinney

AB15

Fairley

CALLUM PTH

4

Borrowstone

Kingswells

Cloghill

Longcairn

Kingswells
Prim Sch

3

KINGSWOOD AVENUE

Long
Cairn

07

Brodiach

F2
1 BROADDYKES CR
2 BROADDYKES VW
3 HUXTERSTONE CT
4 HUXTERSTONE PL

West
Hatton

Cairdhillock

2

Kingswells
Home Farm

Brodiach Burn

WHITERASHES

Cherry
Grove

West
Kingsford

East
Kingsford

A944

B9119

Pinecrest
Farm

Backhill of
Brodiach Farm

P&R

OLD SKENE
RD

06

Backhill

84
85
86

A   B   C   D   E   F

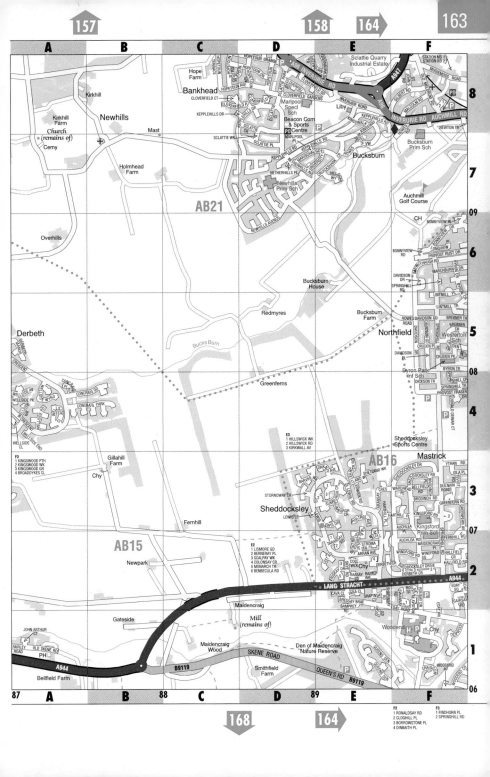

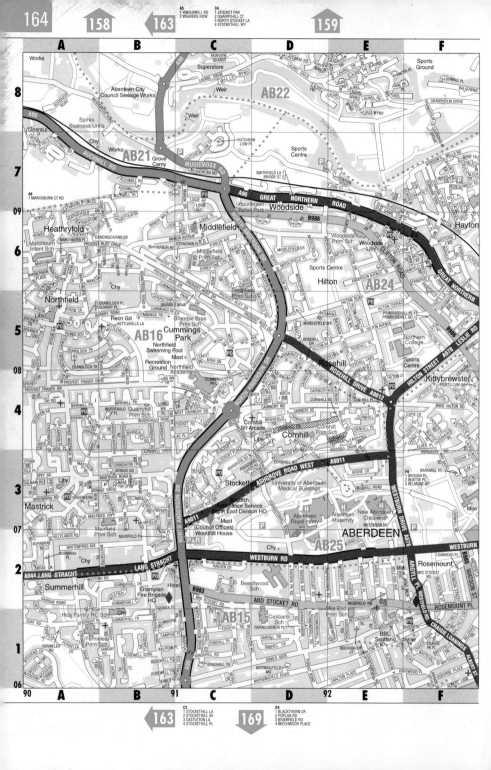

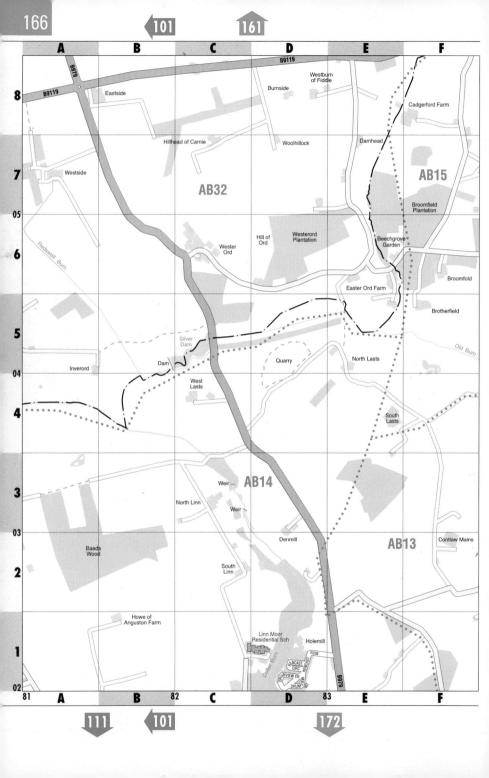

B9119

B9119

8

Eastside

Westside

7

AB32

Hillhead of Carnie

Burnside

Westburn of Fiddle

Woolhillock

Damhead

Cadgerford Farm

AB15

Broomfield Plantation

05

Redswell Burn

6

Wester Ord

Hill of Ord

Westerord Plantation

Beechgrove Garden

Broomfold

Easter Ord Farm

Brotherfield

5

Silver Dam

Dam

Inverord

West Lasts

Quarry

North Lasts

South Lasts

Old Burn

04

4

3

North Linn

Weir

Weir

AB14

03

Baads Wood

Denmill

AB13

Contlaw Mains

2

South Linn

Howe of Anguston Farm

02

Linn Moor Residential Sch

Holemill

ROW

Cullen Burn

NCAST CIRC

MVIEW CR

DRUM

VIEW

B979

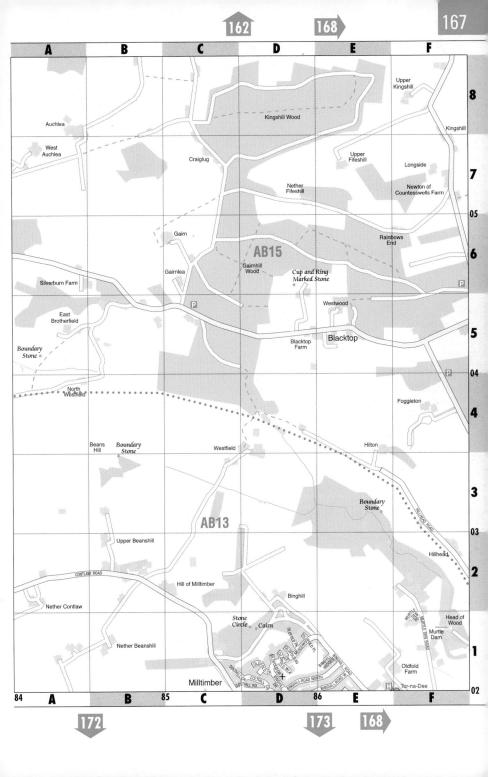

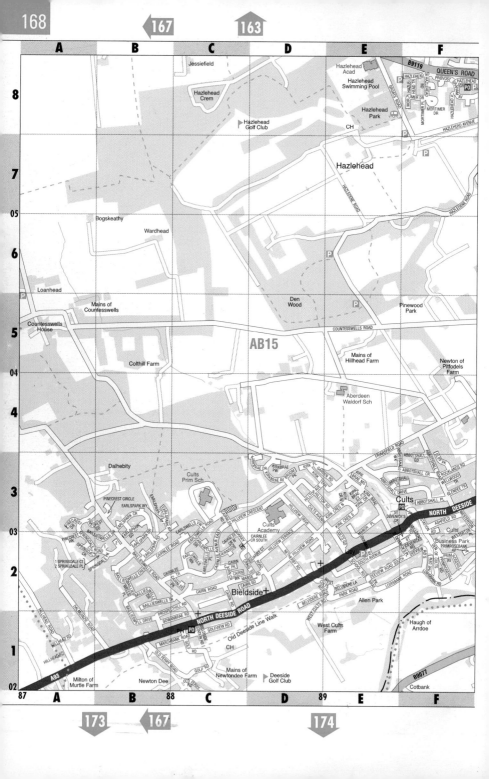

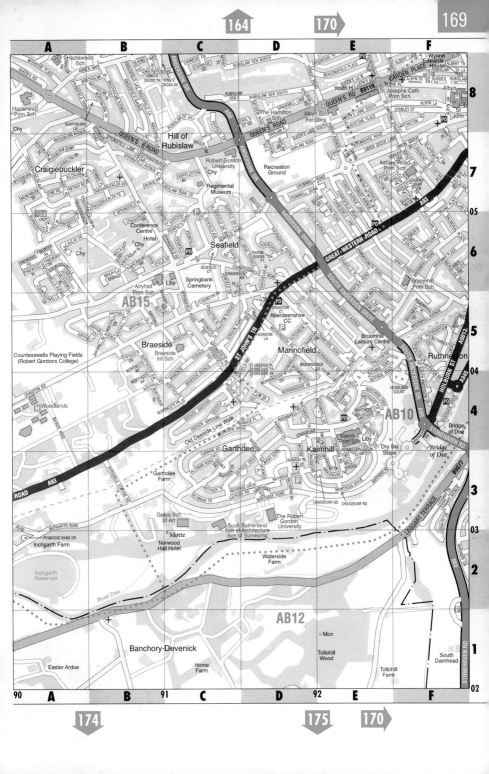

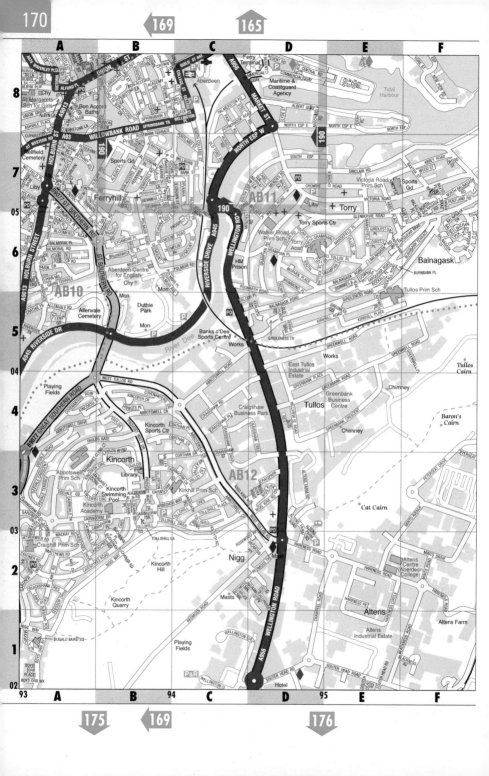

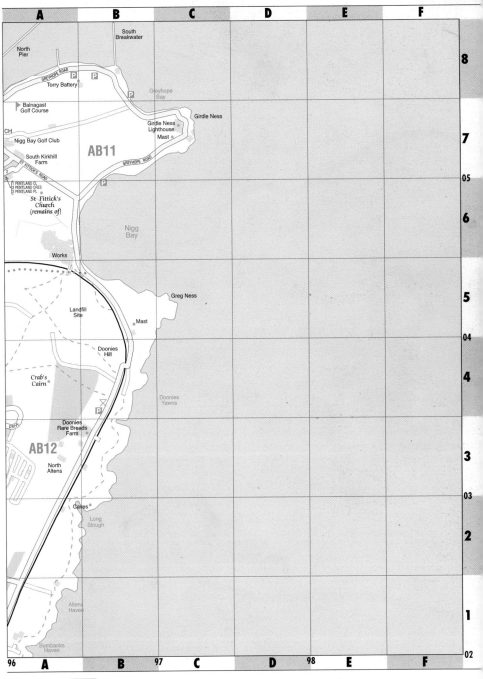

A   B   C   D   E   F

North Pier

South Breakwater

8

GREYHOPE ROAD

P   P

Torry Battery

Greyhope Bay

Balnagast Golf Course

Girdle Ness

Girdle Ness Lighthouse

CH

Nigg Bay Golf Club

Mast

7

AB11

South Kirkhill Farm

ST FITTICK'S ROAD

GREYHOPE ROAD

1 PENTLAND CL
2 PENTLAND CRES
2 PENTLAND PL

P

05

St Fittick's Church (remains of)

Nigg Bay

6

Works

Greg Ness

5

Landfill Site

Mast

04

Doonies Hill

Crab's Cairn

Doonies Yawns

4

P

Doonies Rare Breads Farm

AB12

North Altens

3

03

Caves

Long Slough

2

Altens Haven

1

Burnbanks Haven

02

96   A   B   97   C   D   98   E   F

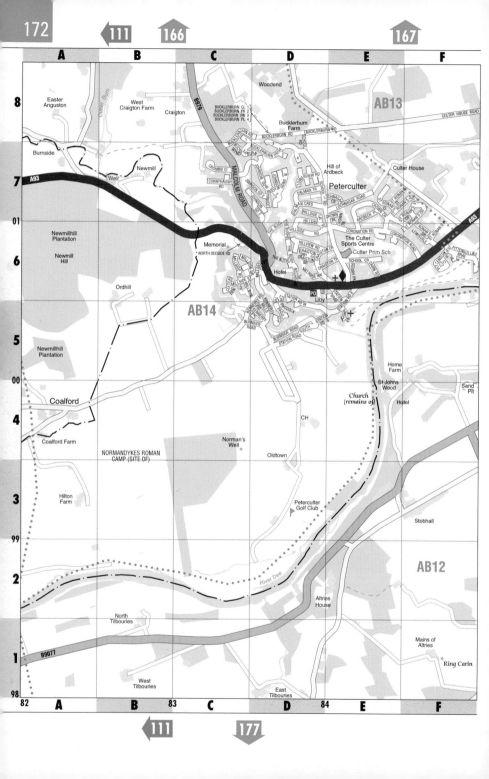

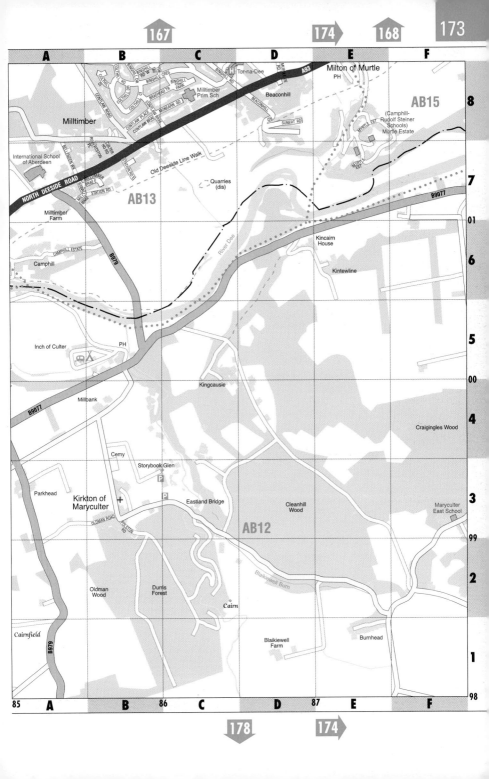

173
168
169

OLD FERRY ROAD

B9077

River Dee

Mid Ardoe Farm

Craighead

Arrdoe House Hotel

Butterywells

Lochend

B9077

Batchart

Jockston

8

7

01

6

5

00

4

3

99

2

1

98

Shannaburn

Heathcot

Townhead Quarry

The Blairs Museum

Blairs College

Westerton

Townhead

Cran Hill

AB12

Hillhead of Heathcot

Rowacks

Jameston Farm

Jameston

Craigingles Wood

Auchlunies

Cowford

Hare Moss

Hill of Blairs

Greenloaning

Newlands Farm

Bishopston

Heathfield

Merchant's Croft

Sunnyside

Clochandighter

Mast

Schoolhill

A   B   C   D   E   F

88   89   90

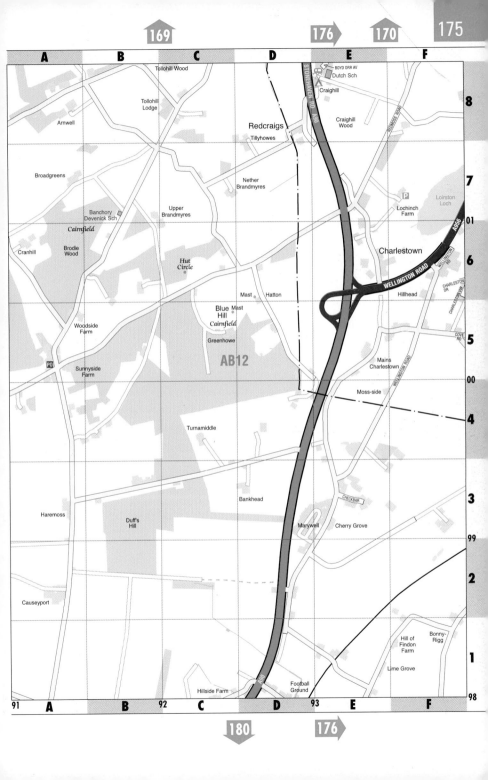

P&R

Hotel

Souter
Head

Lochside

Chy

CRAIGMAR
GD
STRATHBURN

SOUTER HEAD RD
SOUTER HEAD RD

8

DOOLIE
NESS

LOIRSTON WK

LANGDYKES ROAD

BALMORAL RD

FINDON NESS

Caves

DUNLIN RD

LOUANG

Football Gd
Allan Park

7

South
Loirston

Loirston
Prim Sch

WHITEHILLS
WY

PARTAN
SKELLY
AV

EARN'S
HEUGH
WK

SINCLAIR
PL

SINCLAIR PL

LOIRSTON
RD

Cove
Bay

01

PITTOCK

PINEWOOD

REDWOOD

SPARK TR

CHARLESTON

CLASHRODNEY WY

MAR PL

Lib

PH

6

CLASHRODNEY WK
CLASHRODNEY AV

COVE
WYND

PO

STONEYHILL

P

Charlestown
Sch

SCALLA DR

CREEL RD

STONEYHILL
TR

CHARLESTON PL

COVE CRES

CREEL
RD

COVE
RD

COVE
PL

5

AB12

Rigifa
Farm

Colsea Yawn

00

Quarry

Hare Ness

4

South
Blackhill

Blackhills of
Cairnrobin

3

Clashrodney
Bareside Point

99

North Mains
of Findon

2

Blowup Nose

1

Earnsheugh
Bay

98

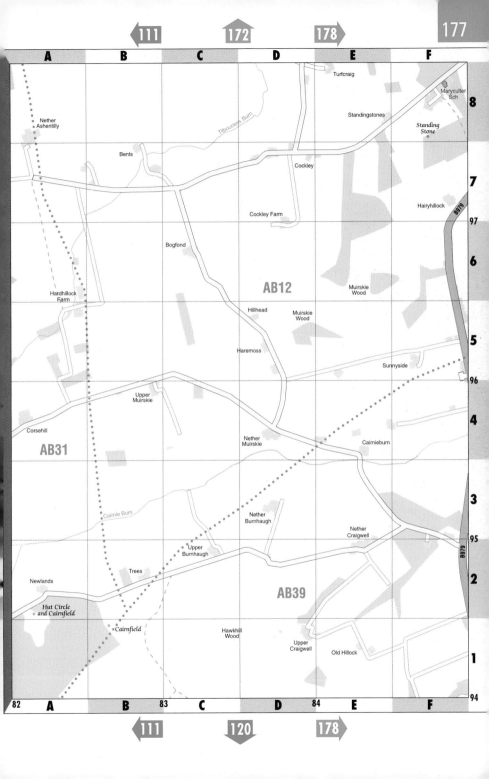

A   B   C   D   E   F

8

Turfcraig

Maryculter
Sch

Standingstones

*Standing
Stone*

Nether
Ashentilly

Bents

Cockley

7

Hairyhillock

B979

Cockley Farm

97

Bogfond

AB12

6

Muirskie
Wood

Hardhillock
Farm

Hillhead

Muirskie
Wood

5

Haremoss

Sunnyside

96

Upper
Muirskie

Corsehill

AB31

Nether
Muirskie

Cairnieburn

4

Cairnie Burn

3

Nether
Burnhaugh

Nether
Craigwell

95

B979

Upper
Burnhaugh

Trees

Newlands

AB39

2

*Hut Circle
and Cairnfield*

• *Cairnfield*

Hawkhill
Wood

Upper
Craigwell

Old Hillock

1

94

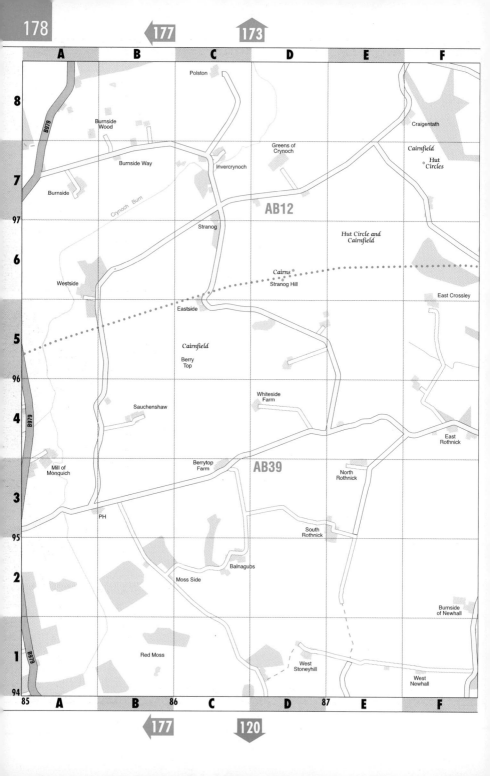

Polston

Burnside Wood

Burnside Way

Greens of Crynoch

Invercrynoch

Craigentath

Cairnfield

Hut Circles

Burnside

Crynoch Burn

AB12

Stranog

Hut Circle and Cairnfield

Westside

Cairns

Stranog Hill

East Crossley

Eastside

Cairnfield

Berry Top

Sauchenshaw

Whiteside Farm

East Rothnick

Mill of Monquich

Berrytop Farm

AB39

North Rothnick

PH

South Rothnick

Balnagubs

Moss Side

Burnside of Newhall

Red Moss

West Stoneyhill

West Newhall

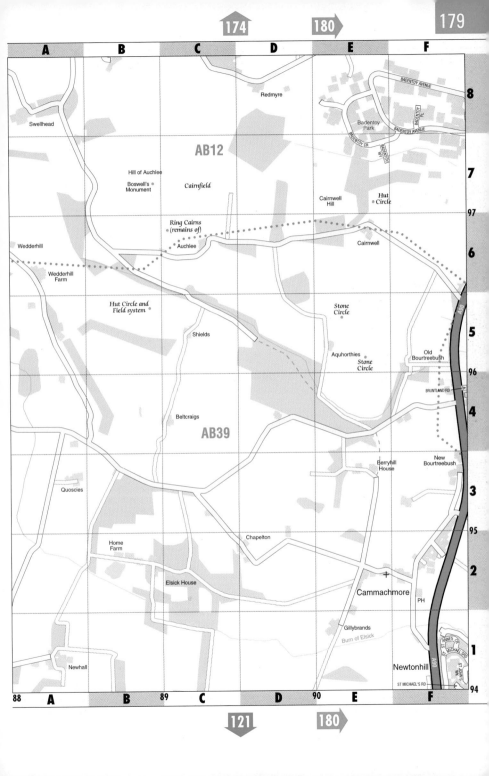

A **B** **C** **D** **E** **F**

8

BADENTOY AVENUE

Swellhead

Badentoy Park

BADENTOY CR

BADENTOY PL

BADENTOY WY

BADENTOY AVENUE

AB12

7

Hill of Auchlee

Boswell's Monument

Cairnfield

Cairnwell Hill

Hut Circle

97

Ring Cairns
(remains of)

Auchlee

Cairnwell

Wedderhill

6

Wedderhill Farm

Hut Circle and Field system

Stone Circle

Shields

Old Bourtreebush

5

Aquhorthies

Stone Circle

96

BRUNTLAND RD

4

Beltcraigs

AB39

Berryhill House

New Bourtreebush

Quoscies

3

95

Chapelton

Home Farm

2

Elsick House

Cammachmore

PH

Gillybrands

Burn of Elsick

1

Newhall

ST ANNES DR

ST MICHAEL'S DR

Newtonhill

ST MICHAEL'S RD

94

88 **A** **B** **89** **C** **D** **90** **E** **F**

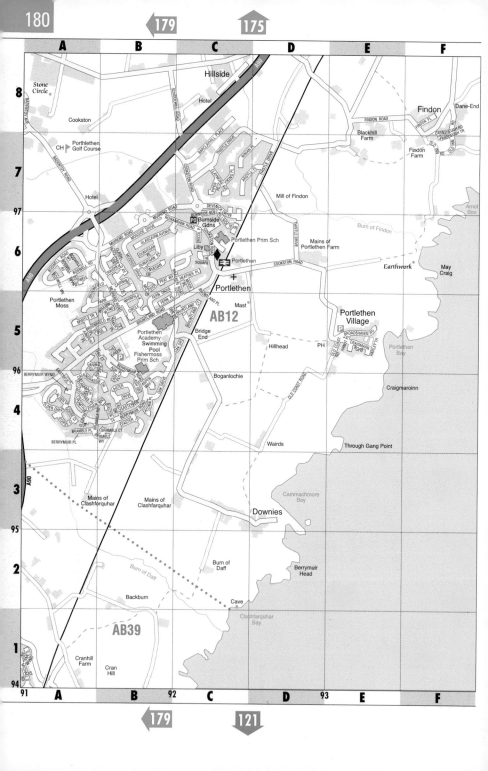

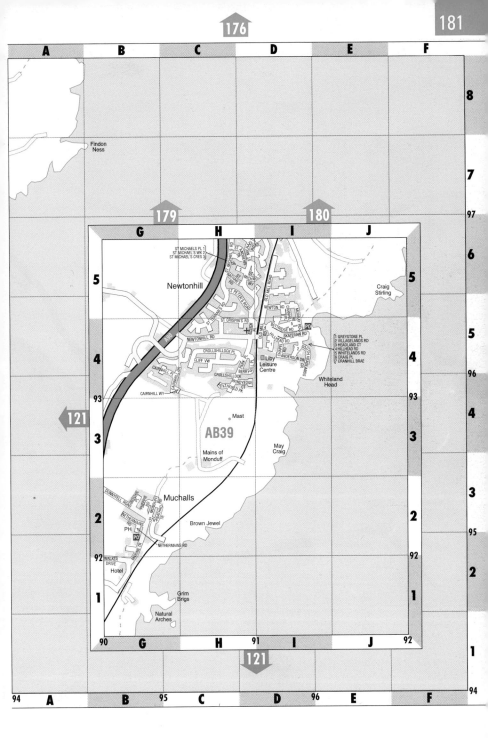

A **B** **C** **D** **E** **F**

8

Findon Ness

7

97

G **H** **I** **J**

6

ST MICHAELS PL 1
ST MICHAEL'S WK 2
ST MICHAEL'S CRES 3

5

Newtonhill

Craig Stirling

ST PETER'S ROAD

ST CRISPIN'S RD

5

NEWTONHILL RD

1 GREYSTONE PL
2 VILLAGELANDS RD
3 HEADLAND CT
4 HILLHEAD RD
5 WHITELANDS RD
6 CRAIG PL
7 CRANHILL BRAE

CROLLSHILLOCK PL

CLIFF VW

Liby
Leisure
Centre

4

CAIRNHILL

CROLLSHILLOCK

WYNDYEDGE CT

FEATHFIELD PK

Whiteland
Head

CAIRNHILL WY

93

121

Mast

AB39

3

Mains of
Monduff

May
Craig

DUNNYFELL ROAD

Muchalls

NETHERMAINS RD

Brown Jewel

2

PH

PO

NETHERMAINS RD

WALKER DRIVE

92

Hotel

Grim
Brigs

1

Natural
Arches

G **H** 91 **I** **J**

90   92

121

A **B** 95 **C** **D** 96 **E** **F**

94   94

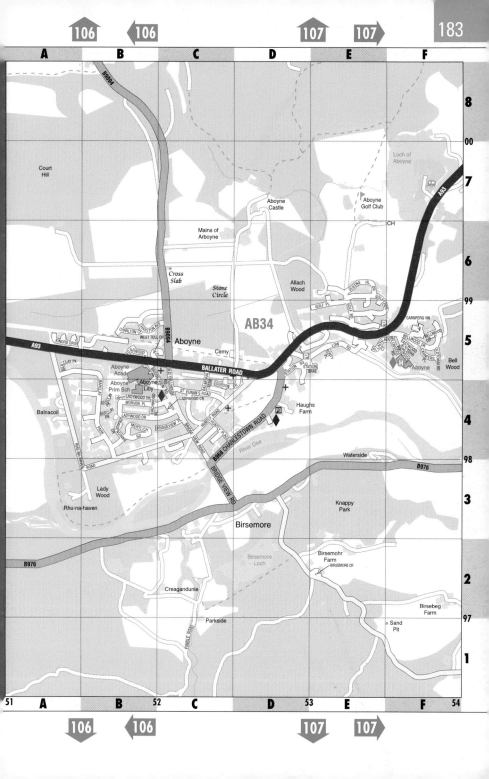

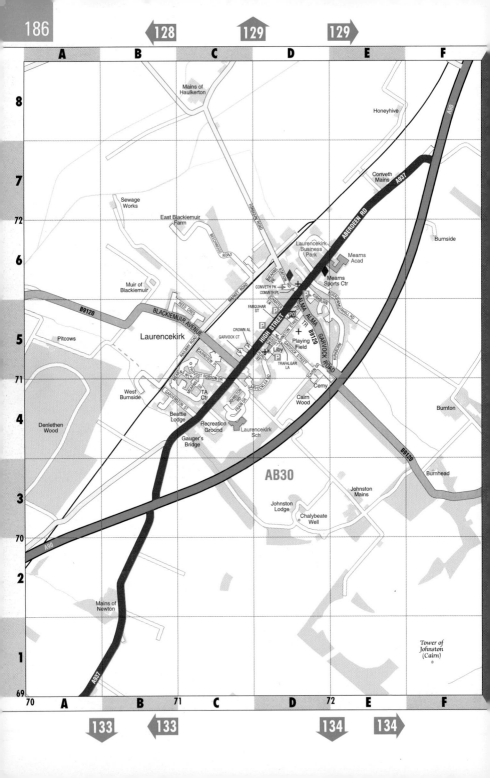

128
129
129

	A	B	C	D	E	F

8

Mains of
Haulkerton

Honeyhive

7

Conveth
Mains

A937

72

Sewage
Works

East Blackiemuir
Farm

ABERDEEN RD

Burnside

6

Laurencekirk
Business
Park

Mearns
Acad

Mearns
Sports Ctr

Muir of
Blackiemuir

CONVETH PK
CONVETH PL

B9120

BLACKIEMUIR AVENUE

REED CRES

FARQUHAR
ST

ALMA

GARVOCK ROAD

5

Pitcows

Laurencekirk

CROWN AL
GARVOCK CT

HIGH STREET

PO

Playing
Field

B9120

71

FAIRVIEW

SCOTT ROBSON DR

GARVOCK LEA RD

JOHNSTON
PARK RD

TRAFALGAR
LA

Cemy

Burnton

West
Burnside

TA
Ctr

Cairn
Wood

4

Denlethen
Wood

Beattie
Lodge

Gauger's
Bridge

Recreation
Ground

Laurencekirk
Sch

Burnhead

B9120

3

AB30

Johnston
Mains

A90

Johnston
Lodge

Chalybeate
Well

70

2

Mains of
Newton

A937

1

Tower of
Johnston
(Cairn)

69

70	A		71	C		72	E		F

133
133
134
134

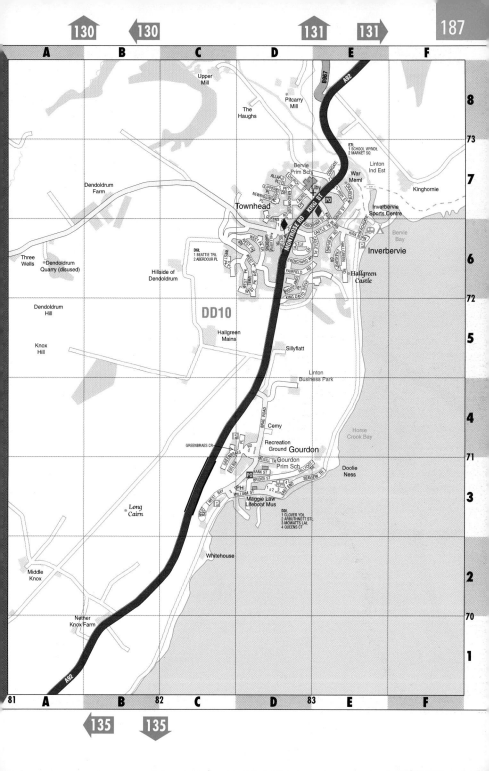

A | B | C | D | E | F

8

73

7

6

72

5

4

71

3

2

70

1

Upper
Mill

Pitcarry
Mill

The
Haughs

E7L
1 SCHOOL WYND L
2 MARKET SQ

Bervie
Prim Sch

Linton
Ind Est

War
Meml

Kinghornie

Townhead

Inverbervie
Sports Centre

Three
Wells

Dendoldrum
Farm

Dendoldrum
Quarry (disused)

Hillside of
Dendoldrum

D6L
1 BEATTIE TRL
2 ABERDOUR PL

Bervie
Bay

Inverbervie

Hallgreen
Castle

DD10

Dendoldrum
Hill

Hallgreen
Mains

Knox
Hill

Sillyflatt

Linton
Business Park

Cemy

Recreation
Ground

Gourdon

Horse
Crook Bay

GREENBRAES CR

Gourdon
Prim Sch

Doolie
Ness

BANK ST

BRIDGE ST

PO

PH

Long
Cairn

WILLIAM ST

Maggie Law
Lifeboat Mus

D3L
1 CLOVER YD L
2 ARBUTHNOTT ST L
3 MOWATTS LAL
4 QUEENS CT

Whitehouse

Middle
Knox

Nether
Knox Farm

81 | A | B | 82 | C | D | 83 | E | F

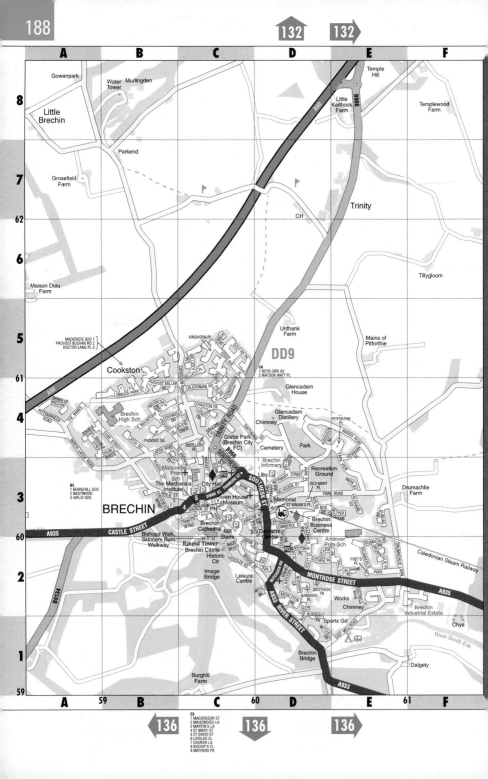

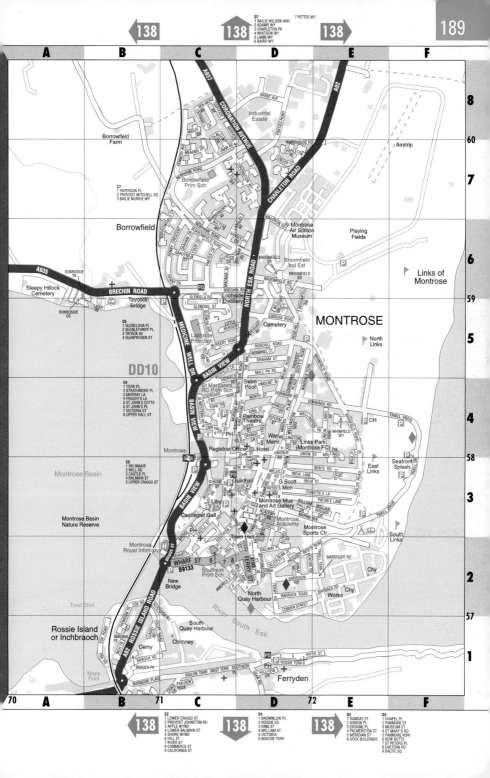

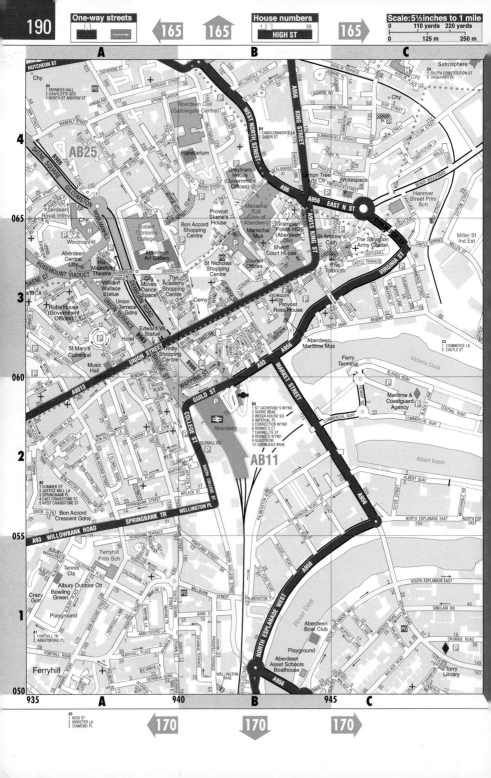

Church Rd **6** Beckenham BR2.......... **53** C6

Place name	Location number	Locality, town or village	Postcode district	Page and grid square
May be abbreviated on the map	Present when a number indicates the place's position in a crowded area of mapping	Shown when more than one place has the same name	District for the indexed place	Page number and grid reference for the standard mapping

Public and commercial buildings are highlighted in magenta **Places of interest** are highlighted in blue with a star ✫

Acad	**Academy**	Comm	**Common**	Gd	**Ground**	L	**Leisure**	Prom	**Promenade**
App	**Approach**	Cott	**Cottage**	Gdn	**Garden**	La	**Lane**	Rd	**Road**
Arc	**Arcade**	Cres	**Crescent**	Gn	**Green**	Liby	**Library**	Recn	**Recreation**
Ave	**Avenue**	Cswy	**Causeway**	Gr	**Grove**	Mdw	**Meadow**	Ret	**Retail**
Bglw	**Bungalow**	Ct	**Court**	H	**Hall**	Meml	**Memorial**	Sh	**Shopping**
Bldg	**Building**	Ctr	**Centre**	Ho	**House**	Mkt	**Market**	Sq	**Square**
Bsns, Bus	**Business**	Ctry	**Country**	Hospl	**Hospital**	Mus	**Museum**	St	**Street**
Bvd	**Boulevard**	Cty	**County**	HQ	**Headquarters**	Orch	**Orchard**	Sta	**Station**
Cath	**Cathedral**	Dr	**Drive**	Hts	**Heights**	Pal	**Palace**	Terr	**Terrace**
Cir	**Circus**	Dro	**Drove**	Ind	**Industrial**	Par	**Parade**	TH	**Town Hall**
Cl	**Close**	Ed	**Education**	Inst	**Institute**	Pas	**Passage**	Univ	**University**
Cnr	**Corner**	Emb	**Embankment**	Int	**International**	Pk	**Park**	Wk, Wlk	**Walk**
Coll	**College**	Est	**Estate**	Intc	**Interchange**	Pl	**Place**	Wr	**Water**
Com	**Community**	Ex	**Exhibition**	Junc	**Junction**	Prec	**Precinct**	Yd	**Yard**

A

Aberchirder 144 E5
Aberdeen 190 B2
Aboyne 183 C5
Alford 154 C4
Altens 170 E1
Annochie 36 F1
Arbuthnott 130 D6
Ardallie 51 E5
Ardgathen 154 A4
Ardlawhill 12 D5
Ardo 49 B6
Arthrath 51 A3
Auchattie 184 B1
Auchenblae 124 B1
Auchendryne 113 E5
Auchleven 71 E7
Auchnagatt 50 C8
Auldyoch 46 C8

B

Backhill 48 B6
Backhill of Fortrie 50 F7
Badenscoth 46 D5
Balgaveny 45 F7
Ballater 182 C4
Balmedie 91 D8
Balnagask 170 F6
Balthangie 22 F2
Banchory 184 B5
Banchory-Devenick 169 B1
Banff 140 D5
Bankhead 163 C8

Barthol Chapel
Barthol Chapel 48 D1
Belfatton 25 F6
Belhelvie 91 B8
Bellabeg 81 B4
Belnacraig 81 D7
Belts of Collonach 117 E8
Benholm 135 D8
Benthoul 101 E2
Berefold 51 B2
Berryhillock 6 C3
Bieldside 168 C2
Birse 107 D4
Birsemore 183 D3
Blackburn 156 A6
Blackhill 26 F7
Blackhouse 147 B7
Blacktop 167 E5
Blairdaff 86 F8
Boddam 40 D1
Bogentory 100 F8
Bogniebrae 31 C4
Bogton 20 B2
Bona Vista 145 B5
Bonnykelly 23 B4
Bonnyton 58 D5
Borrowfield 189 B6
Boyndie 8 D6
Braemar 113 E6
Braeside Aberdeen 169 B5
Braeside Ellon 50 A6
Brechin 188 B3
Brideswell 44 E6
Bridgend 43 D2
Bridge of Alford 154 A6
Bridge of Canny 109 B4
Bridge of Don 160 B1
Bridge of Dun 137 E5

Bridge of Muchalls
Bridge of Muchalls 121 B6
Broadsea 143 B7
Brodiesord 7 D3
Brownhill 36 F1
Buchanhaven 147 C7
Bucksburn 163 E7
Burnhervie 73 D2
Burnside 26 E2
Bush 134 F4

C

Cairnbulg 15 B8
Cairnhill 58 C7
Cairnie 29 D3
Cairnorrie 49 C8
Cammachmore 179 E2
Carnie 101 E4
Castleton 113 F6
Catterline 126 E1
Cauldwells 22 B7
Causewayend 159 C5
Chapel Hill 52 E2
Chapel of Garioch 73 B7
Chapel of Stoneywood 157 D3
Charlestown 175 F6
Clatt 70 C8
Clerkhill 147 C4
Clochcan 37 A2
Clola 38 A2
Clovenstone 88 A8
Coalford 172 A4
Coburty 142 A2
Collieston 64 E3
Colpy 58 A7
Comers 99 D6

Cookney
Cookney 120 F8
Cookston 188 B5
Coplandhill 147 A6
Corgarff 92 F7
Cornhill Aberdeen 164 D4
Cornhill Banff 7 E1
Corse 45 A7
Cothall 89 F6
Cottown 48 D7
Coull 96 F1
Cove Bay 176 C7
Cowbog 23 B6
Cowie 185 F6
Coynach 95 E4
Craigdam 61 C5
Craigearn 87 C5
Craigiebuckler 169 A7
Craigo 133 E3
Crathes 110 E3
Crathie 102 E2
Crawton 126 E2
Crimond 26 D7
Crossbrae 20 D3
Cross of Jackston 59 F7
Crossroads 110 E1
Crovie 3 C3
Cruden Bay 53 A3
Crudie 22 B8
Cullen 1 B4
Cultercullen 76 E7
Cults 168 F3
Cuminestown 22 C1
Cummings Park 164 C5
Cuttyhill 26 C1

D

Danestone 159 B1
Daviot 59 E3
Deebank 184 C3
Denhead Ellon 63 F5
Denhead Peterhead 25 D3
Denmore 160 A4
Derbeth 163 A5
Dinnet 105 F5
Downies 180 D3
Drakemyre 51 A6
Drumblade 44 E7
Drumdollo 44 F5
Drumligair 90 C2
Drumlithie 125 B3
Drumnagorrach 17 E3
Drumoak 111 D6
Drymuir 36 D4
Dubford 3 B1
Dun 137 E6
Duncanstone 56 F1
Dunecht 100 F7
Dunshillock 146 B6
Durno 59 B3
Dyce 158 C6
Dykeside 33 C2

E

Easter Balmoral 102 F1
Eastertown of
   Auchleuchries 51 B4
Echt 100 D4
Edzell 132 A7

Ellon 151 B4
Elrick 161 C1

F

Fairley 162 E4
Farmtown 17 D2
Farnell 137 A2
Ferryden 189 D1
Ferryhill 190 A1
Fetterangus 25 D2
Fettercairn 128 A4
Findon 180 F8
Finnygaud 19 A5
Fintry 21 D5
Finzean 116 C7
Fisherford 46 B2
Flushing 38 F5
Folla Rule 59 D8
Footdee 165 E1
Forbestown 81 C3
Fordoun 129 F6
Fordyce 1 F1
Forgue 31 D4
Fortrie 32 C4
Foveran 77 D6
Fraserburgh 143 E5
Fyvie 47 E5

G

Gallowhills 26 F2
Gardenstown 3 B2
Gariochsford 46 B8
Garlogie 101 C4
Garmond 22 C2
Garthdee 169 D4
Gartly 56 A7
Glenbarry 18 B5
Glenbervie 124 F3
Glenkindie 82 D5
Glenwood 99 E6
Gordonstown Banff 18 C7
Gordonstown Inverurie .46 F5
Gourdon 187 D4
Gowanhill 15 B6
Gowanwell 49 E8
Grange Crossroads 17 A5
Grange Gardens 147 C5
Greenbank 143 A3
Greenburn 158 A2
Greens 35 A5

H

Hallmoss 39 E7
Hassiewells 46 A7
Hatton 52 D4
Hattoncrook 75 C7
Hatton of Fintray 89 C7
Haugh of Glass 42 A6
Hayton 164 F6
Hazlehead 168 E7
Heathryfold 164 A6
Hillhead of Mountblairy ..20 C4
Hill of Rubislaw 169 C7
Hillside Aberdeen 180 C8
Hillside Montrose ...138 C8
Hilton 164 D6
Howe of Teuchar 34 D6
Huntly 148 B5
Hythie 25 F2

I

Inchbare 132 B4
Insch 149 C4
Inver 115 B8
Inverallochy 15 C8

Inverbervie 187 E6
Inverboyndie 140 B6
Inverey 112 E4
Inverkeithny 31 F6
Invernettie 147 C2
Inverugie 39 E7
Inverurie 152 B4
Inverythan 47 D8

J

Johnshaven 135 D6

K

Kaimhill 169 E3
Keig 71 D2
Keilhill 9 F2
Keith Inch 147 F4
Kemnay 87 D7
Kennethmont 56 B3
Kiddshill 36 F3
Kildrummy 83 A8
Kincardine O'Neil 108 B6
Kincorth 170 B3
King Edward 20 F8
Kingswells 162 F3
Kinmuck 75 A2
Kinmundy 153 E2
Kinnaird Park 137 A4
Kinneff 131 D5
Kintore 155 B4
Kirkton 72 A8
Kirkton of Auchterless ..46 F8
Kirkton of Bourtie 74 E7
Kirkton of Craig 138 C2
Kirkton of Culsalmond ..58 E7
Kirkton of Durris 111 B3
Kirkton of Glenbuchat ..81 D6
Kirkton of Logie Buchan .63 E4
Kirkton of Maryculter ..173 B3
Kirkton of Oyne 72 B2
Kirkton of Rayne 58 F5
Kirkton of Skene 101 E7
Kirkton of Tough 85 D3
Kirktown Peterhead ...147 D5
Kirktown St Fergus 27 A2
Kirktown of Alvah 9 B3
Kirktown of Deskford ...6 C4
Kirktown of Fetteresso .185 A4
Kittybrewster 164 F4
Knaven 36 A2
Knock 18 A3
Knockenbaird 149 D8
Knockothie Hill 151 D6
Knowes of Elrick 19 A4

L

Largie 57 C6
Largue 45 D8
Laurencekirk 186 B5
Leddach 161 B2
Leochel-Cushnie 84 B1
Leslie 71 B7
Lethenty 48 C7
Leylodge 88 B4
Leys 25 E3
Lintmill 1 B3
Little Brechin 188 A8
Little Collieston 64 D4
Lochside 134 C3
Logie 133 E2
Logie Coldstone 95 D3
Logie Pert 133 B3
Longhaven 53 D6
Longmanhill 10 B5
Longside 38 D6
Lonmay 14 F1
Lumphanan 98 A3

Lumsden 69 B5
Luthermuir 133 A7
Lyne of Skene 88 A1

M

Macduff 141 F7
Mains of Kinmundy 161 E4
Mannofield 169 D5
Marnoch 18 F1
Marykirk 133 D4
Maryton 138 A3
Marywell 108 A2
Mastrick 164 A3
Maud 36 E7
Meethill 147 A4
Meikle Wartle 59 B6
Memsie 14 A5
Methlick 49 B4
Mid Anguston 111 E8
Mid Ardlaw 13 E6
Middlefield 164 C6
Middle Grange 147 A5
Middlemuir 24 A7
Middleton Park 159 D3
Midmar 99 D6
Migvie 95 D5
Millbreck 38 A4
Millfield 106 C3
Milltimber 173 A8
Milltown of Kildrummy .83 A7
Milltown of Rothiemay .30 D7
Milton 1 B1
Milton of Campfield ..109 A7
Milton of Cushnie 84 A2
Milton of Murtle 173 E8
Mintlaw 146 F5
Mintlaw Station 146 B6
Monboddo 124 C1
Monkshill 48 B7
Montgarrie 154 D7
Montrose 189 E5
Monymusk 86 E6
Mountsolie 13 D2
Muchalls 181 G2
Muir of Alford 84 C6
Muir of Fowlis 84 D2
Muir of Kinellar 88 E4
Muirtack 51 D4
Myrebird 110 E6

N

Netherbrae 11 B2
Nether Kinmundy 38 E2
Netherley 120 E8
Nethermuir 36 C3
New Aberdour 12 E5
Newburgh 77 F8
New Byth 22 D4
New Deer 36 A6
Newhills 163 B8
New Leeds 25 D5
Newmachar 153 D5
New Pitsligo 23 D6
Newtonhill 181 H5
Newtonmill 132 B3
Nigg 170 C2
Nittanshead 23 C4
North Craigo 133 D2
Northfield 164 A5
North Flobbets 48 B1
North Rayne 58 F6
North Water Bridge ..133 A5

O

Old Aberdeen 165 B5
Old Deer 37 D6
Old Kinnernie 100 C8

Oldmeldrum 150 D2
Old Montrose 137 F3
Old Rayne 58 D3
Old Westhall 72 D8
Oldwhat 23 C2
Ordhead 86 C1
Ordie 105 F8
Overbrae 11 D3
Oyne 72 C8

P

Peathill 142 C5
Pennan 12 A8
Perkhill 97 F4
Peterculter 172 E7
Peterhead 147 D4
Pitblae 5 B2
Pitcaple 73 B8
Pitfichie 86 D7
Pitmachie 58 C3
Pitmedden 62 B2
Pittulie 4 F4
Plaidy 21 A5
Port Elphinstone 152 D4
Port Erroll 53 B3
Portlethen 180 C6
Portlethen Village ...180 E5
Portsoy 139 C7
Potterton 91 A6

Q

Quilquox 50 A5

R

Rathen 14 E3
Redcraigs 175 D8
Rhynie 55 D2
Rickarton 119 F3
Roadside of Catterline .126 C2
Roadside of Kinneff ..131 C7
Roanheads 147 E6
Rora 26 E2
Rosehearty 142 B7
Rosehill 164 E5
Rosemount 164 F2
Rossie Island or
    Inchbraoch 189 A1
Rossie Mills 138 B3
Rothienorman 46 F2
Rothney 149 D4
Roughpark 81 A2
Ruthrieston 169 F5
Ruthven 29 E6

S

St Combs 15 C6
St Cyrus 134 D3
St Fergus 27 C3
St Katherines 48 A1
Sandend 1 F4
Sandfordhill 53 D8
Sandhaven 5 A4
Sandyhills 140 E4
Sauchen 86 F1
Schoolhill 101 A1
Scotston 129 D4
Scotstown 140 E6
Scurdie Ness 138 F3
Seafield 169 C6
Seaton 165 C6
Seatown Banff 139 E7
Seatown Buckie 1 A5
Sheddocksley 163 D3
Silverbank 184 F5
South Flobbets 48 B1

South Kirkton 100 E4
South Loirston 176 A7
Stirling 40 C1
Stockethill 164 C3
Stonehaven 185 F7
Stoneywood 158 C2
Strachan 117 D7
Strathdon 81 B3
Strichen 24 F6
Stuartfield 37 D5
Summerhill 164 A2

T

Tarland 96 B3
Tarves 61 E6
Templeton 117 D6
Teuchar 34 B2
The Pole of Itlaw 20 C7
Thornroan 61 E7
Tifty 47 F7
Tillydrone 165 A6
Tillyfourie 86 A3
Tipperty 63 D1
Tocher 58 F7
Tornaveen 98 D5
Torphins 108 F8
Torries 85 D4
Torry 170 E7
Torterston 39 B6
Towie 82 D3
Townhead 187 D7
Trinity 188 E7
Tullos 170 D4
Tullynessle 70 D2
Turriff 145 C3
Tyrie 13 C5

U

Udny Green 62 A1
Udny Station 76 C7
Upper Boddam 57 E5
Upper Boyndlie 13 B5
Upper Lochton 184 C7
Usan 138 E1

W

Waterside 147 A8
Westbank Park 150 B3
Westbrae 145 C3
West Burnside 128 B3
Westhill 161 D4
Whinnyfold 65 B8
Whitecairns 76 D1
Whiteford 59 B1
Whitehills 8 F8
Whitehouse 85 E5
Whitemyres 59 D5
Whiterashes 75 D6
Whitestones 23 A3
Woodhead 48 B5
Woodside 164 D7
Woodside of Arbeadie .184 E6

Y

Ythanbank 50 A1
Ythanwells 45 D5

A

Aalesund Pl 1 AB42 147 C2
Aalesund Rd AB42 147 B2
Abbey Kiln* AB42 37 C7
Abbey La
Aberdeen AB11 170 E7
Peterhead AB42 37 D6
Abbey Pl AB11 170 E7
Abbey Rd AB11 170 F7
Abbey Sq AB11 170 E7
Abbey St AB42 37 D6
Abbots Pl AB12 170 B4
Abbotsford La AB11 190 A1
Abbotsford Pl 2 AB11 190 A1
Abbotshall Cres AB15 168 F3
Abbotshall Dr AB15 168 E3
Abbotshall Gdns AB15 168 F3
Abbotshall Pl AB15 168 F3
Abbotshall Rd AB15 168 F4
Abbotshall Terr AB15 168 E3
Abbotshall Wlk AB15 168 E4
Abbotswell Cres AB12 170 B4
Abbotswell Dr AB12 170 A4
Abbotswell Prim Sch AB12 170 A3
Abbotswell Rd
Aberdeen AB12 170 C4
Peterhead AB42 147 C6
Aberchirder Prim Sch AB54 144 D5
Aberdeen Airport AB21 157 F5
Aberdeen Art Gall* AB25 190 A3
Aberdeen Coll (Gallowgate Centre) AB25 190 B4
Aberdeen Coll Balgownie Ctr AB23 160 A1
Aberdeen Ctr for English AB11 170 B6
Aberdeen Ex & Con Ctr AB23 160 C2
Aberdeen Gram Sch AB25 165 A1
Aberdeen Maritime Mus* AB11 190 B3
Aberdeen Maternity Hospl AB25 164 E3
Aberdeen Music Hall* AB10 190 A3
Aberdeen Rd
Aboyne AB34 96 C3
Alford AB33 154 F3
Huntly AB54 148 F4
Laurencekirk AB30 186 E6
Aberdeen Royal Infmy
Aberdeen AB25 164 D3
Aberdeen AB25 190 A4
Aberdeen Sch for the Deaf AB24 165 D5
Aberdeen Sta AB11 190 B2
Aberdeen Terr 2 AB34 96 C3
Aberdeen Univ (Zoology Department) AB24 165 B6
Aberdeen Waldorf Sch AB15 168 E4
Aberdeenshire Farming Mus* AB42 146 A4
Aberdour Pl 2 DD10 187 D6
Abergeldie Castle* AB35 103 A2
Abergeldie Rd
Aberdeen AB10 169 F6
Ballater AB35 182 D4
Abergeldie Terr AB10 169 F6
Abernethy Rd AB42 147 A5
Aboyne Acad AB34 183 B5
Aboyne Gdns AB10 169 E4
Aboyne Hospl AB34 183 F5
Aboyne Pl
Aberdeen AB10 169 D3
Fraserburgh AB43 143 B4
Aboyne Prim Sch AB34 183 B4
Aboyne Rd AB10 169 D4
Aboyne Terr AB10 169 E3
Acacia Gr 2 AB42 147 A5
Acad Sh Ctr The AB25 190 A3
Academy Gdns AB42 146 C5
Academy Pl AB42 147 C5
Academy Rd
Banff AB45 140 F5
Fraserburgh AB43 143 B6
2 Stonehaven AB39 185 C6
Academy Sq DD10 189 D3
Academy St AB11 190 A2
Academy Way AB51 150 B3
Acorn Pl AB12 180 B4
Adam Pl DD9 132 A7
Adams Way 2 DD10 189 D7
Addison Cres AB45 140 E5
Adelphi La AB11 190 B3
Aden Circ AB42 146 C5
Aden Cres AB42 37 D6
Aden Ctry Pk* AB42 146 A5
Aden Gdns AB42 146 C4
Admirals La 4 AB54 148 E5
Advocates' Rd AB24 165 C3
Affleck Pl AB11 190 B2
Affleck St AB11 190 B2
Affric Pl AB43 143 B4
Afton Rd AB43 143 B4
Ailsa Ct AB43 143 A5
Aird Gn AB45 139 E7
Aird St AB45 139 E6
Airlie Gdns 3 DD9 188 B3
Airlie St DD9 188 B3
Airside Bsns Pk AB21 157 F7
Airways Ind Est AB21 158 A8
Airyhall Ave AB15 169 B5
Airyhall Cres AB15 169 A5
Airyhall Dr AB15 169 B5
Airyhall Gdns AB15 169 B5
Airyhall Pl AB15 169 B5
Airyhall Prim Sch AB15 169 B6
Airyhall Rd AB15 169 B4
Airyhall Terr AB15 169 B5
Airyhill View 2 AB41 77 F8
Albert Den AB25 165 A1
Albert Gdns AB51 152 D6
Albert Gr AB51 150 D3
Albert La
Aberdeen AB10 164 F1
Fraserburgh AB43 143 C7
1 Stonehaven AB39 185 F3
Albert Pl
9 Aberdeen AB25 165 A1
Brechin DD9 188 D2
Oldmeldrum AB51 150 D3
Albert Quay AB11 190 C2
Albert Rd
Ballater AB35 182 D3
Oldmeldrum AB51 150 D3
Albert St
Aberdeen AB25 164 F1
Fraserburgh AB43 143 C7
Inverurie AB51 152 D6
Peterhead AB42 147 F5
Albert Terr
Aberdeen AB10 169 F8
10 Cullen AB56 1 B5
Huntly AB54 148 E3
Oldmeldrum AB51 150 D3
Alberta Pl AB45 140 E6
Albury Gdns AB11 190 A1
Albury Mans AB11 190 A1
Albury Pl AB11 190 A1
Albury Rd AB11 190 A1
Albyn Gr AB10 169 F8
Albyn Hospl AB10 169 F8
Albyn La AB10 169 F8
Albyn Pl AB10 169 E8
Albyn Sch For Girls AB15 169 E8
Albyn Terr AB10 169 F8
Alder Dr AB12 180 A4
Alehousewells Prim Sch AB51 87 C7
Alen Dr AB33 154 C4
Alexander Bell Pl AB43 23 D7
Alexander Cres 5 AB51 87 D7
Alexander Dr
Aberdeen AB24 164 F7
Huntly AB54 148 E5
Alexander Scott's Hospl AB54 148 E4
Alexander St AB52 149 D4
Alexander Terr AB24 165 A6
Alexandra Par AB42 147 F6
Alexandra Terr AB43 143 C5
Alford Acad AB33 154 C3
Alford Bsns Pk AB33 154 E3
Alford Dry Ski Slope* AB33 154 C3
Alford Her Ctr* AB33 154 D3
Alford Pl AB10 170 A8
Alford Prim Sch AB33 154 C3
Alfred St DD10 189 D2
Allachlade Ct AB34 183 E5
Allan Pl AB51 152 C7
Allan St AB10 169 F7
Allandale Gdns AB51 155 C5
Allardice Pl DD10 187 D7
Allardice St
5 Stonehaven AB39 185 E4
2 Stonehaven AB39 185 E4
Allathan Pk AB41 62 B2
Allenvale Gdns AB10 170 A5
Allenvale Rd AB10 170 A5
Allison Cl AB12 176 B8
Allochy Rd AB43 15 C7
Alma Pl AB30 186 D6
Alma Rd AB23 160 B1
Alma Terr AB30 186 D5
Almanythie Rd 2 AB42 147 E6
Alness Cres AB43 143 B4
Alpine Pl AB43 143 A4
Altens Ctr (Aberdeen College) AB12 170 F2
Altens Farm Rd AB12 170 D3
Altens Ind Est AB12 170 E1
Altonrea Gdns AB21 158 C6
Alva Cres AB43 143 B4
Alvah Terr AB45 140 E4
Alwyn Wind AB42 27 B3
America St DD10 189 C2
Amy Row AB39 185 F6
Anchor La DD10 135 C5
Andderson Gdns AB43 143 A6
Anderson Ave AB24 164 E6
Anderson Ct AB43 143 A6
Anderson Dr
Aberdeen AB15 169 C8
Huntly AB54 30 C7
Peterhead AB42 38 D5
Stonehaven AB39 181 I4
Anderson La AB24 164 E6
Anderson Pl AB43 143 B7
Anderson Rd
Aberdeen AB24 164 D6
Ballater AB35 182 D3
Anderson Terr
Aboyne AB34 96 B3
Ellon AB41 151 B5
Anderson Wlk AB51 152 C5
Andover Hill Upper DD9 188 D2
Andover Prim Sch DD9 188 E2
Angus Dr DD10 189 C8
Angus Gdns AB42 25 C1
Angus La 4 AB53 145 D4
Angusfield Ave AB15 169 B7
Angusfield La AB15 169 B8
Ann St Aberdeen AB25 190 A4
Stonehaven AB39 185 E5
Anna Ritchie Sch The AB42 147 C5
Annand Ave AB41 151 B6
Annand Rd AB41 151 B6
Annat Bank AB12 176 C8
Annat Rd DD10 189 D2
Annesley Gr 3 AB31 108 E8
Annesley Pk 5 AB31 108 E8
Annfield Terr AB15 169 E7
Anvil Pl AB43 26 C7
Apple Wynd 3 DD10 189 C2
Aquithie Rd AB51 87 D7
Arbeadie Ave AB31 184 C5
Arbeadie Rd AB31 184 C5
Arbeadie Terr AB31 184 C4
Arbeadie Wood AB31 184 C5
Arbor Ct AB31 184 A4
Arbroath Pl AB12 170 C3
Arbroath Way AB12 170 B3
Arbuthnot Mus* AB42 147 E5
Arbuthnot Terr AB42 147 C5
Arbuthnott House* AB30 130 D6
Arbuthnott Pl 10 AB39 185 E4
Arbuthnott St
2 Montrose DD10 187 D3
7 Stonehaven AB39 185 E4
Archaeolink Prehistory Pk* AB52 72 C8
Ardallie Prim Sch AB42 51 E6
Ardanes Brae AB45 140 E6
Ardarroch Cl AB24 165 C4
Ardarroch Pl AB24 165 D4
Ardarroch Rd AB24 165 C4
Ardbeck Pl AB14 172 E7
Ardeer Pl AB43 143 B4
Ardgith Rd 3 AB41 151 E6
Ardinn Cres AB53 145 F4
Ardinn Rd AB53 145 E4
Ardinn Terr AB53 145 E4
Ardlair Terr AB21 158 C7
Ardlaw Pl AB43 143 A5
Ardmachron Dr 2 AB42 53 B3
Ardmore Distillery* AB52 56 D4
Ardovie Rd DD9 136 E1
Ardtannes Pl 2 AB51 152 D4
Arduthie Gdns AB39 185 C5
Arduthie Rd AB39 185 D5
Arduthie Sch AB39 185 D5
Arduthie St AB39 185 E4
Argyll Cl AB21 157 E4
Argyll Pl
Aberdeen AB25 164 F2
Portlethen AB12 180 C7
Argyll Rd
Aberdeen AB21 157 E4
Fraserburgh AB43 143 B5
Argyll St DD9 188 B4
Arisaig Dr AB43 143 B4
Ark Ct AB43 143 B5
Ark La AB43 5 A4
Armoury La 8 AB42 38 D6
Arn Pl AB41 76 C7
Arnage Ave AB41 151 E5
Arnage Castle* AB41 50 D4
Arnage Cres AB16 164 B3
Arnage Dr AB16 164 A3
Arnage Gdns AB16 164 B3
Arnage Pl AB16 164 B3
Arnage Prim Sch AB41 50 F5
Arnage Terr AB16 164 B3
Arnhall Bsns Pk AB32 161 E1
Arnhall Cres AB32 161 E2
Arnhall Dr AB32 161 F2
Arnot Pl AB12 180 E5
Arran Ave
Aberdeen AB16 163 E2
Peterhead AB42 147 B7
Arran Ct AB43 143 B4
Artlaw Cres AB42 146 E5
Aryburk Row AB21 158 C6
Ash Ct AB12 180 A5
Ash Gr Aberdeen AB21 156 B5
Fraserburgh AB43 143 A6
Portlethen AB12 180 B4
Ash Pl AB12 180 B4
Ash Row 8 AB23 91 C8
Ashdale Cl AB32 161 D3
Ashdale Dr AB32 161 E2
Ashfield Rd AB15 168 F3
Ashgrove AB33 154 D4
Ashgrove Ave AB25 164 F4
Ashgrove Gdns N AB16 164 C3
Ashgrove Gdns S AB16 164 C3
Ashgrove Pl
Aberdeen AB16 164 D3
2 Peterhead AB42 147 B3
Ashgrove Rd AB25 164 F3
Ashgrove Rd W AB16 164 C3
Ash-Hill Dr AB16 164 E3
Ash-Hill Pl AB16 164 E4
Ash-Hill Rd AB16 164 E4
Ash-Hill Way AB16 164 E4
Ashlea Ave AB51 155 C5
Ashley Gdns AB10 169 E7
Ashley Gr AB10 169 F7
Ashley La AB10 169 F7
Ashley Pk Dr AB10 169 E7
Ashley Pk La AB10 169 F7
Ashley Pk N AB10 169 E7
Ashley Pk S AB10 169 F7
Ashley Rd AB10 169 F7
Ashley Rd Prim Sch AB10 169 F7
Ashvale Pl AB10 170 A8
Ashwood Ave AB22 159 D4
Ashwood Circ AB23 159 D5
Ashwood Cres AB22 159 C4
Ashwood Dr AB22 159 D5
Ashwood Gr AB22 159 D5
Ashwood Grange AB22 159 C4
Ashwood Mews AB22 159 D5
Ashwood Par AB22 159 D5
Ashwood Pk AB22 159 D5
Ashwood Pl AB22 159 D5
Ashwood Rd AB22 159 D5
Asloun Castle (remains of)* AB33 84 C5
Aspen Gr AB32 161 C2
Aspen Way AB12 180 B4
Assynt Pl AB43 143 B4
Atholl Pl AB43 143 B5
Atholl Rise AB41 62 A2
Auchenblae Prim Sch AB30 124 B1
Auchinleck Cres AB24 164 F7
Auchinleck Rd AB24 164 F7
Auchinyell Gdns AB10 169 D4
Auchinyell Rd AB10 169 D4
Auchinyell Terr AB10 169 D4
Auchlea Pl AB16 163 F3
Auchlea Rd AB16 163 F2
Auchlethen Dr 1 AB42 52 C4
Auchlossan Ct 5 AB22 165 B8
Auchmacoy Rd 2 AB31 98 E1
Auchmill Rd AB21 163 F8
Auchmill Terr AB21 164 B7
Auchmore Rd AB41 151 C3
Auchnagatt Prim Sch AB41 50 D8
Auchreddie Rd E AB53 36 A5
Auchreddie Rd W 1 AB53 36 A5
Auchriny Circ AB21 158 B3
Auchry Rd AB53 22 B1
Auchterellon Prim Sch AB41 151 B6
Auchterless Prim Sch AB53 46 F8
Auld Kirk Art Gall* AB23 91 A6
Auld Post Office Mus* AB53 145 C4
Auldearn Gdns AB12 170 B3
Auldearn Pl AB12 170 B3
Auldearn Rd AB12 170 B3
Aulton Rd AB42 53 A3
Aulton Way DD10 189 C6
Avenue The
Aberdeen AB13 173 B8
Peterhead AB42 36 E6
Averon Pk AB21 156 A7
Avon Pl AB21 158 B6

B

Back Brae AB44 141 D7
Back Braes DD9 188 C2
Back Hilton Rd AB25 164 F4
Back Path AB45 140 F5
Back Rd DD10 135 C6
Back St 5 Banff AB45 1 F1
Macduff AB44 141 D6
Peterhead AB42 147 E5
Back Wynd
Aberdeen AB25 190 B3
5 Oldmeldrum AB51 150 C3
Backgate AB42 147 E5
Baddifurrow 1 AB51 152 C4
Baden Powell Rd AB53 145 C5
Badenoch Dr AB54 148 E4
Badentoy Ave AB12 179 F8
Badentoy Cres AB12 179 E8
Badentoy Pk AB12 179 E8
Badentoy Pl AB12 179 F8
Badentoy Rd AB12 180 A7
Badentoy Way AB12 179 E7
Bailie Norrie Cres 3 DD10 189 C7
Bailie Wilson Way 1 DD10 189 D7
Baillieswell Dr AB15 168 B2
Baillieswells Cres AB15 168 B2
Baillieswells Dr AB15 168 B2
Baillieswells Gr AB15 168 A2
Baillieswells Pl AB15 168 B2
Baillieswells Rd AB15 168 B2
Baillieswells Terr AB15 168 B2
Bain Cres AB42 146 E4
Bain Dr AB42 146 E4
Bain Gdns 1 AB42 146 E4
Bain Pl 2 AB42 146 E4
Bain Rd AB42 146 E4
Bain Terr AB42 146 E4
Bainzie Rd AB51 152 B8
Baird Rd AB43 24 E6
Baird St AB39 185 E5
Baird Terr AB39 185 E5
Baird Way 6 DD10 189 D7
Bairds Brae AB15 169 A4
Baker Pl 5 AB25 165 A2
Baker St
Aberdeen AB25 190 A4
2 Oldmeldrum AB51 150 C3
Bakersfield Cl 2 AB21 153 D5
Balandro Loan DD10 135 C5
Balbegno Castle* AB30 127 F3
Balbithan View 2 AB51 74 F2
Balfluig Castle (restored)* AB33 154 F2
Balfour Rd AB33 154 C4
Balfron Pl AB15 164 B1
Balgownie Brae AB22 165 A8
Balgownie Cres AB23 165 C8
Balgownie Dr AB22 164 F8
Balgownie Gdns AB22 165 A8
Balgownie Pl AB22 164 F8
Balgownie Prim Sch AB22 165 B8
Balgownie Rd AB22 159 D1
Balgownie Way AB22 165 A8
Ballater Bsns Pk AB35 182 F4
Ballater Prim Sch AB35 182 E5
Ballater Rd AB34 183 C5
Balloch Way AB21 158 C7
Balmain St 4 DD10 189 C3
Balmedie Ctry Pk* AB23 91 D8
Balmedie Ctry Pk Visitor Ctr* AB23 77 D1
Balmedie Leisure Ctr AB23 91 C8
Balmedie Prim Sch AB23 91 D8
Balmellie Pl AB53 145 E4
Balmellie Rd AB53 145 E4
Balmellie St AB53 145 D4
Balmoor Ind Est AB42 147 B6
Balmoor Ret Pk AB42 147 B6
Balmoor Stadium (Peterhead FC) AB42 147 C6
Balmoor Terr AB42 147 C6
Balmoral Ave AB41 151 E5
Balmoral Castle* AB35 102 D2
Balmoral Pl AB10 169 F6
Balmoral Rd AB10 170 A6
Balmoral Terr AB34 183 C4
Balmoral Wynd 1 AB41 151 F5
Balmuir Wood 4 AB34 96 C3
Balnagask Ave AB11 170 F6
Balnagask Circ AB11 170 F6
Balnagask Cres AB11 170 F6
Balnagask Pl AB11 170 F7
Balnagask Rd AB11 170 D5
Balnellan Pl 5 AB35 113 F6
Balnellan Rd 5 AB35 113 F6
Balquhain Castle (remains of)* AB51 73 D6
Baltic Pl
Aberdeen AB11 165 E1
Peterhead AB42 147 F5
Baltic Sq 9 DD10 189 D3
Baltic St DD10 189 D3
Baluss Pl AB42 146 E5
Balvenie Wynd 4 AB41 151 E5
Banchory Acad AB31 184 D4
Banchory Devenick Sch AB12 175 B7
Banchory Mus* AB31 184 C4
Banchory Prim Sch AB31 184 D4
Banff Acad AB45 140 E5
Banff Prim Sch AB45 140 F5
Banff Rd Turriff AB53 22 D5
Turriff AB53 145 D5
Bank Brae AB33 154 D3
Bank La Peterhead AB42 38 D6
Rosehearty AB43 142 C7
Bank Rd AB42 36 E6
Bank St Aberdeen AB24 164 E6
Aberdeen AB11 190 B1
Brechin DD9 188 C3
Montrose DD10 187 D3
Bank Terr AB33 154 D3
Bankhead Acad AB21 158 C1
Bankhead Ave AB21 158 C1
Bankhead Rd AB21 158 C1
Banks o'Dee Sports Ctr AB11 170 C5
Banks of Brechin DD9 188 A4
Banks The DD9 188 A4
Bannerman Pl AB16 164 A6
Barbank St AB45 139 D7
Barbour Brae AB22 159 D1
Barclay Pk AB34 183 A5
Barclay Rd AB51 152 D4
Barclay St 4 AB39 185 E4
Barclayhill Pl AB12 180 C7
Barkmill Rd AB25 164 F3
Barleyhill Cl AB51 88 B6
Barmekin Pk AB32 100 D4
Barnhill Rd AB44 141 C5
Barns Brae DD10 138 D2
Barra Castle* AB51 74 D8

Barra Cres AB43 .... 143 A4
Barra Wlk AB16 .... 163 E2
Barrack La 5 AB43 .... 163 D6
Barrack Rd DD10 .... 189 D2
Barrasgate Rd AB43 .... 143 D7
Barratt Dr AB41 .... 151 B3
Barraview AB51 .... 150 C3
Barringer La AB32 .... 161 F3
Barron Ct AB54 .... 148 D4
Barron St AB24 .... 164 F6
Barthol Chapel Prim Sch AB51 .... 48 D1
Bartlet Pl AB45 .... 140 F6
Barvas Wlk AB16 .... 163 D3
Basin View DD10 .... 189 C4
Bath St Aberdeen AB11 .... 190 A3
Fraserburgh AB43 .... 143 D7
Macduff AB44 .... 141 E7
Peterhead AB42 .... 147 E4
Stonehaven AB39 .... 185 E5
Battery Pk 1 AB42 .... 147 F6
Battle of Harlaw* AB51 .... 73 F7
Battock Pl AB11 .... 170 D6
Battock Terr 1 AB31 .... 98 E1
Bawdley Head AB43 .... 143 B7
Baxter Pl AB11 .... 170 F7
Baxter St AB11 .... 170 F7
Baylands Cres AB42 .... 147 C4
Bayview Cres
Banff AB45 .... 140 F6
Peterhead AB42 .... 147 C4
Bayview Rd
Aberdeen AB15 .... 169 D8
Banff AB45 .... 3 C2
12 Cullen AB56 .... 1 B5
Inverbervie DD10 .... 187 E6
Bayview Rd S AB15 .... 169 D7
Beach Bvd AB11 .... 190 C4
Beach Bvd Ret Pk AB11 .... 165 E2
Beach Leisure Ctr AB24 .... 165 E3
Beach Rd
Johnshaven DD10 .... 135 C6
St Cyrus DD10 .... 134 D3
Stonehaven AB39 .... 185 F5
Beachfield Way 3 AB23 .... 91 C8
Beachgate DD10 .... 187 E6
Beachgate La 3 AB39 .... 185 E4
Beacon Com & Sports Ctr AB21 .... 163 D8
Beacon Dr AB43 .... 143 C4
Beacon Rd DD10 .... 189 D2
Beacon Terr 6 DD10 .... 189 D1
Beaconhill Rd AB13 .... 173 D8
Beaconsfield La 5 AB53 .... 145 C5
Beaconsfield Pl AB15 .... 169 E8
Beaconsfield Terr AB53 .... 145 C5
Bearehill Gdns 1 DD9 .... 188 B3
Beattie Ave AB25 .... 164 F4
Beattie Pl 2 AB25 .... 164 F4
Beattie Terr 1 DD10 .... 187 D6
Beauly Pl AB43 .... 143 A4
Bede House (remains of)* AB51 .... 72 F6
Bede Way AB41 .... 61 E5
Bedford Ave AB24 .... 165 A5
Bedford Pl AB24 .... 165 B4
Bedford Rd AB24 .... 165 A4
Beech Ave AB43 .... 143 A6
Beech Cl 2 AB41 .... 62 A2
Beech Ct 19 AB51 .... 87 D7
Beech Rd
Aberdeen AB16 .... 164 C4
Westhill AB32 .... 161 D2
Beech Tree Rd AB31 .... 184 F5
Beechcroft Terr AB52 .... 149 D4
Beeches The
3 Banchory AB31 .... 184 D4
Mintlaw AB42 .... 146 E4
Beechfield AB51 .... 74 E4
Beechgrove Ave AB15 .... 164 E2
Beechgrove Ct AB15 .... 164 E1
Beechgrove Gdn* AB32 .... 166 E6
Beechgrove Gdns AB15 .... 164 E2
Beechgrove Pl AB15 .... 164 E1
Beechgrove Terr AB15 .... 164 E1
Beechhill Gdns AB15 .... 169 B5
Beechwood Ave
Aberdeen AB16 .... 164 D3
Ellon AB41 .... 151 B5
Beechwood Cl AB32 .... 161 C3
Beechwood Gdns AB32 .... 161 D2
Beechwood Pl
4 Aberdeen AB16 .... 164 D4
2 Ellon AB41 .... 151 B6
Westhill AB32 .... 161 C3
Beechwood Rd
Aberdeen AB16 .... 164 D4
Laurencekirk AB30 .... 186 C6
Beechwood Sch AB15 .... 164 D2
Beldorney Castle* AB54 .... 42 A3
Belgrave Terr AB25 .... 164 F1
Belhaven Rd AB41 .... 62 A2
Bell Ave AB42 .... 147 C2
Bell Terr AB42 .... 147 C2
Bellenden Wlk AB13 .... 173 A7
Bellevue Rd AB45 .... 140 E5
Bellevue Terr AB45 .... 140 F4
Bellfield Rd
Aberdeen AB16 .... 163 F3
Bridge of Don AB23 .... 160 A1
Bell's La AB43 .... 5 A4
Bellswood Cres AB31 .... 184 C5
Bellwood Dr AB34 .... 183 F5
Bellwood Rd AB34 .... 183 F5
Belmont Brae AB39 .... 185 E5
Belmont Gdns 3 AB25 .... 164 F4
Belmont Rd AB25 .... 165 A4
Belmont St AB10 .... 190 A3
Belmuir Gdns AB21 .... 158 B7
Belrorie Circ AB21 .... 158 C7
Beltie Rd AB31 .... 98 D1
Belvidere Cres AB15 .... 164 F1
Belvidere La AB15 .... 168 E2
Belvidere Rd AB15 .... 168 D2
Belvidere St AB25 .... 164 F2
Ben More Ave DD10 .... 189 C8
Benbecula Rd 6 AB16 .... 163 E2
Bennachie Ave 2 AB51 .... 152 C6
Bennachie Leisure Ctr AB52 .... 149 C6
Bennachie View 11 AB51 .... 87 D7
Bents Rd DD10 .... 189 E3
Bents The AB45 .... 1 F3
Benview Gdns AB51 .... 150 D4
Benview Terr AB21 .... 156 B6
Berneray Pl 2 AB16 .... 163 E2
Bernham Ave AB39 .... 185 B5
Bernham Cres AB39 .... 185 B5
Bernham Ct 1 AB39 .... 185 B5
Bernham Pk AB39 .... 185 B5
Bernham Pl 2 AB39 .... 185 B5
Bernham Terr AB39 .... 185 B5
Berry St AB25 .... 190 B4
Berryden Rd
Aberdeen AB25 .... 165 A3
Peterhead AB42 .... 147 B4
Berryhill Pk AB52 .... 72 D8
Berryhill Pl AB39 .... 181 H4
Berryhill View AB52 .... 72 C8
Berrymuir Pl AB12 .... 180 A4
Berrymuir Rd
Macduff AB44 .... 141 E6
Portlethen AB12 .... 180 B5
Berrymuir Wynd AB12 .... 180 A4
Berrywell Gdns AB21 .... 158 B7
Berrywell Pl AB21 .... 158 B7
Berrywell Rd AB21 .... 158 B7
Berrywell Wlk AB21 .... 158 B7
Bervie Brow AB12 .... 176 C8
Bervie Prim Sch DD10 .... 187 D7
Bervie Rd AB43 .... 143 A5
Bethany Gdns AB11 .... 170 A7
Bethlin Mews AB15 .... 162 F4
Bettridge Leisure Ctr AB39 .... 181 I4
Bettridge Rd AB39 .... 181 I4
Beverley Rd AB51 .... 152 E4
Bieldside Sta Rd AB15 .... 168 C1
Biggar Ct AB43 .... 143 A4
Bilbo Gdns AB42 .... 26 E6
Bin Ave AB54 .... 29 C3
Binghill Cres AB13 .... 173 B8
Binghill Dr AB13 .... 167 D1
Binghill Hedges AB13 .... 167 E1
Binghill Pk AB13 .... 173 C8
Binghill Rd AB13 .... 167 E1
Binghill Rd N AB13 .... 167 D1
Binghill Rd W AB13 .... 167 E1
Binview Rd 6 AB56 .... 1 B4
Binview Terr 7 AB56 .... 1 B4
Birch Ave AB32 .... 161 D2
Birch Gr Banchory AB31 .... 184 B4
Ellon AB41 .... 151 E6
Mintlaw AB42 .... 146 D5
Birch Rd AB16 .... 164 D4
Birchfield Pl AB12 .... 176 C6
Birchwood Pl AB34 .... 183 B4
Birkhall Par AB16 .... 164 A4
Birkhall Pl AB16 .... 164 A4
Birnie Pl 25 Boddam AB42 .... 40 D1
Fraserburgh AB43 .... 143 A4
Birsemore Cres AB34 .... 183 E2
Bishop Forbes Cres AB21 .... 156 B6
Bishop's Cl 8 DD9 .... 188 C3
Bishop's Manor (remains of)* AB21 .... 90 D5
Bishopsloch Row AB21 .... 158 C6
Bisset La AB30 .... 186 D5
Blackbraes Rd AB21 .... 153 E5
Blackbraes Way 3 AB21 .... 153 E5
Blackburn Bsns Pk AB21 .... 156 B5
Blackburn Ind Est AB21 .... 156 A6
Blackcraig Rd 3 AB42 .... 53 B3
Blackdog Ind Ctr AB23 .... 91 B5
Blackfriars St DD10 .... 189 C4
Blackhall Cres 6 AB34 .... 96 C3
Blackhall Ind Est AB51 .... 152 B6
Blackhall Rd 3 AB51 .... 152 C6
Blackhall Wynd AB51 .... 152 D5
Blackhill Sta AB51 .... 73 D2
Blackhills Cres AB42 .... 147 B3
Blackhills Pl AB32 .... 161 C3
Blackhills Way AB32 .... 161 C2
Blackhouse Ind Est AB42 .... 147 A7
Blackhouse Terr AB42 .... 147 C7
Blackiemuir Ave AB30 .... 186 B5
Blacklaws Brae AB32 .... 161 D5
Blackness Ave AB12 .... 170 E1
Blackness Rd AB12 .... 170 F1
Black's La AB11 .... 190 C2
Blackthorn Cres 1 AB16 .... 164 D4
Blaikes Quay AB11 .... 190 C2
Blairmore Sch AB54 .... 42 B6
Blairs Coll AB12 .... 174 A6
Blairs Mus The* AB12 .... 174 A6
Blantyre Cres AB43 .... 143 B4
Blantyre St 8 AB56 .... 1 B5
Bleachfield Rd 2 AB22 .... 159 E1
Bleachfield St AB54 .... 148 D4
Blenheim Pl AB25 .... 164 E1
Bloomfield Ct AB10 .... 170 A6
Bloomfield Pl AB10 .... 170 A7
Bloomfield Rd AB10 .... 170 A6
Blythewood Pl AB51 .... 152 E3
Boat Croft 4 AB51 .... 87 C7
Boatie Row AB39 .... 185 F6
Bob Cooney Ct AB25 .... 165 A3
Bodachra Pl AB22 .... 159 E1
Bodachra Rd AB22 .... 159 E1
Boddam Castle (remains of)* AB42 .... 53 F8
Boddam Prim Sch AB42 .... 40 D1
Boddie Pl AB24 .... 165 C3
Bog Rd DD9 .... 188 D3
Bogbeth Rd AB51 .... 87 D6
Bogie Rd 4 AB54 .... 55 E2
Bogie St AB54 .... 148 E4
Bogroy Cres AB45 .... 7 D2
Bogwell La 11 AB39 .... 185 E4
Bon Accord Baths AB11 .... 170 A8
Bon Accord Cres Gdns* AB11 .... 190 A2
Bon Accord Sports Ctr AB24 .... 165 C7
Bona Pl AB43 .... 143 A5
Bon-Accord Cres AB11 .... 190 A2
Bon-Accord Cres La AB11 .... 190 A2
Bon-Accord La AB11 .... 190 A2
Bon-Accord Sq AB11 .... 190 A2
Bon-Accord St AB11 .... 190 A2
Bon-Accord Terr AB11 .... 190 A2
Bonnymuir Pl AB15 .... 164 E2
Bonnyton Rd AB41 .... 62 B2
Bonnyview Dr AB16 .... 163 F6
Bonnyview Pl AB21 .... 163 F6
Bonnyview Rd AB21 .... 163 F6
Bonty Pl AB34 .... 183 E5
Booth Pl AB21 .... 163 E7
Boothby Rd AB43 .... 143 A3
Borrowfield Cres DD10 .... 189 C6
Borrowfield Prim Sch DD10 .... 189 C7
Borrowfield Rd DD10 .... 189 C6
Borrowmuirhill Rd AB30 .... 186 D6
Borrowstone Pl 3 AB16 .... 163 F2
Bosies Bank Way 2 AB42 .... 147 A4
Boswell Ave AB12 .... 180 A6
Boswell Rd AB12 .... 180 A6
Boswell Way AB12 .... 180 A6
Boswell Wlk AB12 .... 180 A6
Boswell Wynd AB12 .... 180 A6
Bothwell Terr 1 AB41 .... 62 B2
Boultenstone Outdoor Ctr* AB36 .... 82 B2
Bourtree Ave AB12 .... 180 A4
Bowling Gn Rd AB53 .... 145 E4
Bowness Rd 6 AB42 .... 53 A3
Boyd Orr Ave AB12 .... 170 A1
Boyd Orr Pl AB12 .... 170 A1
Boyd Orr Wlk AB12 .... 170 A1
Boyd-Orr Ave DD9 .... 188 C4
Boyes La AB54 .... 144 C4
Boyndie Rd AB45 .... 140 D6
Boyndie St AB45 .... 140 F6
Boyndie St W AB45 .... 140 E6
Boyne Castle (remains of)* AB45 .... 2 F3
Boyne Pl 4 AB45 .... 8 F8
Boyne St AB45 .... 8 F8
Bracken Rd AB12 .... 180 B6
Brackens Pl AB53 .... 145 B6
Braco Pl 2 AB45 .... 140 E5
Bracoden Prim Sch AB45 .... 3 D2
Bracoden Rd AB45 .... 3 C2
Bracoden Terr AB45 .... 3 C2
Bradley Terr AB24 .... 165 A6
Brae Cres AB42 .... 146 D4
Brae Rd DD10 .... 187 D4
Brae St 16 AB42 .... 40 D1
Brae The 3 AB53 .... 36 A5
Braecroft Ave AB32 .... 161 E3
Braecroft Cres AB32 .... 161 E4
Braecroft Dr AB32 .... 161 E3
Braefoot Rd AB16 .... 164 E4
Braegowan Rd AB45 .... 3 C2
Braehead AB22 .... 159 F1
Braehead Cres
Peterhead AB42 .... 147 B6
Stonehaven AB39 .... 185 D3
Braehead Dr AB42 .... 53 A3
Braehead Pl 13 AB42 .... 38 D6
Braehead Rd AB42 .... 27 B3
Braehead Terr AB13 .... 173 B8
Braehead Way AB22 .... 159 E2
Braeheads Banff AB45 .... 140 F6
Fraserburgh AB43 .... 15 D6
MacDuff AB44 .... 141 D7
Braeloine Visitor Ctr* AB34 .... 106 C3
Braemar Castle* AB35 .... 113 F7
Braemar Ct AB43 .... 143 C4
Braemar Pl
Aberdeen AB10 .... 169 F6
Ballater AB35 .... 182 C4
Braemar Prim Sch AB35 .... 113 F6
Braemar Rd AB35 .... 182 C4
Braeside Ave AB15 .... 169 C4
Braeside Cres AB39 .... 185 F6
Braeside Inf Sch AB15 .... 169 C5
Braeside Pl AB15 .... 169 C5
Braeside Prim Sch AB41 .... 50 B6
Braeside Terr AB15 .... 169 C4
Braichlie Rd AB35 .... 182 D4
Braiklay Ave AB41 .... 61 E5
Bramble Brae AB16 .... 164 B5
Bramble Brae Prim Sch AB16 .... 164 C5
Bramble Ct AB12 .... 180 B4
Bramble Pl AB12 .... 180 A4
Bramble Rd AB12 .... 180 A4
Bramble Way AB12 .... 180 A4
Brander Mus* AB54 .... 148 D5
Brander Pl AB22 .... 164 E8
Brankie Pl AB51 .... 152 A7
Brankie Rd AB51 .... 152 A8
Braoch Pk DD10 .... 189 B1
Braoch Rd DD10 .... 189 B1
Brebner Cres AB16 .... 163 F5
Brebner Pl 7 AB31 .... 108 E8
Brebner Terr AB16 .... 163 F5
Brechin Bsns Pk DD9 .... 136 C7
Brechin Castle* DD9 .... 188 C2
Brechin Cath DD9 .... 188 C3
Brechin High Sch DD9 .... 188 B4
Brechin Historic Ctr* DD9 .... 188 C2
Brechin Ind Est DD9 .... 188 F2
Brechin Infmy DD9 .... 188 D4
Brechin Rd DD10 .... 189 B6
Brechin Sta DD9 .... 188 D3
Breckview 5 AB41 .... 62 B2
Bredero Dr
Banchory AB31 .... 184 E5
Ellon AB41 .... 151 C3
Bremner Way 9 AB51 .... 87 D7
Brent Ave DD10 .... 189 D8
Brent Field Circ AB41 .... 151 A6
Brent Rd AB21 .... 157 F5
Bressay Brae AB15 .... 163 E2
Bressay Dr AB41 .... 151 B3
Brewery Rd AB43 .... 24 E5
Briar Bank AB21 .... 153 D6
Briar Gdns AB42 .... 146 D4
Brickfield Rd AB39 .... 185 C4
Brickfield Terr 2 AB39 .... 185 C5
Bridge Cres 10 AB31 .... 108 E8
Bridge of Don Acad AB22 .... 159 F1
Bridge of Dun Sta DD10 .... 137 E5
Bridge Pl AB11 .... 190 A2
Bridge Rd Banff AB45 .... 141 A5
Inverurie AB51 .... 87 C7
Bridge Sq AB35 .... 182 E4
Bridge St
Aberdeen AB11 .... 190 A3
Aboyne AB34 .... 96 C2
Ballater AB35 .... 182 D4
Banchory AB31 .... 184 B4
Banff AB45 .... 141 A5
20 Boddam AB42 .... 40 D1
Brechin DD9 .... 188 C2
Cruden Bay AB42 .... 53 B3
Ellon AB41 .... 151 D5
2 Fordyce AB45 .... 1 F1
Fraserburgh AB43 .... 15 D6
Gourdon DD10 .... 187 D3
Montrose DD10 .... 189 C2
Peterhead AB42 .... 147 F5
Portsoy AB45 .... 139 D7
3 Stonehaven AB39 .... 185 D4
Strichen AB43 .... 24 E5
Turriff AB53 .... 22 E4
Woodside AB24 .... 164 D7
Bridge Terr
14 Newburgh AB41 .... 77 F8
Turriff AB53 .... 22 E4
Bridge View Rd AB34 .... 183 C3
Bridgefield 9 AB39 .... 185 E4
Bridgefield Terr 8 AB39 .... 185 E4
Bridgend Cres AB42 .... 52 E4
Bridgend Terr AB53 .... 145 C3
Bridgeview Pl AB34 .... 183 B4
Brierfield Rd 3 AB16 .... 164 D4
Brierfield Terr AB16 .... 164 D4
Briggies Wynd AB51 .... 155 B6
Bright St AB11 .... 170 B6
Brighton Pl
Aberdeen AB10 .... 169 E7
Peterculter AB14 .... 172 D6
Brimmond Cres AB32 .... 161 D2
Brimmond Ctry Pk* AB15 .... 162 D6
Brimmond Dr AB32 .... 161 D2
Brimmond La AB32 .... 161 D2
Brimmond Pl
Aberdeen AB11 .... 170 D6
1 Westhill AB32 .... 161 D2
Brimmond View AB21 .... 158 B2
Brimmond Way AB32 .... 161 D2
Brimmond Wlk AB32 .... 161 D2
Broad St
Aberdeen AB10 .... 190 B3
Fraserburgh AB43 .... 143 D6
4 Peterhead AB42 .... 147 F5
Broaddykes Ave AB15 .... 162 F3
Broaddykes Cl 4 AB15 .... 162 F3
Broaddykes Cres 1 AB15 .... 162 F2
Broaddykes Dr AB15 .... 162 F2
Broaddykes Pl AB15 .... 162 E3
Broaddykes View 2 AB15 .... 162 F2
Broadfold Dr AB23 .... 160 A1
Broadfold Rd AB23 .... 160 A1
Broadford 1 AB51 .... 152 D4
Broadford Gdns AB21 .... 156 B7
Broadlands Gdns AB32 .... 161 B3
Broadsea Rd AB43 .... 143 C7
Broadshaven Rd AB12 .... 180 E5
Broadstraik Ave AB32 .... 161 B2
Broadstraik Brae 1 AB32 .... 161 B2
Broadstraik Cl AB32 .... 161 A3
Broadstraik Dr AB32 .... 161 B2
Broadstraik Gdns AB32 .... 161 A2
Broadstraik Gr AB32 .... 161 A2
Broadstraik Pl 2 AB32 .... 161 B2
Brodick Rd AB43 .... 143 B4
Brodiesord Sch AB45 .... 7 C3
Brodinch Pl AB16 .... 163 F3
Brodinch Rd AB16 .... 163 F3
Bronie Cres 7 AB41 .... 62 B2
Bronieside 2 AB41 .... 62 B2
Brook La AB42 .... 147 F5
Brooke Cres AB23 .... 160 A3
Brookside 1 AB42 .... 147 A8
Broom Pk AB15 .... 168 D3
Broombank Terr AB35 .... 113 E6
Broomfield Cres DD10 .... 189 D6
Broomfield Gdns DD10 .... 189 D6
Broomfield Ind Est DD10 .... 189 D6
Broomfield Pk AB12 .... 180 A5
Broomfield Rd
Montrose DD10 .... 189 D5
Portlethen AB12 .... 180 A5
Broomhill AB43 .... 143 B4
Broomhill Ave AB10 .... 169 F5
Broomhill Leisure Ctr AB10 .... 169 E5
Broomhill Pl AB10 .... 169 F5
Broomhill Prim Sch AB10 .... 169 F6
Broomhill Rd
Aberdeen AB10 .... 169 E4
Stonehaven AB39 .... 185 B4
Turriff AB53 .... 145 D5
Broomhill Terr AB10 .... 169 F5
Broomiesburn Dr AB41 .... 63 D5
Brora Pl AB43 .... 143 B4
Brough Pl 1 AB25 .... 164 F4
Brown St AB24 .... 164 F6
Brownhill Dr 5 AB21 .... 153 D5
Brownhill Pl 1 AB21 .... 153 D4
Brownhill Rd 2 AB21 .... 153 D4
Brownlow Pl 1 DD10 .... 189 D1
Bruan Ct AB43 .... 143 A4
Bruce Brae 1 AB42 .... 38 D6
Bruce Cres Ellon AB41 .... 151 C4
Peterhead AB42 .... 147 A4
Bruce Pl AB51 .... 150 C2
Bruce St AB44 .... 141 C6
Bruce Wlk
Aberdeen AB12 .... 170 C2
Kintore AB51 .... 155 C4
Brucklay Ct
Aberdeen AB21 .... 158 C6
Peterhead AB42 .... 147 B3
Brucklay St AB43 .... 142 C7
Bruinswick Pl AB11 .... 170 B6
Bruntland Ct AB12 .... 180 C5
Bruntland Pl AB12 .... 180 C6
Bruntland Rd
Portlethen AB12 .... 180 B5
Stonehaven AB39 .... 179 F4
Buchan Dr AB21 .... 153 C6
Buchan Pl
Fraserburgh AB43 .... 143 B4
Peterhead AB42 .... 36 E6
Buchan Rd
Aberdeen AB11 .... 170 F6
Fraserburgh AB43 .... 143 B4
Buchan St AB44 .... 141 E7
Buchan Terr AB42 .... 147 C5
Buchanan Gdns AB12 .... 170 B2
Buchanan Pl AB12 .... 170 B3
Buchanan Rd AB12 .... 170 B2
Buchanhaven Prim Sch AB42 .... 147 C6
Buchanness Dr 4 AB42 .... 40 D1
Buchanness Pl 15 AB42 .... 40 D1
Buckie Ave AB22 .... 159 C2
Buckie Cl AB22 .... 159 C2
Buckie Cres AB22 .... 159 C2
Buckie Gr AB22 .... 159 D2
Buckie Rd AB22 .... 159 C2
Buckie Wlk AB22 .... 159 C2
Buckie Wynd AB22 .... 159 C2

Bucklerburn Cl AB14 . . .172 C8
Bucklerburn Dr AB14 . . .172 C7
Bucklerburn Pk AB14 . .172 D7
Bucklerburn Pl AB14 . . .172 D7
Bucklerburn Rd AB14 . .172 C7
Bucklerburn View
AB14 . . . . .172 D7
Bucklerburn Wynd
AB14 . . . . .172 C7
Bucksburn Prim Sch
AB21 . . . . .163 F7
Builg Rd AB31 . . . . .117 C5
Bunstane Terr AB12 . . . .176 C6
Bunzeach Pl 3 AB21 . . . .158 C7
Burgess Dr AB42 . . . . .38 D5
Burgh of Rattray (site of)* AB42 . . . . .16 B4
Burghmuir Circ AB51 . . .152 B6
Burghmuir Dr AB51 . . . .152 B7
Burghmuir Pl AB51 . . . . .152 B6
Burghmuir Way AB51 . . .152 B6
Burn La AB51 . . . . .152 D6
Burn o'Vat Visitor Ctr* AB34 . . . . .105 C6
Burnbank Pl AB11 . . . . . .170 F6
Burnbank Terr AB11 . . . .170 F6
Burnbrae Ave AB16 . . . .164 A2
Burnbrae Cres AB16 . . . .164 A2
Burnbrae Pl AB16 . . . . . .164 A2
Burnbutts Cres AB12 . . .176 C7
Burndale Rd AB21 . . . . . .158 C1
Burnett Hill AB31 . . . . . .184 B5
Burnett Pl
Aberdeen AB24 . . . . .164 F5
Inverurie AB51 . . . . .152 E3
Burnett Rd
Banchory AB31 . . . . .184 B5
16 Kemnay AB51 . . . . .87 D7
Stonehaven AB39 . . . . .185 C6
Burnett St
Laurencekirk AB30 . . . . . . .124 B1
Peterhead AB42 . . . . .37 D5
Burnett Terr AB31 . . . . . .184 B5
Burnhaven Prim Sch
AB42 . . . . .147 D1
Burnieboozle Cres
AB15 . . . . .169 A6
Burnieboozle Pl AB15 . .169 A6
Burns Cres
Fraserburgh AB43 . . . . . . .143 B3
St Combs AB43 . . . . .15 D6
Burns Gdns AB15 . . . . . .169 D7
Burns Pl AB43 . . . . .143 B3
Burns Rd
Aberdeen AB15 . . . . .169 E7
Peterhead AB42 . . . . .147 D6
Burns Terr AB39 . . . . . . .185 C4
Burnshangie Rd 7 AB43 .24 E6
Burnside Buckie AB56 . . . . . .1 B3
Portsoy AB45 . . . . .139 D7
Burnside Ave AB51 . . . . .150 C2
Burnside Bsns Pk
AB42 . . . . .147 C1
Burnside Cres AB42 . . . . .37 D5
Burnside Ct 3 AB42 . . . .146 D5
Burnside Dr
Bridge of Don AB23 . . . . . .160 A1
Dyce AB21 . . . . .158 C5
Burnside Gdns
Aberdeen AB25 . . . . .164 E2
Portlethen AB12 . . . . .180 C6
Stonehaven AB39 . . . . .185 C5
Burnside Pl DD10 . . . . . .189 B1
Burnside Rd
Aboyne AB34 . . . . .96 B3
Dyce AB21 . . . . .158 C5
Huntly AB54 . . . . .148 D5
Laurencekirk AB30 . . . . . . .128 B4
4 Mintlaw AB42 . . . . .146 D5
Peterculter AB14 . . . . .172 C5
Burnside St AB45 . . . . . .139 D7
Burnside Way 2 AB23 . . . .91 C8
Burnside Wlk AB34 . . . . .183 F5
Burnwood Ave AB21 . . . .153 C5
Burnwood Dr AB21 . . . . .153 C5
Bush The AB14 . . . . .172 D6
Bute Way AB16 . . . . .163 E2
Bydand Gdns AB51 . . . . .152 B8
Bydand Pl
Aberdeen AB23 . . . . .160 A3
Huntly AB54 . . . . .148 D5
Byron Ave AB16 . . . . .164 A5
Byron Cres AB16 . . . . . . .163 F6
Byron Ct 2 AB45 . . . . . . .140 E6
Byron Pk Nursery & Inf Sch
AB16 . . . . .163 F4
Byron Sq AB16 . . . . .164 A5
Byron Terr AB16 . . . . . . .163 F5

C

Cabel's La AB11 . . . . .190 C1
Cadenhead Pl AB25 . . . .164 F4
Cadenhead Rd AB25 . . . .164 F4
Cadgers Rd DD9 . . . . . . .136 C2
Cadgers' Rd AB52 . . . . . . .58 B8
Caies La 2 AB53 . . . . . . .145 D5
Caiesdykes Cres AB12 . . .170 A2
Caiesdykes Dr AB12 . . . .170 A2
Caiesdykes Rd AB12 . . . .170 A2
Caird Ave DD10 . . . . .189 B1
Caird Pl AB43 . . . . .5 A4
Cairds Cl AB31 . . . . .184 D6
Cairds Wynd AB31 . . . . .184 C6
Cairn Cres AB15 . . . . . . .168 C2
Cairn Gdns
Aberdeen AB15 . . . . .168 C2
Cairn Gdns *continued*
Laurencekirk AB30 . . . . . . .186 D5
Cairn O'mount Rd
AB30 . . . . .128 B4
Cairn Pk AB15 . . . . .168 C2
Cairn Rd
Bieldside AB15 . . . . .168 C2
20 Kemnay AB51 . . . . .87 D7
Peterculter AB14 . . . . .172 E6
Cairn Wlk AB15 . . . . .168 C2
Cairnadrochit 1 AB35 . .113 F6
Cairnaquheen Gdns
AB15 . . . . .164 D1
Cairnaquheen Pl
AB15 . . . . .164 D1
Cairnbrallan (ruins)* AB54 . . . . .66 E7
Cairnbulg Way 1 AB41 . .151 E5
Cairncatto Rd AB42 . . . .147 D7
Cairncry Ave AB16 . . . . .164 D4
Cairncry Cres AB16 . . . . .164 E4
Cairncry Rd AB16 . . . . . .164 D4
Cairncry Terr AB16 . . . . .164 E4
Cairney Prim Sch AB54 . .29 C3
Cairnfield Circ AB21 . . . .164 A8
Cairnfield Cres AB21 . . .164 A7
Cairnfield Pl AB21 . . . . .164 A7
Cairnfold Rd AB22 . . . . . .165 B8
Cairngorm Cres AB12 . . .170 B3
Cairngorm Dr AB12 . . . .170 A3
Cairngorm Gdns AB12 . .170 B3
Cairngorm Pl AB12 . . . . .170 A3
Cairngorm Rd AB12 . . . .170 A3
Cairngrassie Circ
AB12 . . . . .180 A5
Cairngrassie Dr AB12 . .180 A4
Cairnhill Dr
Fraserburgh AB43 . . . . . . .143 C3
Rosehearty AB43 . . . . .142 B6
Stonehaven AB39 . . . . .181 G4
Cairnhill Pl AB39 . . . . . . .181 G4
Cairnhill Rd
Fraserburgh AB43 . . . . . . .143 C3
Rosehearty AB43 . . . . .142 B6
Cairnhill Way AB39 . . . . .181 G4
Cairnie View AB32 . . . . .161 C4
Cairnlee Ave E AB15 . . . .168 C2
Cairnlee Cres N AB15 . . .168 C2
Cairnlee Cres S AB15 . . .168 D2
Cairnlee Pk AB15 . . . . . .168 B2
Cairnlee Rd AB15 . . . . . .168 B2
Cairnlee Rd E AB15 . . . . .168 C3
Cairnlee Terr AB15 . . . . .168 B2
Cairnorrie Prim Sch
AB41 . . . . .49 B7
Cairnside AB15 . . . . .168 C2
Cairntack Rd AB23 . . . . . .91 A8
Cairntrodlie AB42 . . . . . .147 C5
Cairnvale Cres AB12 . . . .170 A3
Cairnvale Terr AB12 . . . .170 A3
Cairnview Cres AB16 . . . .164 D4
Cairnview Pl AB30 . . . . .186 C5
Cairnwell Ave AB16 . . . . .164 A3
Cairnwell Cres DD10 . . . .189 C8
Cairnwell Dr
Aberdeen AB16 . . . . .164 B3
Portlethen AB12 . . . . .180 B6
Cairnwell Pl AB16 . . . . . .164 A4
Caldhame Gdns DD9 . . . .188 E3
Caldhame Pl DD9 . . . . . .188 E2
Caledonia St DD10 . . . . .189 D2
Caledonian La AB11 . . . .190 A1
Caledonian Pl
Aberdeen AB11 . . . . .190 A1
Montrose DD10 . . . . .189 D2
Caledonian Rd DD9 . . . . .188 C4
California St 9 DD10 . . .189 C2
Callum Cres AB15 . . . . . .162 E4
Callum Path AB15 . . . . . .162 E4
Callum Pk AB15 . . . . .162 E4
Callum Wynd AB15 . . . . .162 E4
Calsayseat Rd AB25 . . . .165 A3
Cameron Ave AB23 . . . . .159 F2
Cameron Ct 4 AB39 . . . .185 D4
Cameron Dr 1 AB23 . . . .159 F1
Cameron Pk AB51 . . . . . . .59 C5
Cameron Pl AB23 . . . . . .160 A1
Cameron Rd 2 AB23 . . . .159 F1
Cameron St
Aberdeen AB23 . . . . .160 A1
Stonehaven AB39 . . . . .185 E4
Cameron Terr AB23 . . . . .160 A1
Cameron Way AB23 . . . . .159 F2
Cammach Circ AB12 . . . .180 A4
Campbell Dr AB45 . . . . . .139 C6
Campbell Hospl AB45 . .139 C7
Campbell Pl AB56 . . . . .1 B5
Campbell St
Banff AB45 . . . . .140 F6
1 Cullen AB56 . . . . .1 B5
Camperdown Rd
AB25 . . . . .164 D2
Camphill Est AB13 . . . . . .173 A6
Camphill Rudolf Steiner Schools Murtle Est
AB15 . . . . .173 F8
Campsie Pl AB15 . . . . . . .164 B1
Campus One AB22 . . . . . .165 A8
Campus Three AB22 . . . .165 A8
Campus Two AB22 . . . . . .165 A8
Canal Cres AB51 . . . . . . .152 E3
Canal Pl AB24 . . . . .165 B3
Canal Rd
Aberdeen AB24 . . . . .165 B3
Inverurie AB51 . . . . .152 E3
Canal St
Aberdeen AB24 . . . . .164 E7
Aberdeen AB24 . . . . .165 B3
Canal View AB51 . . . . . . .152 E3
Candlemaker's La
AB25 . . . . .190 B4
Canina Gdns AB21 . . . . .153 D6
Canmore Pk AB39 . . . . . .185 B5
Canmore Pl 1 AB34 . . . .108 B6
Cantlay Ct 3 AB42 . . . . . . .53 A3
Caperstown Cres
AB16 . . . . .164 B5
Captain Gray Pl 1
AB42 . . . . .147 A6
Carden Pl AB10 . . . . .169 E8
Carding Hill 2 AB41 . . . .151 D6
Carlton Pl AB15 . . . . .164 E1
Carmelite La AB11 . . . . .190 B3
Carmelite St
Aberdeen AB11 . . . . .190 B3
Banff AB45 . . . . .141 A5
Carnegie Cres AB15 . . . .169 C8
Carnegie Gdns AB15 . . . .169 C8
Carnegie St DD10 . . . . . .189 D4
Carnegies Brae 10 AB11 .190 B3
Carnferg Pl AB34 . . . . . .183 F5
Carnie Dr AB25 . . . . .164 F4
Carnoustie Cres AB22 . . .159 E2
Carnoustie Gdns 3
AB22 . . . . .159 E2
Carny St AB44 . . . . .141 D7
Caroline Pl
Aberdeen AB25 . . . . .165 A2
1 Fraserburgh AB43 . . . . .143 D7
Carolines Cres AB41 . . . .151 D6
Carriages The AB51 . . . . .155 C6
Carron Gdns AB39 . . . . .185 D3
Carron Pl AB16 . . . . .164 A4
Carron Terr AB39 . . . . . .185 E4
Carronhall AB39 . . . . . . .185 D4
Carronhill Specl Sch
AB39 . . . . .185 C4
Carters Cl
Mintlaw AB42 . . . . .146 D5
1 Peterhead AB42 . . . . . . .147 E5
Cassie Cl AB12 . . . . .176 B7
Castle (remains of) Peel Ring of Lumphanan* AB31 . . .97 F2
Castle Cres DD10 . . . . . .187 D6
Castle Dr 10 Boddam AB42 .40 D1
Inverallochy AB43 . . . . .15 C7
Castle Fraser, Gdn & Est (NTS)* AB51 . . . . .87 C3
Castle Hill
1 Kintore AB51 . . . . .155 C5
Turriff AB53 . . . . .145 C4
Castle Hillock* AB52 . . . .71 E7
Castle La 4 Banff AB45 . . . . .1 F1
10 Banff AB45 . . . . .140 F6
4 Fordyce AB45 . . . . .1 F1
Rosehearty AB43 . . . . .142 C7
Castle Newe (remains of)* AB36 . . . . .81 D3
Castle of Allardice*
DD10 . . . . .130 F4
Castle of Esslemont (remains of)* AB41 . . . . .62 F4
Castle of Fiddes*
AB39 . . . . .125 F4
Castle of Findon (remains of)* AB45 . . . . .3 B2
Castle of Hall Forest (remains)* AB51 . . . . .88 B6
Castle of King Edward (remains of)* AB45 . . . . .21 A7
Castle of Wardhouse*
AB52 . . . . .57 B3
Castle of Waterton (remains of)* AB41 . . . . .63 D5
Castle Pk Rd 3 AB54 . . . .148 E5
Castle Pl
Inverbervie DD10 . . . . .187 D6
3 Montrose DD10 . . . . .189 C3
Castle Rd Alford AB33 . . . .154 E3
Cruden Bay AB42 . . . . .53 B3
Ellon AB41 . . . . .151 E5
Inverurie AB51 . . . . .155 B4
Peterhead AB42 . . . . .36 E7
Castle Rd Ind Est
AB41 . . . . .151 F5
Castle St
Aberdeen AB10 . . . . .190 B3
Banff AB45 . . . . .140 F6
Brechin DD9 . . . . .188 B3
Ellon AB41 . . . . .151 F5
Fraserburgh AB43 . . . . . . .143 D7
Huntly AB54 . . . . .148 D5
Johnshaven DD10 . . . . .135 C6
Montrose DD10 . . . . .189 C3
Peterhead AB42 . . . . .147 F4
Rosehearty AB43 . . . . .142 D7
Stonehaven AB39 . . . . .185 F3
Castle Terr
Aberdeen AB11 . . . . .190 C3
Buckie AB56 . . . . .1 A5
Fraserburgh AB43 . . . . . . .143 D7
Huntly AB54 . . . . .30 C7
Inverbervie DD10 . . . . .187 E6
Peterhead AB42 . . . . .36 E6
Castle Way AB41 . . . . . . .151 F5
Castle Wynd AB51 . . . . . .155 B4
Castlegait Gall*
DD10 . . . . .189 C3
Castlehill AB11 . . . . .190 C3
Castlehill Dr AB45 . . . . .3 C2
Castleton Cres AB16 . . . .164 C3
Castleton Dr AB16 . . . . . .164 C3
Castleton La 3 AB16 . . . .164 C3
Castleton Pl 7 AB35 . . . .113 F6
Castleton Terr 6 AB35 . . .113 F6
Cathay Terr AB56 . . . . .1 B4
Catherine St AB25 . . . . .190 A4
Catterline Prim Sch
AB39 . . . . .126 E1
Catto Cres
Aberdeen AB12 . . . . .176 C7
Peterhead AB42 . . . . .147 C6
Catto Dr AB42 . . . . .147 C6
Catto Way AB42 . . . . .147 B6
Cattofield Gdns AB25 . . .164 F4
Cattofield Pl AB25 . . . . . .164 F4
Cattofield Terr AB25 . . . .164 F4
Causewayend AB25 . . . . .165 B3
Causewayend Cres
AB54 . . . . .144 E5
Causewayend Pl AB54 . .144 E6
Causewayend Prim Sch
AB25 . . . . .165 B3
Cava Cl AB15 . . . . .163 E2
Cedar Ave AB42 . . . . .147 B4
Cedar Ct AB25 . . . . .165 A4
Cedar Pl AB25 . . . . .164 F3
Cemetery Rd
Fraserburgh AB43 . . . . . . .143 D4
Montrose DD10 . . . . .135 C6
Central Rd AB11 . . . . . . .190 C2
Centre Point AB23 . . . . .160 A3
Chalmers Hospl AB45 . .140 F7
Chalmers La AB53 . . . . .145 D5
Chalmers Pl AB42 . . . . . . .25 C1
Channonry Wynd DD9 . .188 C3
Chanonry The AB24 . . . .165 B6
Chapel Brae
Ballater AB35 . . . . .113 E6
2 Turriff AB53 . . . . .22 C1
Chapel Cl AB51 . . . . .73 B6
Chapel Hillock AB44 . . .141 D6
Chapel La 3 Banff AB45 . . . .8 F8
Portsoy AB45 . . . . .139 E6
1 Turriff AB53 . . . . .145 D4
Chapel of Garioch Prim Sch
AB51 . . . . .73 C7
Chapel Pk 1 AB53 . . . . . . .22 C1
Chapel Pl 1 DD10 . . . . . .189 D3
Chapel Rd
Cruden Bay AB42 . . . . .53 A3
Stonehaven AB39 . . . . .181 I4
Turriff AB53 . . . . .22 C1
Chapel St
Aberdeen AB10 . . . . .165 A1
5 Banff AB45 . . . . .8 F8
Huntly AB54 . . . . .148 D5
Montrose DD10 . . . . .189 D3
Peterhead AB42 . . . . .147 E5
Portsoy AB45 . . . . .139 E6
Turriff AB53 . . . . .145 D4
Chapel Wlk AB54 . . . . .68 F4
Chapelhill Pl 2 AB41 . . .151 D3
Chapelhill Rd
Ellon AB41 . . . . .151 C4
Fraserburgh AB43 . . . . . . .143 B6
Chapelhill Terr 1 AB41 .151 D3
Charles Gdns AB51 . . . . .152 C7
Charles Pl AB51 . . . . .152 C7
Charles St
Aberdeen AB25 . . . . .165 B3
Fraserburgh AB43 . . . . .15 D6
Insch AB52 . . . . .149 C5
Inverallochy AB43 . . . . .15 C8
Charleston Circ AB12 . .176 A5
Charleston Ave AB12 . . .176 A6
Charleston Cres AB12 . .176 A6
Charleston Dr AB12 . . . .175 F6
Charleston Gdns
AB12 . . . . .176 A6
Charleston Gr AB12 . . . .176 A5
Charleston Pl AB12 . . . .176 A6
Charleston Rd AB12 . . . .176 A6
Charleston View AB12 . .175 F5
Charleston Way AB12 . . .176 A6
Charlestown Rd AB34 . . .183 C4
Charlestown Sch
AB12 . . . . .176 A6
Charleton Pk 3 DD10 . . .189 D7
Charleton Pl DD10 . . . . .189 D7
Charleton Rd DD10 . . . . .189 D7
Charlotte Gdns 2 AB25 .190 A4
Charlotte La AB43 . . . . . .143 C7
Charlotte Pl AB25 . . . . . .190 A4
Charlotte St
Aberdeen AB25 . . . . .190 A4
Fraserburgh AB43 . . . . . . .143 C6
Peterhead AB42 . . . . .147 E5
Charlton Ave AB34 . . . . .183 B5
Charlton Cres AB34 . . . . .183 B5
Charter La AB30 . . . . . . .186 D6
Chattan Pl AB10 . . . . . . .169 F7
Checkbar AB12 . . . . .175 E3
Chelsea Pl 6 AB51 . . . . .152 D6
Chelsea Rd 5 AB51 . . . . .152 D6
Cherry Gr AB21 . . . . .156 B5
Cherry Rd AB16 . . . . .164 D4
Cherry Tree Rd AB31 . . .184 D6
Chestnut Pl AB41 . . . . . .151 C3
Chestnut Row AB25 . . . .164 F3
Chestnut Wlk AB41 . . . . . .76 C7
Chevron Cres AB42 . . . . .147 A5
Cheyne Rd AB24 . . . . . . .165 C6
Cheyne Wlk AB21 . . . . . .153 C6
Cheyne's Pl AB53 . . . . . .145 D4
Chievres Pl AB41 . . . . . .151 C3
Chievres Rd AB41 . . . . . .151 C3
Chisholm's La AB53 . . . .145 D5
Chris Anderson Stadium
AB24 . . . . .165 D5
Christian Watt Dr
AB43 . . . . .143 A4
Christie Cres AB39 . . . . .185 D4
Christie Ct 1 AB54 . . . . .148 E5
Christie Gdns AB54 . . . . .148 E5
Christie's La DD10 . . . . .189 D3
Church Ave
Fraserburgh AB43 . . . . .26 D7
Insch AB52 . . . . .149 D5
Church Cres 4 AB53 . . . . .36 A5
Church La
7 Brechin DD9 . . . . .188 C3
18 Kemnay AB51 . . . . .87 D7
Peterhead AB42 . . . . .38 D6
6 Turriff AB53 . . . . .145 C5
Church Pl
12 Boddam AB42 . . . . .40 D1
New Pitsligo AB43 . . . . .23 D7
Church Rd Banff AB45 . . . . .3 C2
Laurencekirk AB30 . . . . . . .133 A7
Potterton AB23 . . . . .91 A6
Church St
Aberdeen AB24 . . . . .164 E6
Aberdeen AB11 . . . . .190 C3
Brechin DD9 . . . . .188 C3
Edzell DD9 . . . . .132 A8
3 Fordyce AB45 . . . . .1 F1
Huntly AB54 . . . . .148 D4
Insch AB52 . . . . .149 C5
Inverallochy AB43 . . . . .15 B8
Inverbervie DD10 . . . . .187 D7
Laurencekirk AB30 . . . . . . .186 D5
Macduff AB44 . . . . .141 C6
New Pitsligo AB43 . . . . .23 D6
Portsoy AB45 . . . . .139 D7
St Combs AB43 . . . . .15 D6
7 Turriff AB53 . . . . .145 C5
Church Terr
Aberdeen AB21 . . . . .156 B5
Fraserburgh AB43 . . . . . . .142 C8
Insch AB52 . . . . .149 D5
Turriff AB53 . . . . .145 C5
Churchhill Rd AB23 . . . . .160 B1
Churchill Dr AB42 . . . . . .147 D7
City Hospl AB24 . . . . . . .190 C4
City Moves Dance Space*
AB25 . . . . .190 A3
City Rd DD9 . . . . .188 C3
Clackriach Castle (remains of)* AB42 . . . . .36 F6
Claremont Gr AB10 . . . . .169 F7
Claremont Pl AB10 . . . . .169 F7
Claremont St AB10 . . . . .169 F7
Clarence St AB11 . . . . . .165 E1
Clarke St AB16 . . . . .164 C6
Clark's La AB24 . . . . .165 C6
Clashfarquhar Cres
AB12 . . . . .180 B6
Clashmach Dr AB54 . . . .148 C4
Clashmach Terr AB54 . . .148 C4
Clashmach View AB54 . .148 C4
Clashnettie Pl AB21 . . . .158 C6
Clashrodney Ave
AB12 . . . . .176 A6
Clashrodney Rd AB12 . . .176 B6
Clashrodney Way
AB12 . . . . .176 A6
Clashrodney Wlk
AB12 . . . . .176 A6
Clatt Prim Sch AB54 . . . . .56 B1
Claymore Ave
Aberdeen AB23 . . . . .160 C3
Portlethen AB12 . . . . .180 C7
Claymore Dr AB23 . . . . . .160 B2
Clergy St AB44 . . . . .141 D6
Clerk St DD9 . . . . .188 C3
Clerkhill Pl 2 AB42 . . . . .147 C4
Clerkhill Prim Sch
AB42 . . . . .147 B5
Clerkhill Rd AB42 . . . . . .147 B4
Cliff Pk AB15 . . . . .168 F4
Cliff View AB39 . . . . .181 H4
Clifton La AB24 . . . . . . .164 F5
Clifton Pl AB24 . . . . .164 F5
Clifton Rd
Aberdeen AB24 . . . . .164 D6
Turriff AB53 . . . . .145 D4
Clinterty Aberdeen Coll
AB21 . . . . .156 C3
Clinton Cres AB43 . . . . . . .23 E6
Clinton Dr AB43 . . . . .5 A4
Clinton Pl
Fraserburgh AB43 . . . . .5 A4
2 New Pitsligo AB43 . . . . . .23 E6
Clipper Pl DD10 . . . . .187 D7
Cloghill Pl 2 AB16 . . . . . .163 F2
Clova Cres AB15 . . . . . . .162 E3
Clova Pk AB15 . . . . .162 E3
Clover Cl AB43 . . . . .143 C7
Clover Mdw AB32 . . . . . .161 B3
Clover Yd 1 DD10 . . . . . .187 D3
Cloverfield Cl AB21 . . . .163 D8
Cloverfield Ct AB21 . . . .163 C8
Cloverfield Gdns
AB21 . . . . .163 D8
Cloverfield Pl AB21 . . . .163 C8
Cloverhill Cres AB22 . . . .159 E1
Cloverhill Rd AB23 . . . . .160 A1
Clune View AB31 . . . . . . .111 C2
Clunie Pl AB16 . . . . .164 A4
Clunie St AB45 . . . . .140 F6
Cluniebank Rd AB35 . . . .113 F5
Cluny Crichton Castle (remains of)* AB31 . . . .109 E6
Cluny Prim Sch AB51 . . . .87 A3
Clyde St AB11 . . . . .190 C2
Cobban's La 2 AB51 . . . .152 D6
Cobden St DD10 . . . . . . .189 D2

Codona's Amusement Pk* AB24 165 E2
Coldhome St 1 AB45 140 F6
Coldstone Ave AB15 162 E3
Coll Wlk AB16 163 E2
College Bounds
Aberdeen AB24 165 B5
Fraserburgh AB43 143 C7
College St AB11 190 A3
Colleonard Cres AB45 140 E4
Colleonard Dr AB45 140 E4
Colleonard Rd AB45 140 D4
Colleonard Sculpture Gdn & Gall* AB45 140 D3
Collieburn Cres AB42 147 C7
Collieston Ave AB23 159 F3
Collieston Circ AB22 159 E3
Collieston Cres AB23 159 F3
Collieston Dr 2 AB23 159 F2
Collieston Path AB22 159 E3
Collieston Pl AB22 159 E2
Collieston Rd AB22 159 E2
Collieston St 1 AB22 159 F2
Collieston Way AB23 159 F3
Colonsay Cres 4 AB16 163 E2
Colpy Rd Ind Est AB51 150 A3
Colpy Way AB51 150 B3
Colquhonnie Castle (remains of)* AB36 81 C3
Colsea Rd AB12 176 C6
Colsea Terr AB12 176 C6
Colthill Circ AB13 173 B8
Colthill Cres AB13 167 C1
Colthill Dr AB13 173 B8
Colthill Rd AB13 167 C1
Colville Pl AB24 165 C3
Commerce La
Aberdeen AB11 190 C3
2 Fraserburgh AB43 143 D6
Commerce St
Aberdeen AB11 190 C3
Brechin DD9 188 D3
Fraserburgh AB43 143 D6
Insch AB52 149 D4
8 Montrose DD10 189 C2
Commercial La 1 AB51 152 D6
Commercial Quay AB11 190 B2
Commercial Rd
Ellon AB41 151 B5
Insch AB52 149 C4
Inverurie AB51 152 E4
Oldmeldrum AB51 150 B2
Commercial St AB44 141 D7
Concert Ct AB10 190 B3
Concraig Gdns AB15 163 A4
Concraig Pk AB15 163 A4
Concraig Pl AB15 163 A4
Condor Cres DD10 189 D7
Conglass Ave AB51 152 A7
Conglass Ct AB51 152 A8
Conglass Dr AB51 152 A8
Conglass Gdns AB51 152 A8
Conglass Gr 3 AB51 152 A7
Conglass Pl AB51 152 A8
Conglass Rd AB51 152 A8
Conglass Way AB51 152 A8
Conglass Wlk 1 AB51 152 A7
Coningham Gdns AB24 165 A6
Coningham Rd AB24 165 A6
Coningham Terr AB24 165 A6
Constitution La AB11 190 C4
Constitution St
Aberdeen AB24 190 C4
Inverurie AB51 152 D6
Peterhead AB42 147 D5
Contlaw Brae AB13 173 B8
Contlaw Pl AB13 173 B8
Contlaw Rd AB13 167 A2
Conveners Wynd DD9 188 B3
Conveth Pk AB30 186 D6
Conveth Pl AB30 186 D6
Conzie Castle (remains of)* AB54 31 B3
Cookston Cres DD9 188 C4
Cookston Rd
Aberdeen AB12 180 D6
Brechin DD9 188 C5
Portlethen AB12 180 C6
Cooper's Brae 10 AB42 38 D6
Cooper's Ct AB41 151 D4
Copeman Ave AB42 147 B4
Copeman Pl AB42 147 B4
Coplandhill Cres AB42 147 B6
Coplandhill Pl 1 AB42 147 A5
Coplandhill Rd AB42 147 B6
Coral Gdns AB42 147 A4
Corbie Dr AB43 143 C4
Cordiner Ct 4 AB42 147 E6
Cordyce Residential Sch AB21 158 C8
Cordyce View AB21 158 A6
Corgarff Castle* AB36 92 D7
Corgarff Prim Sch AB36 92 F7
Cormack Pl 1 AB21 153 C6
Corn Rd AB43 15 B7
Corndavon Terr AB16 164 B3
Cornfield Pl AB53 145 D5
Cornfield Rd AB53 145 D5
Cornhill Dr AB16 164 D4
Cornhill Gdns AB16 164 D4
Cornhill Prim Sch AB16 164 D4
Cornhill Rd
Aberdeen AB25 164 E3
Huntly AB54 144 C5
Cornhill Sh Arc AB16 164 D4
Cornhill Sq AB16 164 D4
Cornhill Terr AB16 164 D3
Cornhill Way AB16 164 D3
Cornyhaugh Rd AB14 172 C7
Coronation Ave DD10 189 C8
Coronation Rd AB14 172 E6
Coronation Way DD10 189 C7
Correction Wynd 5 AB11 190 B3
Corrennie Circ AB21 158 B8
Corrichie Pl AB31 184 E5
Corse Ave AB15 162 E4
Corse Castle (remains of)* AB31 97 D6
Corse Gdns AB15 162 E4
Corse The AB43 26 C7
Corse Wynd AB15 162 F4
Corseduick Pk 1 AB21 153 D5
Corseduick Rd AB21 153 D5
Corsee Hill AB31 184 B4
Corsee Rd AB31 184 A5
Corsehill Gdns AB22 159 F1
Corsekelly Pl AB43 15 D5
Corskie Dr
Aberchirder AB54 144 D5
Macduff AB44 141 D5
Corskie Pl AB44 141 D5
Corsman Gdns 3 AB51 152 C4
Cortes Cres AB43 143 B5
Corthan Cres AB12 170 B4
Corthan Dr AB12 170 C3
Corthan Pl AB12 170 B4
Corunna Pl AB23 160 B1
Corunna Rd AB23 165 D8
Cothal View AB21 158 A8
Cottage Brae AB10 170 A7
Cottages Hall AB54 29 C3
Cotton St AB11 190 C4
Cottown of Balgownie AB23 165 C8
Coubert Rd AB21 153 C6
Coull Gdns
Aberdeen AB22 165 B8
Kingswells AB15 162 E3
Coull Gn AB15 162 E3
Countesswells Ave AB15 169 A6
Countesswells Cres AB15 169 A6
Countesswells Pl AB15 169 A6
Countesswells Rd AB15 168 E5
Countesswells Terr AB15 169 A6
Couper's Rd
Auchenblae AB30 124 A1
Banchory AB31 111 B6
Laurencekirk AB30 128 D4
Courtyard The AB32 161 C2
Cove Circ AB12 176 C6
Cove Cl AB12 176 B6
Cove Cres AB12 176 B6
Cove Gdns AB12 176 C6
Cove Path AB12 176 C6
Cove Pl AB12 176 C6
Cove Rd AB12 175 F5
Cove Way AB12 176 B6
Cove Wlk AB12 176 B6
Cove Wynd AB12 176 B6
Covenanters Dr AB12 170 B4
Covenanters Row AB12 170 A4
Cowan Den AB53 145 E4
Cowgate
Inverbervie DD10 187 E7
Oldmeldrum AB51 150 C3
Stonehaven AB39 185 F3
Cowie Cres AB42 27 B3
Cowie Gdns 2 AB43 26 C7
Cowie La AB39 185 E5
Cowie Wynd 15 AB31 108 E8
Craibstone Ave AB21 158 B3
Craibstone Coll of Ag AB21 157 E2
Craibstone La AB11 190 A2
Craig Gdns AB15 168 C2
Craig House* DD10 138 C2
Craig Lea 1 AB51 87 C6
Craig Pl Aberdeen AB11 190 B1
Stonehaven AB39 181 I4
Craig Rd DD10 189 C1
Craigarbel Cres DD10 187 E6
Craigbank AB51 155 B5
Craigden AB15 163 F1
Craigearn Bsns Pk AB51 155 B2
Craigellie Circ AB43 143 A3
Craigen Terr AB45 3 C2
Craigend Rd AB41 151 A6
Craigendarroch Ave AB16 164 B4
Craigendarroch Circ AB35 182 D5
Craigendarroch Pl AB16 164 B4
Craigendarroch Wlk AB35 182 D5
Craigendinnie Cres AB34 183 B4
Craigewan Cres AB42 147 C6
Craighall Cres AB41 151 D4
Craighead Ave AB12 180 B6
Craighead Dr AB54 148 C4
Craighill Prim Sch AB12 170 A2
Craigie Loanings AB25 164 F1
Craigie Pk AB25 164 F1
Craigie Pk Pl AB25 164 F1
Craigie St AB25 190 A4
Craigiebuckler Ave AB15 169 A7
Craigiebuckler Dr AB15 169 A7
Craigiebuckler Pl AB15 169 A7
Craigiebuckler Terr AB15 169 B7
Craigieburn Pk AB15 169 B6
Craigielea Ave AB15 169 D6
Craigielea Mews AB15 169 D6
Craigievar Castle (NTS)* AB33 97 E8
Craigievar Cres
Aberdeen AB10 169 D3
Ellon AB41 151 E6
Craigievar Gdns AB10 169 D3
Craigievar Pl AB10 169 D4
Craigievar Prim Sch AB33 84 F1
Craigievar Rd AB10 169 E3
Craigievar Terr AB10 169 E3
Craigmarn Rd AB12 180 E5
Craigmaroinn Gdns AB12 176 B8
Craigmyle Rd AB31 108 E8
Craignabo Rd AB42 147 C3
Craigneen Pl 1 AB45 8 F8
Craignook Rd AB21 158 C7
Craigo Prim Sch DD10 133 D2
Craigour Ave 18 AB31 108 E8
Craigour Rd AB31 108 E8
Craigpark AB12 170 D3
Craigpark Circ AB41 151 A6
Craigpark Pl AB41 151 A6
Craigs Rd AB41 151 A6
Craigshaw Bsns Pk AB12 170 D4
Craigshaw Cres AB12 170 D4
Craigshaw Dr AB12 170 C4
Craigshaw Pl AB12 170 C4
Craigshaw Rd AB12 170 C4
Craigshaw St AB12 170 C3
Craigston Ave AB41 151 E5
Craigston Castle* AB53 21 E6
Craigston Gdns AB32 161 F4
Craigston Pl AB32 161 F4
Craigston Rd AB32 161 F4
Craigton Ave AB15 169 C5
Craigton Brae AB31 98 A3
Craigton Cres
Aberdeen AB14 172 D6
1 Banchory AB31 98 A3
Craigton Ct AB10 169 D5
Craigton Dr AB14 172 D6
Craigton Gr AB14 172 D6
Craigton Pk AB15 169 C5
Craigton Rd AB15 169 A4
Craigton Terr
Aberdeen AB15 169 C5
Aberdeen AB14 172 D6
Craigview DD10 187 E7
Craigview Pl AB35 182 E5
Craigview Rd AB35 182 E5
Cramond Terr AB45 140 E5
Cranford Rd AB10 169 E5
Cranford Terr AB10 169 D5
Cranhill Brae AB39 181 I4
Cranhill Pl AB39 181 I5
Cranna View
Huntly AB54 144 E5
Turriff AB53 19 D0
Crathes Castle, Gdn & Est (NTS)* AB31 110 D3
Crathes Pl AB41 151 E5
Crathes Prim Sch AB31 110 D5
Crathie Prim Sch AB35 102 E2
Crathie Terr AB10 170 A5
Crawford Pl 2 AB51 47 A2
Crawpeel Rd AB12 170 D1
Crawton Ness AB12 176 B8
Creel Ave AB12 176 B6
Creel Ct AB12 176 B5
Creel Dr AB12 176 B6
Creel Gdns AB12 176 B6
Creel Pl AB12 176 B5
Creel Rd AB12 176 A5
Creel Wlk AB12 176 B6
Creel Wynd AB12 176 B5
Crescent The AB53 36 A6
Crichie Circ AB51 152 E2
Crimon Pl AB10 190 A3
Crimond Ct AB43 143 C4
Crimond Prim Sch AB43 26 D7
Croft Pl Aberdeen AB16 164 A3
St Cyrus DD10 134 D3
Croft Rd
Aberdeen AB16 164 A2
4 Kemnay AB51 87 D7
Montrose DD10 189 B1
St Cyrus DD10 134 D3
Stonehaven AB39 125 B3
Croft Terr AB16 164 A3
Croftland 4 AB41 62 B2
Croftlands DD10 134 D3
Crollshillock AB39 181 H4
Crollshillock Pl AB39 181 H4
Cromar Cres AB34 96 B3
Cromar Dr 3 AB34 96 C3
Cromar Gdns AB15 162 F3
Cromarty View 1 AB45 140 E6
Crombie Acres AB32 161 B3
Crombie Castle* AB54 18 E3
Crombie Circ AB14 172 C7
Crombie Cirlce AB32 161 C3
Crombie Cl AB32 161 C3
Crombie Dr AB32 161 B3
Crombie Pl
Aberdeen AB11 170 E7
Westhill AB32 161 B3
Crombie Prim Sch AB32 161 D3
Crombie Rd
Aberdeen AB11 190 C1
Westhill AB32 161 B3
Crombie Wynd AB32 161 B3
Cromlet Pk AB51 48 A1
Cromlet Pl AB51 150 D3
Cromwell Gdns AB15 169 D7
Cromwell Rd AB15 169 D7
Crook O'Ness St AB44 141 C7
Crooked La
Aberdeen AB25 190 A4
1 Peterhead AB42 147 F5
5 Turriff AB53 145 D4
Crookfold Gdns AB23 160 A1
Crookfold Pl AB23 160 A1
Cross St
Fraserburgh AB43 143 D7
5 Turriff AB53 145 C4
Cross The 2 AB39 185 F4
Crossfolds Cres AB42 147 B6
Crossgates AB21 158 C1
Crossroads of Braiklay AB41 48 F2
Crossroads Prim Sch AB31 110 F1
Crown Alley AB30 186 C5
Crown Cres AB14 172 E7
Crown La
Aberdeen AB11 190 A2
Turriff AB53 145 D4
Crown Pl AB14 172 D7
Crown St
Aberdeen AB11 190 A1
Turriff AB53 145 D4
Crown Terr
Aberdeen AB11 190 A2
Peterculter AB14 172 E6
Cruden Cres AB16 163 F5
Cruden Pk AB16 163 F5
Cruden Pl AB16 163 F5
Cruden Terr AB39 185 C4
Crudie Sch (Primary) AB53 22 C8
Cruickshank Cres
Aberdeen AB21 163 E7
Aberdeen AB12 170 A2
Cruickshank Ct AB32 161 B2
Cruickshank Pk 7 DD10 138 C8
Cruikshank Botanic Gdns* AB24 165 B6
Cryne Corse Rd
Banchory AB31 119 A6
Stonehaven AB39 124 F8
Cullen House* AB56 1 A4
Cullen Prim Sch AB56 1 B4
Cullen St AB53 139 D7
Cullerlie Farm Pk* AB32 100 E2
Culsh Terr AB53 36 A6
Culstruphan Rd AB36 81 E7
Culter Den AB14 172 C6
Culter House Rd
Aberdeen AB13 173 B7
Milltimber/Aberdeen AB13 172 F8
Culter Prim Sch AB14 172 E6
Culter Sports Ctr The AB14 172 E6
Cultercullen Prim Sch AB41 76 E7
Cults Acad AB15 168 D3
Cults Ave AB15 168 D3
Cults Bsns Pk AB15 168 F3
Cults Gdns AB15 168 E3
Cults Prim Sch AB15 168 C3
Cuminestown Rd AB53 47 E5
Cummings Pk Circ AB16 164 C4
Cummings Pk Cres AB16 164 B5
Cummings Pk Dr AB16 164 B6
Cummings Pk Rd AB16 164 C6
Cummings Pk Terr AB16 164 B5
Cuninghill Ave AB51 152 D4
Cuninghill Rd AB51 152 D4
Cunninghar Rd AB21 153 C5
Cuparstone La AB10 170 A8
Cuparstone Row AB10 170 A7
Curlew Ave 13 AB41 77 F8
Cypress Ave AB23 160 A5
Cypress Gr AB23 160 A5
Cypress Wlk AB23 159 F5

D

Dales Ct AB42 147 B4
Dales Ind Est AB42 147 A1
Dales Pk Prim Sch AB42 147 A3
Dales Rd 2 AB42 147 C2
Dales View Dr AB42 147 A3
Dales View Pl AB42 147 A3
Dalhousie St
Brechin DD9 188 D3
Edzell DD9 132 A7
Dall's La DD9 188 E2
Dalmaik Cres AB14 172 D7
Dalmaik Terr AB14 172 D7
Dalmuinzie Rd AB15 168 A2
Dalrymple Circ AB21 156 B6
Dalrymple Hall & Arts Ctr* AB43 143 E6
Dalrymple St AB43 143 D6
Dalvenie Rd AB31 184 D5
Damacre Rd DD9 188 C3
Damfield Rd AB43 143 C3
Damhead Ind Est AB42 147 A1
Damhead Way AB42 147 B1
Dancingcairns Cres AB16 164 A6
Dancingcairns Pl AB16 164 B7
Danestone Circ AB16 164 C6
Danestone Pl AB23 165 C8
Danestone Prim Sch AB22 159 B1
Danestone Terr AB23 165 C8
Darroch Ct AB35 182 C4
Daun Wlk 4 AB51 87 C6
Davah Rd AB51 152 C5
Davan Pk 1 AB22 165 B8
Davan Pl AB41 151 B6
David McLean Dr AB33 154 C4
David St
Inverbervie DD10 187 E6
Stonehaven AB39 185 E5
Davids La AB51 152 D5
Davidson Cres AB33 154 C3
Davidson Dr
Aberdeen AB16 163 F5
Inverurie AB51 152 B8
Mintlaw AB42 146 E4
Davidson Gdns AB16 163 F5
Davidson Pl
Aberdeen AB16 163 F5
Inverurie AB51 152 B8
St Cyrus DD10 134 D3
Davidston House* AB55 28 C4
Davies Castle Fort* AB56 6 B7
Daviot Prim Sch AB51 59 F3
Dawson Cl AB32 161 B3
Dawson Dr AB32 161 B3
Dawson Wynd AB32 161 B3
Dean Gdns AB32 161 F3
Deans Well AB21 156 B7
Deansloch Cres AB16 164 A5
Deansloch Pl 1 AB16 164 A5
Deansloch Terr AB16 164 A5
Dee Bank Rd AB35 182 D3
Dee La AB31 184 C4
Dee Pl AB11 190 A2
Dee St Aberdeen AB11 190 A2
3 Aboyne AB34 108 B6
Ballater AB35 182 D4
Banchory AB31 184 C3
Deemount Ave AB11 170 C6
Deemount Gdns AB11 170 C6
Deemount Rd AB11 170 B6
Deemount Terr AB11 170 B6
Deer Abbey (remains of)* AB42 37 D7
Deer Rd AB24 164 E6
Deer Rd E AB42 36 E6
Deer Rd W AB42 36 D6
Deeside Ave AB15 169 D4
Deeside Cres AB15 169 C4
Deeside Dr AB15 169 C4
Deeside Gdns AB15 169 C4
Deeside Pk AB15 169 D4
Deeside Pl AB15 169 C4
Deeside Terr AB15 169 C4
Deevale Cres AB12 170 A3
Deevale Gdns AB12 170 A3
Deevale Rd AB12 170 A3
Deevale Terr AB12 170 A3
Deeview Gdns AB31 111 D5
Deeview Rd AB31 184 D5
Deeview Rd S AB15 168 E2
Delgatie Castle* AB53 21 D1
Delgaty Cres AB53 145 E4
Delgaty La AB21 158 B7
Delgaty Terr AB53 145 E5
Dempsey Terr 3 AB24 165 A6
Den of Cults AB15 168 F2
Den of Maidencraig Nature Reserve* AB15 163 E1
Den The AB15 168 F2
Den View AB21 156 A7
Denburn Rd AB10 190 A3
Denburn Way DD9 188 D2
Denhead Cres AB23 91 A6
Denmark St AB43 143 D7
Denmore Gdns AB22 165 B8
Denmore Ind Est AB23 160 B4
Denmore Pl AB23 160 A4
Denmore Rd AB23 160 A4
Dennis Dr DD9 132 D8
Dennis Roger La 1 AB39 185 C5

Dennyduff Rd AB43 . . . 143 B6
Denstrath Rd DD9 . . . 132 D8
Denstrath View DD9 . . . 132 C8
Denview Cres AB23 . . . 91 A6
Denview Rd AB23 . . . 91 A6
Denwell Rd
Insch AB52 . . . 149 D6
Keith AB55 . . . 28 D8
Denwood AB15 . . . 163 F1
Depot Rd AB54 . . . 148 C4
Derbeth Cres AB16 . . . 163 E2
Derbeth Grange AB15 . . . 162 F5
Derbeth Manor AB15 . . . 163 A5
Derbeth Pk AB15 . . . 162 F4
Derbeth Pl AB15 . . . 162 F5
Derbeth Wlk AB15 . . . 162 F5
Derbyhall Ave AB43 . . . 143 C4
Derry Ave AB16 . . . 164 B3
Derry Pl AB16 . . . 164 B3
Desswood Pl AB25 . . . 164 E1
Devanha Cres AB11 . . . 190 A1
Devanha Gdns AB11 . . . 190 A1
Devanha Gdns E AB11 . . . 190 A1
Devanha Gdns W
AB11 . . . 190 A1
Devanha La AB11 . . . 190 A1
Devanha Terr AB11 . . . 190 B1
Devanna Gdns S AB11 . . . 170 B6
Devenick Dr AB12 . . . 180 C7
Devenick Pl AB10 . . . 169 D3
Deveron Rd
Aberdeen AB16 . . . 164 A4
Huntly AB54 . . . 148 C5
Turriff AB53 . . . 145 A5
Deveron St
Huntly AB54 . . . 148 D5
Turriff AB53 . . . 145 B5
Deveron Terr AB45 . . . 140 F5
Deveronside AB45 . . . 141 A6
Deveronside Dr AB53 . . . 145 B5
Devil's Folly AB52 . . . 58 B6
Devonshire Rd AB10 . . . 169 E7
Dewey Ct DD9 . . . 132 D8
Deyhill AB44 . . . 141 E6
Diamond La AB10 . . . 190 A3
Diamond Pl 3 AB10 . . . 190 A3
Diamond St AB10 . . . 190 A3
Dickie Dr
4 Fraserburgh AB43 . . . 26 C7
Peterhead AB42 . . . 147 C7
Dickson Ave 8 DD10 . . . 138 C8
Dickson Terr AB16 . . . 163 F4
Dill Pl AB24 . . . 164 F7
Dill Rd AB24 . . . 164 F7
Dinbaith Pl 4 AB16 . . . 163 F2
Dingwall Dr AB42 . . . 147 D7
Dingwall St AB43 . . . 142 B8
Dinnie Pl AB51 . . . 155 B6
Disblair Ave AB21 . . . 153 C5
Disblair Rd AB21 . . . 153 C5
Distillery Rd
Brechin DD9 . . . 188 C4
Laurencekirk AB30 . . . 128 A4
Oldmeldrum AB51 . . . 150 C4
Dock Bldgs 6 DD10 . . . 189 D2
Dock St DD10 . . . 135 C5
Dock St E AB11 . . . 170 E8
Dock St W AB11 . . . 170 E8
Doctor Lang Pl DD9 . . . 188 B5
Dominies Rd AB24 . . . 164 D5
Don Cres AB51 . . . 152 D4
Don Ct AB24 . . . 164 E7
Don Gdns AB24 . . . 164 E7
Don Pl Aberdeen AB24 . . . 164 F6
Dyce AB21 . . . 158 B6
Don St Aberdeen AB24 . . . 164 F6
Aberdeen AB24 . . . 165 B6
Don Terr AB24 . . . 164 E7
Don View Rd 17 AB51 . . . 87 D7
Donald Ave 6 AB51 . . . 87 C6
Donald Dewar Ct
AB16 . . . 163 F4
Donald Gordon Ct 1
AB51 . . . 150 C2
Donaldson Ct 2 AB54 . . . 148 E5
Donbank Pl AB24 . . . 164 F7
Donbank Prim Sch
AB24 . . . 165 A7
Donbank Terr AB24 . . . 164 F7
Donmouth Cres AB23 . . . 165 D8
Donmouth Ct AB23 . . . 165 D8
Donmouth Gdns AB23 . . . 165 D8
Donmouth Nature Reserve*
AB24 . . . 165 E7
Donmouth Rd AB23 . . . 165 D7
Donmouth Terr AB23 . . . 165 D7
Donside Rd AB33 . . . 154 C4
Donview Gdns 2 AB51 . . . 87 C6
Donview Pl AB24 . . . 164 F7
Donview Rd AB24 . . . 164 F7
Doo'cot Pk AB45 . . . 140 E4
Doolie Ness AB12 . . . 176 B8
Doonies Rare Breads Farm*
AB12 . . . 171 A3
Dorward Pl DD10 . . . 189 D4
Dorward Rd DD10 . . . 189 D4
Double Dykes DD9 . . . 188 A4
Douglas Cl AB42 . . . 147 A7
Douglas Cres AB42 . . . 147 A7
Doune Cres AB44 . . . 141 D5
Dounepark Rd AB45 . . . 141 F2
Dovewells Dr DD9 . . . 188 B4
Downie Way
1 Hillside DD10 . . . 138 D8
3 Kemnay AB51 . . . 87 D7
Downies Brae AB11 . . . 170 E6
Downies Pl AB11 . . . 170 E6
Dowrie Pl 2 AB30 . . . 128 A4
Drinnies Cres AB21 . . . 158 C7
Drinnie's Wood Obsy*
AB42 . . . 37 D8
Drive The DD9 . . . 132 A7
Drostan Dr AB42 . . . 146 E4
Drum Castle, Gdn & Est
(NTS)* AB31 . . . 111 D7
Drum Wynd 3 AB41 . . . 151 E5
Drumachlie Loan DD9 . . . 188 E2
Drumachlie Pk DD9 . . . 188 E2
Drumblade Prim Sch
AB54 . . . 44 D6
Druminnor Castle*
AB54 . . . 55 F1
Drummer's Cnr Sh Ctr
AB42 . . . 147 E5
Drumoak Prim Sch
AB31 . . . 111 D6
Drumrossie St AB52 . . . 149 D5
Drum's La AB25 . . . 190 B3
Drum's Pk* AB53 . . . 47 E5
Drumthwacket Dr
AB12 . . . 180 A4
Drumtochty Castle*
AB30 . . . 123 F3
Drumview Cres AB14 . . . 166 D1
Drumview Rd AB14 . . . 166 D1
Dubford Ave AB23 . . . 159 F4
Dubford Cres AB23 . . . 159 F4
Dubford Gdns AB23 . . . 159 F5
Dubford Gr AB23 . . . 159 F5
Dubford Pk AB23 . . . 159 F3
Dubford Pl AB23 . . . 159 F4
Dubford Rd AB23 . . . 159 F4
Dubford Rise AB23 . . . 159 F5
Dubford Terr AB23 . . . 159 F4
Dubford Wlk AB23 . . . 159 F5
Dubton Rd DD10 . . . 138 C7
Duff Dr 3 AB51 . . . 150 C2
Duff House* AB45 . . . 141 A4
Duff St Aberdeen AB24 . . . 190 C4
Macduff AB44 . . . 141 D6
Turriff AB53 . . . 145 C4
Duff Terr AB45 . . . 7 E1
Dugald Baird Sq AB12 . . . 170 A1
Duke La AB43 . . . 143 D7
Duke St Brechin DD9 . . . 188 B4
Fraserburgh AB43 . . . 143 D7
Huntly AB54 . . . 148 D4
Laurencekirk AB30 . . . 128 B4
Peterhead AB42 . . . 25 C1
Stonehaven AB39 . . . 185 E5
Dulnain Rd AB16 . . . 163 F3
Dumgoyne Pl AB15 . . . 164 B1
Dun Prim Sch DD10 . . . 137 E7
Dunbar St AB24 . . . 165 C5
Dunbar Terr AB54 . . . 148 C4
Dunbennan Rd AB21 . . . 158 C7
Duncan Cres AB42 . . . 147 C6
Duncan Pl AB41 . . . 151 B3
Duncan Rd AB34 . . . 96 B3
Duncan St AB45 . . . 140 E6
Dundarg Castle (remains
of)* AB43 . . . 12 F7
Dundarg Rd AB43 . . . 142 C7
Dundarroch Rd AB35 . . . 182 C4
Dundas Pk DD9 . . . 188 E3
Dundas Rd AB43 . . . 15 B7
Dundonnie St 3 AB42 . . . 40 D1
Dunecht Gdns AB32 . . . 161 C3
Dunecht Prim Sch
AB32 . . . 100 E8
Dunecht Rd AB32 . . . 161 C3
Dungeith Ave AB31 . . . 184 B4
Dunlappie Rd DD9 . . . 132 A7
Dunlin Cres AB12 . . . 176 B7
Dunlin Rd
Aberdeen AB21 . . . 157 E5
Aberdeen AB12 . . . 176 B8
Dunlugas Pl 1 AB53 . . . 145 C6
Dunmail Ave AB15 . . . 168 E2
Dunninald Castle*
DD10 . . . 138 C1
Dunnottar Ave 13 AB39 . . . 185 E4
Dunnottar Castle*
AB39 . . . 126 F6
Dunnottar Rd AB41 . . . 151 E5
Dunnottar Sch AB39 . . . 185 F4
Dunnydeer Gdns
AB52 . . . 149 C5
Dunnydeer Pk AB52 . . . 149 C5
Dunnydeer View AB52 . . . 149 C5
Dunnyfell Rd AB39 . . . 181 G2
Dunrossie Cres DD10 . . . 189 A5
Dunrossie Terr DD10 . . . 189 A6
Dunvegan Ave AB12 . . . 180 B6
Dunvegan Cres AB12 . . . 180 B6
Dunvegan Pl
Ellon AB41 . . . 151 E5
Portlethen AB12 . . . 180 B6
Durie Pl DD9 . . . 132 B7
Duriehill Rd DD9 . . . 132 B7
Durn Ave AB45 . . . 139 D5
Durn Dr AB45 . . . 139 D5
Durn Rd AB45 . . . 139 D5
Durno Pk AB32 . . . 101 E6
Durris Prim Sch AB31 . . . 111 C2
Dutch Sch AB12 . . . 175 E8
Duthie Pl
Aberdeen AB10 . . . 169 D5
Fraserburgh AB43 . . . 143 D3
Duthie Rd AB41 . . . 61 E5
Duthie Terr
Aberdeen AB10 . . . 169 D5
Inverallochy AB43 . . . 15 B8
Duthie's La AB43 . . . 5 A4
Dyce Acad AB21 . . . 158 C6
Dyce Ave AB21 . . . 157 E5
Dyce Dr AB21 . . . 157 E8
Dyce Ind Pk AB21 . . . 158 B4
Dyce Prim Sch AB21 . . . 158 C6
Dyce Sh Ctr AB21 . . . 158 D6
Dyce Sta AB21 . . . 158 A6

E

Earl's Ct 6 AB42 . . . 40 D1
Earl's Ct Gdns AB15 . . . 169 D8
Earlspark Ave AB15 . . . 168 B3
Earlspark Circ AB15 . . . 168 B3
Earlspark Cres AB15 . . . 168 B3
Earlspark Dr AB15 . . . 168 B2
Earlspark Gdns AB15 . . . 168 B2
Earlspark Rd AB15 . . . 168 B2
Earlspark Way AB15 . . . 168 B3
Earlswells Dr AB15 . . . 168 C2
Earlswells Pl AB15 . . . 168 C2
Earlswells Rd AB15 . . . 168 C2
Earlswells View AB15 . . . 168 C2
Earlswells Wlk AB15 . . . 168 C2
Earn's Heugh Ave
AB12 . . . 176 B7
Earn's Heugh Circ
AB12 . . . 176 B7
Earn's Heugh Cres
AB12 . . . 176 B6
Earn's Heugh Pl AB12 . . . 176 B7
Earns Heugh Rd AB12 . . . 176 B7
Earns Heugh View
AB12 . . . 176 B7
Earns Heugh Way
AB12 . . . 176 B6
Earn's Heugh Wlk
AB12 . . . 176 B7
Earnsheugh Rd AB12 . . . 180 F8
Earnsheugh Terr
AB12 . . . 180 F8
East Church St AB45 . . . 1 F1
East Craibstone St 4
AB11 . . . 190 A2
East End DD10 . . . 187 D3
East Glebe AB39 . . . 185 D6
East Gn AB11 . . . 190 B3
East Main Ave AB16 . . . 164 B3
East Mill Rd DD9 . . . 188 E1
East North St
Aberdeen AB24 . . . 190 B4
Peterhead AB42 . . . 147 F5
East Park Rd AB51 . . . 155 C4
East St
Fraserburgh AB43 . . . 15 D6
Montrose DD10 . . . 135 C6
East Tullos Ind Est
AB12 . . . 170 D5
Eastbank DD9 . . . 188 C3
Eastburn Rd AB51 . . . 155 C4
Easter Ct AB12 . . . 180 B4
Easter Dr AB12 . . . 180 B4
Easter Pl AB12 . . . 180 B4
Easterfield Prim Sch
AB53 . . . 32 B4
Easterfield Rd AB53 . . . 145 E4
Eastern Rd 8 DD10 . . . 189 D3
Eastmill Brae DD9 . . . 188 E2
Eastpark St AB54 . . . 148 E5
Eastside Ave AB32 . . . 161 E3
Eastside Dr AB32 . . . 161 E4
Eastside Gdns AB21 . . . 157 F1
Eastside Gn AB32 . . . 161 E4
Eastsyde Pl AB12 . . . 180 A5
Eastwood Terr AB34 . . . 183 F5
Eavern Pl 2 AB51 . . . 150 B3
Ecclesgreig Rd DD10 . . . 134 C4
Echt Prim Sch AB32 . . . 100 E4
Eday Cres AB15 . . . 164 A2
Eday Dr AB15 . . . 163 F2
Eday Gdns AB15 . . . 163 E1
Eday Rd AB15 . . . 163 E2
Eday Sq AB15 . . . 163 F2
Eday Wlk AB15 . . . 163 F2
Eddie Ave DD9 . . . 188 C5
Eden Ct AB31 . . . 184 B4
Eden Dr AB42 . . . 147 B5
Eden Pl AB25 . . . 165 A2
Edgehill Rd AB15 . . . 164 C1
Edgehill Terr AB15 . . . 164 C1
Edgewood Pl AB34 . . . 183 B5
Edindiach Rd AB55 . . . 28 D8
Edingight Wynd 1
AB31 . . . 108 E8
Edinmore Dr AB51 . . . 59 E3
Edinview Gdns AB39 . . . 185 C6
Edmond Gdns AB15 . . . 162 F2
Edmondside 3 AB41 . . . 62 B2
Edward Ave AB45 . . . 140 E4
Edward Pl AB45 . . . 140 E4
Edzell Prim Sch DD9 . . . 132 A7
Eider Ct 2 AB42 . . . 147 B5
Eider Rd AB41 . . . 77 F8
Eigie Cres AB23 . . . 91 C8
Eigie Pk AB23 . . . 91 D8
Eigie Rd AB23 . . . 91 C8
Eigie View AB23 . . . 91 D8
Eigie Wlk AB23 . . . 91 D8
Eilean Rise AB41 . . . 151 B3
Elder Pl AB25 . . . 164 F4
Elevenstones Prim Sch
AB35 . . . 113 F6
Elizabeth Cl 13 AB51 . . . 87 D7
Ellerslie Rd AB21 . . . 158 C1
Ellis St AB42 . . . 147 E5
Ellon Acad AB41 . . . 151 D5
Ellon Acad (annexe)
AB41 . . . 151 D5
Ellon Castle (remains of)*
AB41 . . . 151 E5
Ellon Prim Sch AB41 . . . 151 C5
Ellon Rd AB23 . . . 160 B1
Elm Pl Aberdeen AB25 . . . 164 F3
9 Balmedie AB23 . . . 91 C8
Elmbank Gdns AB51 . . . 150 B3
Elmbank Rd AB24 . . . 165 B3
Elmbank Terr AB24 . . . 165 A4
Elmfield Ave AB24 . . . 165 B4
Elmfield Pl AB24 . . . 165 A4
Elmfield Terr AB24 . . . 165 B4
Elms Rise AB31 . . . 184 C4
Elphin Hill AB41 . . . 151 C7
Elphin St AB43 . . . 12 E6
Elphinstone Rd
Aberdeen AB24 . . . 165 B5
Inverurie AB51 . . . 152 E4
Elrick Circ AB22 . . . 159 E1
Elrick Ctry Pk* AB21 . . . 157 A1
Elrick Gdns AB21 . . . 153 D5
Elrick Prim Sch AB32 . . . 161 D2
Elsick Pl AB39 . . . 181 H4
Endeavour Dr AB32 . . . 161 E1
Endrick Pl AB15 . . . 164 B1
Enterprise Dr AB32 . . . 161 D1
Eriskay Dr AB16 . . . 163 E2
Erroll Pl
Aberdeen AB24 . . . 165 C3
Turriff AB53 . . . 145 D4
Erroll Rd AB53 . . . 145 E4
Erroll St
Aberdeen AB24 . . . 165 C3
Peterhead AB42 . . . 147 E5
Errollston Rd AB42 . . . 53 B3
Erskine Pl 3 DD10 . . . 189 D2
Erskine St
Aberdeen AB24 . . . 165 A4
Montrose DD10 . . . 189 D2
Esk Pk DD9 . . . 188 D2
Esk Pl AB16 . . . 164 A4
Esk Rd DD10 . . . 189 B1
Eskview Terr DD10 . . . 189 C1
Espl The AB42 . . . 147 F6
Esplanade
Aberdeen AB24 . . . 165 D7
Fraserburgh AB43 . . . 143 E4
Essie Circ AB42 . . . 26 E6
Essie Rd AB54 . . . 55 C3
Esslemont Ave AB25 . . . 165 A1
Esslemont Circ AB41 . . . 151 A5
Esslemont Dr AB51 . . . 152 C5
Esslemont Sch AB41 . . . 62 E4
Evan St AB39 . . . 185 D4
Evolve Training & Con Ctr
AB21 . . . 158 B3
Exchange La AB11 . . . 190 B3
Exchange St AB11 . . . 190 B3
Exchequer Row AB11 . . . 190 B3
Exhibition Ave AB23 . . . 160 B1
Exploration Dr AB23 . . . 160 B2

F

Faburn Terr 3 AB31 . . . 98 A3
Fairfield Pl AB51 . . . 155 C5
Fairfield Rd DD10 . . . 187 D6
Fairlands AB51 . . . 152 A8
Fairley Rd
Aberdeen AB15 . . . 163 A1
Kingswells AB15 . . . 162 F2
Fairlie St AB16 . . . 164 C6
Fairney Bsns Pk AB43 . . . 143 A7
Fairview Ave AB22 . . . 159 B1
Fairview Brae AB22 . . . 164 E8
Fairview Circ AB22 . . . 159 A1
Fairview Cres AB22 . . . 159 C1
Fairview Dr AB22 . . . 164 E8
Fairview Gdns
Aberdeen AB22 . . . 159 A1
Inverurie AB51 . . . 152 C6
Fairview Gr 3 AB22 . . . 159 B1
Fairview Grange AB22 . . . 164 C8
Fairview Manor AB22 . . . 159 B1
Fairview Par AB22 . . . 159 B1
Fairview Pk 4 AB22 . . . 159 B1
Fairview Pl AB22 . . . 159 B1
Fairview Rd AB22 . . . 159 A1
Fairview St AB22 . . . 159 B1
Fairview Terr AB22 . . . 159 A1
Fairview Way AB22 . . . 159 B1
Fairview Wlk AB22 . . . 159 C1
Fairview Wynd AB22 . . . 159 C1
Fairway Ave AB51 . . . 152 C5
Fairwinds Pl AB42 . . . 147 A5
Faithlie St AB43 . . . 143 C6
Falconer Pl AB51 . . . 152 C6
Falkland Ave AB12 . . . 176 C7
Fallow Rd AB32 . . . 161 B3
Fara Cl AB15 . . . 163 E2
Farburn Dr AB39 . . . 185 C5
Farburn Ind Est AB21 . . . 158 C5
Farburn Terr AB21 . . . 158 A6
Fare Pk Circ AB32 . . . 161 D4
Fare Pk Cres AB32 . . . 161 E4
Fare Pk Dr AB32 . . . 161 D3
Fare Pk Gdns AB32 . . . 161 D3
Fare View 6 AB31 . . . 108 E8
Farmers Hall 1 AB25 . . . 190 A4
Farmers' La AB42 . . . 147 F5
Farnell Castle* DD9 . . . 137 A2
Farquhar Ave AB11 . . . 170 E6
Farquhar Brae AB11 . . . 170 E6
Farquhar Rd
Aberdeen AB11 . . . 170 E6
Huntly AB54 . . . 148 E5
Farquhar St
Inverbervie DD10 . . . 187 D6
Laurencekirk AB30 . . . 186 D5
Farrier La AB24 . . . 190 B4
Farrochie Gdns AB39 . . . 185 B6
Farrochie Pk AB39 . . . 185 B6
Farrochie Rd AB39 . . . 185 B6
Fassiefern Ave AB23 . . . 160 A3
Fatson's Rd AB43 . . . 143 C6
Faulds Cres
Aberdeen AB12 . . . 170 B4
Montrose DD10 . . . 189 E3
Faulds Gate AB12 . . . 170 A4
Faulds Rd DD10 . . . 189 E3
Faulds Row AB12 . . . 170 B3
Faulds Wynd AB12 . . . 170 B3
Fechil Pl AB41 . . . 151 D4
Fechnie Brae AB21 . . . 156 B6
Fedderate Castle (remains
of)* AB42 . . . 36 B8
Fergus Pl AB21 . . . 158 B7
Ferguson Ave DD9 . . . 188 D4
Ferguson Cres AB42 . . . 146 E5
Ferguson St AB42 . . . 25 C1
Fern Dr AB12 . . . 180 B5
Fern Pl AB12 . . . 180 B5
Fernhill Dr AB16 . . . 164 A3
Fernhill Pl AB16 . . . 164 A3
Fernhill Rd AB16 . . . 163 F2
Fernie Brae
Aberdeen AB11 . . . 170 D5
Banff AB45 . . . 3 B2
Fernie Pl AB43 . . . 143 C7
Fernie Rd AB43 . . . 143 C6
Fernielea Cres AB15 . . . 164 A1
Fernielea Pl AB15 . . . 164 A1
Fernielea Prim Sch
AB15 . . . 164 A1
Fernielea Rd
Aberdeen AB15 . . . 164 A1
Aberdeen AB15 . . . 169 A8
Ferrier Cres AB24 . . . 164 F6
Ferrier Gdns AB24 . . . 164 F6
Ferry Pl AB11 . . . 170 E8
Ferry Rd DD10 . . . 189 D2
Ferry St DD10 . . . 189 D2
Ferryhill Gdns AB11 . . . 190 A1
Ferryhill La AB11 . . . 190 A1
Ferryhill Pl AB11 . . . 190 A1
Ferryhill Prim Sch
AB11 . . . 190 A1
Ferryhill Rd AB11 . . . 190 A1
Ferryhill Terr AB11 . . . 190 A1
Fetach Wlk AB21 . . . 158 B7
Fetterangus Sch AB42 . . . 25 C2
Fettercairn Distillery*
AB30 . . . 128 A4
Fettercairn Prim Sch
AB30 . . . 128 A4
Fetteresso Castle*
AB39 . . . 126 B8
Fetteresso Terr AB39 . . . 185 D5
Fetternear House & Bishop's
Pal (remains of)*
AB51 . . . 87 C8
Fettes Way 7 DD10 . . . 189 D7
Feugh View AB31 . . . 117 D7
Fife Brae 2 AB35 . . . 113 F6
Fife St Banff AB45 . . . 140 F7
Macduff AB44 . . . 141 D6
Turriff AB53 . . . 145 D4
Fifehill Pk AB21 . . . 158 C6
Findhorn Dr 1 AB41 . . . 151 E6
Findhorn Pl 1 AB16 . . . 163 F3
Findlater Castle (remains
of)* AB45 . . . 1 D5
Findlater Dr AB56 . . . 1 B4
Findlater Pl 1 AB45 . . . 140 E5
Findon Ness AB12 . . . 176 C8
Findon Pl AB12 . . . 180 F8
Findon Rd AB12 . . . 180 E8
Finlayson St AB43 . . . 143 C7
Finnan Brae AB11 . . . 170 F7
Fintray Rd AB15 . . . 169 A7
Fintry Prim Sch AB53 . . . 21 D5
Finzean Prim Sch
AB31 . . . 116 C8
Firholme Pl AB51 . . . 152 C5
Firmounth Rd AB34 . . . 105 F5
Firth Dr Banff AB45 . . . 3 C2
MacDuff AB44 . . . 141 C6
Fish St AB11 . . . 190 C3
Fisherford Prim Sch
AB51 . . . 46 A2
Fishermoss Prim Sch
AB12 . . . 180 B5
Fittick Pl AB12 . . . 176 B7
Flory Gdns AB54 . . . 148 D3
Flourmill La AB10 . . . 190 B3
Fold The AB21 . . . 75 C7
Fonthill Gd E AB11 . . . 170 A6
Fonthill Gd W AB11 . . . 170 A7
Fonthill Rd AB11 . . . 190 A1
Fonthill Terr 1 AB11 . . . 190 A1
Forbes Pl AB21 . . . 89 C7
Forbes Rd 8 Banff AB45 . . . 8 F8
Fraserburgh AB43 . . . 5 A4
Forbes St
Aberdeen AB25 . . . 165 A2
Rosehearty AB43 . . . 142 C7
Forbes View 3 AB41 . . . 61 E6
Forbesfield La AB15 . . . 169 E7
Forbesfield Rd AB15 . . . 169 E7
Fordoun Rd AB30 . . . 186 C7
Fordyce Ave AB53 . . . 36 A6

Fordyce Castle* AB45 ....1 F1
Fordyce Joiner's Workshop & Visitor Ctr* AB45 ....1 E1
Fordyce Prim Sch AB45 ....1 F1
Fordyce Rd AB53 ....36 A6
Fordyce St AB43 ....142 B8
Fordyce Terr AB53 ....36 A5
Fore St DD10 ....135 C6
Forehill Prim Sch AB22 ....159 C4
Forest Ave AB15 ....169 E7
Forest Ave La AB15 ....169 E7
Forest Dr AB39 ....185 C4
Forest Pk AB39 ....185 B4
Forest Rd
Aberdeen AB15 ....164 D1
Kintore AB51 ....155 B5
Forest Way AB54 ....148 C4
Foresters Ave AB21 ....158 C3
Forestside Dr AB31 ....184 D6
Forestside Rd AB31 ....184 D6
Forglen Cres AB53 ....145 C5
Forgue Prim Sch AB54 ....31 D3
Forgue Rd AB51 ....47 A2
Forman Dr AB42 ....147 C4
Formartine Rd AB24 ....165 A6
Forrest Pl 4 AB42 ....147 C4
Forrest Rd AB42 ....147 C4
Forrestal St DD9 ....132 D8
Forresterhill Rd AB16 ....164 C4
Forsyth Dr AB23 ....91 D8
Forsyth Rd AB23 ....91 D8
Forties Field Cres AB41 ....151 A6
Forties Field Rd AB41 ....151 A6
Forties Rd
Aberdeen AB21 ....157 E5
Montrose DD10 ....189 D8
Fortree Rd AB41 ....151 C3
Forvie Ave AB22 ....159 E2
Forvie Circ AB22 ....159 E3
Forvie Cl AB22 ....159 E3
Forvie Cres AB22 ....159 E2
Forvie La AB22 ....159 E2
Forvie National Nature Reserve* AB41 ....64 B2
Forvie Path AB22 ....159 E2
Forvie Pl AB22 ....159 E2
Forvie Rd AB22 ....159 E3
Forvie St AB22 ....159 E3
Forvie Terr AB22 ....159 E2
Forvie Visitor's Ctr* AB41 ....64 D3
Forvie Way AB22 ....159 E2
Foudland Cres AB52 ....149 C5
Fountain Pk AB45 ....140 E6
Fountain St AB45 ....140 E6
Fountainhall Rd AB25 ....164 E1
Foveran Path AB22 ....159 E3
Foveran Prim Sch AB41 ....77 D7
Foveran Rise AB22 ....159 D3
Foveran St AB22 ....159 D3
Foveran Way AB22 ....159 D2
Fowler Ave AB16 ....164 C6
Fowlershill Gdns 6 AB22 ....165 B8
Fowlie's La 9 AB53 ....145 D4
Fowlsheugh Nature Reserve* AB39 ....126 F2
Frain Dr AB30 ....186 C4
Fraser Cres AB43 ....15 B7
Fraser Ct AB54 ....148 C4
Fraser Dr AB32 ....161 C2
Fraser Pl
Aberdeen AB25 ....165 B3
Alford AB33 ....154 D3
Inverallochy AB43 ....15 C8
Kemnay AB51 ....87 D7
Fraser Rd
Aberdeen AB25 ....165 A3
Alford AB33 ....154 D3
Fraser St AB25 ....165 B3
Fraserburgh Acad AB43 ....143 C5
Fraserburgh Fc AB43 ....143 D6
Fraserburgh Her Ctr* AB43 ....143 D7
Fraserburgh Hospl AB43 ....143 B5
Fraserburgh Leisure Ctr AB43 ....143 D5
Fraserburgh N Prim Sch AB43 ....143 C7
Fraserburgh S Pk Sch AB43 ....143 C5
Fraserfield Gdns AB23 ....160 A1
Fraser's La 4 DD10 ....189 C4
Frederick St
Aberdeen AB24 ....190 B4
Inverallochy AB43 ....15 C7
French Dr AB33 ....154 D4
Friarsfield Rd AB15 ....168 E3
Friendship Terr AB10 ....169 F7
Frithside St AB43 ....143 D6
Froghall Ave AB24 ....165 B3
Froghall Gdns AB24 ....165 B3
Froghall Pl AB24 ....165 B4
Froghall Rd AB24 ....165 B3
Froghall Terr AB24 ....165 B3
Froghall View AB24 ....165 B4
Fungle Rd AB34 ....183 C1
Fyfe Pk AB51 ....87 D7
Fyvie Castle (NTS)* AB53 ....47 E6
Fyvie Prim Sch AB53 ....47 E5

G

Gadie Cres AB16 ....164 A4
Gadie Braes AB42 ....147 E6
Gadwall Pl 1 AB42 ....147 B5
Gaelic La AB10 ....190 A3
Gairn Circ AB10 ....170 A6
Gairn Cres AB10 ....170 A6
Gairn Mews AB10 ....170 A6
Gairn Rd AB10 ....170 A6
Gairn Terr AB10 ....170 A6
Gairnshiel Ave AB16 ....164 B4
Gairnshiel Pl AB16 ....164 B4
Gairsay Dr AB15 ....164 A2
Gairsay Rd AB15 ....163 F2
Gaitside Cres AB10 ....169 C3
Gaitside Dr AB10 ....169 C3
Gaitside Pl AB10 ....169 D3
Gaitside Rd AB10 ....169 C3
Gaitside Terr AB10 ....169 C3
Gallica Dr AB21 ....153 D6
Gallowgate AB25 ....190 B4
Gallowhill DD9 ....188 C4
Gallowhill Rd
Aboyne AB34 ....108 B6
Fraserburgh AB43 ....143 B6
Gallowhill St 6 AB45 ....140 F6
Gallowhill Terr
Aberdeen AB21 ....158 D7
Fraserburgh AB43 ....143 B6
Gamrie Brae AB45 ....3 C2
Gannochy Cres DD10 ....189 C6
Garden Cres AB45 ....3 C2
Garden Pl 4 AB42 ....53 B3
Garden Rd AB15 ....168 D3
Garden St AB44 ....141 D6
Gardenston St AB30 ....186 B4
Gardiner's Brae AB45 ....140 F5
Gardner Cres AB12 ....169 F2
Gardner Dr AB12 ....170 A2
Gardner Rd AB12 ....170 A2
Gardner Wlk AB12 ....170 A2
Gardyne St DD10 ....189 C6
Garioch Rd AB51 ....152 D6
Garlogie Mill Power House Mus* AB32 ....101 C4
Garmaddie La 1 AB21 ....158 C7
Garrison Rd DD10 ....189 D2
Garrol Pl 1 AB30 ....128 A4
Garthdee Cres AB10 ....169 E4
Garthdee Dr AB10 ....169 E4
Garthdee Gdns AB10 ....169 E4
Garthdee Rd AB10 ....169 D3
Garthdee Terr AB10 ....169 E4
Gartly Prim Sch AB54 ....56 A6
Garvock Ave DD10 ....189 C8
Garvock Ct AB30 ....186 C5
Garvock Rd AB30 ....186 D5
Garvock St AB30 ....186 D5
Garvock Wynd AB11 ....165 E1
Garvocklea Gdns AB30 ....186 C4
Gas St AB51 ....150 C4
Gatehouse La AB51 ....152 E5
Gaval Ct 2 AB42 ....25 C1
Gaval St AB42 ....25 C2
Gaveny Pl AB44 ....141 E5
Gaw St AB43 ....143 B7
Gdns The AB51 ....152 E5
Gean Ct 5 AB23 ....91 C8
Gean Dr AB21 ....156 B5
Geary Pl AB42 ....147 A5
Gellatly Pl DD9 ....188 C4
Gellymill Rd AB44 ....141 B5
Gellymill St AB44 ....141 D7
George Gdn Ave AB42 ....147 C7
George Rd AB42 ....147 D6
George St
Aberdeen AB25 ....190 A4
9 Banff AB45 ....140 F6
Fraserburgh AB43 ....143 C7
Huntly AB54 ....148 D4
Insch AB52 ....149 D5
Macduff AB44 ....141 D7
Montrose DD10 ....189 C3
George Terr AB39 ....185 D4
George V Ave AB54 ....148 C3
Gerrard St AB25 ....190 A4
Gerries Yd AB42 ....147 F5
Gibson Pl 2 DD10 ....189 D2
Gight Castle* AB41 ....48 E6
Gilbert Rd AB21 ....163 F8
Gilcomston Pk AB25 ....190 A3
Gilcomston Stps AB25 ....190 A4
Gillahill Pl AB16 ....164 B3
Gillahill Rd AB16 ....164 B3
Gillespie Cres AB25 ....164 E4
Gillespie Pl AB25 ....164 F4
Gindera Rd DD10 ....189 D5
Girdleness Rd AB11 ....170 E5
Girdleness Terr AB11 ....170 D5
Girdlestone Pl AB11 ....170 E6
Gladstone Pl
Aberdeen AB24 ....164 E7
Aberdeen AB15 ....169 E8
Dyce AB21 ....158 B6
Gladstone Rd
Huntly AB54 ....148 E4
Peterhead AB42 ....147 F6
Gladstone Terr
New Deer AB53 ....36 A5
Turriff AB53 ....145 C4
Glamourhaugh Ave AB54 ....148 D3
Glamourhaugh Cres 1 AB54 ....148 D3
Glascairn Ave AB12 ....180 B6
Glashieburn Ave AB23 ....159 E3
Glashieburn Prim Sch AB22 ....159 E3
Glass Prim Sch AB54 ....42 A6
Glebe Pk Aboyne AB34 ....108 B6
Banchory AB31 ....184 D4
Glebe Pk (Brechin City FC) DD9 ....188 C4
Glebe Pk Cres 9 AB56 ....1 B4
Glebe Rd AB51 ....152 D5
Glebe Terr AB32 ....101 E6
Glebe The Brechin DD9 ....132 A7
2 Kemnay AB51 ....87 D6
Glebefield 12 AB42 ....38 D6
Glebefield Terr AB42 ....147 C4
Glebeland AB32 ....101 E6
Glen Ave AB21 ....158 B6
Glen Dr AB21 ....158 B6
Glen Gdns AB21 ....158 B6
Glen O'Dee AB31 ....184 A6
Glen O'Dee Hospl AB31 ....109 D3
Glen Rd Aberdeen AB21 ....158 B6
Banchory AB31 ....98 A3
Glenbervie House* AB39 ....124 F3
Glenbervie Prim Sch AB39 ....125 B3
Glenbervie Rd
Aberdeen AB11 ....190 C1
Laurencekirk AB30 ....124 F3
Stonehaven AB39 ....125 B3
Glenbuchat Castle* AB36 ....81 F6
Glenbuchty Pl AB43 ....143 B7
Glencadam Distillery* DD9 ....188 D4
Glenclova Pl 1 DD10 ....189 C5
Glendale Rd AB42 ....147 C5
Glendee Terr AB15 ....168 F3
Glendronach Distillery* AB54 ....31 E3
Gleneagles Ave AB22 ....159 E2
Gleneagles Ct AB51 ....152 C5
Gleneagles Dr 2 AB22 ....159 E2
Gleneagles Gdns 1 AB22 ....159 E2
Glenesk Ave DD10 ....189 C5
Glenesk Distillery* DD10 ....138 D8
Glenfarquhar Castle (remains of)* AB30 ....124 A3
Glenfarquhar Rd AB30 ....124 B2
Glenglassaugh Distillery* AB45 ....2 A3
Glenhome Ave AB21 ....158 B5
Glenhome Cres AB21 ....158 B6
Glenhome Ct AB21 ....158 C6
Glenhome Gdns AB21 ....158 B5
Glenhome Terr AB21 ....158 B5
Glenhome Wlk AB21 ....158 C6
Glenisla Rd DD10 ....189 C5
Glenlethnot Pl 2 DD10 ....189 C5
Glenogil St DD10 ....189 C5
Glenprosen St 4 DD10 ....189 C5
Glenshee Rd 11 AB35 ....113 F6
Glentanar Cres AB21 ....158 C7
Glenugie Cres AB42 ....147 C1
Glenugie Dr AB42 ....147 C1
Glenugie Gdns AB42 ....147 B1
Glenugie View AB42 ....147 C1
Glenury Cres AB39 ....185 E6
Glenury Rd AB39 ....185 E6
Glenwood Pk AB51 ....99 E6
Golden Knowes Ct AB45 ....140 D6
Goldenknowes Rd AB45 ....140 D6
Golf Cres Aboyne AB34 ....183 E6
Inverurie AB51 ....152 B5
Golf Pk
1 Cruden Bay AB42 ....53 A3
Inverurie AB51 ....152 B5
Golf Pl Aboyne AB34 ....183 E5
Inverurie AB51 ....152 C5
Golf Rd Aberdeen AB24 ....165 D4
Aberdeen AB15 ....168 C1
Aboyne AB34 ....183 E5
Ballater AB35 ....182 D4
Ellon AB41 ....151 C6
Peterhead AB42 ....147 C7
Golf Rd Pk DD9 ....188 C5
Golf Terr AB52 ....149 C5
Golf Wlk AB51 ....152 B5
Golfview Cres 3 AB51 ....87 C6
Golfview Rd AB15 ....168 C1
Goodhope Rd AB21 ....164 A8
Gordon Ave
Aberdeen AB23 ....160 A1
Boddam AB42 ....40 D1
Inverurie AB51 ....152 B7
Gordon Cl
11 Boddam AB42 ....40 D1
Westhill AB32 ....161 D3
Gordon Cres
Aboyne AB34 ....183 C4
Inverurie AB51 ....152 A7
Portsoy AB45 ....139 D6
Gordon Ct 1 AB54 ....148 D4
Gordon Dr AB51 ....152 A7
Gordon Gdns
5 Inverurie AB51 ....152 B7
Westhill AB32 ....161 E3
Gordon Gr AB41 ....151 C5
Gordon Highlanders Regimental Mus* AB15 ....169 C7
Gordon La
Aberdeen AB10 ....169 D5
Fraserburgh AB43 ....12 E5
Gordon Lennox Cres AB23 ....160 A3
Gordon Pl
Aberdeen AB23 ....159 F2
Alford AB33 ....154 C4
Ellon AB41 ....151 C5
Inverurie AB51 ....152 B7
Rothienorman AB51 ....46 F2
Gordon Prim Sch AB54 ....148 E5
Gordon Rd
Aberdeen AB15 ....169 C5
Alford AB33 ....154 C4
Bridge of Don AB23 ....160 A1
Inverurie AB51 ....152 B8
15 Kemnay AB51 ....87 D7
Turriff AB53 ....145 C5
Gordon Schools The AB54 ....148 E5
Gordon St
Aberdeen AB11 ....190 A2
13 Boddam AB42 ....40 D1
Fraserburgh AB43 ....15 D6
Huntly AB54 ....148 D4
Gordon Terr
Aberdeen AB15 ....169 D5
Dyce AB21 ....158 B6
Insch AB52 ....149 D4
Inverurie AB51 ....152 A7
Peterhead AB42 ....147 D7
Gordon Way AB54 ....148 C3
Gordon Wlk AB51 ....152 B7
Gordondale Rd AB15 ....164 E1
Gordon's Mills Cres AB24 ....164 F7
Gordon's Mills Pl AB24 ....165 A7
Gordon's Mills Rd AB24 ....164 F7
Gorse Circ AB12 ....180 A4
Gort Rd AB24 ....165 A7
Gourdon Prim Sch DD10 ....187 D3
Gowanbrae Rd AB15 ....168 B1
Gowans Rd 8 AB53 ....145 C5
Graeme Ave AB21 ....158 B6
Graham Cres DD10 ....189 C6
Graham St DD10 ....189 D5
Graham Terr AB33 ....154 C3
Grampian Ct AB33 ....154 C4
Grampian Kart Club* AB45 ....8 C6
Grampian Pl AB11 ....170 D6
Grampian Rd
Aberdeen AB11 ....190 C1
Alford AB33 ....154 C4
Grampian Terr AB31 ....98 E1
Grampian Transport Mus* AB33 ....154 D4
Grampian View DD10 ....138 D2
Granary Pl 3 AB43 ....143 D6
Granary St AB54 ....148 D4
Grandholm Cres AB22 ....164 F8
Grandholm Dr AB22 ....164 F8
Grandholm Gr AB22 ....164 F7
Grandholm St AB24 ....164 F6
Grange Gdns AB42 ....147 C5
Grange Pk Pl 1 AB42 ....147 B4
Grange Pk Rd AB42 ....147 B4
Grange Rd AB42 ....147 B6
Granitehill Pl AB16 ....164 C4
Granitehill Rd AB16 ....164 B6
Grant Cl AB32 ....161 D3
Grant Ct AB42 ....147 E5
Grant Rd AB31 ....184 C4
Grant St Banff AB45 ....8 F8
Banff AB45 ....140 F6
Buckie AB56 ....1 A3
14 Cullen AB56 ....1 B5
Granton Pl AB10 ....169 F8
Granville Pl AB10 ....169 E6
Grassic Gibbon Ctr* AB30 ....130 E6
Grattan Pl AB43 ....143 D5
Gray St Aberdeen AB10 ....169 F6
Fraserburgh AB43 ....143 C6
Gray's La AB53 ....145 D5
Grays Sch of Art AB10 ....169 C3
Great Northern Rd AB24 ....164 D7
Great Southern Rd AB12 ....170 A4
Great Stuart St 2 AB42 ....147 F6
Great Western Rd AB10 ....169 E6
Green Castle* AB30 ....128 C7
Green Hadden St AB11 ....190 B3
Green Mdws AB51 ....86 F1
Green Rd AB54 ....148 D3
Green St AB42 ....53 B2
Green The Banff AB45 ....3 C2
Portlethen AB12 ....180 B5
Greenbank Bsns Ctr AB12 ....170 E4
Greenbank Cres AB12 ....170 E4
Greenbank Pl AB12 ....170 D4
Greenbank Rd AB12 ....170 D4
Greenbrae Ave AB23 ....160 A3
Greenbrae Circ AB23 ....160 A4
Greenbrae Cres AB23 ....160 A4
Greenbrae Dr AB23 ....159 F4
Greenbrae Gdns N AB23 ....160 A4
Greenbrae Gdns S AB23 ....160 A4
Greenbrae Pl 3 AB42 ....147 B4
Greenbrae Prim Sch AB23 ....160 A3
Greenbrae Wlk AB23 ....160 A4
Greenbraes Cres DD10 ....187 C4
Greenbraes Rd DD10 ....187 C3
Greenburn Dr AB21 ....158 B1
Greenburn Pk AB21 ....158 C1
Greenburn Rd AB21 ....158 B1
Greenburn Rd N AB21 ....158 A2
Greenburn Terr AB21 ....163 D8
Greenfern Ave AB16 ....163 F3
Greenfern Pl AB16 ....164 A3
Greenfern Rd AB16 ....163 F3
Greenhill Rd AB42 ....147 F5
Greenhole Pl AB23 ....159 F2
Greenmore Gdns AB24 ....164 F5
Greens Rd AB21 ....153 D5
Greens Terr AB21 ....153 D5
Greens The 2 AB42 ....146 D5
Greens Way AB21 ....153 D5
Greenwell Pl AB12 ....170 F5
Greenwell Rd AB12 ....170 E5
Gregness Gdns AB11 ....170 E5
Greig Pl AB39 ....185 D4
Greyhope Rd AB11 ....171 A8
Greystone Pl
Alford AB33 ....154 C3
Stonehaven AB39 ....181 I4
Greystone Rd AB33 ....154 C3
Groats Rd AB15 ....168 E8
Grosvenor Pl 10 AB25 ....165 A1
Grosvenor Terr 1 AB25 ....165 A1
Grove Cres AB16 ....164 E3
Grove Rd AB51 ....87 D6
Grove Terr 2 AB31 ....108 E8
Guestrow 9 AB10 ....190 B3
Guild St AB11 ....190 B2
Gulleymoss Gdns AB32 ....161 E4
Gullymoss Pl AB32 ....161 E4
Gullymoss View AB32 ....161 E4
Gurney St AB39 ....185 E5
Guthrie Pk DD9 ....188 D2
Guthrie's Haven AB45 ....140 E6

H

Hacklaw Pl 1 AB42 ....53 B3
Hadden St AB11 ....190 B3
Haddo Cres 2 AB41 ....77 F7
Haddo Ctry Pk* AB41 ....49 D1
Haddo House (NTS)* AB41 ....49 C1
Haddo La AB41 ....61 E6
Hall Cres AB44 ....141 E6
Hall Rd AB42 ....27 B2
Hallfield Cres AB16 ....163 F2
Hallfield Rd AB16 ....163 F2
Hallgreen Castle* DD10 ....187 E6
Hallgreen Rd DD10 ....187 E6
Halliday Pl AB42 ....147 A6
Halsey Dr DD9 ....132 C8
Hamewith Ave AB39 ....185 C3
Hamilton Pl AB15 ....164 E1
Hamilton Rd AB43 ....143 B7
Hamilton Sch The AB15 ....169 D8
Hammerfield Ave AB10 ....169 E5
Hammersmith Rd AB10 ....169 E6
Hanover St
Aberdeen AB11 ....190 C4
Fraserburgh AB43 ....143 D7
Peterhead AB42 ....147 D5
Hanover St Prim Sch AB11 ....190 C4
Harbour La AB45 ....3 B3
Harbour Pl Banff AB45 ....8 F8
Banff AB45 ....140 F6
Montrose DD10 ....135 C5
Harbour Rd Banff AB45 ....3 B2
Fraserburgh AB43 ....143 D6
Harbour St Banff AB45 ....3 B3
1 Boddam AB42 ....40 D1
Cruden Bay AB42 ....53 B2
Peterhead AB42 ....147 F4
Harcourt Rd AB15 ....164 D2
Hardgate AB11 ....190 A2
Hardgate La AB10 ....170 A6
Hardie Ct AB54 ....144 D5
Hareburn Terr AB23 ....91 B5
Harehill Rd AB22 ....159 E1
Hareness Circ AB12 ....170 E1
Hareness Pk AB12 ....170 E2
Hareness Rd AB12 ....170 D2
Harestones Stone Circ (remains of) The* AB53 ....32 C3
Harlaw Bsns Ctr AB51 ....152 C8
Harlaw Dr AB51 ....152 D7
Harlaw Pl AB15 ....169 D7
Harlaw Rd
Aberdeen AB15 ....169 D7
Inverurie AB51 ....152 D7
Harlaw Terr AB15 ....169 D7
Harlaw Way AB51 ....152 C8
Harley Terr AB12 ....180 E5

Harris Dr AB24 165 A6
Harris Pl AB43 143 B4
Harrow Rd AB24 165 C6
Harthill Castle* AB52 72 E8
Harthill Pl AB16 163 E3
Hartington Rd AB10 169 F8
Harvest Hill AB32 161 B3
Harvey Pl AB45 140 E6
Hatton (Cruden) Prim Sch
AB42 52 D4
Hatton (Fintray) Prim Sch
AB21 89 C7
Hatton Castle (remains of)*
AB53 33 F5
Hatton Ct 2 AB21 89 B7
Hatton Farm Gdns 2
AB42 52 D4
Hatton Farm Rd AB42 52 C4
Hatton Rd AB53 145 E4
Haudagain Ret Pk
AB24 164 C7
Haugh Path AB43 12 D6
Haughton Ctry Pk*
AB33 154 D5
Haughton Pl AB33 154 C4
Hawthorn Cres
Aberdeen AB16 164 B4
Ballater AB35 182 E4
6 Mintlaw AB42 146 D5
Hawthorn Ct 3 AB35 182 E4
Hawthorn Gr AB35 182 E4
Hawthorn Pl AB35 182 E4
Hawthorn Rd 5 AB42 147 B5
Hay Cres AB42 147 D6
Hay St AB42 53 B3
Hayfield Cres AB24 164 E4
Hayfield Pl
Aberdeen AB24 164 E5
2 Peterhead AB42 147 A6
Hay's Ct AB33 154 D3
Hay's Way AB32 161 D3
Hay's Wlk AB33 154 D3
Hayton Rd AB24 164 F6
Haywood Dr AB45 139 D6
Hazel Dr AB32 161 D2
Hazledene Rd AB15 168 E7
Hazlehead Acad AB15 168 E8
Hazlehead Ave AB15 168 F8
Hazlehead Cres AB15 168 F8
Hazlehead Gdns AB15 168 F8
Hazlehead Pk* AB15 168 E8
Hazlehead Pl AB15 168 F8
Hazlehead Prim Sch
AB15 169 A8
Hazlehead Rd AB15 168 F8
Hazlehead Swimming Pool
AB15 168 E8
Hazlehead Terr AB15 168 F8
Hazlewood Sch AB15 169 A8
Headland Ct
Aberdeen AB10 169 F4
Stonehaven AB39 181 I4
Heath Dr AB42 147 B3
Heath Row AB31 184 C5
Heather Pl AB12 180 C6
Heathfield Pk AB39 181 H4
Heathryfold Circ
AB16 164 A6
Heathryfold Cl AB16 164 B6
Heathryfold Dr AB16 164 A6
Heathryfold Pl AB16 164 A6
Helen Row AB39 185 F6
Henderson Circ AB42 147 A5
Henderson Cres AB51 155 B5
Henderson Dr
Kintore AB51 155 B5
Westhill AB32 161 C2
Henderson Pk AB42 147 A5
Henderson Rd AB43 143 B5
Henry La 3 AB42 36 E6
Henry Pl AB44 141 D5
Herd Cres DD10 135 C6
Hermitage Ave AB24 165 B5
Heron Cres AB41 151 C3
Heron Rd 5 AB51 87 C7
Hetherwick Rd AB12 170 A2
Hexagon The AB43 143 D6
High Gn AB45 3 C2
High Pen La DD9 132 B7
High Shore AB45 141 A6
High St Aberdeen AB24 165 B5
Auchenblae AB30 124 B1
Banchory AB31 184 B4
Banff AB45 140 F5
Brechin DD9 188 C3
Cuminestown AB53 22 C1
Edzell DD9 132 B7
Fraserburgh AB43 143 D7
Insch AB52 149 D5
Inverbervie DD10 187 E7
Inverurie AB51 152 E4
Kemnay AB51 87 D7
Laurencekirk AB30 186 D5
Macduff AB44 141 D6
Montrose DD10 189 C3
New Aberdour AB43 12 E5
New Deer AB53 36 A6
New Pitsligo AB43 23 E6
Peterhead AB42 147 D7
Pittulie AB43 4 F4
St Combs AB43 15 D5
Stonehaven AB39 185 F4
Strichen AB43 24 E6
Turriff AB53 145 D4
Highfield Ave AB31 184 C5
Highfield Ct 4 AB39 185 C7
Highfield Gdns 3 AB39 185 C7
Highfield Way AB39 185 C7
Highfield Wlk AB53 145 D5
Highland Her Ctr*
AB35 113 E6
Highview Gr DD10 134 C3
Highwood AB31 184 C5
Hill of Banchory S AB31 184 E5
Hill of Banchory W
AB31 184 D6
Hill Pl DD10 189 C2
Hill Rd DD10 138 C8
Hill St Aberdeen AB25 190 A4
Cruden Bay AB42 53 B2
6 Montrose DD10 189 C2
Peterhead AB42 53 B4
Portsoy AB45 139 D7
Rosehearty AB43 142 C7
Hillbrae Way AB21 153 E4
Hillcrest AB43 143 B5
Hillcrest Pl AB16 164 C5
Hillcrest Rd AB53 145 C5
Hillcroft Rd AB31 184 B5
Hillfoot Terr DD10 187 D3
Hillhead Dr AB41 151 C3
Hillhead Pl AB41 151 D4
Hillhead Rd
Aberdeen AB15 167 F3
Ellon AB41 151 D3
Stonehaven AB39 181 I4
Hillocks Way AB21 163 E7
Hillside
Fraserburgh AB43 23 E6
Pitmedden AB41 62 A2
Hillside Cres
Aberdeen AB14 172 D7
Westhill AB32 161 E4
Hillside Dr 8 AB35 113 F6
Hillside Gdns AB32 161 E4
Hillside Pl AB14 172 D7
Hillside Rd
Aberdeen AB14 172 D6
Westhill AB32 161 E4
Hillside Terr AB12 180 C7
Hillside View AB32 161 E4
Hillswick Rd 3 AB16 163 E3
Hillswick Wlk 1 AB16 163 E3
Hilltop Ave
Aberdeen AB15 168 D3
Westhill AB32 161 D5
Hilltop Cres AB32 161 D4
Hilltop Dr AB32 161 D4
Hilltop Gdns AB32 161 E4
Hilltop Rd AB15 168 D3
Hillview
Aberchirder AB54 144 D5
8 Strichen AB43 24 E6
Hillview Ave AB32 161 E4
Hillview Cres
Aberdeen AB15 168 C3
Montrose DD10 189 D1
Rosehearty AB43 142 C7
Hillview Dr AB15 168 D3
Hillview Gdns DD10 187 D6
Hillview Rd
Aberdeen AB12 170 D4
Banchory AB31 184 C5
Cults AB15 168 D2
Laurencekirk AB30 124 B2
Peterculter AB14 172 D6
Westhill AB32 161 E4
Hillview Terr AB15 168 D2
Hillylands Rd AB16 164 A2
Hilton Ave AB24 164 D5
Hilton Circ AB24 164 E4
Hilton Dr AB24 164 E5
Hilton Hts AB24 164 E5
Hilton Pl AB24 164 F5
Hilton Rd AB24 164 E5
Hilton St AB24 164 F4
Hilton Terr AB24 164 E5
Hilton Wlk AB24 164 E5
His Majestys Theatre*
AB25 190 A3
Hobshill Pl 5 AB42 52 C4
Holburn Pl AB10 170 A6
Holburn Rd AB10 169 F7
Holburn St AB10 169 F4
Holland Pl AB25 165 A3
Holland St AB25 165 A3
Holly Dr AB39 185 C4
Holly Tree Rd AB31 184 D6
Hollybank Cres AB31 184 B5
Hollybank Pl AB10 170 A7
Holmdale Pl 2 AB53 145 C5
Holy Family RC Sch
AB15 164 B1
Homelea AB32 161 B2
Hope St AB42 147 D6
Hopecroft Ave AB21 158 B1
Hopecroft Dr AB21 158 B1
Hopecroft Terr AB21 158 B1
Hopetoun Ave AB21 163 C8
Hopetoun Cres AB21 163 C8
Hopetoun Ct AB21 163 D8
Hopetoun Dr AB21 163 D8
Hopetoun Gn AB21 163 D8
Hopetoun Grange
AB21 158 A1
Hopetoun Rd AB21 163 C8
Hopetoun Terr AB21 163 C8
Horn's Brae 1 AB44 141 C6
Hosefield Ave AB15 164 E2
Hosefield Rd AB15 164 E2
Hospital Rd Ellon AB41 151 C6
Hillside DD10 138 C8
Hospital St John AB10 169 F8
Houghton Dr 2 DD10 138 D8
House of Dun (NTS)*
DD10 137 F6
House of Monymusk*
AB51 86 F6
House of Schivas*
AB41 49 F3
Howatt Pk AB43 5 A4
Howburn Ct AB11 170 A7
Howburn Pl AB10 170 A7
Howe Moss Ave AB21 157 D6
Howe Moss Cres
AB21 157 D6
Howe Moss Dr AB21 157 D5
Howe Moss Pl AB21 157 D6
Howe Moss Terr AB21 157 D7
Howes Cres AB16 164 A6
Howes Dr AB16 164 A6
Howes Rd AB16 163 F5
Howes View AB21 163 E7
Howie La AB14 172 E5
Howieslap AB51 155 D4
Howieson Pl AB51 152 B8
Hudson St AB39 185 E5
Hume St DD10 189 C3
Hunter Ave AB39 185 C6
Hunter Dr AB39 185 C6
Hunter Pl
Aberdeen AB24 165 D3
Stonehaven AB39 185 C6
Huntly Castle* AB54 148 E6
Huntly Nordic Ski & Outdoor
Ctr* AB54 148 D6
Huntly Pl AB34 183 C4
Huntly Rd
Aberchirder AB54 144 C4
Aboyne AB34 183 C4
Huntly St AB10 190 A3
Huntly Sta AB54 148 E4
Huntly Swimming Pool
AB54 148 E5
Hutcheon Gdns AB23 165 C8
Hutcheon Low Dr
AB21 164 C7
Hutcheon Low Pl
AB21 164 C7
Hutcheon St
Aberdeen AB25 190 A4
5 Macduff AB44 141 C6
Hutchison Terr AB10 169 D5
Hutton Pl AB16 164 A5
Hutton Rd AB21 157 E6
Huxterstone Ct 3 AB15 162 F2
Huxterstone Dr AB15 162 F2
Huxterstone Pl 4 AB15 162 F2
Huxterstone Terr
AB15 162 F2
Hythe The 4 AB44 141 C6

I

Ilderton Pl 2 AB31 184 D4
Imperial Pl 4 AB11 190 B3
Inch Rd AB41 65 G4
Inch Terr DD10 189 B1
Inchbrae Dr AB10 169 D3
Inchbrae Rd AB10 169 D3
Inchbrae Terr AB10 169 C3
Inchdrewer Castle (remains
of)* AB45 8 F3
Inchgarth Rd AB15 169 A3
Inchley Pl 17 AB31 108 E8
Inchley Terr 4 AB31 108 E8
Inchmarlo Rd AB31 184 A4
India La DD10 189 D3
India St DD10 189 D3
Infirmary Rd DD9 188 D3
Infirmary St DD9 188 D3
Ingleside 6 AB41 62 B2
Ingram Wlk AB12 170 C2
Inkbottle Way 1 AB39 185 C7
Inkbottle Wlk 2 AB39 185 C7
Inn Brae AB42 38 D6
Insch Bsns Pk AB52 149 D7
Insch Prim Sch AB52 149 D5
Insch Sta AB52 149 C4
Insch War Meml Hospl
AB52 149 D4
Institute St AB45 139 E7
Institution St AB44 141 C7
Institution Terr AB45 140 F5
International Sch of
Aberdeen AB13 173 A7
Intown Rd AB23 160 B2
Inverallochy Castle (remains
of)* AB43 15 B5
Inverallochy Prim Sch
AB43 15 C7
Invérarity Cres 5 DD10 138 C8
Inverbervie Sports Ctr
DD10 187 E7
Inverboyndie Ind Est
AB45 140 B6
Invercauld Gdns AB16 164 B4
Invercauld Pl AB16 164 B4
Invercauld Rd
Aberdeen AB16 164 B4
Ballater AB35 182 C4
3 Braemar AB35 113 F6
Inverey Castle (remains of)*
AB35 112 E4
Invergarry Pk DD10 134 D4
Inveriscandye Rd DD9 132 B7
Invermarkie Wynd 3
AB31 98 E1
Invernettie Rd AB42 147 C4
Inverquhomery Rd 4
AB42 38 D6
Inverugie Castle (remains
of)* AB42 39 E7
Inverugie Rd AB42 147 A6
Inverugie Wynd 2
AB41 151 F5
Inverurie Acad AB51 152 D5
Inverurie Hospl AB51 152 D4
Inverurie Rd AB21 158 A1
Inverurie St AB30 124 B1
Inverurie Sta AB51 152 E6
Inverurie Swimming Ctr
AB51 152 D5
Iona Ave AB42 147 B7
Ironfield La AB39 185 F5
Irvine Pk 3 AB21 153 C6
Irvine Pl
Aberdeen AB10 169 F6
3 Fraserburgh AB43 26 C7
Inverurie AB51 152 B8
Irvine Way AB51 152 B8
Isla Pl AB16 163 F3
Islay Ct AB41 151 B3
Ivanhoe Pl AB10 169 C4
Ivanhoe Rd AB10 169 C3
Ives Rd AB42 147 E6
Ivy Pl AB39 185 C4

J

Jack's Brae AB25 165 A1
Jackson St AB51 152 D5
Jackson Terr AB24 165 C3
Jamaica St
Aberdeen AB25 165 A3
Peterhead AB42 147 F5
James Mitchell Pl
AB42 146 E5
James Presly Ct AB54 148 D3
James St
Aberdeen AB11 190 C3
Macduff AB44 141 D6
3 Oldmeldrum AB51 150 C3
Peterhead AB42 147 F5
James Stott Rd AB42 147 A7
Jarvis Pl AB43 143 A4
Jasmine Pl AB24 190 B4
Jasmine Terr AB24 190 B4
Jasmine Way AB24 190 B4
Jenner Pl DD9 188 C5
Jesmond Ave AB22 159 D2
Jesmond Ave N AB22 159 D2
Jesmond Circ AB22 159 C4
Jesmond Dr AB22 159 D5
Jesmond Gdns AB22 159 C4
Jesmond Gr AB22 159 C4
Jesmond Rd AB22 159 E3
Jesmond Sq AB22 159 D2
John Arthur Ct AB15 163 A1
John Gray Dr 14 AB51 87 D7
John Morrison Cres 1
AB42 36 E6
John Pk Pl AB22 164 E8
John Sorrie Dr AB51 152 A6
John St Aberdeen AB25 190 A4
Dyce AB21 158 B5
Montrose DD10 189 D4
2 Stonehaven AB39 185 F3
Johns Brae AB44 141 D6
Johnshaven Prim Sch
DD10 135 B5
Johnson Gdns E AB14 172 C7
Johnson Gdns N AB14 172 D7
Johnson Gdns W
AB14 172 D7
Johnston Pk AB53 145 D5
Johnston Rd AB30 186 C4
Johnston St AB30 186 D5
Jopp's La AB25 190 A4
Jubilee Cres AB45 8 F8
Jubilee Hospl AB54 148 D3
Judy's La 8 AB56 1 B4
Juniper Pl AB12 180 A5
Jura Pl AB16 163 E2
Justice Mill Brae
AB11 170 A8
Justice Mill La 2 AB11 190 A2
Justice St AB10 190 C3
Jute St AB24 165 B3

K

Kaimhill Circ AB10 169 E4
Kaimhill Gdns AB10 169 E4
Kaimhill Prim Sch
AB10 169 E4
Kaimhill Rd AB10 169 E4
Kartstart* AB21 158 C4
Katrine Terr AB41 151 B6
Keig Prim Sch AB33 71 C2
Keil Brae AB51 150 D3
Keir Circ AB32 161 C3
Keir Hts AB23 91 C8
Keith Ave AB23 91 C8
Keith Cres 12 AB23 91 C8
Keith Gdns
Blackburn AB21 156 B6
1 Fraserburgh AB43 26 D7
Keith Hall* AB51 74 C4
Keith Pl 1 AB39 185 F4
Keith St AB42 147 F4
Keithhall Prim Sch
AB51 74 D3
Keithhall Rd AB51 152 F3
Keithleigh Gdns AB41 62 A2
Keithmuir Gdns AB31 111 C5
Keithmuir La AB31 111 D5
Keithmuir Rd AB31 111 D5
Kellands Ave AB51 152 D5
Kellands Prim Sch
AB51 152 D5
Kellands Rd AB51 152 C5
Kellands Rise AB51 152 C5
Kembhill Pk AB51 87 C7
Kemnay Acad AB51 87 D7
Kemnay House* AB51 87 D6
Kemnay Pl AB15 169 B7
Kemnay Prim Sch
AB51 87 D6
Kemnay Rd AB51 152 E2
Kemp St AB16 164 C6
Kemp's La 8 AB53 145 D4
Kencast Circ AB14 166 D1
Kencast Row AB14 166 D1
Kendal Rd AB51 87 D7
Kenfield Cres AB15 169 C6
Kenfield Pl AB15 169 C6
Kennedy Ave DD10 189 C7
Kennedy Ct AB54 148 D4
Kennedy Pl AB43 143 C3
Kennedy Rd AB43 143 C4
Kennerty Mills Rd
AB14 172 D6
Kennerty Pk AB14 172 D5
Kennerty Rd AB14 172 C5
Kennethmont Prim Sch
AB54 56 C4
Kent Gdns AB43 143 B6
Kepplehills Dr AB21 163 C8
Kepplehills Rd AB21 163 D7
Kepplestone Ave
AB15 169 C7
Kerloch Cres
Banchory AB31 184 E5
8 Torphins AB31 108 E8
Kerloch Gdns AB11 170 D5
Kerloch Pl AB11 170 C5
Kessock Pl AB43 143 D4
Kessock Rd AB43 143 D4
Kessock Rd Ind Est
AB43 143 D4
Kestrel Rd 10 AB41 77 F8
Kettlehills Cres AB16 164 B5
Kettlehills La AB16 164 B5
Kettlehills Rd AB16 164 A5
Kettock Gdns AB22 159 D1
Kidd St 1 AB10 190 A3
Kildrummy Castle*
AB33 82 F7
Kildrummy Prim Sch
AB33 69 B1
Kildrummy Rd
Aberdeen AB15 169 A7
Ellon AB41 151 E5
Kilmarnock Dr 5 AB42 53 A3
Kilsyth Rd AB12 170 C3
Kimberley Ct 5 AB51 47 A2
Kinaldie Cres AB15 169 A7
Kincardine Castle (remains
of)* AB30 128 C6
Kincardine Com Hospl
AB39 185 C5
Kincardine O'Neil Prim Sch
AB34 108 B6
Kincardine O'Neil War Meml
Hospl AB31 108 E8
Kincardine Rd AB31 108 E8
Kincardine St DD10 189 D4
Kincorth Acad AB12 170 B3
Kincorth Circ AB12 170 A3
Kincorth Cres AB12 170 B4
Kincorth Pl AB12 170 A4
Kincorth Sports Ctr
AB12 170 B4
Kincorth Swimming Pool
AB12 170 B3
Kindrochit Castle (remains
of)* AB35 113 F5
Kindrochit Dr 10 AB35 113 F6
Kinellar Prim Sch
AB21 156 B6
King David Dr DD10 187 D5
King Edward Ct AB44 141 E5
King Edward Prim Sch
AB45 20 F8
King Edward St AB43 143 C6
King St Aberdeen AB24 164 E6
Aberdeen AB10 190 B3
Huntly AB54 148 D4
Inverbervie DD10 187 D7
Inverurie AB51 152 D7
3 Montrose DD10 189 D1
10 Oldmeldrum AB51 150 C3
Peterhead AB42 147 D5
Rosehearty AB43 142 C8
Stonehaven AB39 185 F4
Kinghorn Pl DD9 188 C5
Kings Coll (University of
Aberdeen) AB24 165 B5
Kings Coll Con & Visitor Ctr*
AB24 165 C5
King's Cross Ave AB15 169 B8
King's Cross Rd AB15 169 B8
King's Cross Terr
AB15 169 B8
King's Deer Pk* AB30 122 F1
King's Gate AB15 169 A8
King's Rd AB39 185 D4
Kingscliff Sporting Lodge*
AB41 49 A6
Kingsfield Pl 2 AB51 155 C5
Kingsfield Rd AB51 155 E3
Kingsford Rd
Aberdeen AB16 163 F3

Kingsford Rd *continued*
Alford AB33 ...154 D3
Kingsford Sch AB16 ...163 F3
Kingshill Ave AB15 ...164 C1
Kingshill Rd AB15 ...164 C1
Kingshill Terr AB15 ...164 C1
Kingsland Pl AB25 ...190 A4
Kings's Cres AB24 ...165 C3
Kingston Gdns AB41 ...151 E6
Kingswalk AB21 ...163 E8
Kingsway AB21 ...163 E8
Kingswell La 7 AB45 ...140 F6
Kingswell Pk AB45 ...140 F6
Kingswells Ave AB15 ...162 F3
Kingswells Cres AB15 ...162 F5
Kingswells Dr AB15 ...162 E3
Kingswells Prim Sch AB15 ...162 F3
Kingswells View AB32 ...161 D4
Kingswood Ave AB15 ...162 F3
Kingswood Cres AB15 ...162 F3
Kingswood Dr AB15 ...162 F3
Kingswood Gdns AB15 ...162 F2
Kingswood Gr 3 AB15 ...162 F3
Kingswood Mews AB15 ...162 E3
Kingswood Path 1 AB15 ...162 F3
Kingswood Rd AB15 ...162 F3
Kingswood Wlk 2 AB15 ...162 F3
Kininmonth Sch AB42 ...25 D3
Kinkell Rd AB15 ...169 A7
Kinloch Rd AB42 ...27 B2
Kinmonth Rd AB39 ...125 B3
Kinmundy Ave AB32 ...161 E3
Kinmundy Dr
Peterhead AB42 ...147 B5
Westhill AB32 ...161 E3
Kinmundy Gdns
Peterhead AB42 ...147 A4
Westhill AB32 ...161 E3
Kinmundy Gn AB32 ...161 E3
Kinmundy Rd
Newmachar AB21 ...153 D5
Peterhead AB42 ...147 A4
Kinmundy Wlk AB42 ...147 B5
Kinnaber Rd DD10 ...138 D8
Kinnaird Pl
2 Aberdeen AB24 ...165 A6
Brechin DD9 ...188 D2
Kinnaird Rd AB43 ...143 C7
Kinnairdy Castle* AB54 ...31 D8
Kinneff Prim Sch DD10 ...131 D7
Kinneskie Rd AB31 ...184 B4
Kinnies La 1 AB54 ...144 C4
Kinord Circ 2 AB22 ...165 B8
Kinord Dr AB34 ...183 A5
Kinord Rd AB41 ...151 B7
Kintore Bsns Pk AB51 ...155 A8
Kintore Gdns AB25 ...165 A2
Kintore Pl 6 AB25 ...165 A2
Kintore Prim Sch AB51 ...155 B4
Kintore St AB30 ...124 B1
Kirk Brae
Aberdeen AB15 ...168 E3
Fraserburgh AB43 ...143 D7
Oldmeldrum AB51 ...150 D3
Kirk Brae Ct AB15 ...168 E3
Kirk Brae Mews AB15 ...168 E3
Kirk Burn DD10 ...187 E6
Kirk Cres N AB15 ...168 E3
Kirk Cres S AB15 ...168 E3
Kirk Dr AB15 ...168 E3
Kirk La 3 AB44 ...141 C6
Kirk Pk AB21 ...153 C5
Kirk Pl AB15 ...168 D3
Kirk Rd AB39 ...185 D5
Kirk St
Oldmeldrum AB51 ...150 C3
Peterhead AB42 ...147 D5
Kirk Terr AB15 ...168 D3
Kirk View AB31 ...98 A3
Kirkbrae 1 AB41 ...61 E6
Kirkbrae Ave AB15 ...168 D3
Kirkbrae Dr AB15 ...168 D3
Kirkbrae Terr AB53 ...36 A5
Kirkbrae View AB15 ...168 D3
Kirkburn AB30 ...186 D6
Kirkburn Dr AB42 ...147 C5
Kirkgate AB42 ...37 D6
Kirkhill AB53 ...22 D4
Kirkhill Dr
Aberdeen AB21 ...157 E7
Oldmeldrum AB51 ...150 D3
Kirkhill Ind Est AB21 ...157 D7
Kirkhill Pl Aberdeen AB11 170 E5
Dyce AB21 ...157 E5
Kirkhill Prim Sch AB12 ...170 C3
Kirkhill Rd
Aberdeen AB11 ...170 D5
Dyce AB21 ...157 E6
Potterton AB23 ...91 A6
Kirkhill View AB21 ...156 B6
Kirkland 3 AB51 ...87 D6
Kirklands 1 AB41 ...49 B4
Kirkton Ave
Aberdeen AB21 ...158 A8
Westhill AB32 ...161 B3
Kirkton Cres AB43 ...143 D4
Kirkton Dr AB21 ...157 F8
Kirkton Gdns AB32 ...161 B3
Kirkton Pk
Chapel of Garioch AB51 ...73 B7
Daviot AB51 ...59 E2
Kirkton Rd
Fraserburgh AB43 ...143 C3
Stonehaven AB39 ...185 B5
Westhill AB32 ...161 B3
Kirktonhill Pl AB30 ...133 D4
Kirktonhill Rd AB30 ...133 D4
Kirktown Brae AB43 ...143 D2
Kirkwall Ave 2 AB16 ...163 E3
Kirkwood Cres AB45 ...139 D5
Kitchenhill View AB42 ...36 E6
Kittybrewster Prim Sch AB24 ...165 A5
Kittybrewster Ret Pk AB24 ...165 A4
Knock Ave AB45 ...8 F8
Knock Castle* AB35 ...182 A3
Knock La 7 AB45 ...8 F8
Knock St Banff AB45 ...8 F8
Peterhead AB42 ...37 D4
Knock View AB42 ...37 D5
Knockdhu Distillery* AB54 ...18 A3
Knockhall Castle* AB41 ...63 F1
Knockhall Rd Ellon AB41 ...77 F8
6 Newburgh AB41 ...77 F8
Knockie Rd AB53 ...145 B5
Knockothie Brae AB41 ...151 D6
Knockothie Hill 1 AB41 ...151 C6

L

Laburnum Gr AB42 ...147 B4
Laburnum La 11 AB42 ...38 D6
Laburnum Wlk AB16 ...164 D4
Ladder Rd The AB36 ...66 A1
Lade Cres AB21 ...158 C2
Ladeside Gdns AB51 ...152 E2
Ladeside Rd
Brechin DD9 ...188 C2
Inverurie AB51 ...152 E3
Ladysbridge Hospl AB45 ...8 E7
Ladywell Pl AB11 ...170 E5
Ladywell Rd AB51 ...155 B6
Ladywood Cres AB34 ...183 C4
Ladywood Dr AB34 ...183 B4
Laggan Pl AB41 ...151 B7
Laing Ct AB51 ...152 E5
Laing St AB44 ...141 D7
Laingseat Rd AB23 ...91 A6
Laird Gdns AB22 ...159 C1
Lairds Pk AB21 ...89 C7
Laird's Wlk AB42 ...40 D1
Laithers Cres AB53 ...145 C5
Lamb Way 5 DD10 ...189 D7
Lamond Pl AB25 ...165 A3
Lamondfauld La 6 DD10 ...138 C8
Lamondfauld Rd DD10 ...138 C8
Landale Rd AB42 ...147 D5
Landends AB30 ...128 D4
Lane The AB51 ...86 F1
Lang Stracht AB15 ...163 E2
Lang Stracht The AB33 ...154 D4
Langdykes Cres AB12 ...176 B8
Langdykes Dr AB12 ...176 B8
Langdykes Rd AB12 ...176 B8
Langdykes Way AB12 ...176 C8
Langley Ave DD10 ...189 D6
Langstane Pl AB11 ...190 A2
Larch Rd AB16 ...164 C4
Larch Wood Gdns* AB55 ...28 A6
Larg Dr AB32 ...161 B3
Latch Gdns DD9 ...188 B4
Latch Rd DD9 ...188 B4
Lathallan Grange DD10 ...135 D6
Laurel Ave AB22 ...164 E8
Laurel Braes AB22 ...164 E8
Laurel Cres DD10 ...187 D7
Laurel Ct 1 AB39 ...185 C4
Laurel Dr AB22 ...164 C8
Laurel Gdns AB22 ...164 E8
Laurel La AB22 ...159 C1
Laurel Pk AB22 ...164 E8
Laurel Pl AB22 ...164 E8
Laurel Rd AB22 ...164 E8
Laurel Terr
Aberdeen AB22 ...164 E8
9 Pitmedden AB41 ...62 B2
Laurel View AB22 ...164 D8
Laurel Wynd AB22 ...164 E8
Laurelwood Ave AB25 ...164 F4
Laurencekirk Bsns Pk AB30 ...186 D6
Laurencekirk Sch AB30 ...186 D4
Lavender Pk 4 AB51 ...155 C4
Laverock Hill AB41 ...151 C6
Laverock Rd 8 AB41 ...77 F8
Law of Balgreen* AB45 ...10 D1
Law of Doune Rd AB44 ...141 C5
Law The* AB45 ...3 D4
Lawrence Rd AB52 ...58 A7
Laws Dr AB12 ...170 A2
Laws Rd AB12 ...170 A2
Lawson Ave AB31 ...184 C5
Lawson Cres AB31 ...184 C4
Lawson Dr AB21 ...158 A7
Lawson Pl AB31 ...184 C4
Lawsondale Ave AB32 ...161 F2
Lawsondale Dr AB32 ...161 F2
Lawsondale Terr AB32 ...161 F3
Lea Rig AB32 ...161 B3
Leadside Rd AB25 ...165 A1
Learny Pl AB15 ...169 E7
Leask Ave AB42 ...147 C4
Lecht 2090 Ski Ctr* AB36 ...79 C3
Lecht Rd AB36 ...79 C3
Leddach Gdns AB32 ...161 C3
Leddach Pl AB32 ...161 C3
Leddach Rd AB32 ...161 C3
Lee Cres AB22 ...159 C3
Lee Cres N AB22 ...159 C3
Lee Mar DD10 ...138 B6
Leeds Terr 2 AB42 ...25 D5
Leggart Ave AB12 ...169 F3
Leggart Cres AB12 ...169 F2
Leggart Terr AB12 ...169 F2
Leighton Gdns AB41 ...151 B5
Leith Hall, Gdn & Est (NTS)* AB54 ...56 C4
Lemon Pl AB24 ...190 C4
Lemon St AB24 ...190 C4
Lemon Tree Arts Ctr* AB24 ...190 B4
Lemonbank Pl AB44 ...141 D6
Lendrum Pl AB53 ...145 B6
Lennox Terr AB54 ...148 E4
Lerwick Rd AB16 ...163 E3
Leslie Cres Alford AB33 ...154 C4
Westhill AB32 ...161 C3
Leslie Pl AB51 ...152 E3
Leslie Rd AB24 ...164 F5
Leslie Terr AB25 ...165 A4
Leslie's La AB53 ...145 D4
Lethen Wlk AB12 ...180 A4
Lethnot Rd DD9 ...132 A7
Letter Rd AB32 ...88 A1
Leven Ave AB41 ...151 B6
Lewis Ct AB15 ...163 D3
Lewis Dr AB16 ...163 E3
Lewis Pl AB43 ...143 B3
Lewis Rd
Aberdeen AB16 ...163 E3
Fraserburgh AB43 ...143 B3
Lewisvale AB14 ...172 F6
Leys Dr 5 AB43 ...26 C7
Leys Gdns AB21 ...156 B6
Leys Rd AB31 ...184 E4
Leys The AB44 ...141 E7
Leys Way 7 AB51 ...87 C6
Library Gdns 12 AB43 ...24 E6
Lickleyhead Castle* AB52 ...71 F6
Licklyhead Way AB21 ...158 C7
Liddell Pl AB21 ...158 B7
Liddles Cl 6 DD9 ...188 C3
Lilac Gr 1 AB42 ...147 B3
Lilac Pl AB16 ...164 B4
Lily Loch Rd AB39 ...185 B5
Lilybank Pl AB25 ...164 F4
Lime St AB11 ...165 E1
Linden Gdns AB44 ...141 D6
Lindsay Pl DD9 ...132 B7
Lindsay St AB10 ...190 A3
Lingbank Terr 1 AB42 ...147 A4
Links Ave DD10 ...189 E4
Links Pk (Montrose FC) DD10 ...189 E4
Links Pl AB11 ...165 E1
Links Rd
Aberdeen AB23 ...165 D8
Banff AB45 ...139 E7
Fraserburgh AB43 ...143 D5
Peterhead AB42 ...27 B3
Links St AB11 ...165 E1
Links Terr AB42 ...147 C5
Links View
Aberdeen AB24 ...165 D4
Cruden Bay AB42 ...53 A2
Peterhead AB42 ...27 B2
Linksfield Gdns AB24 ...165 C4
Linksfield Pl AB24 ...165 C4
Linksfield Rd
Aberdeen AB24 ...165 C4
3 Peterhead AB42 ...147 C4
Linn Moor Residential Sch AB14 ...166 D1
Linn of Dee Pl 2 AB35 ...113 E6
Linn of Dee Rd AB35 ...113 E6
Lintmill Brae AB41 ...63 F5
Lintmill Pl AB16 ...163 F5
Lintmill Terr AB16 ...163 F5
Linton Bsns Pk DD10 ...187 E5
Linton Ind Est DD10 ...187 E7
Linton The AB51 ...86 F1
Lismore Gdns 1 AB16 ...163 E2
Little Belmont St AB10 ...190 A3
Little Chapel St 7 AB10 ...165 A1
Little Farrochie Pl AB39 ...185 C5
Little Nursery DD10 ...189 C5
Little Wynd DD9 ...132 A7
Littlejohn St
Aberdeen AB25 ...190 B4
Huntly AB54 ...148 D4
Littlewood Pl AB33 ...154 D4
Loan Dykes DD10 ...138 D7
Loan The AB45 ...1 F1
Loanhead Pk AB51 ...59 E3
Loanhead Pl AB25 ...164 F2
Loanhead Terr AB25 ...165 A2
Loanhead Wlk 3 AB25 ...165 A2
Loch La AB45 ...8 F8
Loch of Strathbeg Nature Reserve* AB43 ...15 F1
Loch of Strathbeg Visitor Centre, Starnafin* AB43 ...15 D1
Loch St Aberdeen AB25 ...190 A3
Banff AB45 ...8 F8
Rosehearty AB43 ...142 C8
Loch View
1 Fraserburgh AB43 ...26 C7
Westhill AB32 ...161 C4
Loch Way 4 AB51 ...87 D6
Lochans The DD10 ...134 C3
Lochburn Brae AB51 ...155 B6
Lochburn Dr AB51 ...155 B6
Lochnagar Cres AB14 ...172 D7
Lochnagar Rd AB14 ...172 E7
Lochpots Prim Sch AB43 ...143 B5
Lochpots Rd AB43 ...143 B5
Lochside Ave AB23 ...159 F3
Lochside Cres
Aberdeen AB23 ...159 F3
Montrose DD10 ...189 C6
Lochside Distillery* DD10 ...189 C6
Lochside Dr AB23 ...159 F3
Lochside Pl
Aberdeen AB23 ...159 F3
4 Peterhead AB42 ...147 A4
Lochside Prim Sch DD10 ...189 C5
Lochside Rd
Aberdeen AB23 ...159 F3
Montrose DD10 ...134 C3
Peterhead AB42 ...147 A4
Lochside Terr AB23 ...160 A3
Lochside Way AB23 ...159 F3
Lochview Dr AB23 ...160 A3
Lochview Pl AB23 ...159 F3
Lochview Way AB23 ...160 A3
Lodge Wlk
Aberdeen AB10 ...190 B3
1 Fraserburgh AB43 ...143 D6
Peterhead AB42 ...147 E4
Lodging Brae AB45 ...139 E7
Logie Ave
Aberdeen AB16 ...164 C7
11 Cullen AB56 ...1 B5
Logie Ave W AB43 ...26 C8
Logie Coldstone Prim Sch AB34 ...95 D3
Logie Dr Buckie AB56 ...1 B5
Fraserburgh AB43 ...26 C7
Logie Dum Sch AB51 ...59 C1
Logie Gdns AB16 ...164 C7
Logie House* AB51 ...73 A8
Logie Pl AB16 ...164 B6
Logie Rd Ellon AB41 ...63 D2
Fraserburgh AB43 ...26 D7
Logie Terr AB16 ...164 C6
Loirsbank Rd AB15 ...168 E2
Loirston Ave AB12 ...176 B7
Loirston Cl AB12 ...176 B7
Loirston Cres AB12 ...176 C8
Loirston Ct AB12 ...176 B8
Loirston Manor AB12 ...176 C7
Loirston Pl
Aberdeen AB11 ...170 E6
Cove Bay AB12 ...176 C7
Loirston Prim Sch AB12 ...176 B7
Loirston Rd AB12 ...176 C7
Loirston Way AB12 ...176 B8
Loirston Wlk AB12 ...176 B8
Lomond Cres AB41 ...151 B6
Lonach Cres AB54 ...30 C7
Long Cl AB41 ...151 D4
Long Straight The AB51 ...155 A6
Long Wlk Pl AB16 ...164 B4
Long Wlk Rd AB16 ...164 B4
Long Wlk Terr AB16 ...164 B4
Longate AB42 ...147 E5
Longhaven Prim Sch AB42 ...53 C6
Longlands Pl AB16 ...164 B5
Longside Rd AB42 ...146 E5
Longside Sch AB42 ...38 D5
Longview Terr AB16 ...163 F6
Lord Hay's Gr AB24 ...165 C7
Lost Gall The* AB36 ...80 D6
Louden Pl AB21 ...158 C7
Louisville Ave AB15 ...169 D7
Lovat St AB42 ...25 D5
Love La
4 Fraserburgh AB43 ...143 D6
Peterhead AB42 ...147 E5
5 Stonehaven AB39 ...185 F3
Low Rd AB34 ...183 E5
Low Shore Banff AB45 ...8 F8
Macduff AB44 ...141 C7
Low St Banff AB45 ...140 F5
Fraserburgh AB43 ...12 E5
New Pitsligo AB43 ...23 E6
Portsoy AB45 ...139 D7
Low Wood Rd AB39 ...185 D4
Lower Balmain St 4 DD10 ...189 C2
Lower Blantyre St 2 AB56 ...1 B5
Lower Cowgate AB51 ...150 C3
Lower Craigo St 1 DD10 ...189 C2
Lower Denburn AB25 ...190 A3
Lower Grange AB42 ...147 B5
Lower Hall St DD10 ...189 C4
Lubbock Pk Gdns DD9 ...188 B4
Lumphanan Prim Sch AB31 ...98 A3
Lumsden Prim Sch AB54 ...69 B4
Lumsden Way AB23 ...77 C1
Lunan Ave DD10 ...189 C7
Luncarty Pl AB53 ...145 B6
Lusylaw Rd AB45 ...140 D5
Luthermuir Prim Sch AB30 ...133 B7
Lyne of Skene Sch AB32 ...88 A1

M

Maberly St AB25 ...190 A4
MacDonald Rd AB39 ...185 C4
Macallan Rd 3 AB51 ...155 C4
MacAulay Dr AB15 ...169 A6
MacAulay Grange AB15 ...169 B6
MacAulay Pl AB15 ...169 B6
MacAulay Wlk AB15 ...169 B6
MacAuley Gdns AB15 ...169 B6
Macbeth Pl 4 AB31 ...98 A3
MacDiarmid Dr 1 DD10 ...138 C8
Macduff Distillery* AB45 ...141 B4
Macduff Ind Est AB44 ...141 E6
Macduff Marine Aquarium* AB44 ...141 D7
Macduff Prim Sch AB44 ...141 E5
MacGregor Rd AB43 ...15 B7
MacGregor St 1 DD9 ...188 C3
MacKay Rd AB12 ...170 A2
MacKenzie Ave AB30 ...124 B1
MacKenzie Ct AB42 ...147 C2
MacKenzie Gdns DD9 ...188 B4
MacKie Acad AB39 ...185 D6
MacKie Ave AB41 ...61 E6
MacKie Cres AB41 ...61 E6
MacKie Pl AB25 ...165 A1
MacKie's La AB53 ...145 D4
MacLean Terr AB45 ...139 E7
MacNab Ave DD10 ...189 C6
Maconochie Pl AB43 ...143 D4
Maconochie Rd AB43 ...143 D5
Maggie Law Lifeboat Mus* DD10 ...187 D3
Maggie's Hoosie* AB43 ...15 C8
Maiden Castle (Fort)* AB51 ...72 F7
Maiden St AB42 ...147 E5
Maidencraig Pl AB16 ...163 F2
Main Rd
Aberdeen AB21 ...156 B5
Banchory AB31 ...98 A2
Hillside DD10 ...138 C8
Main St
Aberchirder AB54 ...144 C4
Alford AB33 ...154 E3
Banff AB45 ...3 B2
Cruden Bay AB42 ...53 B3
Cuminestown AB53 ...22 B1
Ellon AB41 ...77 F7
Fraserburgh AB43 ...143 C7
Fyvie AB53 ...47 E5
Garmond AB53 ...22 C3
Hatton AB42 ...52 C4
Huntly AB54 ...69 B4
Inverallochy AB43 ...15 C8
Laurencekirk AB30 ...133 A7
Longside AB42 ...38 D6
Montrose DD10 ...135 C5
New Byth AB53 ...22 E4
Portsoy AB45 ...139 E7
Rothienorman AB51 ...47 A2
Sandhaven AB43 ...5 A4
Sauchen AB51 ...87 A1
Turriff AB53 ...145 C4
Mains Circ AB32 ...161 F3
Mains Ct AB32 ...161 F3
Mains View AB32 ...161 F3
Maisondieu La 2 DD9 ...188 C3
Maisondieu Prim Sch DD9 ...188 B3
Maitland Cres AB51 ...152 B8
Maitland Path AB51 ...152 B8
Maitland Wlk AB51 ...152 B8
Major La
9 Oldmeldrum AB51 ...150 C3
4 Oldmeldrum AB51 ...150 C3
Malcolm Rd
Aberdeen AB21 ...163 F8
Banff AB45 ...140 E5
Peterculter AB14 ...172 C7
Malcolm's Mount AB39 ...185 B5
Malcolm's Mount W AB39 ...185 B5
Malcolm's Way AB39 ...185 B4
Mall Pk Rd DD10 ...189 D5
Mall The DD10 ...189 D5
Mallard Ct 12 AB41 ...77 F8
Mallard Dr 3 AB42 ...147 B5
Mallard Rd 11 AB41 ...77 F8
Maltings The DD10 ...189 E4
Mameulah Cres AB21 ...153 D5
Mameulah Ct 1 AB21 ...153 D6
Mameulah Rd AB21 ...153 D6

Mameulah View 2
AB21 153 D6
Manner St AB44 141 D7
Manor Ave AB16 164 B6
Manor Dr AB16 164 C7
Manor Pl AB15 168 E2
Manor Terr AB16 164 C6
Manor Wlk AB16 164 B6
Man's Hill Ave AB39 185 D5
Manse Croft AB31 117 C7
Manse Gdns 3 AB53 145 C4
Manse La
Aberdeen AB21 89 B7
2 Turriff AB53 145 C4
Manse Pl Boddam AB42 40 C1
6 Peterhead AB42 52 C4
Manse Rd
Bieldside AB15 168 C2
Brechin DD9 132 B7
4 Hillside DD10 138 C8
Huntly AB54 55 D1
Inverurie AB51 152 D4
Methlick AB41 49 B3
3 Peterhead AB42 52 C4
Potterton AB23 91 A6
Turriff AB53 145 C4
Udney AB41 62 A1
Westhill AB32 101 E6
Manse St
Fraserburgh AB43 143 D7
Peterhead AB42 25 D5
Manse Terr
23 Boddam AB42 40 D1
7 Peterhead AB42 52 C4
Turriff AB53 145 C5
Manse Wlk AB41 61 F5
Mansefield Pl
Aberdeen AB11 170 E6
2 Banchory AB31 184 E4
2 Fraserburgh AB43 26 D7
Mansefield Rd AB11 170 E6
Manson Rd AB51 150 C2
Maple Pl AB12 176 C6
Mar Lodge Est (NTS)*
AB35 112 F4
Mar Rd Ballater AB35 113 E6
Huntly AB54 70 C7
Marchbank Rd AB15 168 B1
Marchburn Ave AB16 164 A6
Marchburn Cres AB16 164 A6
Marchburn Ct Rd 1
AB16 164 A6
Marchburn Dr AB16 163 F6
Marchburn Inf Sch
AB16 164 A6
Marchburn Pl AB16 164 A6
Marchburn Rd AB16 164 A6
Marchburn Terr AB16 164 B6
Marchfield Dr 1 AB51 152 B7
Marchfield Pl 2 AB51 152 B7
Marchmont Pl AB12 176 C8
Marchmont St AB12 176 C8
Marconi Rd AB43 143 B7
Marconi Terr AB43 143 B7
Marcus Cres AB21 156 B7
Marcus Dr AB21 156 B7
Marcus Gdns AB21 156 B7
Marcus Rd AB21 156 B6
Maree Terr AB41 151 B6
Margaret Clyne Ct
AB12 170 A3
Margaret Pl AB10 169 F5
Margaret St
5 Aberdeen AB10 165 A1
1 Stonehaven AB39 185 E4
Marine Ave DD10 189 D3
Marine Ct AB11 190 A1
Marine La AB11 190 A1
Marine Terr
Aberdeen AB11 190 A1
Portsoy AB45 139 D7
Stonehaven AB39 181 G1
Marischal Coll (University of Aberdeen) AB25 190 B4
Marischal Gdns AB21 163 D7
Marischal Mus* AB10 190 B3
Marischal St
Aberdeen AB11 190 B3
Peterhead AB42 147 E5
4 Stonehaven AB39 185 F3
Market Brae AB41 151 D6
Market Hill Ellon AB41 151 D6
3 Peterhead AB42 38 D6
Market La
Aberdeen AB24 165 B5
Stonehaven AB39 185 E4
10 Strichen AB43 24 E5
4 Turriff AB53 145 D5
Market Pl
4 Inverurie AB51 152 E6
New Pitsligo AB43 23 E6
Market Pl Sch AB51 152 E5
Market Rd AB30 186 C5
Market Sq
2 Inverbervie DD10 187 E7
Laurencekirk AB30 124 B1
11 Oldmeldrum AB51 150 C3
1 Oldmeldrum AB51 150 C3
15 Stonehaven AB39 185 E4
Market St
Aberchirder AB54 144 C4
Aberdeen AB11 190 B3
Brechin DD9 188 C4
Ellon AB41 151 D4
Greenburn AB21 158 A2
Huntly AB54 148 C4
Insch AB52 149 D5
Macduff AB44 141 C6
Market St continued
Montrose DD10 189 D4
2 Peterhead AB42 36 E6
Turriff AB53 145 C5
Market Stance 7 AB34 96 C3
Market Terr 9 AB43 24 E6
Markethill Ind Est
AB53 145 D5
Markethill Prim Sch
AB53 145 C5
Markethill Rd AB53 145 D5
Marlpool Pl AB21 163 D7
Marlpool Specl Sch
AB21 163 D8
Marquis Rd AB24 164 F6
Marsh Pl AB12 180 B5
Mart Rd AB33 154 D3
Martin Ave AB39 185 C6
Martin Brae AB51 152 C5
Martin Dr AB39 185 C6
Martin Pl AB39 185 C6
Martin Rd AB52 149 D5
Martin Terr DD10 131 C7
Martin's La 3 DD9 188 C3
Mary St AB39 185 E4
Maryculter E Sch
AB12 173 F3
Maryculter Sch AB12 177 F8
Maryfield Cres AB51 152 C6
Maryfield Pl 1 AB51 152 C6
Marykirk Prim Sch
AB30 133 D4
Marykirk Rd DD10 138 D8
Maryville Pk AB15 164 C1
Maryville Pl AB15 164 C1
Marywell La AB51 99 C6
Marywell St AB11 190 A2
Mastrick Cl AB16 164 B3
Mastrick Dr AB16 164 A3
Mastrick Junc AB16 164 A3
Mastrick Rd AB16 164 B3
Mathers Pk 9 DD9 188 C3
Mathers Pl 1 AB41 77 F8
Mathieson La 4 AB31 98 E1
Matthew Dr AB42 147 A4
Matthews Rd AB12 170 A2
Maud Hospl AB42 36 E6
Maud Prim Sch AB42 36 E6
Maud Rly Sta Mus*
AB42 36 F6
Maud Sta Bsns Pk
AB42 36 E6
Mavis Bank 7 AB41 77 F8
Maxwell Cres AB12 170 A1
Maxwell Pl AB43 143 B6
Maxwell Pl Ind Est
AB43 143 A6
May Baird Ave AB25 164 F3
Mayfield Gdns
Aberdeen AB15 169 D7
Insch AB52 149 D4
Mayfield Rd
St Cyrus DD10 134 D3
Turriff AB53 145 E4
Mayfield Terr AB52 149 D4
McCombie Cres 7 AB51 87 D7
McGregor Closet
AB42 147 A7
McGregor Cres AB42 147 A7
McIntosh's La 3 AB53 145 D4
McBey Way AB41 77 C6
McDonald Dr AB41 151 C6
McDonald Gdns AB41 151 D6
McDonald St 1 AB54 148 E4
McEwan Gall* AB35 104 A4
McGill Terr DD10 187 D3
McIver Terr AB54 148 C4
McKay Rd AB44 141 C6
McVeagh St AB54 148 D5
Meadow Ave AB54 148 D5
Meadow Croft 1 AB51 74 F2
Meadow Ct 1 AB54 144 D5
Meadow Dr AB51 150 C3
Meadow La AB24 165 A7
Meadow Pl
Aberdeen AB24 165 A7
1 Inverurie AB51 152 B8
Meadow Rd
2 Inverurie AB51 152 B8
Turriff AB53 22 C1
Meadow St AB54 148 D5
Meadowbank Pl 1
AB53 145 C5
Meadowbank Rd
AB53 145 B6
Meadowlands Ave
AB32 161 E4
Meadowlands Cl 1
AB15 161 E5
Meadowlands Cres
AB32 161 E5
Meadowlands Ct 3
AB32 161 E5
Meadowlands Dr
AB32 161 D5
Meadowlands Pk
AB32 161 D5
Meadowlands Pl
AB32 161 D5
Meadowlands Way 2
AB32 161 E5
Meadows Dr AB51 150 C3
Meadows The
Aberdeen AB13 167 D1
Ellon AB41 63 D5
Meadows Vale AB51 150 C2
Meadows Way AB41 151 F4
Meadowside DD10 187 D7
Mealmarket St AB24 190 B4
Mearns Acad AB30 186 E6
Mearns Cl 4 AB51 152 B8
Mearns Dr
Laurencekirk AB30 186 C4
Montrose DD10 189 C7
Stonehaven AB39 185 C6
Mearns Pk AB30 186 D6
Mearns Sports Ctr
AB30 186 E6
Mearns St AB11 190 C3
Mearns Wlk
Laurencekirk AB30 186 B4
Stonehaven AB39 185 C5
Meavie Pl AB45 140 E6
Medicine Well Dr
DD10 189 C5
Meethill Pl AB42 147 B4
Meethill Prim Sch
AB42 147 C3
Meethill Rd AB42 147 B5
Meikle Gdns AB32 161 D3
Meikle Mill DD9 188 D2
Meiklemill Farm Ind Est
AB41 151 A4
Meiklemill Prim Sch
AB41 151 B4
Meldrum Acad AB51 150 B4
Meldrum Dr AB21 153 D5
Meldrum Meg Way
AB51 150 B2
Meldrum Prim Sch
AB51 150 C3
Melgum Rd AB34 96 B3
Melrose Cres AB44 141 D6
Melrose Pl AB51 155 B3
Melrose Wlk AB14 172 D6
Melville Gdns DD10 189 D3
Melville Rd DD10 189 D3
Menie Cl 10 AB23 91 C8
Menie Cres 4 AB23 91 C8
Menie House* AB23 77 D3
Menzies Rd AB11 190 B1
Merchant St AB42 147 E4
Merchants Quay 3
AB42 147 E4
Mercury Lone DD10 134 D3
Mercury Terr DD10 134 D3
Meridian St 5 DD10 189 D2
Merkland La AB24 165 D4
Merkland Pl AB24 165 C4
Merkland Rd AB24 165 C4
Merkland Rd E AB24 165 C4
Merlin Terr 9 AB41 77 F8
Meston Wlk AB24 165 B5
Methlick Prim Sch
AB41 49 B4
Mews The AB31 184 D3
Mid St Banff AB45 7 E1
Fraserburgh AB43 143 C6
Inverallochy AB43 15 C8
Mid Street AB43 15 D6
Montrose DD10 135 C6
Peterhead AB42 147 D7
Rosehearty AB43 142 C8
Mid Stocket Mews
AB25 164 F2
Mid Stocket Rd AB15 164 C2
Midchingle Rd AB11 190 C2
Middleburgh Rd AB43 143 C4
Middlefield Cres
AB24 164 D6
Middlefield Pl AB24 164 D6
Middlefield Prim Sch
AB16 164 C6
Middlefield Terr AB24 164 D6
Middlefield Wlk AB24 164 D5
Middlemuir Rd AB51 152 C6
Middleton Circ AB22 159 C3
Middleton Cl AB22 159 C3
Middleton Cres AB22 159 C3
Middleton Dr AB22 159 C3
Middleton Path AB22 159 C3
Middleton Pk DD9 188 D2
Middleton Pk Prim Sch
AB22 159 D3
Middleton Pl
Aberdeen AB22 159 F1
Insch AB52 58 D3
Middleton Rd
Aberdeen AB22 159 C3
Insch AB52 58 D3
Middleton Terr AB22 159 C3
Middleton Way
Aberdeen AB22 159 C3
Inverurie AB51 152 C7
Midmar Castle*
AB51 100 A4
Midmar Cres AB15 162 F4
Midmar Pk AB15 162 F4
Midmar Prim Sch AB51 99 D6
Midmar View AB15 162 F3
Midmar Wlk AB15 162 F4
Midmill Bsns Pk AB51 155 D2
Migvie Ave AB15 162 F4
Migvie Castle (remains of)*
AB34 95 D5
Migvie Gdns AB15 162 F4
Migvie Gr AB15 162 F4
Migvie Lea AB15 162 F4
Mildens Row AB39 185 E6
Mile End AB42 147 C3
Mile End Pl 2 AB42 147 C3
Mile End Prim Sch
AB15 164 E1
Mile-End Ave AB15 164 E2
Mile-End La AB15 164 F2
Mile-End Pl AB15 164 E2
Mile-End S AB10 170 A6
Mill Ct AB24 164 D7
Mill La Montrose DD10 189 C2
Peterhead AB42 37 D4
Mill Lade Wynd AB22 164 C8
Mill of Forest Gr AB39 185 B3
Mill of Forest La 6
AB39 185 C4
Mill of Forest Rd
AB39 185 B4
Mill o'Forest Prim Sch
AB39 185 B4
Mill Pl Aboyne AB34 96 B3
Montrose DD10 133 D3
Mill Rd Aboyne AB34 96 B3
Huntly AB54 148 E4
Inverurie AB51 152 E1
2 Montrose DD10 189 C3
Oldmeldrum AB51 150 D2
Turriff AB53 145 C4
Mill St MacDuff AB44 141 D7
Montrose DD10 189 D4
Millan Ct 7 AB31 98 A3
Millan Pk 5 AB31 98 A3
Millan View 6 AB31 98 A3
Millarsmires End 4
AB22 159 E2
Millbank La AB25 165 A3
Millbank Pl AB25 165 A3
Millburn Ave AB43 15 D6
Millburn Ct AB44 141 E5
Millburn Pl AB43 143 A5
Millburn Rd AB51 150 B2
Millburn St AB11 190 B1
Millden Rd AB15 168 F3
Milleath Wlk 2 AB21 158 C7
Millend 3 AB41 77 F7
Miller Gdns
Fraserburgh AB43 143 A6
Newmachar AB21 153 D5
Miller St AB11 190 C3
Miller St Ind Est AB11 190 C3
Millers Visitor & Ret Ctr The* AB51 99 F5
Millfield Ave 2 AB51 152 C7
Millfield Dr AB51 152 C7
Millfield Pl AB51 152 C7
Millfield Terr 1 AB51 152 C7
Millgrove Rd AB21 158 C2
Millhill Brae AB21 158 C1
Millpark Rd AB41 151 A6
Millside Dr AB14 172 C6
Millside Rd AB14 172 C6
Millside St AB14 172 C6
Millside Terr AB14 172 C6
Millstone Pl 8 AB51 87 D7
Milltimber Brae AB13 173 A7
Milltimber Brae E
AB13 173 A7
Milltimber Prim Sch
AB13 173 C8
Millwood Rd AB41 151 B6
Milnamair 1 DD10 189 C3
Milne's Wynd DD10 135 C6
Milton Dr AB51 87 C6
Milton of Arbuthnott
AB30 130 D6
Milton of Crathes Visitor Ctr The* AB31 110 D3
Milton View AB51 87 C6
Minden Cl AB23 160 B1
Mineralwell View
AB39 185 E6
Minister La
8 Aberdeen AB10 165 A1
2 Aberdeen AB10 190 A3
Mintlaw Acad AB42 146 C5
Mintlaw Prim Sch
AB42 146 E5
Mintlaw Rd AB42 25 D1
Minto Ave AB12 170 F3
Minto Circ 2 AB51 87 C7
Minto Dr AB12 170 F2
Minto Rd AB12 170 F2
Minty's La 2 AB53 145 D4
Mitchell Ave AB54 148 C5
Mitchell Dr DD9 188 D1
Mitchell Gdns AB21 156 B7
Mitchell Pl AB42 37 D4
Modley Ave AB41 151 B4
Modley Cl AB41 151 B4
Modley Ct AB41 151 B4
Modley Pl AB41 151 C5
Moir Ave AB16 164 C5
Moir Cres AB16 164 C5
Moir Dr AB16 164 C5
Moir Gn AB16 164 C5
Monaltrie Ave AB35 182 E5
Monaltrie Cl AB35 182 E6
Monaltrie Cres AB35 182 D5
Monaltrie Rd AB35 182 E4
Monaltrie Way AB35 182 E5
Monarch Terr 5 AB16 163 E2
Monboddo Rd 16 AB31 108 E8
Monboddo St AB30 124 B1
Monduff Rd AB39 181 G2
Monearn Gdns AB13 173 B8
Monquhitter Prim Sch
AB53 22 C1
Montbletton Pl AB44 141 E5
Monteach Rd AB41 49 C7
Montgarrie Rd AB33 154 D4
Montgomery Rd AB24 164 F7
Montrose Acad DD10 189 D3
Montrose Air Sta Mus*
DD10 189 D6
Montrose Basin Nature Reserve* DD10 189 A3
Montrose Basin Wildlife Ctr*
DD10 138 B3
Montrose Cl AB21 157 E5
Montrose Dr AB10 169 E3
Montrose Mus & Art Gall*
DD10 189 D3
Montrose Rd
Aberdeen AB21 157 E5
Inverbervie DD10 187 D6
Montrose Royal Infmy
DD10 189 B2
Montrose Sports Ctr
DD10 189 E3
Montrose St DD9 188 D2
Montrose Sta DD10 189 C4
Montrose Way AB21 157 E5
Monument Cl AB42 147 C2
Monymusk Arts Ctr*
AB51 86 E5
Monymusk Prim Sch
AB51 86 E6
Monymusk Terr AB15 169 A7
Monymusk Walled Gdn*
AB51 86 F6
Moor Pl AB12 180 C6
Morar Ct AB41 151 A6
Moray Pl AB15 164 C1
Moray Rd AB43 143 C7
Moray St AB44 141 E7
Moray View 4 AB45 140 E6
Morgan Rd AB24 164 D4
Morlich Ave AB41 151 B6
Mormond Ave AB43 143 C5
Mormond Cres AB42 146 E4
Mormond Pl
Inverallochy AB43 15 B7
Strichen AB43 24 F6
Mormond View 1 AB42 25 D5
Morningfield Mews
AB15 164 D1
Morningfield Rd AB15 164 D1
Morningside Ave
Aberdeen AB10 169 D4
4 Inverurie AB51 152 A7
Morningside Cres
Aberdeen AB10 169 D4
7 Inverurie AB51 152 A7
Morningside Dr AB51 152 A7
Morningside Gdns
Aberdeen AB10 169 E5
2 Inverurie AB51 152 A7
Morningside Gr AB10 169 D5
Morningside Pk AB51 152 A8
Morningside Pl AB10 169 D5
Morningside Rd
Aberdeen AB10 169 D5
5 Inverurie AB51 152 A7
Morningside Terr
Aberdeen AB10 169 D4
6 Inverurie AB51 152 A7
Morphie Dr DD10 134 D3
Morrison Ct 1 AB42 36 E7
Morrison Dr AB10 169 C4
Morrison Pl
6 Kemnay AB51 87 D7
Peterhead AB42 53 A3
Morrison Way AB51 155 C2
Morrison's La AB53 145 D4
Morrone Birkwood National Nature Reserve*
AB35 113 D5
Mortimer Dr AB15 168 F8
Mortimer Pl AB15 168 F8
Mortimer's La AB51 152 C7
Mortlich Gdns AB34 183 B4
Morven Ave DD10 189 C8
Morven Circ AB32 161 D4
Morven Cres
Peterhead AB42 147 B6
Westhill AB32 161 D3
Morven Dr AB32 161 D3
Morven Gdns AB32 161 D3
Morven Pl
Aberdeen AB11 170 D6
Aboyne AB34 183 B4
Morven View 1 AB34 96 C3
Morven Way AB35 182 E6
Morven-View Rd AB45 3 C2
Mosman Gdns AB24 164 D5
Mosman Pl AB24 164 E5
Moss Rd
Aberchirder AB54 144 C5
Huntly AB54 55 D1
Moss St AB55 28 E7
Mosscroft Ave AB32 161 C1
Mosside Cres AB12 180 B6
Mosside Dr AB12 180 B6
Mosside Pl 2 AB32 161 D2
Mounie Castle* AB51 60 A3
Mount Ave DD10 189 D4
Mount Pleasant AB23 165 D8
Mount Rd DD10 189 D4
Mount St
Aberdeen AB25 165 A2
Banchory AB31 184 B5
Mounthooly AB24 165 C3
Mounthooly Way
AB24 165 C3
Mountskip Cres DD9 188 B4
Mountskip Rd DD9 188 B4
Mountview Gdns 4
AB25 165 A2
Mowatshill Rd AB42 147 B4
Mowatts La 3 DD10 187 D3

Muchalls Castle* AB39 121 B6
Mugiemoss Rd AB21 163 F8
Muir of Dinnet National Nature Reserve* AB34 105 D6
Muir Rd AB43 14 B5
Muirend Rd AB12 180 B6
Muiresk Dr AB53 145 B5
Muirfield Pl AB16 164 B2
Muirfield Prim Sch AB16 164 B2
Muirfield Rd AB16 164 B3
Muirs The AB54 55 D2
Muirton Cres AB21 158 C7
Mull Way AB16 163 E2
Mulloch View 2 AB34 106 A5
Mundi Cres AB21 153 D6
Mundurno Rd AB22 159 D1
Murcar Ind Est AB23 160 A5
Murison Dr AB43 142 B7
Murray Ave 2 AB41 61 E5
Murray La 3 DD10 189 C4
Murray Pl AB39 185 D3
Murray Rd AB39 181 I5
Murray St DD10 189 C4
Murray Terr
Aberdeen AB11 170 B6
Alford AB33 154 C3
Murray's La AB11 190 C1
Murtle Den Rd AB13 167 F1
Museum of Farming Life* AB41 62 A3
Museum of Scottish Lighthouses* AB43 143 D8
Museum St 3 DD10 189 D3
Myrtle Est AB15 173 E7
Myrtle Terr AB12 180 A5
Myrus Ave AB45 141 D4
Myrus Circ AB44 141 E5

N

Napier Pl AB30 133 D4
Napier Terr AB30 133 D5
Narrow La 4 AB42 147 E5
Natural Arches & Cliff Stacks* AB42 53 D5
Neil Burn Dr 4 AB34 108 B6
Nellfield Pl AB10 170 A7
Nellfred Terr AB51 152 C7
Nelson Ct AB24 165 C3
Nelson La AB24 165 C3
Nelson Pl AB54 148 D4
Nelson St
Aberdeen AB24 165 C3
Huntly AB54 148 D4
Ness Circ AB41 151 B7
Ness Pl AB16 164 A3
Nether Aden Rd AB42 146 E5
Nether Blackhall AB51 152 A6
Nether Caldhame DD9 188 E3
Nether Davah Ct 2 AB51 152 B5
Nether Davah Pl 1 AB51 152 B5
Nether Davah Way AB51 152 B5
Netherby Rd AB15 168 D2
Netherhill La AB42 27 B2
Netherhills Ave AB21 163 D7
Netherhills Pl AB21 163 D7
Netherkirkgate AB10 190 B3
Netherley Pl 2 AB35 182 E4
Netherley Prim Sch AB39 120 C8
Nethermains Rd AB39 181 G2
Nethermuir Rd AB42 36 D6
Netherview Ave AB21 158 C7
Netherview Pl AB21 158 B6
Netherview Rd AB21 158 B6
Neuk The AB21 156 B7
Nevada Ct 5 AB21 153 C6
Nevis Bsns Pk AB22 159 D1
New Aberdeen Childrens Hospl AB25 164 E3
New Aberdour Prim Sch AB43 12 E6
New Byth Prim Sch AB53 22 E4
New Deer Sch AB53 36 A5
New Gd AB45 3 C3
New Pier Rd AB11 170 F8
New Pitsligo & St John's Sch AB43 23 D6
New Pk Pl AB16 164 A3
New Pk Rd AB16 164 A3
New Rd Huntly AB54 148 E4
Montrose DD10 135 C6
New St 17 Boddam AB42 40 D1
Peterhead AB42 147 E6
Stonehaven AB39 185 E4
New View Ct 9 AB56 1 B5
New Wynd DD10 189 C3
Newbigging Dr 5 AB39 185 C4
Newbigging Pl DD10 187 D7
Newburgh Circ AB22 159 D4
Newburgh Cres AB22 159 E3
Newburgh Dr AB22 159 D3
Newburgh Mathers Prim Sch AB41 77 F8
Newburgh Path AB22 159 D3
Newburgh Pl AB22 159 E3
Newburgh Rd AB22 159 E4
Newburgh St AB22 159 D3
Newburgh Way AB22 159 D3
Newhame Rd DD10 189 C7
Newhills Ave AB21 163 D6
Newhills Prim Sch AB21 163 D7
Newlands Ave AB10 169 E5
Newlands Cres AB10 169 E5
Newlands Dr AB51 155 C5
Newlands Rd AB42 146 D4
Newmachar Prim Sch AB21 153 D6
Newmanswalls Ave DD10 189 C6
Newton Rd
Aberdeen AB16 164 C6
Dyce AB21 157 E6
Mintlaw AB42 146 D5
Peterhead AB42 27 B2
Stonehaven AB39 181 I5
Newton Terr AB21 163 F8
Newtonhill Rd AB39 181 H4
Newtown Dr AB44 141 E7
Nicol Ct AB35 182 E4
Nicol Pl AB12 180 C6
Nicol Rd 2 AB51 155 C4
Nicol's Brae AB44 141 C7
Nigg Kirk Rd AB12 170 C3
Nigg Way AB12 170 A1
Ninian Pl AB12 180 C7
Ninian Rd AB21 157 E6
Noble St AB43 143 C7
Norfolk Rd AB10 169 E5
North Anderson Dr AB15 164 C2
North Balnagask Rd AB11 170 F7
North Beach Rd AB23 91 C8
North Braeheads 2 AB43 143 D7
North Castle St 13 AB56 1 B5
North Deeside Rd
Aberdeen AB13 173 A7
Aboyne AB34 108 A6
Peterculter AB14 172 C6
North Deskford St 3 AB56 1 B4
North Donside Rd AB23 160 A1
North East Falconry Ctr* AB54 43 A8
North Esk Rd
Brechin DD9 132 B7
Montrose DD10 189 D4
North Espl E AB11 190 C2
North Espl W AB11 190 B1
North Grampian Circ AB11 170 D6
North High St AB45 139 D7
North La
Fraserburgh AB43 143 D7
Peterhead AB42 147 D7
North Latch Rd DD9 188 A4
North Pl AB42 25 C1
North Rd Insch AB52 149 C4
Peterhead AB42 147 A8
North Silver St AB10 190 A3
North St
Aberchirder AB54 144 D4
Fraserburgh AB43 143 D7
Huntly AB54 144 C4
Inverurie AB51 152 C7
Mintlaw AB42 146 D6
Montrose DD10 189 D4
1 Peterhead AB42 147 E6
Rosehearty AB43 142 B8
Strichen AB43 24 E6
North St Andrew St 3 AB25 190 A4
North Stocket La 3 AB16 164 C4
Northburn Ave AB15 169 B8
Northburn La AB15 169 A8
Northcote Ave AB15 169 B4
Northcote Cres AB15 169 B5
Northcote Hill AB15 169 B4
Northcote Pk AB15 169 B4
Northcote Rd AB15 169 C4
Northern Coll AB24 164 F5
Northern Rd AB51 155 B6
Northfield Acad AB16 164 C5
Northfield Farm Mus* AB43 12 C2
Northfield Gdns 4 AB42 52 C4
Northfield Pl
Aberdeen AB25 165 A1
3 Ellon AB41 151 B5
Northfield Swimming Pool AB16 164 B5
Novar Pl AB25 165 A2
Nursery La
Brechin DD9 188 D1
Inverurie AB51 152 E5
Nursery Pk DD9 188 D2
Nursery Rd DD10 189 C5

O

Oak Cres AB32 161 D2
Oak Dr AB12 180 B4
Oak Tree Ave AB31 184 E6
Oak View 6 AB23 91 C8
Oakbank Gdns 7 AB51 150 C3
Oakbank Sch AB15 164 D1
Oakhill Cres AB15 164 D1
Oakhill Rd
Aberdeen AB15 164 D1
Kintore AB51 155 C4
Ogilvie Ave AB54 148 D3
Ogilvie Cres AB51 155 B5
Ogilvie Pl AB45 140 E5
Ogilvie St 2 AB45 8 F8
Ogilvie Terr DD10 189 C1
Ogston Rd AB41 151 B5
Ogstonmill 1 AB21 89 B7
Old Aberdeen Rd
3 Ellon AB41 61 E5
Laurencekirk AB30 129 F7
Old Castlegate 11 AB45 140 F6
Old Chapel Rd AB51 152 B7
Old Chapel Wlk 3 AB51 152 C7
Old Church Rd
Aberdeen AB11 170 D5
Buckie AB56 1 A4
Old Coast Rd AB12 180 D4
Old Course Ave AB51 152 B5
Old Ferry Rd AB15 168 B1
Old Ford Rd AB11 190 B1
Old Gamrie Rd AB44 141 E6
Old Inn Rd AB12 180 F7
Old Kemnay Rd AB51 152 D3
Old Line Rd AB35 182 C5
Old Mart Pl DD9 188 D3
Old Mart Rd 14 AB31 108 E8
Old Meldrum Rd AB21 158 D1
Old Military Rd
Alford AB33 97 F8
Ballater AB35 113 E1
Banchory AB31 98 A6
Huntly AB54 56 A7
Old Mill Cres AB23 91 C8
Old Mill Rd AB39 181 I4
Old Mkt Pl AB45 141 A5
Old Pier AB39 185 F3
Old Port Rd AB51 152 E5
Old Rayne Prim Sch AB52 58 D3
Old Rd
Aberchirder AB54 144 D5
Huntly AB54 148 E4
Old Rectory Ave AB41 151 D4
Old Road AB23 91 C8
Old Royal Sta The* AB35 182 D4
Old Sch 1 AB42 146 D5
Old Sch Rd AB53 22 D5
Old Skene Rd
Aberdeen AB15 163 A1
Kingswells AB15 162 F1
Westhill AB32 161 C3
Old Sta Pl AB35 182 E5
Old Sta Rd AB51 152 E5
Old Sta Sq DD10 134 D3
Old Strichen Rd AB43 143 B3
Old Toll Rd AB54 148 E3
Old Tollhouse Rd AB34 183 C5
Oldcroft Pl AB16 164 C3
Oldcroft Terr AB16 164 C3
Oldfold Ave AB13 167 D1
Oldfold Cres AB13 167 D1
Oldfold Dr AB13 167 D1
Oldfold Pk AB13 167 D1
Oldfold Pl AB13 167 D1
Oldfold Wlk AB13 167 D1
Oldmachar Acad AB22 159 D3
Oldman Rd AB12 173 B3
Oldmeldrum Rd
Aberdeen AB21 153 C6
Ellon AB41 62 A2
Oldmill Rd AB11 190 A2
Oldtown Pl AB16 164 B6
Oldtown Rd AB34 183 F5
Oldtown Terr AB16 164 A6
Omar Ave DD10 189 B5
Orange La DD10 189 D4
Orchard The 2 AB24 165 C4
Orchard Gr Ellon AB41 76 C7
3 Peterhead AB42 147 B3
Westhill AB32 100 D4
Orchard Pl AB24 165 C4
Orchard Rd AB24 165 C4
Orchard St AB24 165 C4
Orchard Wlk 1 AB24 165 C4
Ord St AB15 169 B8
Ordiquhill Prim Sch AB45 18 C7
Orkney Ave AB16 163 E3
Osborne Pl AB25 164 F1
Oscar Pl AB11 170 D6
Oscar Rd AB11 170 D6
Overhill Gdns AB22 159 E1
Overton Ave AB21 158 C5
Overton Circ AB21 158 B5
Overton Cres AB21 158 C5
Overton Pk AB21 158 C5
Overton Way AB21 158 B5
Overton Wlk AB21 158 C6
Oyne Prim Sch AB52 72 D8
Oyne Rd AB15 169 A7

P

Paddock The AB14 172 D6
Palmerston Pl AB11 190 B1
Palmerston Rd AB11 190 B2
Palmerston St 4 DD10 189 D2
Panmure Gdns AB23 91 A6
Panmure Pl DD10 189 D3
Panmure Row 5 DD10 189 D3
Panmure St
Brechin DD9 188 C3
2 Montrose DD10 189 D3
Panmure Terr DD10 189 D3
Pannanich Rd AB35 182 E5
Panter Cres DD10 189 C6
Pantoch Dr 2 AB31 184 F5
Pantoch Gdns 1 AB31 184 F5
Pantoch Way AB31 184 F5
Paradise Rd AB51 87 D7
Park Brae AB15 168 E2
Park Cres Banff AB45 7 E1
Ellon AB41 151 C4
Oldmeldrum AB51 150 D4
Peterhead AB42 36 E6
Portsoy AB45 139 C6
Park Dr Portsoy AB45 139 D7
Stonehaven AB39 185 C6
Park Gr Aberdeen AB23 91 A8
Brechin DD9 188 E3
Park La Aberdeen AB24 190 C4
Huntly AB54 56 A7
Oldmeldrum AB51 150 D4
3 Peterhead AB42 147 F5
Park Pl Aberdeen AB24 190 B4
Brechin DD9 188 D3
3 Peterhead AB42 52 D4
Stonehaven AB39 181 H4
Park Rd Aberdeen AB15 168 E2
Aberdeen AB24 190 C4
Brechin DD9 188 D3
Ellon AB41 151 C4
Oldmeldrum AB51 150 D4
Portsoy AB45 139 C7
Park Rd Ct AB24 165 D3
Park St Aberdeen AB24 190 C4
Fraserburgh AB43 143 C7
Huntly AB54 148 E4
Park St N AB54 148 E5
Park Terr
Aberdeen AB23 91 A8
Ellon AB41 151 C4
Park View
Aberchirder AB54 144 C4
Brechin DD9 188 E4
Mintlaw AB42 146 C4
Peterhead AB42 52 D4
Parkhill AB51 87 D6
Parkhill Ave AB21 158 C5
Parkhill Circ AB21 158 B5
Parkhill Cres AB21 158 C5
Parkhill Rd
Alford AB33 154 C4
Peterhead AB42 147 D6
Parkhill Way AB21 158 B5
Parkside
Montrose DD10 135 C6
Westhill AB32 161 D2
Parkvale 5 AB42 38 D6
Parkview AB42 146 C4
Parkway E AB23 160 B2
Parkway The AB22 159 E2
Partan Skelly Ave AB12 176 B7
Partan Skelly Way AB12 176 B7
Pass of Ballater AB35 182 D6
Pat McBoyle Ct 1 AB54 148 D5
Paterson Pl 1 DD10 189 C7
Paterson St AB44 141 D7
Patey Rd AB41 151 C3
Paton's La DD10 189 E3
Peacock's Cl AB10 190 C3
Pearse St DD9 188 B3
Peat Way AB12 180 B6
Peggy's Gdn AB31 111 B3
Pennan Rd
Aberdeen AB24 165 A7
Ellon AB41 151 D6
Pennan Way AB41 151 D7
Penny Pl 3 AB42 147 A5
Pentland Cl AB11 170 F7
Pentland Cres AB11 171 A7
Pentland Pl
Aberdeen AB11 170 F6
Peterhead AB42 147 A6
Pentland Rd AB11 170 F7
Peregrine Rd AB32 161 C1
Perkhill Rd AB31 98 A3
Perry Rd DD9 132 D8
Persley Cres AB16 164 C6
Petergrange Rd AB42 147 B5
Peterhead Acad AB42 147 D6
Peterhead Com Hospl AB42 147 D4
Peterhead Maritime Heritage Ctr* AB42 147 C3
Peterhead Swimming Pool AB42 147 D6
Peterhead Ugie Hospl AB42 147 C7
Peterseat Dr AB12 170 F3
Peterwell Rd AB53 47 E4
Peth of Minnonie AB53 48 B3
Pettens Cl AB23 91 D8
Pettens St AB23 91 C8
Pheppie Rd AB39 181 G2
Philorth Ave AB43 143 C4
Phingask Rd AB43 143 C4
Phoenix Pl AB21 158 C3
Picktillum Ave AB25 164 F4
Picktillum Pl AB25 164 F4
Pictavia Ex* DD9 136 B6
Pine View
Fraserburgh AB43 143 A6
Huntly AB54 148 C5
Pine View *continued*
Mintlaw AB42 146 D5
Pinecrest Circ AB15 168 B3
Pinecrest Dr AB15 168 A3
Pinecrest Gdns AB15 168 A3
Pinecrest Wlk AB15 168 A2
Pinewood Ave AB15 169 A6
Pinewood Pl
Aberdeen AB15 169 A6
Cove Bay AB12 176 C7
Peterhead AB42 147 A4
Pinewood Rd AB15 169 A6
Pinewood Terr AB15 169 A6
Pinkie Gdns 3 AB21 153 D4
Pinkie Rd AB21 153 D5
Pintail Pl AB42 147 B5
Piper Pl AB12 180 C7
Pirie's Ct AB24 164 F6
Pirie's La
Aberdeen AB24 164 F5
Fraserburgh AB43 5 A4
3 Inverurie AB51 152 D6
5 Turriff AB53 145 D5
Pitblae Gdns AB43 143 B3
Pitblae Pl AB43 143 A3
Pitchaidlie Pl 1 AB45 1 F1
Pitfichie Castle* AB51 86 D7
Pitfichie La 4 AB21 158 C7
Pitfichie Pl AB21 158 C7
Pitfodels Sta Rd AB15 169 B3
Pitforthie Pl DD9 188 E4
Pitfour Cres 1 AB42 25 C1
Pitfour Ct AB42 147 B4
Pitfour Pl AB42 146 E4
Pitfour Prim Sch AB42 146 C5
Pitlurg Castle* AB55 28 D4
Pitmedden Ave AB21 158 B7
Pitmedden Cres AB10 169 E3
Pitmedden Dr AB21 158 B7
Pitmedden Gdn (NTS)* AB41 62 A2
Pitmedden Mews AB21 158 B7
Pitmedden Prim Sch AB41 62 B2
Pitmedden Rd
Aberdeen AB10 169 E4
Dyce AB21 158 A8
Overton AB21 89 E5
Pitmedden Read Ind Est AB21 157 F8
Pitmedden Terr AB10 169 E4
Pitmedden Way AB21 158 B7
Pitmunie Pl 3 AB51 87 C7
Pitmurchie Rd AB34 108 A7
Pitodrie Stadium (Aberdeen FC) AB24 165 D4
Pitsligo Castle (remains of)* AB43 142 D7
Pitsligo St AB43 142 B6
Pitstruan Pl AB10 169 F6
Pitstruan Terr AB10 169 F6
Pittendriech Rd DD9 188 A4
Pittendrum Gdns AB43 5 A4
Pittengullies Brae AB13 172 F6
Pittengullies Circ AB14 172 F6
Pittodrie La AB24 165 C4
Pittodrie Pl AB24 165 C4
Pittodrie St AB24 165 C4
Pittrichie View AB21 75 C7
Pittulie Castle* AB43 142 F7
Place of Tilliefoure* AB51 72 B2
Plane Tree Rd AB16 164 D4
Plane Trees 3 AB53 22 C1
Planetarium* AB25 190 B4
Pleasure Wlk AB42 147 F4
Plover Pl AB41 151 B4
Poet's Pl DD9 188 E2
Police La 4 AB43 24 E6
Polinar Pl AB51 152 D4
Polmuir Ave AB11 170 B6
Polmuir Pl AB11 170 B6
Polmuir Rd AB11 190 A1
Polo Gdns AB21 158 C3
Polston Rd AB12 173 B3
Polwarth Rd AB11 170 C6
Pool La AB42 147 F4
Poplar Cres AB42 147 B4
Poplar Rd 2 AB16 164 D4
Port Elphinstone Prim Sch AB51 152 D3
Port Erroll Sch AB42 53 B3
Port Henry Rd 3 AB42 147 E6
Port Rd 2 AB51 152 E6
Portal Cres AB24 165 A5
Portal Terr AB24 165 A5
Portland St AB11 190 B1
Portlethen Acad AB12 180 B5
Portlethen Prim Sch AB12 180 C6
Portlethen Sta AB12 180 C6
Portree Ave AB16 163 E3
Portsoy Cres AB41 151 E6
Portsoy Gr AB41 151 F6
Portsoy Pl 2 AB41 151 E6
Portsoy Prim Sch AB45 139 D6
Poultry Mkt La AB10 190 B4
Powis Circ AB24 165 A5
Powis Cres AB24 165 A5
Powis La AB25 165 B3
Powis Pl AB24 165 A3
Powis Terr AB24 165 A4
Poynernook Rd AB11 190 B2

Premnay Prim Sch AB52 .... 71 E7
Primrose Bank Dr AB15 .... 169 A2
Primrosebank Ave AB15 .... 168 F2
Primrosehill Ave AB15 .. 168 F2
Primrosehill Dr AB24 .. 164 F5
Primrosehill Gdns 1 AB24 .... 164 F5
Primrosehill Pl 2 AB24 164 F5
Primrosehill Rd AB15 .. 168 F2
Prince Albert Mews 4 AB10 .... 165 A1
Prince Arthur St AB25 .. 164 F1
Prince St AB42 .... 147 D6
Princes St
Aberdeen AB24 .... 190 B4
Huntly AB54 .... 148 D4
Inverurie AB51 .... 152 C7
Princess Cres AB21 .... 158 C7
Princess Dr AB21 ...... 158 C6
Princess Rd
Aberdeen AB21 .... 158 C7
Stonehaven AB39 ...... 185 D5
Princess Royal & Duke of Fife Meml Pk* AB35 .. 113 E6
Pringle Ave AB41 .... 61 E5
Printfield Terr AB24 .... 164 F6
Printfield Wlk AB24 .... 164 F6
Priory Pk AB14 .... 172 E6
Privet Hedges AB16 .... 164 C4
Prospect Ct AB11 ...... 170 B6
Prospect Terr
Aberdeen AB11 .... 190 B1
Dyce AB21 .... 158 C3
2 Banchory AB31 .... 98 A3
Prospecthill Rd AB15 .. 168 B1
Provost Barclay Dr 4 AB39 .... 185 C4
Provost Buchan Rd DD9 .... 188 B5
Provost Cordiner Rd AB41 .... 151 C4
Provost Craig Rd AB35 .... 182 D4
Provost Davidson Dr AB41 .... 151 C4
Provost Dr AB51 .... 150 D3
Provost Florence Dr AB51 .... 150 C2
Provost Fraser Dr AB16 .... 163 F4
Provost Gordon Terr AB45 .... 140 E6
Provost Graham Ave AB15 .... 168 F8
Provost Johnston Rd 2 DD10 .... 189 C2
Provost Millar Ave DD9 .... 188 B4
Provost Milne Dr AB43 .... 143 C4
Provost Mitchell Rd 2 DD10 .... 189 C7
Provost Noble Ave AB43 .... 143 A5
Provost Peter Cres DD10 .... 187 D7
Provost Rd DD9 .... 188 B4
Provost Reid's Rd DD10 .... 189 D2
Provost Robson Dr AB30 .... 186 C5
Provost Ross House* AB11 .... 190 B3
Provost Rust Dr AB16 .. 163 F6
Provost Scott's Rd DD10 .... 189 D5
Provost Skene's House* AB25 .... 190 B4
Provost Sq DD9 .... 188 B4
Provost St AB54 .... 148 E4
Provost Stewart Pl 3 AB39 .... 185 C4
Provost Watt Dr AB12 .. 170 B3
Provost's Circ AB51 .... 152 C7
Prunier Dr AB42 .... 147 A6
Prunier Pl AB42 .... 147 A6
Pusey Pl AB42 .... 147 C2
Putachie Path 4 AB53 .. 145 C4

Q

Quarry Ct AB15 .... 168 D2
Quarry Pl
2 Aberdeen AB16 .... 164 A5
1 Mintlaw AB42 .... 146 D4
Quarry Rd
Aberdeen AB16 .... 164 A5
Aberdeen AB15 .... 168 C3
Fraserburgh AB43 ...... 143 D7
Mintlaw AB42 .... 146 C4
Peterhead AB42 .... 52 D4
Quarryhill Ct 2 AB16 .. 164 C4
Quarryhill Prim Sch AB16 .... 164 B4
Quayside Banff AB45 .... 140 F7
Fraserburgh AB43 ...... 143 D6
Queen Mary St AB43 .. 143 B6
Queen St
Aberdeen AB24 .... 164 E6
Aberdeen AB10 .... 190 B3
Huntly AB54 .... 148 E4
Inverurie AB51 .... 152 C7
Montrose DD10 .... 189 D4
Peterhead AB42 .... 147 D6
Queen St *continued*
Rosehearty AB43 .... 142 C7
Queen's Ave AB15 ...... 169 C7
Queens Cl AB43 .... 143 C6
Queen's Cl DD10 .... 189 D3
Queens Cres
Portsoy AB45 .... 139 D6
Rosehearty AB43 .... 142 C7
Queen's Cres 7 AB42 .... 40 D1
Queens Ct 4 DD10 ...... 187 D3
Queens Den AB15 ...... 163 E1
Queen's Dr 5 AB56 .... 1 B4
Queen's Gate AB45 .... 139 D6
Queen's Gdns
Aberdeen AB15 .... 169 E8
Stonehaven AB39 ...... 185 D5
Queens Hill Dr AB34 .... 183 E6
Queen's La 8 AB42 ...... 40 D1
Queen's La N AB15 .... 169 E8
Queen's La S AB15 .... 169 D7
Queens Rd
Fraserburgh AB43 ...... 143 C6
Inverbervie DD10 ...... 187 D7
Queen's Rd
Aberdeen AB15 .... 163 E1
Aboyne AB34 .... 106 B3
Ballater AB35 .... 182 D4
22 Boddam AB42 .... 40 D1
Stonehaven AB39 ...... 185 D4
Turriff AB53 .... 145 C4
Queen's Terr AB10 .... 169 F8
Queen's Wlk 9 AB42 .... 40 D1

R

Raasay Gdns AB16 .... 163 E2
Raasay Rd AB42 .... 147 B7
Rae Circ AB51 .... 152 B8
Rae St AB53 .... 145 D4
Raeburn Pl
Aberdeen AB25 .... 190 A4
Ellon AB41 .... 151 B6
Raeden Ave AB15 ...... 164 D2
Raeden Cres AB15 .... 164 C2
Raeden Ct AB15 .... 164 C2
Raeden Pk Rd AB15 .... 164 D2
Raeden Pl AB15 .... 164 C2
Raeholm Rd 3 AB22 .... 159 E1
Raemoir La 2 AB31 .... 184 D5
Raemoir Rd AB31 ...... 184 D5
Raemoss Rd AB42 ...... 147 E6
Raik Rd AB11 .... 190 B2
Railway Pl DD10 .... 189 D2
Railway Rd AB30 ...... 186 C5
Railway Terr AB51 .... 152 E3
Rainbow Theatre* DD10 .... 189 D4
Rainnieshill Cl 1 AB21 .. 153 E5
Rainnieshill Gdns 2 AB21 .... 153 E5
Rainnieshill Rd AB21 .. 153 E5
Rainnieshill Way AB21 .... 153 D5
Ramsay Cres AB10 .... 169 D4
Ramsay Gdns AB10 .... 169 D3
Ramsay Pl AB10 .... 169 D3
Ramsay Rd
Banchory AB31 .... 184 C4
Stonehaven AB39 ...... 185 C4
Ramsay St Brechin DD9 .. 132 B7
1 Montrose DD10 ...... 189 D2
Ramsay Terr AB43 .... 143 A5
Rannes St AB52 .... 149 D4
Rannoch Rd 1 AB41 .... 151 B6
Rappahouse End 1 AB22 .... 159 E1
Rashieley Rd 2 AB51 .. 152 C4
Rathen Prim Sch AB43 .. 14 E3
Rathen Rd AB43 .... 15 B7
Rattray Pl 1 AB24 ...... 165 A6
Rattray Rd AB42 .... 147 D7
Ravenscraig Castle* AB42 .... 39 D7
Ravenscraig Rd AB42 .. 147 C6
Raxton Pl AB21 .... 158 C7
Rayne N Prim Sch AB51 .... 58 F6
Rearie Cl 4 AB21 ...... 153 C6
Rectory Dr 3 AB43 ...... 24 E6
Rectory Rd AB53 ...... 145 B5
Red Inch Circ 1 AB41 .... 77 F7
Redcloak Cres AB39 .. 185 B6
Redcloak Dr AB39 .... 185 B6
Redcloak Pk AB39 .... 185 B6
Redcloak Way AB39 .. 185 B6
Redfield Cres DD10 .. 189 C4
Redfield Rd DD10 .... 189 C4
Redhall Pl AB30 .... 129 E6
Redmoss Ave AB12 .... 170 D2
Redmoss Cres AB12 .. 170 D4
Redmoss Pk AB12 ...... 170 D2
Redmoss Pl AB12 ...... 170 C2
Redmoss Rd AB12 .... 170 C1
Redmoss Terr AB12 .... 170 D2
Redmoss Wlk AB12 .... 170 C2
Redmyre Prim Sch AB30 .... 129 F6
Redwood Cres AB12 .. 176 C6
Reed Cres AB30 .... 186 C5
Reform St DD10 .... 189 D4
Regent Quay AB11 .... 190 C3
Regent Rd AB11 .... 190 C2
Regent Wlk AB24 ...... 165 C5
Reid St AB45 .... 141 A5
Reidfield Pl AB43 .... 15 D5
Reidhaven Pl 6 AB56 ...... 1 B5
Reidhaven St Banff AB45 .. 8 F8
Reidhaven St *continued*
2 Banff AB45 .... 140 F6
7 Cullen AB56 .... 1 B4
Reisque Ave AB21 ...... 153 D6
Rennie's Ct 6 AB11 .... 190 B3
Rennies La AB54 ...... 144 D4
Rennie's Wynd AB11 .. 190 B3
Renny Cres DD10 ...... 189 C6
Rhu-na-Haven Rd AB34 .... 183 A4
Rhynie Prim Sch AB54 .. 55 D2
Richmond Ave
3 Huntly AB54 .... 55 D2
Peterhead AB42 .... 147 A5
Richmond Gdns 1 AB54 .55 D2
Richmond La 3 AB54 .. 148 D4
Richmond Pl AB35 .... 182 E4
Richmond Rd AB54 .... 148 D3
Richmond St AB25 .... 165 A2
Richmond Terr
Aberdeen AB25 .... 165 A2
2 Huntly AB54 .... 55 D2
Peterhead AB42 .... 147 C5
Richmond Wlk AB25 .. 165 A2
Richmondhill Ct AB15 .. 164 D1
Richmondhill Pl AB15 .. 164 D1
Richmondhill Rd AB15 .... 164 D1
Ricketts Ct DD9 .... 132 D8
Riddoch La AB53 ...... 145 D5
Riddoch Rd 3 AB53 .... 145 D5
Ridgeway Gr AB22 .... 159 C1
Riggs The 9 AB42 .... 38 D6
Ringway Rd AB42 ...... 147 A8
Ritchie Pl
Aberdeen AB24 .... 164 F7
Stonehaven AB39 ...... 181 G2
River St Brechin DD9 .. 188 D2
Montrose DD10 .... 189 C2
River View AB42 ...... 147 A8
Riverside Dr
Aberdeen AB10 .... 169 F4
Huntly AB54 .... 148 C5
Insch AB52 .... 58 D3
Peterhead AB42 .... 147 C7
Stonehaven AB39 ...... 185 C3
Riverside Pk AB51 .... 152 D3
Riverside Pl AB51 .... 152 D4
Riverside Rd
Ellon AB41 .... 151 B3
Inverurie AB51 .... 87 C7
Montrose DD10 .... 189 B2
Riverside Terr AB10 .. 170 A5
Riverview Dr AB21 .... 158 C7
Riverview Pl AB41 .... 151 C3
Robbie Cl 11 AB23 .... 91 C8
Robbie's Rd AB43 .... 143 A3
Robert Gordon Univ AB15 .... 169 C7
Robert Gordon Univ The AB10 .... 169 D3
Robert Gordon's Coll AB25 .... 190 A3
Robert St AB39 .... 185 E5
Robertson Rd AB43 .. 143 A6
Robertson Pl AB13 .... 173 B8
Rockall Pl AB11 .... 170 E6
Rockall Rd AB11 ...... 170 E6
Rocklands Rd AB15 .... 168 F3
Rocksley Dr 19 AB42 .... 40 D1
Roderick Dr AB43 .... 5 A4
Rodney St AB39 .... 185 E5
Rolland Ct AB39 ...... 125 B3
Rolland Pl AB39 ...... 125 B3
Rolland Rd AB39 ...... 125 B3
Ronaldsay Rd 1 AB15 .. 163 F2
Roscobie Pk AB31 .... 184 A5
Rose Ave AB42 .... 147 B3
Rose Hill DD10 .... 189 D5
Rose La
1 Inverurie AB51 ...... 152 D5
Portsoy AB45 .... 139 E7
Rose Pl Aberdeen AB10 .. 165 A1
Peterhead AB42 .... 147 B3
Rose St Aberdeen AB10 .. 170 A8
2 Peterhead AB42 ...... 147 F5
Roseacre AB45 .... 139 D6
Roseacre Cres AB53 .. 145 E4
Rosebank
8 Oldmeldrum AB51 .... 150 C3
6 Oldmeldrum AB51 .... 150 C3
Rosebank Gdns AB11 .. 190 A1
Rosebank Pl AB11 .... 170 A7
Rosebank Terr AB11 .. 190 A1
Rosebery St AB25 .... 164 E2
Rosehearty Sch AB43 .. 142 B7
Rosehill Ave AB24 .... 164 D5
Rosehill Cres
Aberdeen AB24 .... 164 E5
Banchory AB31 .... 184 B4
Rosehill Ct DD10 ...... 189 D5
Rosehill Dr AB24 ...... 164 D5
Rosehill La AB31 ...... 184 B5
Rosehill Pl AB24 ...... 164 E5
Rosehill Rd DD10 ...... 189 D5
Rosehill Terr AB24 .... 164 E5
Rosemount Pl
Aberdeen AB25 .... 164 F1
3 Hillside DD10 .... 138 C8
Rosemount Prim Sch DD10 .... 138 C8
Rosemount Rd DD10 .. 138 C8
Rosemount Sq 2 AB25 .. 165 A1
Rosemount Terr 1 AB25 .... 165 A2
Rosemount Viaduct AB25 .... 190 A3
Rosewell Dr AB15 .... 164 B1
Rosewell Gdns AB15 .. 164 B1
Rosewell Pk AB15 .... 164 B1
Rosewell Pl AB15 .... 164 B1
Rosewell Terr AB15 .. 164 B1
Rosewood Ave AB12 .. 170 C2
Roslin Pl AB24 .... 190 C4
Roslin St AB24 .... 165 D3
Roslin Terr AB24 ...... 190 C4
Ross Cres AB16 .... 164 B3
Ross St AB44 .... 141 D6
Rossie Island Rd DD10 .... 189 B1
Rossie Sq 2 DD10 .... 189 D1
Rossie Terr DD10 .... 189 D1
Rothiemay Prim Sch AB54 .... 30 D7
Rothienorman Prim Sch AB51 .... 47 A2
Rothney Ct AB52 ...... 149 C4
Rousay Dr AB15 ...... 163 F2
Rousay Pl AB15 ...... 163 F1
Rousay Terr AB15 .... 163 F2
Row The AB43 .... 26 D7
Rowan Ave AB54 ...... 148 C6
Rowan Circ AB42 .... 146 D5
Rowan Dr
7 Balmedie AB23 .... 91 C8
Westhill AB32 .... 161 C2
Rowan Gr AB41 .... 76 C7
Rowan Pl Ellon AB41 .. 151 C4
Fraserburgh AB43 .... 143 B6
Rowan Rd AB16 ...... 164 D4
Rowan Terr 1 AB42 .... 52 D4
Rowan Tree Rd AB31 .. 184 D6
Rowanbank 2 AB42 .... 147 B4
Rowanbank Rd AB12 .. 180 B6
Royal Cornhill Hospl AB25 .... 165 A3
Royal Lochnagar Distillery* AB35 .... 115 E8
Royfold Cres AB15 .... 169 C8
Rubislaw Den N AB15 .. 169 C8
Rubislaw Den S AB15 .. 169 C8
Rubislaw of Hill AB15 .. 169 C8
Rubislaw Pk Cres AB15 .... 169 B7
Rubislaw Pk Rd AB15 .. 169 B7
Rubislaw Pl AB10 .... 170 A8
Rubislaw Terr AB10 .. 169 F8
Rubislaw Terr La AB10 .... 169 F8
Ruby La AB10 .... 190 A3
Ruby Pl AB10 .... 190 A3
Rugosa Circ AB21 .... 153 D6
Runcie's La AB43 .... 5 A4
Russell Ct 6 AB43 .... 26 C7
Russell Rd AB11 ...... 190 B1
Russell St
Montrose DD10 .... 189 D3
Peterhead AB42 .... 37 D6
Ruthrie Rd AB10 ...... 169 E4
Ruthrie Terr AB10 .... 169 E4
Ruthriehill Rd AB21 .. 158 C3
Ruthrieston Circ AB10 .. 169 F5
Ruthrieston Cres AB10 .... 169 F5
Ruthrieston Pl AB10 .. 169 F5
Ruthrieston Rd AB10 .. 169 E5
Rutland Cres DD10 .. 189 C5
Ryeland AB41 .... 62 A2

S

St Aidan Cres AB31 .... 184 E4
St Andrew St
Aberdeen AB25 .... 190 A4
Brechin DD9 .... 188 B4
Peterhead AB42 .... 147 E5
St Andrew's Cath AB10 .... 190 C3
St Andrews Dr AB43 .. 143 B6
St Andrew's Dr 10 AB53 .. 145 D4
St Andrew's Gdns AB51 .... 152 D5
St Andrews Prim Sch AB43 .... 143 C6
St Andrews Sch AB51 .. 152 D5
St Andrews Terr AB39 .. 181 H5
St Andrew's Terr 1 AB35 .... 113 E6
St Annes Cres AB39 .. 179 F1
St Anne's Wynd AB39 .. 180 A1
St Bridget Cres AB39 .. 185 C4
St Brydes Rd 1 AB51 .... 87 D6
St Catherine St AB45 .. 140 F6
St Catherine St W AB45 .... 140 E6
St Catherine's Wynd 1 AB10 .... 190 B3
St Clair St AB24 ...... 190 B4
St Clair Way 4 AB41 .... 77 F8
St Clair Wynd 3 AB41 .... 77 F8
St Clement St AB11 .. 165 E1
St Combs Ct AB45 .... 140 E5
St Combs Prim Sch AB43 .... 15 C6
St Comb's Rd AB45 .... 139 E7
St Congan's Cres AB53 .... 145 B4
St Congant's Den AB53 .... 145 E4
St Crispin's Rd AB39 .. 181 H4
St Cyrus National Nature Reserve* DD10 ...... 134 D2
St Cyrus National Nature Reserve Visitor Ctr* DD10 .... 134 D2
St Cyrus Prim Sch DD10 .... 134 E3
St David St 5 DD9 .... 188 C3
St Devenick's Cres AB15 .... 168 E3
St Devenicks Mews AB15 .... 168 F2
St Devenick's Pl AB15 .. 168 E3
St Drostans La AB43 .... 12 E6
St Duthac Cres AB31 .. 184 E5
St Eunan's Rd AB34 .. 183 C4
St Fergus Prim Sch AB42 .... 27 B3
St Fittick's Rd AB11 .. 171 A7
St Helena Ct 18 AB42 .... 40 D1
St James's Cres AB51 .. 152 E4
St James's Pl AB51 .. 152 A3
St John's Cotts 5 DD10 .. 189 C4
St John's Gdns 10 AB51 .. 87 D7
St John's Pl
Aberdeen AB11 .... 190 A2
6 Montrose DD10 ...... 189 C4
St John's Rd AB21 .... 163 F8
St John's Terr AB15 .. 169 C5
St John's Wlk AB39 .. 179 F1
St Josephs Cath Prim Sch AB10 .... 169 F8
St Kieran Cres AB39 .. 185 C3
St Machar Acad AB24 .. 165 B5
St Machar Cres 1 AB31 .. 184 E4
St Machar Dr AB24 .... 165 A5
St Machar Pl AB24 .... 165 C6
St Machar Prim Sch AB24 .... 165 A6
St Machar Rd AB24 .... 165 A6
St Machars Cath AB24 .. 165 B6
St Magnus Pl 4 AB42 .. 147 B5
St Magnus Rd AB43 .... 5 A3
St Margaret's Pl AB15 .. 164 B1
St Margarets RC Prim Sch DD10 .... 189 C4
St Margarets Sch for Girls AB10 .... 170 A8
St Marnan Rd AB31 ...... 98 E1
St Mary St
4 Brechin DD9 .... 188 C3
Peterhead AB42 .... 147 D5
St Mary Terr 3 AB42 .... 25 D5
St Mary's Cath AB10 .. 190 A3
St Mary's Dr AB41 .... 151 D4
St Mary's Pl
Aberdeen AB11 .... 190 A2
Ellon AB41 .... 151 D3
St Mary's Rd 4 DD10 .. 189 D3
St Michael's Cres AB39 .... 181 I5
St Michaels Pl AB39 .. 181 I5
St Michael's Rd AB39 .. 181 H5
St Michael's Way AB39 .... 181 H5
St Michael's Wlk AB39 .... 181 H5
St Nathalan Cres AB31 .... 184 E4
St Nathan's Rd AB39 .. 181 H5
St Nicholas Cres 1 AB31 .... 184 D4
St Nicholas Dr AB31 .. 184 E4
St Nicholas La AB10 .. 190 B3
St Nicholas Rd AB31 .. 184 D4
St Nicholas St AB10 .. 190 B3
St Ninians Cl AB24 .... 165 C6
St Ninian's Pl
Aberdeen AB24 .... 165 C6
Brechin DD9 .... 188 D3
4 Turriff AB53 .... 145 C5
St Olave Pl 4 AB42 ...... 53 A3
St Paul St AB25 .... 190 B4
St Peter La AB24 ...... 165 C3
St Peter St
Aberdeen AB24 .... 165 C3
Peterhead AB42 .... 147 E5
St Peter's Gate 3 AB24 .. 165 C4
St Peters Pl 7 DD10 .. 189 D3
St Peters RC Sch AB24 .... 165 C5
St Peter's Rd
Montrose DD10 .... 189 D3
Stonehaven AB39 ...... 181 H5
St Ronan's Circ AB14 .. 172 E7
St Ronan's Cres AB14 .. 172 E7
St Ronan's Dr AB14 .. 172 E6
St Ronan's Pl AB14 .. 172 F6
St Swithin St AB10 .... 169 E8
St Tarquins Pl 6 AB45 ...... 1 F1
St Ternan's Rd AB39 .. 181 H4
Salisbury Pl AB10 ...... 169 F6
Salisbury Rd AB35 .... 182 D4
Salisbury Terr AB10 .. 169 F6
Salmon La 6 AB39 .... 185 E4
Saltoun Pl AB43 .... 143 D6
Salvation Army Citadel The* AB10 .... 190 C3
Samprey Rd AB15 .... 163 E1
Sanday Rd AB15 ...... 164 B1
Sandford Ct 1 AB42 .. 147 C4
Sandford Pl 5 AB42 .... 40 D1
Sandford Terr AB42 .. 147 C5
Sandhaven Meal Mill* AB43 .... 5 A3
Sandhaven Prim Sch AB43 .... 5 A4
Sandilands Dr AB24 .. 165 A6
Sandyhill Rd AB45 .... 140 E4

Saphock Pl AB51 152 C6
Satrosphere* AB24 190 C4
Scalloway Pk AB43 143 A5
Scalpay Wlk 3 AB16 163 E2
Scatha Ritchie Pl AB43 143 B7
Schivas Rd AB42 147 C4
School Ave AB24 165 C5
School Brae AB43 23 E6
School Cres
Aberdeen AB14 172 E6
5 Newburgh AB41 77 F8
School Dr AB24 165 C5
School Hill
Banchory AB31 184 D4
Ellon AB41 151 C5
Turriff AB53 145 D4
School La
3 Aberchirder AB54 144 D5
Ballater AB35 182 D4
2 Inverurie AB51 152 D5
Macduff AB44 141 C7
Turriff AB53 145 C4
School Pk 5 AB43 24 E6
School Pl
Aberdeen AB24 165 D5
School Pl
1 New Pitsligo AB43 23 E6
School Rd
Aberdeen AB24 165 C5
Aboyne AB34 96 C3
Alford AB33 154 C3
9 Ballater AB35 113 F6
Banchory AB31 98 A3
Banff AB45 1 F1
9 Banff AB45 8 F8
Cults AB15 168 E2
Drumlithie AB39 125 B3
Ellon AB41 77 F8
Huntly AB54 29 E5
Inverurie AB51 152 E3
Kintore AB51 155 C4
Kirktown AB42 27 B3
3 Laurencekirk AB30 128 A4
Laurencekirk AB30 133 B7
New Deer AB42 36 E6
Newmachar AB21 153 D5
Peterculter AB14 172 D7
Peterhead AB42 147 B3
Stonehaven AB39 185 C5
Turriff AB53 47 E5
School St
Fraserburgh AB43 143 D7
New Pitsligo AB43 23 E6
School Terr AB24 165 D5
School Wlk AB24 165 D5
School Wynd
Inverbervie DD10 187 E7
St Cyrus DD10 134 D3
Schoolhendry St AB45 139 E7
Schoolhill AB25 190 A3
Schoolhill Rd
Aberdeen AB12 180 B8
Ellon AB41 151 D5
Sclattie Circ AB21 163 D8
Sclattie Cres AB21 163 D8
Sclattie Pk AB21 163 D8
Sclattie Pl AB21 163 D7
Sclattie Quarry Ind Est AB21 158 C1
Sclattie Wlk AB21 163 C7
Scolty Pl AB31 184 E5
Scolty View AB31 184 E5
Scotston Pl DD10 134 D3
Scotston Terr DD10 134 D3
Scotstown Gdns AB23 165 C8
Scotstown Moor Nature Reserve* AB23 159 E4
Scotstown Prim Sch AB22 159 F1
Scotstown Rd
Aberdeen AB23 159 F3
Peterhead AB42 147 B7
Scott Cres DD10 138 C8
Scott Ct AB54 148 C5
Scott Dr AB54 148 C5
Scott Gr AB23 91 A8
Scott St DD9 188 D2
Scott Sutherland Sch of Architecture School of Surveying AB10 169 D3
Scottish Amb Service N E Division HQ AB25 164 C3
Scurdie Ness AB12 176 C8
Scylla Dr AB12 176 A6
Scylla Gdns AB12 176 B6
Scylla Gr AB12 176 B6
Sea St AB56 1 B5
Seafield Ave AB15 169 C6
Seafield Cres
Aberdeen AB15 169 C6
Banff AB45 140 E6
Seafield Ct AB15 169 C6
Seafield Dr E AB15 169 C7
Seafield Dr W AB15 169 C7
Seafield Gdns AB15 169 C6
Seafield Pl 6 Banff AB45 8 F8
Cullen AB56 1 B4
Portsoy AB45 139 E6
Seafield Rd
Aberdeen AB15 169 C6
Buckie AB56 1 B3
Peterhead AB42 147 C4
Seafield St Banff AB45 8 F8
Banff AB45 140 E6
Seafield St *continued*
4 Cullen AB56 1 B5
Portsoy AB45 139 D6
Seafield Terr AB45 139 C6
Seaforth Rd AB24 165 D3
Seaforth St 7 AB43 143 D6
Seagate
Montrose DD10 189 C2
3 Peterhead AB42 147 F6
Seal Craig Gdns AB12 176 B8
Seamount Rd AB25 190 B4
Seaton Ave AB24 165 C5
Seaton Cres AB24 165 D6
Seaton Dr AB24 165 D6
Seaton Gdns AB24 165 C6
Seaton Pl AB24 165 C6
Seaton Pl E AB24 165 C6
Seaton Prim Sch AB24 165 D6
Seaton Rd AB24 165 D5
Seatown Pl AB43 15 C8
Seaview Ave AB23 160 A5
Seaview Circ AB23 160 A4
Seaview Cl AB23 160 A5
Seaview Cres AB23 160 A4
Seaview Dr AB23 160 A4
Seaview Pl
Aberdeen AB23 160 A5
Montrose DD10 189 B1
Seaview Rd
Aberdeen AB23 165 C8
Banff AB45 1 F3
24 Boddam AB42 40 D1
Peterhead AB42 27 B3
Seaview Terr
Gourdon DD10 187 D3
Johnshaven DD10 135 C5
Sedge Pl AB12 180 A5
Selbie Dr AB51 152 C5
Selbie Pl
Inverurie AB51 152 D5
Montrose DD10 187 D4
Seton Dr AB54 148 D5
Seton Terr 8 Ellon AB41 62 B2
Huntly AB54 148 D5
Seton Way 2 AB51 150 C2
Settrington St AB54 148 D4
Shand Ct 2 AB44 141 C6
Shand St AB44 141 C6
Shand Terr AB44 141 C6
Shannoch Dr 1 AB51 87 D7
Shannocks View AB53 145 B6
Shapinsay Ct AB15 163 E2
Shaw Circ AB32 161 C3
Sheddocksley Dr AB16 163 F2
Sheddocksley Rd AB16 163 F3
Sheddocksley Sports Ctr AB15 163 F4
Shepherd Pl AB12 170 A3
Sheriffs Brae 8 AB45 140 F6
Sherwood Pl AB53 36 A5
Shetland Wlk AB16 163 E3
Shieldhill Gdns AB12 176 C8
Shielhill Gdns AB22 159 E1
Shillinghill AB45 139 D7
Ship St AB42 147 F4
Shiprow
Aberdeen AB11 190 B3
Peterhead AB42 147 F4
Shoe La AB10 190 B4
Shore Brae 2 AB11 190 B3
Shore La AB11 190 C3
Shore St
Fraserburgh AB43 143 D7
Inverallochy AB43 15 C8
Macduff AB44 141 C6
Portsoy AB45 139 E7
Rosehearty AB43 142 C8
Sandhaven AB43 5 A4
Shore Wynd 5 DD10 189 C2
Shorehead Banff AB45 139 D7
Stonehaven AB39 185 F3
Short Loanings AB25 165 A2
Shunnery O'Brian AB51 152 E3
Sidney Cres 4 AB42 52 D4
Sillerton La AB12 170 B3
Silver Gdns 12 AB39 185 E4
Silver Pitt Gdns 3 AB42 147 A4
Silver Way DD10 189 C7
Silverburn Cres AB23 160 A2
Silverburn Pl AB23 160 A2
Silverburn Rd AB22 159 E1
Silverhillock AB45 7 E1
Simpson Ave 1 AB51 47 A2
Simpson Pl AB44 141 D7
Simpson Rd AB23 165 C8
Sims Rd 5 AB54 55 D2
Sinclair Cres
Aberdeen AB21 153 C5
Cove Bay AB12 176 C7
Sinclair Gdns DD10 138 D8
Sinclair Pl
Aberdeen AB12 176 C7
Fraserburgh AB43 143 A5
Sinclair Rd AB11 190 C1
Sinclair Terr AB12 176 C7
Sir Patrick Geddes Way AB35 182 E5
Skateraw Rd AB39 181 I4
Skelly Rock AB12 176 C8
Skelton St AB42 147 D6
Skene House* AB32 101 A8
Skene Pl AB21 158 B6
Skene Prim Sch AB32 101 D6
Skene Rd AB15 163 D1
Skene Sq AB25 190 A4
Skene Sq Prim Sch AB25 165 A2
Skene St
Aberdeen AB25 190 A3
Macduff AB44 141 D7
Peterhead AB42 147 E6
Skene Terr AB10 190 A3
Skerry Dr AB42 147 C3
Skerry Pk 14 AB42 40 D1
Skinner Ave AB51 152 C5
Skinner Rd AB42 38 D6
Skye Rd AB16 163 E2
Slackadale Gdns AB53 145 B6
Slains Ave
Aberdeen AB22 159 D2
Ellon AB41 151 E6
Slains Castle (remains of)* AB41 64 F4
Slains Circ AB22 159 D2
Slains Cres AB41 151 E5
Slains Ct AB42 147 C3
Slains La AB22 159 E2
Slains Rd AB22 159 D2
Slains Sch AB41 64 D5
Slains St AB22 159 D2
Slains Terr AB22 159 D2
Slateford Rd DD9 132 A7
Sleigh Cres 6 AB43 24 E6
Slessor Dr AB12 170 A1
Slessor Rd AB12 170 A2
Slug Rd Banchory AB31 110 D2
Stonehaven AB39 185 A7
Sluie Dr AB21 158 C7
Smiddy Field 2 AB41 49 B4
Smiddy La AB41 151 D4
Smiddy Pk DD10 131 C7
Smiddy Rd AB39 125 B3
Smiddyhill Rd AB43 143 A3
Smith Cres AB54 144 D5
Smith Rd AB45 140 E5
Smithbank Rd DD9 188 C4
Smithfield Dr AB16 164 D5
Smithfield La AB24 164 D7
Smithfield Prim Sch AB16 164 C5
Smithfield Rd AB24 164 E6
Smithy La
7 Peterhead AB42 38 D6
11 Strichen AB43 24 E6
6 Turriff AB53 145 D4
Smithy Rd 3 AB51 47 A2
Smithyhaugh Rd AB16 163 F6
Sneesbin Hillock* AB45 8 F2
Snipe St AB41 151 B4
Social Club Rd AB42 40 C1
Society La AB24 164 E6
Somerset Cres AB52 149 C5
Souter Circ AB32 161 E4
Souter Gdns AB32 161 E3
Souter Head Rd AB12 170 D1
Souter St AB44 141 D6
Souterford Ave AB51 152 E6
Souterford Ave Bsns Pk AB51 152 E6
Souterford Cres 1 AB51 152 E6
Souterford Dr AB51 152 E6
Souterford Rd AB51 152 E6
Souterford Wynd 3 AB51 152 E6
South Anderson Dr AB10 169 E6
South Ave AB15 168 E2
South Castle St 1 AB56 1 B4
South Coll St AB11 190 B1
South Constitution St 1 AB11 190 C4
South Crown St AB11 190 A1
South Deskford St 4 AB56 1 B4
South Espl E AB11 190 C1
South Espl W AB11 190 B1
South Grampian Circ AB11 170 D6
South Harbour Rd AB43 143 D3
South Headlands Cres AB39 181 I4
South High St AB45 139 D6
South La AB42 147 D7
South Lodge Dr AB39 185 C6
South Mount St AB25 165 A1
South Rd Ellon AB41 151 D4
Insch AB52 149 D4
Oldmeldrum AB51 150 C3
Peterhead AB42 147 C1
South Silver St AB10 190 A3
South St Huntly AB54 144 D4
Mintlaw AB42 146 E5
Montrose DD10 135 C5
Southesk Pl
Aberdeen AB21 158 B7
Montrose DD10 189 C1
Southesk Prim Sch DD10 189 C2
Southesk St
Brechin DD9 188 C3
Montrose DD10 189 C2
Southesk Terr DD9 188 D2
Southview Terr AB54 144 C4
Soy Ave AB45 139 D6
Soy Burn Gdns AB45 139 C6
Spa St AB25 190 A3
Spademill La AB15 169 D8
Spademill Rd AB15 169 D8
Spalings The 2 AB34 108 B6
Spark Terr AB12 176 C6
Spey Rd AB16 164 A3
Spey Terr AB16 164 A3
Spires Bsns Units AB21 164 A8
Spital AB24 165 C4
Spital Wlk AB24 165 B4
Spittal The AB42 26 D1
Spring Gdn AB25 190 A4
Spring Tyne AB32 161 B3
Springbank 1 AB42 147 C3
Springbank Pl 3 AB11 190 A2
Springbank St AB11 190 A2
Springbank Terr
Aberdeen AB11 190 A2
Peterhead AB42 147 B3
Springdale Cres AB15 168 A2
Springdale Ct AB15 168 B2
Springdale Pk AB15 168 A2
Springdale Pl AB15 168 B2
Springdale Rd AB15 168 A2
Springfield Ave AB15 169 B7
Springfield Gdns
Aberdeen AB15 169 B6
Springfield Gdns *continued*
Peterhead AB42 36 D7
Springfield La AB15 169 B7
Springfield Pl AB15 169 B6
Springfield Rd
Aberdeen AB15 169 A8
2 Kemnay AB51 87 D7
Springhill Cres AB16 163 F5
Springhill Rd 2 AB16 163 F3
Springhill Terr AB16 163 F4
Spurryhillock Ind Est AB39 185 B4
Square DD10 135 C6
Square The
5 Aboyne AB34 96 C3
Banchory AB31 184 B4
7 Banff AB45 1 F1
5 Cullen AB56 1 B5
Ellon AB41 151 D5
Fetterangus AB42 25 C1
Huntly AB54 148 D5
Inverurie AB51 86 E6
Portlethen AB12 180 C6
Portsoy AB45 139 D7
6 Rhynie AB54 55 D2
Rosehearty AB43 142 C7
Stuartfield AB42 37 D4
2 Tarves AB41 61 E6
Torphins AB31 108 E8
Turriff AB53 22 E5
Stable Cl AB51 59 E3
Staffa St AB42 147 B7
Stafford St AB25 165 A3
Stanley St AB10 169 F8
Station Brae
Aberdeen AB14 172 E6
Aboyne AB34 183 E5
Ellon AB41 151 B5
6 Fraserburgh AB43 143 D6
Station Mews AB21 163 F8
Station Pl
2 Cruden Bay AB42 53 A3
Longside AB42 38 E6
Montrose DD10 135 C6
Peterhead AB42 147 C5
Station Rd
Aberdeen AB21 163 F8
Banchory AB31 184 D4
Boddam AB42 40 C1
Cruden Bay AB42 53 A3
3 Cullen AB56 1 B5
Cults AB15 168 F3
Dyce AB21 158 A6
Ellon AB41 151 B5
Fordoun AB30 129 E6
Fraserburgh AB43 15 B8
Hatton AB42 52 D4
Insch AB52 56 D4
Inverurie AB51 152 E6
Kemnay AB51 87 D6
Laurencekirk AB30 186 D6
Longside AB42 38 D6
2 Maud AB42 36 E7
Milltimber AB13 173 B7
Mintlaw AB42 146 C5
Newmachar AB21 153 D6
Peterhead AB42 147 D5
4 Rothienorman AB51 47 A2
St Cyrus DD10 134 D3
Stonehaven AB39 125 B3
13 Torphins AB31 108 E8
Turriff AB53 145 D3
Station Rd E
Milltimber AB13 173 B7
Peterculter AB14 172 E5
Station Rd S AB14 172 D5
Station Rd W AB14 172 D6
Station Sq
Aboyne AB34 183 D5
Ballater AB35 182 E4
Station Terr AB42 38 D6
Stell Rd AB11 190 B2
Stephen's La 15 AB41 77 F8
Steven Rd AB54 148 B4
Stevenson Ct 3 AB25 165 A1
Stevenson Rd AB43 143 D8
Stewart Cl 2 AB33 154 E3
Stewart Cotts 2 AB42 52 C4
Stewart Cres
Aberdeen AB16 164 B4
Alford AB33 154 E3
Stewart Csescent AB16 164 A5
Stewart Dr AB33 154 E4
Stewart Gr 1 AB33 154 E3
Stewart La Alford AB33 154 E3
2 Huntly AB54 148 E4
Stewart Pk Pl AB24 164 D5
Stewart Pl 3 AB33 154 E3
Stewart Rd AB33 154 E3
Stewart Terr AB16 164 A5
Stewart Way AB33 154 E3
Stewart Wlk 4 AB33 154 E3
Stirling St AB11 190 B3
Stocket Par 1 AB16 164 C4
Stockethill Ave 2 AB16 164 C3
Stockethill Cres AB16 164 C3
Stockethill La 1 AB16 164 C3
Stockethill Pl 4 AB16 164 C3
Stockethill Way 4 AB16 164 C4
Stonefield Dr AB51 152 A7
Stonehaven Leisure Ctr AB39 185 F6
Stonehaven Rd AB10 169 F4
Stonehaven Sta AB39 185 F5
Stonehaven Tolbooth Mus* AB39 185 F4
Stoneybank Gdns AB53 36 A5
Stoneybank Terr 2 AB53 36 A5
Stoneyhill Terr AB12 176 C6
Stoneyton Terr AB21 158 B1
Stoneywood Pk AB21 158 C4
Stoneywood Pk Ind Est AB21 158 C4
Stoneywood Pk N AB21 158 C4
Stoneywood Prim Sch AB21 158 C2
Stoneywood Rd AB21 158 C2
Stoneywood Terr AB21 158 C3
Stornoway Cres AB15 163 D3
Storybook Glen* AB12 173 C3
Stracathro Hospl DD9 132 D4
Stracathro Public Sch DD9 132 C4
Strachan Pl AB16 164 C6
Strachan Prim Sch AB31 117 D7
Strachan's La AB10 170 A7
Strachan's Pk DD9 188 D3
Straik Pl AB32 161 C2
Straik Rd AB32 161 B2
Strait La AB53 145 D5
Strait Path AB45 140 F5
Straloch Ave 4 AB21 153 D5
Stranathro Terr AB39 181 G2
Strathbeg Ct AB43 143 A5
Strathbeg Pl 3 AB22 165 B8
Strathburn Gdns AB51 152 C6
Strathburn Prim Sch AB51 152 C6
Strathburn St AB12 176 B8
Strathdon Sch AB36 81 A3
Strathmore Dr AB16 164 A4
Strathmore Pl 2 DD10 189 C4
Street The AB42 26 E1
Strichen Ct AB43 143 B3
Strichen Prim Sch AB43 24 F6
Strichen Rd AB43 143 C3
Stroma Terr AB16 163 E2
Stronsay Ave AB15 164 A1
Stronsay Cres AB15 164 A2
Stronsay Dr AB15 164 A1
Stronsay Pl AB15 164 A1
Stuart Cres 1 AB41 61 E5
Stuart La 3 AB45 140 F6
Stuart St 4 AB45 140 F6
Stuartfield Prim Sch AB42 37 D4
Sugarhouse La AB11 190 C3
Suie Rd AB33 154 A8
Sumburgh Cres AB16 163 E3
Summer Brae 3 AB21 153 D5
Summer Pl AB21 158 B6
Summer St
Aberdeen AB24 164 F6
Aberdeen AB10 165 A1
Summerfield Pl
Aberdeen AB24 190 C4
Inverallochy AB43 15 C7
Summerfield Terr
Aberdeen AB24 190 B4
Inverallochy AB43 15 C7
Summerfield Wlk AB43 15 C7
Summerhill Cres AB15 164 B2
Summerhill Dr AB15 164 B2
Summerhill Rd AB15 164 B1
Summerhill Terr AB15 164 B1
Summers Rd AB43 142 C7
Sunert Rd AB13 173 D8
Sunnybank Pl AB24 165 B4
Sunnybank Prim Sch AB24 165 B4
Sunnybank Rd AB24 165 B4
Sunnyhill Pl AB53 145 C5
Sunnyside Ave
Aberdeen AB24 165 B4
Banchory AB31 111 D5
Sunnyside Cres AB31 111 D6
Sunnyside Dr
Alford AB33 154 D4
Banchory AB31 111 D6
Sunnyside Gdns
Aberdeen AB24 165 B4
Banchory AB31 111 D6
Sunnyside La AB31 111 D6

Sunnyside Rd AB24 165 B4
Sunnyside Royal DD10 138 C8
Sunnyside Terr AB24 165 B4
Sunnyside View AB51 155 C3
Sunnyside Wlk AB24 165 B3
Sunset Wood AB31 184 B5
Sutherland Ave 5 AB42 147 E6
Sutherland Pl AB45 139 C7
Swan Pl AB41 151 B4
Swan Rd AB41 151 B3
Swan St DD9 188 C3
Swanley Cotts AB39 120 A2
Swann Pl AB35 182 D4
Sycamore Pl
Aberdeen AB11 170 B6
Huntly AB54 148 C5
5 Mintlaw AB42 146 D5

T

Tailyour Cres DD10 189 C6
Talisman Dr AB10 169 C3
Talisman Rd AB10 169 C3
Tanfield Ave AB24 164 F6
Tanfield Wlk AB24 164 F6
Tannery Ct 3 AB45 140 E5
Tannery St AB45 140 E6
Taransay Cres AB16 163 E3
Taransay Rd AB16 163 E2
Tarbothill Rd 4 AB22 165 B8
Target Rd AB45 139 C7
Tarlair Rd AB44 141 F7
Tarlair St AB44 141 E7
Tarland Prim Sch AB34 96 C3
Tarves Prim Sch AB41 61 E5
Tay Rd AB16 164 A4
Taylor Cres
Peterhead AB42 26 E6
Stonehaven AB39 185 C4
Taylor Dr AB54 144 D5
Tayock Ave 3 DD10 189 C5
Teal St AB41 151 B4
Tedder Rd AB24 165 A6
Tedder St AB24 165 A6
Temperance La The 2 AB54 144 C4
Temple of Theseus* AB42 37 D7
Temple View AB45 141 A5
Tern Pl AB23 160 A4
Tern Rd AB12 176 B7
Terpersie Castle* AB33 70 C3
Teuchar Pk 4 AB53 22 B1
Teuchar Rd AB53 22 B1
Teviot Pl DD10 189 E3
Teviot Rd AB16 163 F3
Thainstone Agricultural Ctr* AB51 74 B1
Thainstone Bsns Ctr AB51 74 B1
Thainstone Ct AB51 74 B1
Theatre La AB11 190 B3
Thistle Dr AB12 180 D7
Thistle Gdns 7 AB42 146 D5
Thistle La AB10 165 A1
Thistle Pl AB10 170 A8
Thistle Rd AB21 157 E5
Thistle St AB10 170 A8
Thomas Glover Pl AB22 165 B8
Thompson Terr AB43 143 B5
Thomson Rd AB45 140 E5
Thomson St AB25 164 F2
Thomson Terr
Montrose DD10 189 B1
Stonehaven AB39 185 C4
Thomson's La 4 AB51 152 D6
Thores Rd AB42 147 C7
Thorngrove Ave AB15 169 D6
Thorngrove Cres AB15 169 D6
Thorngrove Pl AB15 169 D6
Thornhill Rd AB53 22 C1
Thornton Castle* AB30 128 E2
Threadneedle St 3 AB42 147 E5
Tillybrake Ind Est AB31 184 E5
Tillybrake Rd AB31 184 D5
Tillybrake Rise
Banchory AB31 184 D5
Drumoak AB31 111 C5
Tillybrig AB32 100 E8
Tillycairn Castle (remains of)* AB51 86 C2
Tillydrone Ave AB24 165 B6
Tillydrone Rd AB24 165 A7
Tillydrone Sh Ctr AB24 165 A7
Tillydrone Terr AB24 165 A6
Tillyduff Gdns AB43 15 D5
Tillyfar Gdns AB53 145 B5
Tilquhillie Castle* AB31 110 C1
Tilquillie Pl AB31 184 E6
Tipperty Prim Sch AB41 63 D2
Tiree Cres AB16 163 E2
Toch Hill Pl AB30 129 E6
Tocher St AB44 141 D6
Tochieneal Cnr AB56 1 B3
Todhead Gdns AB12 176 C8
Todlaw Wlk AB21 158 C7
Tolbooth The* AB11 190 C3
Tolbooth Wynd 2 AB42 147 E5
Tollohill Cres AB12 170 C3
Tollohill Dr AB12 170 B3
Tollohill Gdns AB12 170 C3
Tollohill La AB12 170 B2
Tollohill Pl AB12 170 C3
Tollohill Sq AB12 170 B3
Tolmount Cres DD10 189 C7
Tolquhon Ave AB41 61 E6
Tolquhon Castle (remains of)* AB41 61 F3
Tolquhon Pl 2 AB41 151 E5
Tophead Pl AB42 26 E6
Topping Gdns AB43 143 B6
Tor-na-Dee Hospl AB13 173 D8
Tornashean Gdns AB21 158 C7
Torphins Prim Sch AB31 108 E8
Torry Acad AB11 170 D6
Torry Rd AB54 148 C4
Torry Sports Ctr AB11 170 D6
Torry St AB54 148 D4
Tortorston Dr AB42 39 C5
Tortorston Rd AB42 39 C5
Tough Prim Sch AB33 85 D4
Towerhill AB42 147 C1
Towerhill Pl AB42 147 C2
Towerview Rd AB14 172 D7
Towie Barclay Castle* AB53 33 E2
Towie Castle (remains of)* AB33 82 E3
Towie Prim School AB33 82 D3
Town House The* AB39 185 F3
Townhead Ave AB51 152 B7
Townhead Dr 6 AB51 152 B7
Townhead Gdns 3 AB51 152 B7
Townhead Pl AB51 152 B7
Townhead Rd AB51 152 B7
Townhead Terr 4 AB51 152 B7
Tradlin Circ AB21 156 A6
Trafalgar La AB30 186 D5
Traill Dr DD10 189 E3
Traill Terr DD10 189 E2
Tree Rd AB41 61 E6
Trenchard Way DD10 187 D6
Triity Quay AB11 190 B3
Trinity Fields Cres DD9 188 C5
Trinity La AB11 190 B3
Trinity Rd DD9 188 C4
Trinity St AB11 190 B3
Troup View AB45 3 C2
Tuach Rd 3 AB51 155 C5
Tuach View 1 AB51 155 C4
Tullich Rd AB35 182 E4
Tullochgorum Gdns 2 AB42 38 D6
Tullos Circ AB11 170 D6
Tullos Cres AB11 170 E6
Tullos House (remains of)* AB51 73 A4
Tullos Pl AB11 170 E6
Tullos Prim Sch AB11 170 F6
Tullynessle Prim Sch AB33 154 A8
Tummel Rd AB41 151 B6
Tumulus Way AB51 155 C2
Turfhill Rd AB53 36 A6
Turin Way AB41 77 C6
Turlundie Terr AB43 23 D7
Turnberry Cres AB22 159 F2
Turnberry Ct AB22 159 F2
Turnberry Dr AB51 152 C5
Turnberry Gdns AB23 159 F2
Turner St AB44 141 C6
Turnishaw Hill AB41 151 C6
Turriff Acad AB53 145 D4
Turriff Cottage Hospl AB53 145 E4
Turriff FC AB53 145 D4
Two Mile Cross AB10 169 E3
Tyrie Gdns AB52 149 D5
Tyrie Prim Sch AB43 13 C5

U

Udny Castle* AB41 62 A1
Udny Gn Prim Sch AB41 62 A1
Udny Pl AB41 151 E5
Ugie Dr AB42 146 E4
Ugie Pl AB16 164 A3
Ugie Rd AB42 147 C7
Ugie St AB42 147 E6
Ugie View 1 AB43 24 E6
Ugiebank Pl AB42 147 B7
Uist Rd AB16 163 E2
Union Glen AB11 190 A2
Union Gr
Aberdeen AB10 169 F7
Fraserburgh AB43 143 C6
Union Gr La AB10 169 E7
Union La Ellon AB41 151 D4
Rosehearty AB43 142 C7
Union Pl DD10 189 D3
Union Rd MacDuff AB44 141 C6
Montrose DD10 189 D4
Union Row
Aberdeen AB10 190 A2
Dyce AB21 158 B6
Montrose DD10 189 E4
Union St
Aberdeen AB10 190 A3
Brechin DD9 188 C2
Edzell DD9 132 A8
Ellon AB41 151 C5
Montrose DD10 189 D4
Peterhead AB42 147 F5
Rosehearty AB43 142 C7
Union Terr AB10 190 A3
Union Terr Gdns* AB10 190 A3
Union Wynd AB10 190 A3
University Ct AB21 163 D7
University of Aberdeen Medical Bldgs AB25 164 D3
University Rd AB24 165 B5
Uphill La 1 AB42 147 E4
Upper Arbeadie Pl AB31 184 C5
Upper Arbeadie Rd AB31 184 B6
Upper Craigo St 5 DD10 189 C3
Upper Denburn AB25 190 A3
Upper Farburn Rd AB21 157 F5
Upper Hall St 8 DD10 189 C4
Upper Lochton E AB31 184 C7
Upper Mastrick Way AB16 164 A4
Upper Westfield Prim Sch AB22 159 F2
Upperboat Pl 3 AB51 152 D4
Upperboat Rd AB51 152 C5
Upperkirk Gate 2 AB54 148 D4
Upperkirkgate AB10 190 B3
Upperton Ind Est AB42 147 A1
Urie Cres AB39 185 E5
Urievale Rd AB51 59 B1
Urquhart Cres AB42 27 B2
Urquhart La AB24 165 D3
Urquhart Pl 2 AB24 190 C4
Urquhart Rd
Aberdeen AB24 165 D3
Oldmeldrum AB51 150 C3
Peterhead AB42 27 B3
Turriff AB53 22 E5
Urquhart St AB24 165 D3
Ury Dale AB51 152 E5
Ury Mdws AB51 152 A8
Usan Ness AB12 176 C8
Usan Rd DD10 189 D1

V

Valentine Cres AB22 159 D2
Valentine Dr AB22 159 C1
Valentine Rd AB22 159 C2
Valley Cres AB12 170 C3
Valley Gdns AB12 170 B3
Victoria Ct AB51 152 D6
Victoria Gdns AB45 140 E6
Victoria Pl Banff AB45 140 E6
Brechin DD9 188 D2
Cullen AB56 1 B5
Victoria Rd
Aberdeen AB11 190 C1
Alford AB33 154 C4
Ballater AB35 182 D4
Huntly AB54 148 D4
Maud AB42 36 E7
Peterhead AB42 147 D6
Victoria Rd Prim Sch AB11 170 E7
Victoria Sq 5 DD10 189 D1
Victoria St
Aberdeen AB10 170 A8
Cullen AB56 1 B5
Dyce AB21 158 B6
Fraserburgh AB43 143 D6
Insch AB52 149 C5
Inverurie AB51 152 D6
7 Montrose DD10 189 C4
Stonehaven AB39 185 E4
7 Turriff AB53 145 C4
Victoria Terr
Inverbervie DD10 187 D6
Inverurie AB51 152 E3
Kemnay AB51 87 D6
Turriff AB53 145 D4
View Gdns 2 AB42 40 D1
View Terr AB25 165 A2
Viewbank Pl DD9 188 E3
Viewfield Ave AB15 169 C6
Viewfield Cres AB15 169 C6
Viewfield Gdns AB15 169 B7
Viewfield Pl 1 AB35 182 D4
Viewfield Rd
Aberdeen AB15 169 C6
Ballater AB35 182 D4
Fraserburgh AB43 143 C6
Viewmount Rd AB31 184 D4
Viking Pl AB12 180 C7
Village Farm Ct 9 AB31 108 E8
Villagelands Rd AB39 181 I4
Virginia St AB11 190 C3
Volum St AB42 147 F5

W

Waldron Rd DD10 189 D7
Wales St AB11 190 C4
Walker Ave AB45 140 F5
Walker Dr AB39 181 G1
Walker La AB11 190 C1
Walker Pl AB11 190 C1
Walker Rd AB11 190 C1
Walker Rd Prim Sch AB11 170 D6
Wallace Cres
Peterhead AB42 147 A7
1 Turriff AB53 145 C4
Wallace Rd AB51 152 E5
Wallace St 2 AB42 147 E4
Wallace Way AB42 147 A7
Wallace Wynd 3 AB39 185 F3
Wallacebrae Ave 2 AB22 159 A1
Wallacebrae Cres AB22 159 B1
Wallacebrae Dr AB22 159 B1
Wallacebrae Gdns 2 AB22 159 B1
Wallacebrae Path 1 AB22 159 B1
Wallacebrae Pl AB22 159 A1
Wallacebrae Rd AB22 159 B1
Wallacebrae Terr AB22 159 A1
Wallacebrae Wlk 1 AB22 159 A1
Wallacebrae Wynd AB22 159 B1
Wallfield Cres AB25 164 F1
Wallfield Pl AB25 164 F1
Walton Rd AB21 157 E3
Wapping St AB11 190 B2
Ward Rd AB43 142 C7
Ward St AB42 53 B3
Wardes Rd AB51 152 E4
Wardhead Pl AB16 163 F3
Wardhouse Rd DD10 189 D7
Wards La AB44 141 E7
Wards Rd DD9 188 E4
Ware Rd AB42 147 D7
Warrack Terr DD10 189 D4
Water La
Aberdeen AB11 190 C3
Banff AB45 141 A6
Ellon AB41 151 D4
1 Turriff AB53 145 D5
Water Path AB45 140 F6
Water St AB43 24 E6
Waterloo Quay AB11 165 E1
Watermill Rd AB43 143 A6
Waters of Philorth Nature Reserve* AB43 15 A7
Waters The AB30 124 B1
Waterside Ct 1 AB51 87 C7
Waterside Pl AB42 147 A8
Waterside Rd
Montrose DD10 189 E2
Peterhead AB42 147 A8
Strathdon AB36 81 D2
Waterside Way AB42 147 A7
Waterson Dr DD9 188 C4
Waterton Rd AB21 158 C2
Watson Ave AB54 148 D3
Watson Cres AB42 147 A5
Watson Gdns AB43 143 B6
Watson La AB25 164 F2
Watson St
Aberdeen AB25 164 F2
Banchory AB31 184 C4
Watson Watt Pl DD9 188 C4
Watt Cres AB51 152 D6
Watt's La AB44 141 C7
Waughton Pl DD10 135 C6
Waul Pk AB43 143 C7
Waulkmill Cres AB16 164 A6
Waulkmill Rd 1 AB16 164 A5
Wavell Cres AB24 164 F7
Waverley Pl AB10 170 A8
Weavers Row 2 AB16 164 A5
Webster Rd AB12 170 A2
Weigh-house Sq 3 AB11 190 B3
Well St Peterhead AB42 147 D7
Rosehearty AB43 142 B8
Wellbrae AB51 59 E3
Wellbrae Terr
Aberdeen AB15 169 C6
Inverurie AB51 59 E2
Wellfield Cres 3 AB53 145 C5
Wellfield La 2 AB54 144 D5
Wellfield Terr AB54 144 D5
Wellgrove Cres AB32 161 C2
Wellgrove Dr AB32 161 C2
Wellgrove Rd AB32 161 C2
Wellheads Cres AB21 158 B4
Wellheads Dr AB21 158 A5
Wellheads Ind Est AB21 158 B3
Wellheads Pl AB21 158 B4
Wellheads Rd AB21 158 C5
Wellheads Terr AB21 158 B3
Wellheads Way AB21 158 B4
Wellington Brae AB11 190 B1
Wellington Circ AB12 170 C1
Wellington Gdns DD10 189 D4
Wellington Pk DD10 189 D4
Wellington Pl AB11 190 B2
Wellington Rd AB12 175 E6
Wellington St
Aberdeen AB11 165 E1
Montrose DD10 189 D4
Wellpark AB51 59 E3
Wellpark Gdns AB51 155 C5
Wellpark Rd AB51 155 B6
Wellside Ave AB15 163 A4
Wellside Circ AB15 163 A4
Wellside Cl AB15 163 A4
Wellside End AB15 163 A4
Wellside Gdns AB15 162 F4
Wellside Pk AB15 163 A4
Wellside Pl AB15 162 F4
Wellside Rd AB15 163 A4
Wellside Wlk AB15 163 A4
Wellside Wynd AB15 163 A4
Wellwood Terr AB15 168 F3
West Bay DD10 187 C3
West Brae DD10 135 C5
West Cairncry Rd AB16 164 B4
West Church St AB45 1 F1
West Craibstone St 5 AB11 190 A2
West Ct AB54 148 C4
West Cults Rd AB15 168 D1
West End AB45 8 F8
West Fountain St 5 AB45 140 E6
West Glebe AB39 185 D6
West Haven Cres AB43 15 B8
West High St AB51 152 D6
West Mount St AB25 165 A2
West N St AB24 190 B4
West Pk
Fraserburgh AB43 15 D5
Inverbervie DD10 187 D6
West Pk Ave DD10 187 D6
West Pk Cres DD10 187 D6
West Pk Gr DD10 187 D6
West Pk Pl DD10 187 C6
West Pk St AB54 148 D5
West Pk Terr DD10 187 D6
West Rd
Fraserburgh AB43 143 B4
Peterhead AB42 147 C5
West Shore Rd Ind Est AB43 143 B7
West Skene St AB44 141 D7
West St
Fraserburgh AB43 15 D6
Montrose DD10 135 C5
Strichen AB43 24 E6
West Terr DD10 189 C1
West Toll Cres AB34 183 B5
West Tullos Rd AB12 170 B4
Westbank Pk AB51 150 B3
Westbrae Cres AB53 145 C5
Westburn Ave AB51 152 A6
Westburn Ct 2 AB25 165 A2
Westburn Dr
Aberdeen AB25 164 E3
Inverurie AB51 152 A6
Westburn Gdns AB51 152 A6
Westburn Pl AB51 152 A6
Westburn Rd AB25 164 C2
Westdyke Ave AB32 161 C2
Westdyke Ct AB32 161 B2
Westdyke Dr AB32 161 B2
Westdyke Gdns AB32 161 B2
Westdyke Pl AB32 161 C2
Westdyke Terr AB32 161 B2
Westdyke Way AB32 161 B2
Westdyke Wlk AB32 161 C2
Westend Gdns 1 AB51 150 B3
Western Ave AB41 151 B4
Western Pl AB41 151 B3
Western Rd
Aberdeen AB24 164 E6
Insch AB52 149 B5
Inverurie AB51 152 D6
Montrose DD10 189 C3
Western Rd N DD10 189 C4
Westerton Cres AB16 164 A6
Westerton Pl
Aberdeen AB16 164 B6
Cults AB15 168 F3
Westerton Prim Sch AB16 163 F5
Westerton Rd AB15 168 F3
Westerwards AB45 139 C6
Westfield Ave
Inverurie AB51 152 C6
Stonehaven AB39 185 D5
Westfield Ct AB39 185 D5
Westfield Gdns
Inverurie AB51 152 C6
Westhill AB32 161 D3
Westfield Pk AB39 185 D5
Westfield Rd
Aberdeen AB25 164 F2
Inverurie AB51 152 D6
Stonehaven AB39 185 D5
Turriff AB53 145 B5
Westfield Specl Sch AB43 143 B5
Westfield Terr AB25 164 F1
Westhill Acad AB32 161 E3
Westhill Bsns Pk AB32 161 B1
Westhill Cres AB32 161 C3
Westhill Dr AB32 161 E2
Westhill Grange AB32 161 C3
Westhill Hts AB32 161 D4
Westhill Pl 9 AB53 145 C5
Westhill Prim Sch AB32 161 E3
Westhill Rd AB32 161 F3
Westholme Ave AB15 169 B8
Westholme Cres N AB15 169 B8
Westholme Terr AB15 169 A8

Westray Cres AB15 .....164 B2
Westray Pk AB43 .....143 B4
Westray Rd AB15 .....164 A2
West's Way AB54 .....144 D5
Westshore Rd AB43 ...143 B7
Westwood **2** DD9 .....188 B3
Westwood Cres AB32 ...161 D3
Westwood Dr AB32 ...161 D3
Westwood Gr AB32 ...161 D3
Westwood Pl AB32 ...161 D3
Westwood Way AB32 ...161 D3
Westwood Wlk AB32 ...161 D3
Wharf St DD10 .....189 C2
Wheatland **1** AB41 .....62 A2
Whin Path AB21 .....156 B7
Whin Pk Pl AB16 .....164 A4
Whin Pk Rd AB16 .....164 B5
Whinfield Rd DD10 ...189 E4
Whinfield Way DD10 ...189 E4
Whinhill Cres **5** AB45 ...140 F6
Whinhill Gate AB11 ...190 A1
Whinhill Gdns AB11 ...170 B6
Whinhill Rd
  Aberdeen AB11 .....190 A1
  Banff AB45 .....140 D5
Whinhill Terr AB45 ...140 E5
Whinpark Circ AB12 ...180 B5
Whisky Brae AB41 .....151 C5
Whistleberry Castle (remains
  of)* DD10 .....131 E6
White Gates **2** AB42 ...147 A8
White Ship Ct **2** AB43 ...24 E6
Whiteford Gdns AB51 ...59 C1
Whiteford Pl AB51 .....59 B1
Whiteford Rd AB51 .....59 B1
Whitehall Pl AB25 .....164 F1
Whitehall Rd AB15 .....164 E1
Whitehall Terr AB25 ...164 F1
Whitehill Pl AB42 .....147 B3
Whitehills Cres AB12 ...176 B7

Whitehills Prim Sch
  AB45 ....8 F7
Whitehills Rise AB12 ...176 B6
Whitehills Way AB12 ...176 A7
Whitehorse Terr **1** AB23 ..91 C8
Whitehouse St **6** AB10 .165 A1
Whitelands Rd AB39 ...181 I4
Whiteley Well Dr
  AB51 ....152 B8
Whiteley Well Pl **3**
  AB51 ....152 B8
Whitemyres Ave AB16 ...164 A2
Whitemyres Pl AB16 ...164 B2
Whiterashes AB15 .....162 F1
Whites Pl DD10 .....189 D4
Whitestripes Ave
  AB22 ....159 C2
Whitestripes Cres
  AB22 ....159 D2
Whitestripes Dr AB22 ..159 C3
Whitestripes Path
  AB22 ....159 D2
Whitestripes Pl AB22 ..159 D2
Whitestripes Rd AB21 ..158 F7
Whitestripes St AB22 ..159 D2
Whitestripes Way
  AB22 ....159 D3
Whitson Way **4** DD10 ..189 D7
Widgeon Way AB41 ...151 B4
Wildgoose Dr **2** AB21 ..153 C6
Wilkie Ave AB16 .....164 C6
William Mackie Cres **1**
  AB39 ....185 C6
William Mackie Rd
  AB39 ....185 C6
William Phillips Dr
  DD10 ....189 D3
William Rodger Dr
  DD10 ....189 E3
William St
  11 Banchory AB31 ...108 E8
  Fraserburgh AB43 .....15 B8
  Montrose DD10 .....187 C3

William St continued
  4 Montrose DD10 .....189 D1
Williams Cres AB43 ...143 C5
Williamson Pl **3** AB45 ..140 E6
Willow Gr Gdns AB21 ..156 B6
Willow Wynd AB12 .....180 B5
Willowbank Rd
  Aberdeen AB11 .....190 A1
  Peterhead AB42 .....147 B3
Willowdale Pl AB24 ...190 B4
Willowgrove Dr AB21 ..156 B5
Willowpark Cres AB16 ..164 B2
Willowpark Pl AB16 ...164 B3
Willowpark Rd AB16 ...164 B3
Wilson Cres AB45 .....8 F8
Wilson Pl **12** AB51 .....87 D7
Wilson Rd
  Banchory AB31 .....184 C5
  Peterhead AB42 .....140 F5
Wilson St AB42 .....147 E6
Wilson's Pk DD9 .....188 C3
Windford Rd AB16 .....163 F2
Windford Sq AB16 .....163 F2
Windhill St AB42 .....37 C4
Winding Brae **6** AB42 ...38 D6
Windmill Brae AB11 ...190 A2
Windmill La AB11 .....190 A2
Windmill Rd AB42 .....147 A6
Windmill St AB42 .....147 E6
Windy Brae AB45 .....140 D6
Windyedge AB51 .....152 C5
Windyedge Ct AB39 ...181 H4
Wingate Pl AB24 .....165 A6
Wingate Rd AB24 .....165 A6
Wiseman Terr AB42 .....27 B3
Wishart Ave DD10 .....189 D5
Wishart Gdns DD10 ...189 D5
Witchden Rd DD9 .....188 D2
Witchhill Rd AB43 .....143 B4
Wood St
  Aberdeen AB11 .....170 F7
  Banff AB45 .....140 E6
  Portsoy AB45 .....139 E7
Woodburn Ave AB15 ...169 A7

Woodburn Cres AB15 ..169 A7
Woodburn Gdns AB15 ..169 A7
Woodburn Pl AB15 .....169 A7
Woodburn Rd AB21 ...156 A6
Woodcot Brae AB39 ...185 D4
Woodcot Ct **2** AB39 ...185 D4
Woodcot Gdns **1** AB39 .185 D4
Woodcot La AB39 .....185 D4
Woodcot Pk AB39 .....185 D4
Woodcroft Ave AB22 ...159 C5
Woodcroft Gdns AB22 ..159 C5
Woodcroft Gr AB22 ...159 C5
Woodcroft Rd AB22 ...159 C5
Woodcroft Wlk AB22 ...159 C5
Woodend Barn Arts Ctr*
  AB31 ....110 B4
Woodend Cres AB15 ...163 F1
Woodend Dr AB15 .....164 A1
Woodend Hospl AB15 ..163 F1
Woodend Pl AB15 .....169 A8
Woodend Rd AB15 .....164 A1
Woodend Terr AB15 ...164 A1
Woodhill Pl AB15 .....164 C1
Woodhill Rd AB15 .....164 C1
Woodhill Terr AB15 ...164 C2
Woodland Gdns AB51 ...59 D3
Woodland Wynd AB33 ...85 C7
Woodlands AB53 .....145 D5
Woodlands Cres AB53 ..145 D4
Woodlands Dr
  Aberdeen AB21 .....157 E6
  Ellon AB41 .....151 D6
Woodlands Edge
  AB41 ....151 D6
Woodlands Hospl
  AB15 ....169 A4
Woodlands Pl
  Banchory AB31 .....184 E6
  Inverbervie DD10 .....187 D6
Woodlands Rd
  Aberdeen AB21 .....157 E6
  Banchory AB31 .....184 D6
Woodlea Gdns AB41 .....76 C7
Woodlea Gr AB41 .....76 C7

Woodside Cres
  Banchory AB31 .....184 C5
  Mintlaw AB42 .....146 C4
Woodside Pl
  1 Banchory AB31 .....184 D5
  1 Mintlaw AB42 .....146 C4
Woodside Prim Sch
  AB24 ....164 E6
Woodside Rd
  Aberdeen AB23 .....160 A3
  Banchory AB31 .....184 C5
  Torphins AB31 .....108 E8
Woodside Terr AB31 ...184 D5
Woodstock Rd AB15 ...164 C1
Woodview Ct **14** AB39 ..185 E4
Woodview Pl **2** AB39 ..185 E4
Woolmanhill AB25 .....190 A4
Woolmanhill Hospl
  AB25 ....190 A3
Wrights' & Coopers' Pl
  AB24 ....165 B6
Wrights Wlk AB32 .....161 E3
Wynd The **6** AB53 .....145 C4
Wyndford La AB32 .....161 F3
Wyness Ct AB51 .....152 D5
Wynne Edwards House*
  AB10 ....169 F8
Wyverie Ct AB51 .....150 C4

Y

York Pl Aberdeen AB11 ..165 E1
  2 Cullen AB56 ....1 B4
  1 Montrose DD10 .....189 C4
York St Aberdeen AB11 ..165 E1
  Peterhead AB42 .....147 D5
York Terr DD10 .....189 C4
Youngson's La **7** AB53 .145 D4
Ythan Pl AB41 .....151 C4
Ythan Rd AB16 .....163 F3
Ythan Terr AB41 .....151 C4
Yule Sq AB54 .....148 E5